JUSTICE AND PEACE

JUSTICE AND PEACE

A Christian Primer

Third Edition
Revised and Expanded

J. Milburn Thompson

ORBIS BOOKS
Maryknoll, New York 10545

ORBIS BOOKS
Maryknoll, New York 10545

Founded in 1970, Orbis Books endeavors to publish works that enlighten the mind, nourish the spirit, and challenge the conscience. The publishing arm of the Maryknoll Fathers and Brothers, Orbis seeks to explore the global dimensions of the Christian faith and mission, to invite dialogue with diverse cultures and religious traditions, and to serve the cause of reconciliation and peace. The books published reflect the views of their authors and do not represent the official position of the Maryknoll Society. To learn more about Maryknoll and Orbis Books, please visit our website at www.maryknollsociety.org.

Copyright © 2019 by J. Milburn Thompson

Published by Orbis Books, Box 302, Maryknoll, New York 10545-0302.

Manufactured in the United States of America.

Library of Congress Cataloging-in-Publication Data

Names: Thompson, Joseph Milburn, 1947– author.
Title: Justice and peace : a Christian primer / J. Milburn Thompson.
Description: Third edition, revised and expanded. | Maryknoll, NY : Orbis
    Books, [2019] | Includes bibliographical references and index.
Identifiers: LCCN 2018053161 (print) | LCCN 2019001021 (ebook) | ISBN
    9781608337897 (e-book) | ISBN 9781626983281 (pbk.) | ISBN 9781608337897
    (ebk.)
Subjects: LCSH: Christianity and justice. | Social justice. |
    Peace—Religious aspects—Christianity.
Classification: LCC BR115.J8 (ebook) | LCC BR115.J8 T46 2019 (print) | DDC
    261.8—dc23
LC record available at https://lccn.loc.gov/2018053161

Contents

Introduction

Peace is both a gift of God and a human work. It must be constructed on the basis of central human values: truth, justice, freedom, and love.

National Conference of Catholic Bishops,
The Challenge of Peace: God's Promise and Our Response (1983), #68

The life and words of Jesus and the teaching of his Church call us to serve those in need and to work actively for social and economic justice. As a community of believers, we know that our faith is tested by the quality of justice among us, that we can best measure our life together by how the poor and the vulnerable are treated.[1]

National Conference of Catholic Bishops,
Economic Justice for All (1986), #8

The almost universal response to the September 11, 2001, terrorist attacks was, "This changes everything." The way Americans and others looked at the world did indeed change. Such changes are the rule, not the exception. The world changed dramatically, for example, with the collapse of communism in Europe, symbolized by the dismantling of the Berlin Wall in 1989. Such dramatic changes generally mean that humanity is faced with different problems rather than fewer problems.

Dramatic changes in global politics call for innovative thinking and imaginative analysis. Now is a good time for Christian citizens to take a fresh look at international relations and foreign policy.

OBJECTIVES AND AUDIENCE

This is a starter book, a primer. It is written for college students, thoughtful Christians, and anyone who is concerned about global issues and wants to learn more. It is intended for budding scholars, not established experts. It strives to be scholarly in the sense of being well researched, accurate, and balanced in seeking the truth. The scope of this text precludes any pretense of making major contributions to the understanding of or the solution to the myriad problems it reviews. Indeed, there is a certain amount of hubris involved in even attempting a book that addresses such diverse disciplines and so many controversies. No author can pretend to be proficient in history, economics, politics, ecology, international relations, ethics, and theology. Rather, the goal is to inform citizens well enough that they can be active participants in public policy debates and catalysts for constructive change in the contemporary world. Participation and transformation are the responsibilities of all citizens in a democracy, and certainly of Christian citizens.

This is therefore a getting-started book as well.[2] Information, understanding, and rigorous critical analysis are necessary first steps for creating a more just and peaceful world. Analysis, however, is not sufficient; society needs to be changed.

Public policy primarily reflects values and interests. For example, should the alleviation of global hunger be a goal of foreign policy or is national self-interest its only objective? Should a particular piece of legislation serve the basic needs of the poor or the welfare of corporations? These are fundamentally questions about values and interests. Once one decides which values public policy should serve, the process of translating those values into appropriate policies remains complex and often controversial. However, citizens can and should participate in the discussion and in the development of policies and systems. When citizens "leave it to the experts," they simply ensure that the expert's values and interests become policy.

Any study of American foreign policy and of the global situation must be undertaken from some perspective. Every analyst, whether located in the Pentagon, a university, or the local cafe, brings assumptions, values, goals, and objectives to debates about international relations. This particular book brings a *Christian perspective* to bear on the world situation.

A Christian perspective is grounded in the conviction that God is sovereign and that God's reign is loving and just. By creating human beings in God's own image, God has bestowed on each and every person an intrinsic dignity and an infinite value. This human dignity is nourished and developed in community. Humanity is God's people—a family—called to love and care for one another and for the earth. As co-creators with God, human beings are responsible for creating a just community conducive to the flowering of each person's potential.

Such a perspective means that an exploration of the contemporary global situation is crucial. Christians are called to care for brothers and sisters, near and far. Christians should be concerned about what public policies do for and to people. There should be no gulf between faith (our relationship with God) and everyday life.[3] Christians are called to live their faith in the world, and this means that politics, economics, and social policy are important.

This study will operate on three interrelated levels. The first level focuses on the reality of the situation. The first step is to ask what ethicist Daniel Maguire calls "reality revealing questions."[4] What is going on? Who is doing what to whom? The goal here is to seek information and gather the facts, to *see* reality.

The second level involves analysis and evaluation. The task now is interpretation, to *judge* what should be done. One's perspective is brought to bear on the facts, seeking insight and surfacing possible solutions. What are the causes of this problem? What are the objectives and consequences of various solutions? Analysis is complex, and there will be differences of opinion. Often these disagreements are rooted in the values and interests that are brought to the investigation. For example, nearly everyone agrees that terrorism should be prevented and resisted. The differences in the proposals regarding terrorism are rooted both in different values and goals—to take revenge on evil terrorists or to reconcile them into a just community, for example—and in different interpretations of the causes of the problem and the consequences of various solutions.

The third level moves to commitment and *action*. Reasonable solutions must be sought and implemented; strategies for change need to be devised and deployed. This, too, is complex, difficult, and often frustrating. Sometimes creative solutions fail to be realized. Other times solutions fall short of resolving the problem or bring with them new problems. There are times, too, when remedies work, and real progress can be celebrated. Obviously this process of reflection and action is ongoing, as Christians move in faith and hope toward the kingdom God has promised.

There is a spiritual dimension that corresponds to this conceptual and ethical framework. Peace activist Ammon Hennacy once wrote:

> Love without courage and wisdom is sentimentality, as with the ordinary church member. Courage without love and wisdom is foolhardiness, as with the ordinary soldier. Wisdom without love and courage is cowardice, as with the ordinary intellectual. Therefore one with love, courage, and wisdom is one in a million, who moves the world, as with Jesus, Buddha, and Gandhi.[5]

The Eastern Christian tradition repeats the Jesus Prayer, "Lord Jesus Christ, Son of the living God, have mercy on me a sinner," as a form of centering mantra. An alternative, based on the quote from Ammon Hennacy, might be, "God, my mother, teach me the compassion, the wisdom, and the courage of your heart."

These three virtues correspond helpfully to the three levels of social analysis. A *compassionate heart* is essential for seeing those who are poor and suffering in our midst. Without compassion a statistic such as "one in every five American children is poor" elicits only indifference and apathy. Compassion is essential, but not sufficient. Unless we pause to seek *wisdom*—to gather information and interpret it carefully—we may do more harm than good. And without the *courage* to raise our voices and to get our hands dirty in the struggle to change society, compassion is mere sentimentality, and wisdom is academic in the worst sense of the word. Compassion, wisdom, and courage give a spiritual dimension to the seeing, judging, and acting[6] that are essential for social analysis.

This book, then, is an introduction to the obstacles to justice and peace found in the contemporary world.[7] It seeks to inform the reader through a critical analysis of the pressing problems facing humanity early in the twenty-first century and to transform both the reader and the world.

The book begins by establishing a theological foundation, based on Christian values and principles, for social analysis. It then traces the major trends in the development of the contemporary world—colonialism, the industrial/technological revolutions, and the Cold War and globalization. Succeeding chapters focus on the obstacles to a more just and peaceful world: the global gap between the rich and the poor, and the need for sustainable development; climate change, the population explosion, and environmental destruction; violations of human rights; war, conflict, and peace; and weapons and disarmament. Finally, the epilogue reflects directly on the meaning of Christian citizenship and the call to action, and suggests resources for action on behalf of justice and peace and for further study. Although the book focuses on global issues and foreign policy, it also attends to related domestic issues.

This organization of the book makes sense, but the chapters could easily be organized differently. Not only is humanity interdependent, but the issues facing humanity are deeply interrelated. Each of the issues addressed here, for example, is a genuine "security" issue, a threat to peace. The words of Pope Paul VI point to the interrelated themes of the book, "If you want peace, work for justice."

The study questions after each chapter aim to stimulate further discussion of the issues raised in the text rather than test comprehension of the material. The "For Reflection" sidebars in the text are also to provoke reflection and discussion.

REVISIONS TO THE SECOND EDITION

A book on global issues inevitably needs to be updated. The first edition of this book was published in 1997, and the second edition in 2003. Since then we have come to recognize that climate change, as a result of global warming, is not an issue for our grandchildren but is upon us; we are experiencing its consequences. The globalization of the world's economy is increasing economic inequity rather than spurring human development. Human rights are extensively acknowledged, yet widely violated. Ultranationalism is challenging democracy; violence and conflict are widespread; terrorism is a constant threat; and new weapons and a new arms race are looming. An investigation of these issues has been woven into the book, and they are a significant focus of various chapters. There has been a concerted effort to bring the statistics and situations throughout the book up-to-date. The election of Donald J. Trump as president of the United States halfway through this process has necessitated a revision of the revision in several places.

There are other changes worth noting, especially for those who have used the book in teaching. The theological foundation in chapter 1 is substantially the same, as is the history in chapter 2. Chapter 3, on "Poverty, Economic Justice, and Human Development," covers much of the same territory as previous editions, but with a consistent global focus, more attention to economic inequity, and a section on practical solutions to poverty. Chapter 4, on "Climate Change, Resource Depletion, and Environmental Destruction," has been largely rewritten with a focus on global warming and the consequences of and response to climate change. Chapter 5, on "Human Rights," has a new section on torture and has been consistently updated. In chapter 6, "Conflict, War, and Peace," the section on "The Global Landscape of Conflict and War" has been extended significantly. Finally, chapter 7, on "Weapons and Disarmament," considers weapons of long-term destruction other than land mines, and has new sections on "Targeted Killing and Armed Drones," "Cyberattacks and Space Defense," and "Gun Safety in the United States."

ACKNOWLEDGMENTS

Teaching and learning is a communal activity. I have presented this material in the classroom for over forty years. The responses of students have refined these ideas and transformed me again and again. I am grateful to all those students and dedicate this book to them.

I appreciate those who presented this material to me—my teachers and academic colleagues. I hope this book will be as good a teacher as the books and articles I have read in researching it. I look forward to the responses of colleagues and students, to continuing the conversation.

When I wrote the first edition of this book, I was teaching at what is now the University of Saint Joseph in West Hartford, Connecticut, which I thank for the incentive to write this book and for the time to write it. Father John J. Stack, now deceased, was an important mentor for me in those years. In 2001, I moved to Bellarmine University, which is located in my hometown, Louisville, Kentucky. My new colleagues in the theology department at Bellarmine, Fathers George Kilcourse and Clyde Crews, old friends from our graduate studies at Fordham University, supported me in working on the revised edition published in 2003. The three of us are now retired.

This revision has been a retirement project begun in mid-2014. My colleagues in the current theology department at Bellarmine—Gregory Hillis,

Deborah Prince, Joseph Flipper, Justin Klassen, Hoon Choi, and especially Elizabeth Hinson-Hasty, the department chair—have given me constant encouragement and support. In addition, Robert Kingsolver, dean of Bellarmine's School of Environmental Studies, gave me insightful and helpful feedback on chapter 4, and Louis Hehman, a former student, offered me responses to the first two chapters. Patricia Allen, the Humanities secretary, helped in numerous ways. The friendship of David and Judy Sisk has constantly boosted my morale.

My editor at Orbis Books, Jill O'Brien, has been wonderful. She has been patient with an author who routinely extended deadlines and who had gotten way too long-winded over four years of work. She was brilliant and efficient in pulling the manuscript together into final form.

My wife, Mary Ann, a professor of community health nursing, is at once a tough critic and a strong advocate. Without her love, encouragement, and prodding I couldn't have produced this book.

CHRISTIAN FAITH, JESUS, AND CATHOLIC SOCIAL TEACHING

You are the light of the world. A city built on a hill cannot be hid. No one after lighting a lamp puts it under the bushel basket, but on the lampstand, and it gives light to all in the house. In the same way, let your light shine before others, so that they may see your good works and give glory to your Father in heaven. (Matt 5:14–16)

To set out on the road to discipleship is to dispose oneself for a share in the cross (cf. John 16:20). To be a Christian, according to the New Testament, is not simply to believe with one's mind, but also to become a doer of the word, a wayfarer with and a witness to Jesus. This means, of course, that we never expect complete success within history and that we must regard as normal even the path of persecution and the possibility of martyrdom.
National Conference of Catholic Bishops,
The Challenge of Peace: God's Promise and Our Response (1983), #276

This book explores issues of justice and peace that face humanity in the twenty-first century. Christians need to understand these issues in order to create a global community that is more just and at peace. This chapter will try to make explicit *why* Christians should work for justice and make peace. It will attempt to build a theological foundation or framework for approaching social issues as Christian disciples.

CHRISTIAN FAITH

Faith is a *relationship* with God; Christian faith is a relationship with God as revealed by Jesus, the Christ. It is important to understand faith as a relationship and not primarily as a set of beliefs or a checklist of moral requirements. Creeds and commandments are important for persons of faith because they begin to name the God who loves us and they guide us in our response to God. But the relationship of each person with God is primary and central.

As with any relationship, faith is rooted in experience. Since God is spirit, it is sometimes difficult for modern people, convinced of the efficacy of the scientific method and closed off to mystery and transcendence, to open themselves to experience the Spirit. There are endless human experiences that tend to pull us beyond ourselves, such as falling in love, the birth of a child, the death of someone we love, or even a breathtaking sunrise. Faith, however, always requires the leap that acknowledges the presence of God's Spirit.

Like lovers bursting to recount the experience of being in love,[1] an encounter with transcendent mystery begs to be shared, reflected upon, and responded to. Religious believers gather with other people of faith in community to tell stories of God, to seek to understand their relationship with God (doing theology), to celebrate their faith (worshiping God), and to respond to it (right living). This is how "church" is formed and tradition passed on. Eventually, the narratives about God and faith are written down in scripture. Creeds are formulated, liturgy is designed, and principles are put into practice. All of this happens in response to the human relationship with God that rightfully becomes the core and compass of human life.

Jesus and the Spirit

Jesus was a person of faith. "The most crucial fact about Jesus was that he was a 'spirit person,' a 'mediator of the sacred,' one of those persons in human history for whom the Spirit was an experiential reality."[2] At the center of Jesus's life was an intimate and continuous relationship with the divine Spirit. Jesus was the culmination of a stream of Spirit persons in the Jewish tradition—Abraham and Sarah, Moses, David, and the prophets—and others following in Jesus's wake throughout history—Peter and Paul; John Chrysostom and Augustine; Benedict, Francis and Clare of Assisi, and Ignatius; Thomas Aquinas and Teresa of Avila; Mother Teresa of Calcutta and Thomas Merton, to name just a few.

Jesus knew God in a very personal way. He had visions of God at his baptism by John (Matt 3:13–17), in the desert (Matt 4:1–11), and on the mountaintop (Matt 17:1–13).[3] Jesus sought out isolated places where he prayed to God throughout the night (Matt 14:23; Mark 1:35). In a culture afraid to utter the Almighty's name, Jesus called God *Abba* (Mark 14:35), Aramaic for "Papa." As the Spirit's healing and liberating power flowed through Jesus, he taught about God and faith "with authority," that is, on the basis of his own profound experience of the divine mystery at the heart of reality. At the beginning of his public ministry Jesus applied the words of Isaiah the prophet to himself:

> The Spirit of the Lord is upon me,
>> because he has anointed me to bring good news to the poor.
> He has sent me to proclaim release to the captives
>> and recovery of sight to the blind,
>>> to let the oppressed go free,
> to proclaim the year of the Lord's favor. (Luke 4:18–19)

Jesus invited everyone he met to faith, to encounter the same Spirit he knew and to live in relationship with God.

The Politics of Compassion

Who is the God whom Jesus knew and obeyed and revealed? "For Jesus, compassion was the central quality of God and the central moral quality of a life centered on God."[4] "Be compassionate (merciful) as your Father is compassionate (merciful)" (Luke 6:36). Moreover, Jesus, "God-with-a-face,"[5] is the embodiment of divine compassion in the world. Jesus not only proclaimed the message of the Father's mercy, he lived it.

The Hebrew word translated as "compassion" (*rachamim*) is the plural of the word for womb (*rechem*).[6] It connotes giving life, nourishing, caring, and tenderness, a warm embrace. Mercy or compassion is often used in referring to God (as God's name or essence) in the Hebrew Scriptures. "The Lord, the Lord, a God merciful [*rachum*] and gracious [*henum*], slow to anger, and abounding in steadfast love [*hesed*] and faithfulness [*emet*]" (Exod 34:6). "God's being God is revealed in his mercy. Mercy is the expression of his divine essence."[7]

For Jesus, then, God is like a mother who feels for and loves *all* the children of her womb.[8] As followers of Jesus, Christians are to imitate God, being compassionate toward one another. Compassion is both a feeling—being moved by the suffering of others as Jesus so often was—and a way of living, a willingness to share that suffering and do something about it. In and through Jesus, God shares the suffering of humanity and transforms it into new life.[9]

"For Jesus, compassion was more than a quality of God and an individual virtue: it was a social paradigm, the core value of life in community. To put it boldly, compassion for Jesus was political."[10] When compassion led Jesus to touch a leper, heal a woman with constant menstruation, feed the hungry, forgive sinners, or share a meal with tax collectors and prostitutes, it was moving him to challenge the dominant sociopolitical paradigm of his social world. Thus, Jesus was engaged in what might be called the "politics of compassion," in contrast to the "politics of purity" that dominated his social world.

In the first century, Jewish society was structured around avoiding anything that would make one religiously unclean. The biblical roots of this purity system were found in the book of Leviticus, especially in the verse, "You shall be holy, for I the Lord your God am holy" (Lev 19:2). Set in the context of laws about ritual and religious purity, the holiness of the Jewish community was defined in terms of purity.

This purity system tended to be hierarchical and exclusionary. It divided those who were born into the tribe of Levites and priests from those who were not, the righteous who observed the purity laws from sinners who were unclean and impure, the whole and the well from the handicapped and the ill, the rich (blessed by God) from the poor, males from females, and Jews from Gentiles. In effect, the purity system created a world with sharp social boundaries, a world where many were treated as outcasts.[11]

In opposition to the teaching of the Pharisees and of Jewish leaders to "Be holy [pure] as God is holy," Jesus, based on his interpretation of the God of mercy in the Hebrew Scriptures and his experience of the Spirit,[12] proclaimed, "Be compassionate as God is compassionate." Jesus's call to compassion can be seen as a radical challenge to the theology and the politics of the dominant social system of the time, a social structure that placed an oppressive burden on the poor and the marginalized.

Jesus's parables and sayings often indicted the purity system and those who used it for power and privilege. In the parable of the Good Samaritan (Luke 10:29–37), for example, it is probable that the priest and the Levite passed by the man beaten by robbers because they were afraid of becoming ritually unclean by drawing too close to him. The Samaritan, who was by definition impure, acted compassionately toward the wounded man and became the model for loving one's neighbor. Speaking in the style of the prophets of Israel, Jesus denounced the Pharisees and other religious leaders for their rigorous following of the religious codes to the neglect of practicing "justice and mercy and faith."[13] Indeed, the string of Jesus's denunciations of the Pharisees and leaders collected in Luke 11 and Matthew 23 are dense with allusions to the purity system and the Pharisaic preoccupation with the outside and external, the law and duty, to the neglect of the spirit and the heart, of justice and compassion.

Here, Jesus stands in the tradition of the Hebrew prophets, who reminded the people of Israel that God was more concerned with justice and mercy and righteousness than with ritual or periodic fasting.

> I hate, I despise your festivals,
> > and I take no delight in your solemn assemblies. . . .
> But let justice roll down like waters
> > and righteousness like an ever-flowing stream. (Amos 5:21, 24)

> Is not this the fast that I choose:
> > to loose the bonds of injustice,
> > to undo the thongs of the yoke,

> to let the oppressed go free,
>> and to break every yoke?
> Is it not to share your bread with the hungry,
>> and bring the homeless poor into your house . . . ? (Isa 58:6–7)[14]

Sincere worship and humble fasting are good and important, of course, but the Hebrew prophets and Jesus pointed out that such rituals became outrageous hypocrisy if not accompanied by justice and mercy for the oppressed and the poor.

Jesus's healings and exorcisms and practice of table fellowship shattered the purity boundaries of his social world. Jesus touched lepers who were so unclean that they were literally cast out of the city, and he was touched by a hemorrhaging woman (Mark 5:25–34) and had his feet washed by an unclean woman when he was at dinner at Simon's house (Luke 7:36–50). Jesus entered a graveyard to free a man of a "legion" of unclean spirits who then entered a herd of unclean pigs (Mark 5:1–20). Jesus frequently "reclined at table" with impure social outcasts such as tax collectors and sinners. Indeed, the community of disciples gathered around Jesus negated the exclusive boundaries of the purity system. Jesus's followers included women, some of whom financially supported his itinerant community (Luke 8:1–3), tax collectors, common laborers, the marginalized, the healed, and the forgiven. The inclusive community of Jesus's disciples embodied a radically alternative social vision rooted in compassion and justice.[15]

An Inclusive Early Church

The Christian movement in the early church was characterized by the inclusiveness of compassion rather than the exclusiveness of the purity system. Even an Ethiopian eunuch, a man at the bottom of the purity system, was baptized into the church without hesitation (Acts 8:26–40). And in his letter to the Galatians, Paul resoundingly declared the unity of all in the Spirit of Christ: "There is no longer Jew or Greek, there is no longer slave or free, there is no longer male and female; for all of you are one in Christ Jesus" (Gal 3:28).[16]

The apostles, filled with the spirit of Christ, founded communities that were inclusive and egalitarian, generous and loving. The Acts of the Apostles describes the Christian community at Jerusalem in this way:

> All who believed were together and had all things in common; they would sell their possessions and goods and distribute the proceeds to all, as any had need. Day by day, as they spent much time together in the temple, they broke bread at home and ate their food with glad and generous hearts, praising God and having the goodwill of all the people. And day by day the Lord added to their number those who were being saved. (Acts 2:44–47)[17]

Evangelical theologian Ronald Sider characterizes the practice of the Jerusalem community as "unlimited liability" for each other and "total availability" to each other.[18]

When, through a unique set of historical circumstances, the Jerusalem community became impoverished, Paul took up a great collection from the Gentile churches to bring to the church in Jerusalem. Thus Paul logically enlarged the scope of Christian unity and generosity to the universal church, giving us a model of interchurch sharing. And when Paul heard about class divisions in Eucharistic celebrations at Corinth, he angrily declared that if wealthy Christians were feasting while poor believers went hungry, then they were not eating the Lord's Supper at all, but profaning the body of Christ (1 Cor 11:17–34). On the basis of the practice of the early church and the meaning of the Eucharist, Sider concludes, "As long as any Christian anywhere in the world is hungry, the Eucharistic celebration of all Christians everywhere in the world is imperfect."[19] Along the same lines, we might legitimately wonder if Christ is really present at a racially segregated Eucharist, noting that eleven o'clock Sunday morning probably remains the most segregated hour in the week in the United States, as Martin Luther King Jr. observed.[20]

Jesus's Third Way

Jesus's politics of compassion addressed not only the Jewish purity system but also the violent oppression of the Roman Empire.[21] In the first century, Israel was occupied by the Romans, who ruled somewhat indirectly through Jewish leaders. Roman rule was domineering and exploitative, and the Jews understandably resented it. Thus, revolutionary sentiment and messianic expectations were high in Jesus's social world.

The Jewish people were expecting God to send them a messiah, someone like David, who would throw out the Romans and reestablish the kingdom of Israel. And there were Jewish groups, some called Zealots, who were ready to engage in violent resistance to Roman rule. The politics of Jesus's world were highly charged. Indeed, the Pharisees and the Essenes hoped that their faithful following of the purity laws and the holiness code would persuade God to send the messiah.[22]

Ordinary people—the peasants, shepherds, housekeepers, fisherfolk, shopkeepers, and merchants—experienced a double oppression by both Roman rulers and Jewish leaders. The taxes paid to the Romans, which amounted to as much as 40 percent of their income, drove many people into debt. These taxes were collected by fellow Jews who not only collaborated with the hated Romans but also enriched themselves in the process. And the religious leaders burdened the people with the onus of the purity system, adding religious guilt to their economic woes.[23]

In this oppressive context Jesus proclaimed the good news that the reign of God was at hand, offering liberation, justice, and mercy. It was a welcome message. Understanding this social context, doubly oppressive and tense with revolutionary fervor, helps to make sense of some of Jesus's sayings and of events that at first seem strange to contemporary Christians.

Jesus's Sermon on the Mount, as reported in Matthew 5–8 and Luke 6:20–49, is a challenging statement of his alternative way and of the politics of compassion. This teaching of Jesus has been a stumbling block for his followers throughout Christian history. Eileen Egan, a longtime advocate of peace and justice in the Catholic Worker tradition, once said that she thought all of theology might be understood as a way to get around the Sermon on the Mount. She thought Christians should walk through it instead.[24] Is it possible to practice this ethic outlined by Jesus?

The first step in a realistic interpretation of the Sermon on the Mount is to see it in the context of Jesus's social world. Biblical scholar Walter Wink provides surprising insight by applying this method to one of the most perplexing passages in Jesus's discourse.[25]

> "You have heard that it was said, 'An eye for an eye and a tooth for a tooth.' But I say to you, Do not resist an evildoer. But if anyone strikes you on the right cheek, turn the other also; and if anyone wants to sue you and take your coat, give your cloak as well; and if anyone forces you to go one mile, go also the second mile." (Matt 5:38–41; see also Luke 6:29–31)

Is Jesus asking his followers to be human doormats, cowardly and complicit in the face of injustice? No—his message is not as simple as that.

Wink argues persuasively that the Greek word *antistenai*, translated as "resist not evil" in the King James version of the Bible, should be more accurately rendered, "Do not take revenge on someone who does you wrong," as is found in the Good News version. The sense is not to retaliate against violence with violence. But if Jesus counsels his followers not to *fight* back, neither does he allow *flight* in response to injustice. Rather, he calls for courageous and *creative resistance*, and he gives his audience—people who know about injustice first-hand—three examples of his alternative or "third way" to respond.

In the first example, the reference to the right cheek is key. The ancient world was a right-handed world, where even to gesture with the left hand was offensive and insulting. The best way to hit the right cheek with the right hand is with the back of the hand. (Try acting out the scene.) So Jesus is saying: when someone gives you the back of their hand, turn your other cheek to them. A backhand slap was the normal way of reprimanding inferiors, and it still carries the connotation of putting someone down. (Masters backhanded slaves; husbands, wives; men, women; Romans, Jews.) The expected response is cowering submission. Jesus counsels neither hitting back nor turning tail, but rather turning the other cheek, which is an act of remarkably courageous resistance. It allows the inferior in the relationship to assert her or his equal humanity with the oppressor, and it forces the oppressor to take stock of the relationship and perhaps of the social system that supports such inequality. It is risky, to be sure, but it is a creative way to challenge an unhealthy relationship and an unjust system. Both Gandhi and Martin Luther King Jr. grasped this well and molded this idea into a tool for resisting social injustice and creating a more just community.

In Jesus's second example someone is being sued for his coat or outer garment by a creditor. Indebtedness was the most pressing social problem in first-century Palestine, and only the poorest person would have nothing but his coat to serve as collateral.[26] Now he is being hauled into court to have even that stripped away, contrary to the law of Moses.[27]

Jesus recommends a creative and unexpected response in this situation. The people of the time wore only an outer garment and an inner garment. In effect, Jesus would have the debtor say, "Here, take not only my coat, but my underwear as well. Then, you'll have everything!" and walk out of the court naked, leaving the red-faced creditor with a coat in one hand and underwear in the other. The creditor would be embarrassed and shamed—and unmasked. This is not a respectable moneylender but a loan shark who perpetuates a system that has reduced an entire social class of his own people to landlessness and destitution. This burlesque offers the creditor the chance to see the human consequences of these practices and to repent, and it empowers the oppressed to take the initiative and burst the delusion that this is a just system. It is a brave and ingenious form of resistance.

Jesus's third example refers to a practice of the Roman occupation troops. When Roman troops were moving about, a soldier could force a civilian to carry his sixty-five-pound pack for him, but only for one mile. To force a civilian to go further risked severe penalties under military law. Jesus's executioners used this procedure in forcing Simon of Cyrene to carry the cross (Mark 15:21). This policy was a bitter reminder to the Jews that they were a subject people even in the Promised Land. Imagine, then, the soldier's surprise when, upon arrival at the next mile marker, he absent-mindedly reaches for his gear, looking for his next human pack-mule, and the Jew says with a smile, "That's all right, I'll carry it for another mile," and strides off down the road. Going the second mile knocks the oppressor off balance and reveals the injustice of the situation. It also affirms the dignity of the oppressed by allowing the victim to seize the initiative. Without shedding blood or even raising one's voice in anger, the oppressed person has started down the road to liberation.

Given such an interpretation, this passage becomes a different sort of stumbling block to Christian discipleship. Rather than being dismayed by the idea of complacency or submissiveness in the face of evil and injustice, which at first glance seems implied by Jesus's sayings, one can be put off by the courage and creativity called for by Jesus. But if the Christian disciple is to stumble over this teaching, it should be by the challenge of creative resistance, Jesus's third way between the ordinary options of fight or flight in response to injustice.

In Matthew's Gospel Jesus goes on to say,

> "You have heard that it was said, 'You shall love your neighbor and hate your enemy.' But I say to you, Love your enemies and pray for those who persecute you, so that you may be children of your Father in heaven; for he makes his sun rise on the evil and on the good, and sends rain on the righteous and the unrighteous. For if you love those who love you, what reward do you have? Do not even the tax collectors do the same? And if you greet only your brothers and sisters, what more are you doing than others? Do not even the Gentiles do the same? Be perfect [compassionate], therefore, as your heavenly Father is perfect [compassionate]." (Matt 5: 43–48).

Love of enemies is challenging indeed, but love expressed in nonviolent resistance has the power to free the oppressed from docility and the oppressor from sinful exploitation, affirming the image of God in both. Jesus teaches that this is the way that is consistent with the nature of God, who is compassion, and with our relationship with God, who calls us to create a just community through love.

Jesus lived what he taught, as the events of his life attest. He rode into Jerusalem on a donkey rather than a white horse, and he was crucified at the hands of the Romans at the insistence of the Jewish leaders. The inscription that Pilate put on his cross read, "The King of the Jews." Jesus's suffering in love redeemed humanity from personal and social sin and established the kingdom of God. Jesus rejected dominating power and insisted instead on the power of love.[28] As John Dominic Crossan notes, "[T]he Christian Bible presents the radicality of a just and nonviolent God repeatedly and relentlessly confronting the normalcy of an unjust and violent civilization."[29]

The Christian community eschewed violence and warfare and embraced nonviolence and peace, even in the face of persecution, during the first three centuries of its existence. There are multiple and complex reasons why Christians refused military participation during this period, but the basic reason was its incompatibility with Christian love. This practice of pacifism changed rather dramatically in 313 CE, when the Roman Empire in effect became the Holy Roman Empire after the conversion of the Emperor Constantine.[30] By 416 CE, only Christians could serve in the army of the Roman Empire.[31]

Christian Conversion and Social Transformation

At the beginning of his public ministry, Jesus is presented as traveling through Galilee, proclaiming a message of *metanoia,* or conversion, in response to the coming of the reign of God.[32] This notion of conversion is central to understanding the message of Jesus and the meaning of Christian discipleship. Basically, conversion means turning from selfishness toward love by placing God and the teachings of Jesus at the center of life. Conversion, then, is a call to "Be compassionate as your Father is compassionate." St. Paul puts it this way: "Let each of you look not to your own interests, but to the interests of others. Let the same mind be in you that was in Christ Jesus, who, . . . emptied himself, . . . and became obedient to the point of death—even death on a cross" (Phil 2:4–5, 7–8).

Conversion of the heart, then, means that Christians are to be socially subversive and that disciples of Christ must work to transform the world.[33] Conversion means to turn around; subversion means to turn over. The implication is that the Christian, like a plow moving through a field, will turn society over, from oppression to justice, from violence to peace. "The Christian is called not only to change his [or her] own heart but also to change the social, political, economic, and cultural structures of human existence. Conversion is not addressed to the heart alone."[34]

CATHOLIC SOCIAL TEACHING

Foundations

The social teaching of the churches—Catholic, Orthodox, and Protestant—attempts to interpret the social dimension of Christian discipleship in the context of the contemporary world.

The World Council of Churches (WCC), which includes nearly all Orthodox and Protestant churches, has held international assemblies every eight years since its founding in 1948. The 10th Assembly was held in Busan, Republic of Korea, in the fall of 2013 (see its website at www.oikoumene.org). The documents produced by these world assemblies have emphasized the theme of a "responsible society" and have clearly expressed the notion that justice demands the transformation of social structures.[35] In recent years there has also been a particular focus on justice, peace, and the integrity of creation. The National Council of Churches (NCC), the comparable body in the United States, has likewise given consistent and concerted attention to issues of justice and peace, as have the national assemblies of the various Protestant denominations (such as, for example, the Presbyterian Church, USA).

"Catholic social teaching" refers to the body of work produced by the popes, the Second Vatican Council, the Vatican synods, and the national conferences of Catholic bishops, beginning with the encyclical *Rerum Novarum (The Con-*

dition of Labor), issued by Pope Leo XIII in 1891.[36] The documents produced by the Vatican address global concerns of the universal church (see the website for the Vatican at www.vatican.va), and those of bishops' conferences tend to take more national or regional perspectives on justice and peace issues (see, for example, the website for the United States Conference of Catholic Bishops at www.usccb.org).

Catholic social thought has not developed in a systematic manner. Sometimes popes and bishops' conferences have decided to address specific issues that seemed pressing at a particular moment in history. Thus Pope Leo XIII addressed labor conditions in 1891; Pope John XXIII wrote on human rights and the arms race in 1963; Pope Paul VI took on poverty and development in 1967; the Latin American bishops, poverty and liberation in 1968 (at Medellín) and in 1979 (at Puebla); and the US Catholic bishops published statements on the arms race and deterrence in 1983 and the US economy in 1986. Other social encyclicals have been produced to mark the anniversary of a previous encyclical, such as *Quadragesimo Anno* by Pope Pius XI, *Octogesima Adveniens* by Pope Paul VI, and *Centesimus Annus* by Pope John Paul II, to mark the fortieth, eightieth, and hundredth anniversaries, respectively, of *Rerum Novarum (The Condition of Labor)* (1891). These documents tend to have a broader, more general scope, while also engaging issues of the day. Although there is much cross-referencing among these documents and a certain consistency both in theory and in positions taken, there is no conscious philosophical or theological foundation adopted and developed, nor do they expound a clear economic, social, or political theory. Although Catholic social thought has paid much more attention to its biblical basis since the Second Vatican Council (1962–1965), its use of scripture has remained uneven. Nevertheless, the Magisterium (the pope and the bishops) of the Catholic Church has managed to produce a substantial and credible body of social teaching, one that, unfortunately, has been referred to as "our best kept secret."[37]

The documents comprising Catholic social teaching over the past hundred years fill a thick volume, and theological reflection on this body of thought fills many more volumes.[38] While it is not possible here to give a thorough overview of Catholic social thought, it is important to note several key themes related to the issues addressed in this book.

First, Catholic social teaching unambiguously affirms that the church and individual Christians are to be *engaged in the work of transforming the world*. This is clearly expressed in a famous sentence from the document produced by an international Synod of Bishops in 1971, *Justice in the World*: "Action on behalf of justice and participation in the transformation of the world fully appear to us as a constitutive dimension of the preaching of the Gospel, or, in other words, of the church's mission for the redemption of the human race and its liberation from every oppressive situation."[39] Working for justice is not peripheral or optional, but rather central and essential for a life lived in relationship with God. Faith affects every aspect of the believer's life, including the social, cultural, economic, and political dimensions. "Our faith is not just a weekend obligation, a mystery to be celebrated around the altar on Sunday. It is a pervasive reality to be practiced in homes, offices, factories, schools, and businesses across our land."[40]

Second, the two values that form the foundation of Catholic social thought are *human dignity*, realized in *community*. The human person is both sacred and social. The church's profound commitment to the values of human dignity and community is based on the biblical stories of *creation* and of God's *covenant* with the people of Israel.

Human beings are created in the image and likeness of God (Gen 1:27) and as such are gifted with an unearned and inestimable value and dignity. Each person is obligated to respect this human dignity and to treat one another as sacraments of God and as sisters and brothers. Through the call of Abraham and his descendants and through God's revelation to Moses at Sinai, God established a covenant with the Hebrew people.

God acted in the history of the people of Israel, liberating them from bondage in Egypt and thus demonstrating compassion, faithfulness, and concern for justice and freedom. At Sinai God promised to take care of the people if they would keep the covenant with God. Chapters 20–23 in the book of Exodus detail the code that is to characterize their lives: faithful worship of God alone, care for one another, creation of a just community, and a special concern for the vulnerable members of the community—widows and orphans, the poor, and strangers. Thus the people of Israel are called into community, a just community that becomes the norm of their faithful response to God's love for them.[41]

Principles

These two values, then, human dignity and just community, rooted in the stories of creation and covenant, are the foundation for the major principles developed in Catholic social teaching. Although listings of the principles may differ somewhat, those most relevant to the themes developed in this book are human rights, social sin, solidarity, participation, the preferential option for the poor, peacemaking, and care for creation. Each will receive at least a brief reflection here.

The meaning of *human rights* and the development of this principle in Catholic social thought will be explored in chapter 5. Clearly the concept of human rights is rooted in the creation of humanity in the image of God and in the obligations of life in community. Pope John XXIII provides the fullest exposition of human rights from the church's perspective in his encyclical *Peace on Earth* (*Pacem in Terris*) (1963).[42]

Whenever the church talks about human rights, it is careful to give equal attention to human responsibility. Catholic social thought has used human rights as a normative framework for addressing the minimal obligations of any society or polity in a pluralistic world.[43] In other words, the least that can be expected of any government is to create a society where basic human needs (food, water, health care, education, shelter, and safety) are met, and where there is the opportunity to develop one's potential and to participate in society through work and through the political process. Each person, then, has the responsibility to use his or her gifts for the betterment of society and to participate in creating a more just community.

There is an abiding awareness in Catholic social thought that evil and sin tend to become embedded in the structures and institutions of society, that is, there is a consciousness of *social sin* or the "structures of sin." This concept is deeply rooted in the theology of the Hebrew prophets who accused Israel of infidelity and who functioned as the conscience of the nation.

The social sciences have convincingly argued that all knowledge is socially constructed—that is, that each person is so enmeshed in culture and society that it is virtually impossible to understand or know anything outside of our social framework.[44] This adds an empirical dimension to the concept of social sin. Thus, for example, racism transcends the sum total of individual acts of discrimination and can become institutionalized and self-perpetuating in a society.[45] The same claim can be made for other social sins, such as sexism, heterosexism, violence, ethnic hatred, and materialism or consumerism.

In his encyclical *On Social Concern*, Pope John Paul II speaks of "'structures of sin,' which . . . are rooted in personal sin, and thus always linked to the concrete acts of individuals who introduce these structures, consolidate them and make them difficult to remove. And thus they grow stronger, spread, and become the source of other sins, and so influence people's behavior."[46] Pope John Paul II then points to two interrelated actions and attitudes that seem to him to be at the root of structures of sin in the contemporary world—"the all-consuming desire for profit" and "the thirst for power." They give rise to "certain forms of modern imperialism" and to "real forms of idolatry: of money, ideology, class and technology."[47] Certainly race, ethnicity, and gender could be added to the idolatries mentioned by the pope.

> **For Reflection**
>
> It is generally easier to see the social sin of other nations than it is to see the sinful structures of one's own nation. The anti-Semitism of Nazi Germany clearly transcended the acts of individuals and became the sin of the nation. The same was true of apartheid in South Africa. What are the social sins of contemporary America? Of the Catholic Church? How can social redemption be accomplished?

If evil is structured into a society, its remedy must include social transformation, that is, changing the structures and institutions of society. Christian responsibility, then, must include both *charity*, personal acts of compassion in response to individual suffering, and *justice*, social and political action aimed at transforming the root causes of evil and suffering. Christians should be found in soup kitchens, tutoring programs, and inner-city clinics, and on picket lines, in political campaigns, and congressional lobbies.[48]

Pope John Paul II recommends the virtue of *solidarity* as the antidote to structures of sin. He sees solidarity as the moral virtue and social attitude that corresponds to the reality of global interdependence.

> [Solidarity] then is not a feeling of vague compassion or shallow distress at the misfortunes of so many people, both near and far. On the contrary, it is a firm and persevering determination to commit oneself to the common good; that is to say to the good of all and of each individual, because we are all really responsible for all.[49]

Solidarity is diametrically opposed to the desire for profit or a thirst for power. It calls for a readiness to sacrifice oneself for the sake of the other and to serve the neighbor, as opposed to a willingness to exploit or oppress the other for one's own advantage. Because of the unity and interdependence of humanity, the virtue of solidarity is a commitment to recognize the equality of persons and peoples, to share the goods of creation with all, and to work with others as partners on behalf of development, justice, and peace.[50]

Likewise, Pope Francis understands solidarity on three levels: practical acts that meet the real needs of the poor, working to change the structural causes of poverty, and the creation of a new attitude or perspective that thinks in terms of community. As he writes in *Evangelii Gaudium,*

> In this context we can understand Jesus' command to his disciples: "You yourselves give them something to eat!" (Mark 6:37): it means working to eliminate the structural causes of poverty and to promote the integral development of the poor, as well as small daily acts of solidarity in meeting the real needs which we encounter. The word "solidarity" is a little worn and at times poorly understood, but it refers to something more than a few sporadic acts of generosity. It presumes the creation of a new mindset which thinks in terms of community and the priority of the life of all over the appropriation of goods by a few.
>
> Solidarity is a spontaneous reaction by those who recognize that the social function of property and the universal destination of goods are realities which come before private property. . . . Changing structures without generating new convictions and attitudes will only ensure that

those same structures will become, sooner or later, corrupt, oppressive, and ineffectual.[51]

Solidarity, then, encompasses acts both of charity and of justice, motivated by a mindset resolutely focused on community and the common good.

Increasingly, Catholic social thought has understood social justice in terms of *participation*.[52] "Social justice implies that persons have an obligation to be active and productive participants in the life of society and that society has a duty to enable them to participate in this way."[53] The principle of participation is rooted in the created dignity of the human person, who is endowed with freedom and charged with self-determination, and in the obligations of a just community.

The church's understanding of participation is broad and inclusive, and it involves reciprocal obligations on the part of individuals and society. Pope John Paul II and the American and Canadian bishops have stressed both the right to civil or *political* participation and the right to meaningful work, or *economic* participation.[54] As citizens and workers, persons should have the opportunity and the obligation to participate in a whole range of voluntary organizations and associations, including political parties and unions, and in the full spectrum of political and economic decisions. Nations, as well, large and small, rich and poor, should have the opportunity and the obligation to participate in international organizations such as regional associations, the World Trade Organization (WTO), and the United Nations.[55] It is the principle of participation that empowers persons and nations to have a voice in decisions that affect them.

There is a balanced appreciation of the role of the government in Catholic social thought. On the one hand, the principle of *subsidiarity*, which insists that larger communities should not usurp the proper role and authority of smaller communities, tends to decentralize power and to limit the authority of central governments.[56] On the other hand, the principle often called *socialization* insists on the proper role of central government, especially in the increasingly complex contemporary world, to help promote the common good and to advocate for the poor.[57] National government should not render citizens and local communities powerless by throwing its weight around where inappropriate, but government should not fail to exercise power where it is needed. Both individual initiative and government intervention can be proper forms of participation.

In their pastoral letter on the American economy, the US Catholic bishops highlight the *preferential option for the poor*.[58] The bishops stated that Christians must judge the morality and the justice of public policies from the perspective of the poor:

> Decisions must be judged in light of what they do *for* the poor, what they do *to* the poor, and what they enable the poor to do *for themselves*. The fundamental moral criterion for all economic decisions, policies, and

institutions is this: They must be at the service of *all people, especially the poor.*[59]

This option for the poor and the powerless is a remarkably challenging way to invite contemporary Christians to "Be compassionate as your Father is compassionate."

The US bishops adapted this principle from their brother bishops in Latin America. In 1968 the Latin American Bishops Conference met at Medellín, Colombia, to reflect on the implications of the Second Vatican Council and especially its *Pastoral Constitution on the Church in the Modern World.* That document said that "the church has always had the duty of scrutinizing the signs of the times and of interpreting them in the light of the gospel."[60] The most significant "sign of the time" in Latin America was the crushing poverty of the overwhelming majority of people and the glaring gap between the rich and the poor. At Medellín the church began to move haltingly from the side of the rich to stand with the poor. When the Latin American bishops met again in 1979 in Puebla, Mexico, they articulated this move as the "preferential option for the poor."[61] This Latin American theology was consistent with Pope Paul VI's encyclical *On the Development of Peoples* (1971) and, after being picked up by the US bishops, was also employed by Pope John Paul II in his *On Social Concern* (1987, ##42–45).[62] The option for the poor is a key principle of Catholic social teaching.

The preferential option for the poor has deep biblical roots. God's compassionate and caring concern for the poor is a dominant theme in the Hebrew Scriptures and in the message and ministry of Jesus and the early Christian community. The commitment of God's people to the covenant was manifested in their treatment of the widow, the orphan, and the stranger. In *Evangelii Gaudium,* Pope Francis takes pains to establish the New Testament basis of the option for the poor:

> God's heart has a special place for the poor, so much so that he himself "became poor" (2 Cor 8:9). The entire history of our redemption is marked by the presence of the poor. Salvation came to us from the "yes" uttered by a lowly maiden from a small town on the fringes of a great empire. The Savior was born in a manger, in the midst of animals, like children of poor families; . . . he was raised in a home of ordinary workers and worked with his own hands to earn his bread. When he began to preach the Kingdom, crowds of the dispossessed followed him, illustrating his words: "The Spirit of the Lord is upon me, because he has anointed me to preach good news to the poor" (Luke 4:18). He assured those burdened by sorrow and crushed by poverty that God has a special place for them in his heart: "Blessed are you poor, yours is the Kingdom

of God" (Luke 6:20); he made himself one of them: "I was hungry and you gave me food to eat," and he taught them that mercy towards all of these is the key to heaven (cf. Matt 25:5ff.).[63]

Jesus identified himself with the hungry, the thirsty, the stranger, the naked, the sick, and the imprisoned—with "the least of these" (Matt 25:31–46).

Who are the poor? "[T]he poor are the economically disadvantaged, the materially deprived, who as a consequence suffer powerlessness, exploitation and oppression."[64] Poverty, then, is primarily an economic and material reality in this usage. The US bishops acknowledge the many spiritual and physical diminishments affecting people but add that material poverty compounds these problems.[65] The option for the poor calls Christians and the church to stand with the hungry, the homeless, the have-nots, those without access to adequate education, employment, or basic health care—those on the margins of society.

The "option" or choice for the poor is not optional. "Rather it is a decisive action and a deliberate choice, reflecting values as well as desires, flowing from the core of . . . faith."[66] Standing with the poor,[67]

A Latin American churchman whose life illustrates the preferential option for the poor is Dom Hélder Câmara (1909–1999). Dom Hélder was Archbishop of Olinda and Recife in northern Brazil from 1964 until his retirement in 1985, a period that directly corresponded to the military regime in Brazil. He turned the resplendent residence of the archbishop into a community center and moved into three rooms at the back of a church in Recife. He had no car or chauffeur; he would simply set off toward his destination and inevitably one of his flock would offer him a ride. He tried to persuade the bishops gathered at Vatican II to give their gold crosses to the poor and wear wooden crosses as he did. When the powers that be sent an assassin to his home, Dom Hélder greeted the man and fixed him tea. The man was so taken aback by the humility and goodness of Dom Hélder that he could not do his job. Câmara continually worked with the poor and spoke out on their behalf, so the military regime banned him, forcing the media to treat him as if he did not exist. Many others in the Latin American church who opposed the violent oppression of the poor, such as Archbishop Óscar Romero in El Salvador, were martyred during this period.

being present to the poor, seeing the world from the perspective of the poor, working with the poor, advocating for the poor, this is *essential* to being a follower of Christ. Christians stand with the poor because God stands with the poor. "This is why I want a Church which is poor and for the poor," writes Pope Francis. "We are called to find Christ in [the poor], to lend our voice to their causes, but also to be their friends, to listen to them, to speak for them and to embrace the mysterious wisdom which God wishes to share with us through them."[68] Given the scandalous extent and depth of poverty in the United States and in the world (see chapter 3), the preferential option for the poor is a radical challenge. How is it possible that there can be rich Christians in a hungry world?[69]

Care for creation has gradually received the attention in Catholic social teaching that the contemporary ecological crisis deserves. John Paul II included passing mention of ecological concerns in two of his social encyclicals and also addressed the issue in his World Day of Peace Message in 1990. The US bishops and other bishops' conferences (notably the Philippines) produced statements on the issue. Pope Benedict XVI included a section on the ecological crisis in his 2009 encyclical *Charity in Truth* (##48–51), and he focused on the topic in his 2010 World Day of Peace message, "If You Want to Cultivate Peace, Protect Creation."[70] This developing, contemporary teaching culminates with Pope Francis's 2015 encyclical devoted to the environment, *Laudato Si': On Care for Our Common Home.*[71] The theological literature on theology and ecology continues to proliferate and progress.[72]

Prior to the contemporary environmental crisis, Western Christianity's largely unexamined environmental ethic was one of human domination over the earth.[73] The environmental crisis spurred the church to develop an ecological theology and to examine its environmental ethic. John Paul II and Benedict XVI moved the Catholic Church from a position of human domination over earth to one of human stewardship of earth. They teach that creation is a gift of God entrusted to humanity to care for and cultivate. "Human beings legitimately exercise a *responsible stewardship over nature,* in order to protect it, to enjoy its fruits and to cultivate it in new ways, with the assistance of advanced technologies, so that it can worthily accommodate and feed the world's population" (*Charity in Truth,* #50). Human beings, created in God's image, are seen as co-creators with God and as stewards or caretakers of earth and its resources. Benedict also made Vatican City the world's first carbon-neutral state (it is also the world's smallest state)—an accomplishment that may speak more loudly and profoundly about the church's commitment to environmental responsibility than its documents.[74]

This environmental ethic of human stewardship for the natural world is theologically defensible and environmentally helpful. Genesis is clear that God created the world and remains in charge of it. "Everything that exists belongs to God, who has entrusted it to man, albeit not for his arbitrary use. . . . Man thus has a duty to exercise responsible stewardship over creation, to care for it and to cultivate it" ("If You Want to Cultivate Peace, Protect Creation," #6). The "dominion" (Gen 1:26, 28) given to human beings can persuasively be understood in terms of responsibility rather than authority. Humans are to care for and cultivate the earth so that the human community can flourish.

Pollution of the air, water, and land and overconsumption of natural resources harm human beings, especially the poor, and threaten the future of humankind. Wise environmental practices are in the enlightened self-interest of humanity. A stewardship ethic can justify and motivate important changes in human behavior and significant social transformations.

In his 2015 encyclical, *Laudato Si': On Care for Our Common Home,* Pope Francis takes church teaching a step further, away from the worrying anthropocentrism (human-centeredness) of stewardship, to a theocentric, relationship ethic of human kinship with nature. Stewardship does not give intrinsic value to creation, nor does it acknowledge human relationship with and dependence on nature. Pope Francis, consciously and clearly, draws on his namesake to connect humanity with nature and to focus on care for creation and the option for the poor. "[St. Francis] shows us just how inseparable the bond is between concern for nature, justice for the poor, commitment to society, and interior peace" (#10). Pope Francis rejects anthropocentrism as an inadequate Christian anthropology with disastrous results for the poor, the vulnerable, and the biotic community (##115–21). He develops an integral ecology in which each organism and ecosystem has intrinsic value beyond its usefulness, and everything in nature and in society is interrelated and interconnected (##138–42). This is an ecological theology and environmental ethic that is sound, in tune with contemporary cosmology and evolutionary biology, and potentially responsive to the ecological crisis.

Pope Francis connects the despoliation of nature with the exploitation of the poor and oppressed. Climate change and poverty are two manifestations of humanity's fundamental problem—a technological and consumerist worldview that treats both nature and people as resources to be used. Our "throwaway culture" (#22) leaves us drowning in our wastes and gagging in pollution, and it results in abortion of defenseless embryos and exploitation of the poor. The only adequate response is to overcome individualism, apathy, and self-centeredness and forge a mindset based on community, compassion, and love. In *Laudato Si'*, Pope Francis offers a prophetic critique of the prevailing consumerist worldview and calls for a fundamental conversion of mind and heart.[75]

Finally, peacemaking (a central issue in chapters 6 and 7) has been another prominent and consistent theme in Catholic social thought. The Catholic tradition, at least from the fourth century on, has not taken a pacifist position. Rather, it has justified war as a rule-governed exception to the moral presumption in favor of peace. Indeed, when the US bishops, in their pastoral letter *The Challenge of Peace,* affirmed nonviolence as a legitimate position for Christians to hold, many hailed this as significant progress.[76] Although it has not uttered a definitive "no" to war or military intervention as a last resort, the contemporary church has been a vocal advocate for peace in four specific ways:

1. By promoting and working for justice—through development, human rights, and participation—the church has sought to overcome the causes of war. Pope John XXIII's advocacy of human rights in his encyclical *Peace on Earth* was an important step in this direction. Following John XXIII, Pope Paul VI said that "the new name for peace is development," a sentiment reiterated by popes John Paul II and Francis.[77] The church has clearly identified the connection between working for justice and making peace and has not been fooled into thinking that calm in the midst of injustice, oppression, hostility, or hatred is genuine peace.[78] Justice and forgiveness are the only sure foundations for peace.[79]

2. By developing the just-war tradition and applying it to policies and situations, the church has insisted that military intervention and warfare are *moral* questions, not merely tools of the state or techniques of *realpolitik*. And the church's moral analysis has yielded important conclusions, such as the condemnation of "any act of war aimed indiscriminately at the destruction of entire cities or of extensive areas along with their population. . . ,"[80] its prohibition on the use of nuclear weapons,[81] and the "strictly conditioned moral acceptance of nuclear deterrence . . . as a step on the way toward progressive disarmament."[82]

By persuasively articulating the criteria of the just-war tradition, the Roman Catholic Magisterium has provided a moral framework that has significantly influenced public policy discussions and the policies themselves. The decision about military intervention in the Persian Gulf (1991), for example, was debated largely in terms of the just-war tradition, and the Pentagon took pains to persuade the public that it was fighting the war within the bounds of the principle of discrimination.[83] Recently, the church has increasingly fostered nonviolence, with its insistence on conflict resolution, diplomacy, and alternatives to violence. Indeed, Pope John Paul II and his successors sometimes come across as at least practical pacifists in their continual calls for peace and their criticisms of war and violence.[84]

3. By decrying the arms race and the misplaced priorities evident in military spending, the church has functioned as a moral check on an irrational situation. In the words of the Second Vatican Council, "the arms race is an utterly treacherous trap for humanity, and one which injures the poor to an intolerable degree."[85] Again, the church is making the connection between justice and peace, pointing out not only the danger of accumulating weapons of mass destruction, but also the theft from the poor represented by extravagant military spending.

4. By supporting institutions designed to promote peace, the church has played a constructive role in creating the conditions for peace. By reminding the world of the fact of interdependence and by calling for the virtue of solidarity that is necessary for creating a just global community, the church has

advocated a world order that is essential for justice and peace.[86] The church continually supports and suggests strengthening the United Nations and other regimes that foster cooperation and conflict resolution. And the church has been willing, sometimes behind the scenes, as in the Cuban Missile Crisis (John XXIII) and in Poland (John Paul II), and sometimes more publicly, as in El Salvador (archbishops Romero and Rivera), to participate directly in conflict resolution.

Given that contemporary Catholic social teaching was partly developed in a Cold War world characterized by a deep polarization of competing ideologies, there is a remarkable *balance* in Catholic social thought. To the polarizations of "either/or," Catholic social thought responds with "both/and." Catholic social teaching affirms both the value and dignity of each human person and the value of the community, both individual freedom and the common good, both human rights and human responsibility, both personal sin and structures of sin and the redemption of persons and nations and all of creation, both the obligation of society to enable persons to participate in political and economic life and the responsibility of the person to participate in society, both the principle of subsidiarity or decentralization of decision making and the principle of socialization or the proper role of government, both nonviolence and the justified use of force.

There is much to be said for this balance in Catholic social teaching. It focuses on seeking the truth rather than getting trapped in a one-sided ideology that is popular at the moment. It allows the church to criticize both capitalism and socialism and to call for the integral or holistic development of the human person. It also allows the church to be critical and constructive without being politically partisan.

The danger of such balance, however, is the tendency to be dispassionate or lukewarm when a situation calls for the passionate defense of justice or a bruising condemnation of oppression. If we are to be considered true allies of Christ in the tradition of Hebrew prophets, there are times when the church and Christians should be prophetic—when we should, and indeed, *must*, take sides. Indeed, the preferential option for the poor and the church's clear stand on behalf of human dignity, human rights, just community, peacemaking, and stewardship of creation call for precisely such committed advocacy and action. Reason and truth are not obstacles to a passion for justice and peace; selfishness and apathy are the problems.

Undoubtedly, there are many who would urge the church to take even stronger stands for justice and peace, but the record of the Christian community as a justice seeker and peacemaker is, on the whole, positive and constructive. Included in that record is the witness and service of individual Christians whose lives have introduced neighbors and friends to Catholic social thought and the social teaching of the churches. Some of these Christian witnesses have become well-known, including Dorothy Day, Dom Hélder Câmara, Saint Óscar Romero, Jean Donovan, Martin Luther King Jr., Desmond Tutu, Mother Teresa, Cesar Chavez, Helen Prejean, and Philip and Daniel Berrigan.[87] Those who practice justice and peace are eloquent witnesses to the healing presence and reconciling power of God in our world. Their stories may be the best entry point into the social witness of the church.

STUDY QUESTIONS

1. Is the idea that faith is a relationship with God meaningful for you?

2. What is the message of Jesus? What makes you think that Jesus was or was not interested in justice and peace issues? Is the gospel message relevant to social, economic, and political issues?

3. Can you think of a personal experience where Jesus's Third Way could have offered you an alternative between fighting or fleeing?

4. Catholic social teaching has been called the church's "best kept secret." What strategies would you propose for getting this message out to people in the church and into society? What is the message? What are the central themes in Catholic social teaching?

5. How can Christians follow Christ in a consumer society? How should rich Christians respond to a hungry world? What would it mean to take seriously the "preferential option for the poor?"

6. In what ways do you think the church has been successful in being an advocate for justice and a peacemaker? In what ways has the church fallen short in these roles?

2

THE TWENTY-FIRST CENTURY: HOW DID WE GET HERE?

[T]he most fundamental task is for our community of faith to understand and act on two fundamental ideas. The first is drawn from the Beatitudes: "Blessed are the peacemakers, they will be called children of God." The second is the familiar call of Pope Paul VI: "If you want peace, work for justice." These two deceptively simple statements outline the key elements of our mission: To be Christian is to be a peacemaker and to pursue peace is to work for justice.

National Conference of Catholic Bishops,
"Concluding Word," *The Harvest of Justice Is Sown in Peace* (1993)

On September 11, 2001, our world changed. The terrorist attack that destroyed the World Trade Center in New York City, damaged the Pentagon in Washington, DC, and killed three thousand ordinary people, was so brutal as to be incredible. As an act of terrorism it was brilliant. There are no better symbols of American (and Western) economic and military power than the World Trade Center and the Pentagon. The coordination, skill, and sophistication of this new type of suicide bombing and the commonplace character of its victims did indeed terrorize a complacent American populace. Why would someone hate America so much as to forfeit his life to kill thousands of average Americans? Is there an effective and moral response to terrorism?

World politics had already changed dramatically at the beginning of the last decade of the twentieth century (1989–1991) with the collapse of Communism in Eastern Europe and the Soviet Union, which signaled the end of the Cold War. This positive political development, however, had little practical effect on realities such as global economic inequality, population pressures, or environmental destruction. Poverty has bedeviled humanity from its origins, but modern economic systems, the global economy, and ecological concerns are relatively new. Violence has always been a scourge for humankind, but today we have the ability to combine medieval brutality with hi-tech sophistication.[1] The aim of this chapter is to trace the three major trends or historical movements that set up the current economic, political, and environmental situations.

Obviously, this is a look at the big picture. Understanding these historical megatrends is important if humanity is to overcome the obstacles to a more just and peaceful world. Trying to remedy a problem without addressing its history is like trying to rid a yard of dandelions without pulling up their roots. It simply does not work.

The three historical movements that have produced the contemporary world are colonialism, the industrial/technological revolution, and the large-scale trends that characterize the latter half of the twentieth century—the Cold War, democratization, and globalization. Each will be examined in turn.

COLONIALISM

Commemorating Christopher Columbus

In 1992 the peoples of the Americas commemorated the five hundredth anniversary of Columbus landing in what we now call the Caribbean. There was much controversy about this anniversary. While earlier generations in the United States might have unabashedly danced in the streets in honor of this quincentennial, and some wished to do so, many people were too aware of the ambiguities for a wholehearted celebration.[2] This paragraph's first sentence was carefully crafted to attend to some of the politically sensitive issues raised by this anniversary, and dissecting that sentence can introduce those issues.

First, "the peoples of the Americas": Columbus found what came to be called the Americas (North, South, and Central). He first landed in what is today the Dominican Republic, and he explored the Caribbean on subsequent journeys. Columbus, so the story goes, thought he was in India, so he called the people who were here "Indians."

Next, "landing," not discovery. As the comedian and social commentator Dick Gregory used to say, "How do you 'discover' a land that is already occupied?" Yet in elementary school I learned that Columbus discovered America in 1492. There is a good deal of hubris and more than a touch of racism in the notion that until Europeans set foot in a place, it does not really exist. The Americas were a "New World" for the Europeans, but these lands were already home for the indigenous people.

"Caribbean." The Carib people were found on many of the islands in the sea named after them when Columbus arrived. The Carib people were nearly exterminated—wiped out by the diseases and the swords brought over by the Europeans. When whites arrived in the Americas there were perhaps 100 million aborigines living in the Western Hemisphere. Within about a century that number was reduced by nearly 90 percent. "The demographic disaster that struck the hemisphere's aborigines after 1492 has no equal in history, not even the Black Death."[3]

"Commemorate." It is, in part, because we are acutely aware of the fate of native peoples, resulting from Europeans coming to the Americas, that we remembered, rather than celebrated, this anniversary. The European "settlement" of the Americas was a mixed tragedy. From the perspective of the aboriginal peoples the settlement was a conquest that led to the exploitation of their labor and resources, the loss of their land and freedom, and their death.

This is surely one of the worst stories of exploitation and oppression in all of human history. There were, of course, winners and losers in this sad saga. Europe and some Europeans benefited immensely from the exploitation of the resources of the Americas, and there was a mutual enrichment that eventually developed from the mingling of these cultures and peoples. But despite benefits that may have accrued for the overall good of humanity from colonialism, the central story is one of inhumanity and injustice. An additional and equally unjust chapter in the story is the enslavement of Africans to work on the plantations in the Caribbean and the Americas. Put simply, white people from Europe exploited the people, lands, and resources of black, brown, red, and yellow people all over the globe. That is the story and the legacy of colonialism.

Thus far, the tale of colonialism has been introduced through the prism of the commemoration of the five hundredth anniversary of Columbus landing in the Americas. It is beyond the scope of this book to explore colonialism in detail,[4] but it is important to communicate the breadth of European colonialism and a sense of what it meant to those who were colonized.

Europe Colonizes the World

The colonial period began around 1500 and lingers into the present, although nearly all colonies have now gained political (though not necessarily economic) independence. During this period only a handful of countries escaped direct colonization, most notably China, Japan, and Turkey.[5] No country, however, escaped the impact of European military and economic power. Indeed, these exceptions avoided direct colonization principally because of the balance of power among contending European colonizers.

In the case of China, for example, the European powers and the United States agreed on an Open Door policy after the British navy defeated China in the Opium Wars of 1839–1842. This agreement was designed to block Russia and Japan from actually annexing Chinese territory, thereby keeping the wealth, technology, and resources of China open to the exploitation of all. Through its victory, Britain won the "right" to profitably export deadly opium *into* China.[6]

Another set of figures indicates the extent of European colonial control. "In the year 1800, Europe, its colonies, and its former colonies already covered 55 percent of the world's land surface. By 1914, that figure reached an astonishing 84 percent of the land surface."[7] Given the indirect colonial control of countries like China and Turkey, virtually every people on earth has experienced the domination or influence of Europeans.

Phase One—1500–1815

The colonial period of European expansion can be divided into two phases.[8] The first phase, from 1500 to 1815, was characterized by exploration and trade. Spain and Portugal, and later the Netherlands, were the dominant powers during this period.

As Marco Polo learned, the crafts and goods of the Orient were at first superior to those of Europe. By the sixteenth century, Europe was beginning to trade on a more equal basis with the East. The goal of the European powers regarding the East was to establish trading posts and trade routes, and to compete favorably with each other for the goods of the Orient. The Europeans found Africa to be inhospitable for settlement because of disease, climate, and terrain. Thus, they tended to establish heavily armed forts in African ports for the sake of trade.

In Central and South America, however, Spain and Portugal established colonies. Here the environment was amenable and the natives were easily conquered because the Europeans had swords, guns, and horses. The Europeans came in and took over. Mexico provides a good example of what happened in this first phase of colonization.

When Hernán Cortéz landed on the coast of Mexico in 1519 with perhaps six hundred soldiers, he encountered the Aztec Empire that had swallowed Mexico during the seventy-year rule (1427–1496) of its great leader Tlacaelel. The Aztecs were themselves foreign conquerors of the various peoples in Mexico. They had demanded onerous tribute from the indigenous people, and sacrificed tens of thousands of them to their gods. The Aztec Empire was ruthless and exploitative.

The Aztec capital, Tenochtitlan, on the site of today's Mexico City, with its sparkling canals and huge market, was superior to the stinking burgs of medieval Europe. "It could boast archives of bark books, a magnificent calendar, and priests versed in math and astronomy. All Aztec children went to school."[9]

The sophistication of the Aztec civilization, however, did not include metals, horses, or the wheel. When Cortéz brandished his sword, fired his blunderbuss and cannons, and ran his horses, he easily defeated the woefully ill-armed Aztecs. When he declared himself a god, he found a willing reception among the oppressed indigenous people. After Cortéz conquered the capital, he melted down the exquisite jewelry from the Aztec treasury into gold bars. The

Spanish soldiers raped the women, took the land, and enslaved the people. Angered by human sacrifice, the Spanish killed the Aztec priests and scribes, and burned their bark books, reducing this pre-Columbian culture to ashes. In their sadistic cruelty and their single-minded search for wealth, the Spaniards managed to make the Aztec tyranny pale in comparison.

The indigenous people dropped from overwork in the mines and on the plantations, despaired because of the destruction of their culture, and died from the diseases brought by the Europeans—smallpox, malaria, influenza, measles, typhoid, dysentery, etc.—to which they had no resistance. "The net result of this ruthless exploitation was that the native population declined from seventeen million in 1522 to a mere one million by 1608. Here, surely, is a piece of genocide that rivals any in history!"[10]

By the seventeenth century, Spain had set up a system of "trade" with its colonies that was enshrined in law. The colony sent gold and silver, sugar and tobacco to Spain, and the "mother" country sent back consumer goods. "Bales of tobacco leaves floated to Seville; the Spanish worked these into cigarettes and returned them to Mexico City."[11] Manufacturing was a monopoly of Spain and strictly forbidden to the colonies. All trade was required to use Spanish ships. Thus did colonization cripple the economies of the colonies with economic dependency.

Spain set up two systems within its colonies that have left a lasting legacy throughout Latin America—the hacienda and a three-tiered caste structure. The hacienda was a large, nearly self-sufficient plantation growing sugar, cotton, or, later, coffee (an import from Africa, via the Middle East, to the New World). The hacienda was owned by a landlord and worked by indebted peasants under the supervision of a foreman. This pattern of a landed elite and impoverished, landless peasants still endures throughout Latin America and in much of the Two-Thirds World. A 1975 World Bank survey of eighty-three former colonies found that, typically, only 3 percent of landowners controlled 79 percent of farmland.[12]

Intermarriage between the Spanish and the Indians created a three-tiered caste system in most of Latin America. At the top were the "pure" Europeans, often well educated and wealthy, called *creoles*. Next were the *mestizos*, or mixed bloods, who occupied a middle role. At the bottom were the Indians or indigenous peoples, who continue to be the poorest people in the lowliest positions. In some places, such as Brazil, Cuba, and Puerto Rico, the slave trade added Africans to this mix. Color and class continue to present problems of justice in much of Latin America.

Along with the sword came the cross. In Mexico, at least, the first Franciscan and Dominican missionaries tried to convert the Indians and to protect them from the murderous and greedy soldiers. Bartolomé de las Casas, for example, boldly denounced the inhumane treatment of the Indians to some temporary effect. After Juan Diego's vision of the dark Virgin of Guadalupe in 1531, Indians flocked to the church. By the beginning of the seventeenth century, however, the early missionaries had moved on to other parts of Central America and California. They were replaced by bishops, appointed by the King of Spain, and Spanish priests who were often aristocrats seeking their fortune in Mexico. Now the church became a direct agent of Spanish imperialism and itself a large landowner in the hacienda system. The religious message to the peasants was that the Lord would reward their humble obedience in the next life. Through the power of the church, Spain was able to rule for almost three centuries with barely an army present.[13]

The sixteenth through the eighteenth centuries established the global dominance of Europe and the economic patterns that endure to the present. The basic pattern was that Europe got wealthy and the colonies became impoverished and dependent. This happened because the colonizers established the rules of the game to benefit themselves. The colonial relationship was lopsidedly exploitative. Europe stole the rich resources of the colonies and then used the colonies as a market for European goods. This plundered wealth strengthened Europe for even greater plunder. Within the colonies a similar system prevailed. The wealthy elite, who now possessed the land, became richer through the labor of the peasants under their control. Whether one's perspective is global or domestic, the rich became richer and more powerful because they developed a system that exploited others for their benefit. Here lie the roots of injustice in much of the contemporary world.

Phase Two—1815–1945

The nineteenth century was the zenith of the British Empire. In 1815 Great Britain defeated Napoleon. With France subdued and Spain in decline, Britain ruled the seas. "By 1914, fully one-quarter of all humanity was under the rule of this relatively tiny island state, and it was literally true that the sun never set on the British Empire."[14]

The wealth garnered from the colonial system fueled the Industrial Revolution, which in turn strengthened the power of the colonial system. "It was in part the cash of Liverpool, centre of the triangular trade in slaves, cotton and rum between West Africa, the West Indies and Britain, that financed the mills of South Lancashire, the cradle of the industrial revolution."[15] The British plunder of the Bengal region of India in the mid-eighteenth century provided London with enough capital to be midwife to the birth of the Industrial Revolution. In turn, the Industrial Revolution gave the European states, and especially Britain, a considerable technological advantage. This commercial and military advantage quickly converted mutual trade relations with the East into the lopsided exploitation that characterized the colonial system. In other words, the colonial powers *caused* the underdevelopment of the colonies. British economic policy in India is one example.

Before Britain arrived in India, there was a thriving textile industry based in small shops. When this inexpensive cloth began to compete with the developing textile mills in England, Britain imposed export restrictions (such as a 75 percent tariff) on Indian goods. This diminished cotton exports to Britain in the period of 1815–1832 by a factor of thirteen. In Bengal, the British went so far as to deliberately break the little fingers of thousands of Indian weavers so they could no longer practice their craft. This ruthless policy resulted in massive unemployment.

> The net effect of this policy of enforced complementarity of the British and Indian economies was that the non-agricultural population decreased from 45 percent of the whole in early 1800 to only 26 percent by 1940. Simply put, India had been well on its way toward becoming an industrial, diversified economy. This was reversed by the British.[16]

Through such practices, Britain underdeveloped India.

British trade policy toward its colonies worked as follows: The colony could only export to or import from Britain using only British ships. The manufacture of certain goods that might compete with those produced in Britain was forbidden, and the whole protectionist system was buttressed by tariffs.[17] It was such policies that caused the British subjects who had relocated to the North American colonies to revolt. For example, at one time, no wool or cloth could be produced in the colonies except for local use, and steel furnaces and rolling mills were forbidden. Goods often had to be shipped to England even if their destination was the colony next door. And, of course, there were the taxes and tariffs that burdened the colonials. In North America there was a successful revolt. In Asia and Africa these policies stood.[18]

Although Britain was the dominant power in the nineteenth century, it was not without rivals. In Africa the competition became so sharp that the European powers gathered at the Congress of Berlin in 1884 and carved up the map of Africa into zones of control. The countries created at Berlin bore no resemblance to the natural frontiers or the historical boundaries of various tribes and peoples. Traditional enemies were often lumped together in one state, while in other instances, single tribes were divided into two or three different countries. The casual arrogance of the Congress of Berlin continues to reap a bitter harvest of ethno-nationalist conflict and political chaos in contemporary Africa.[19]

The Congress of Berlin acknowledged Great Britain's control of Uganda and Kenya. Britain was interested in East Africa, and especially Kenya, in part, to protect its trade routes to Asia through the Suez Canal. The colonial administrators decided that Kenya, with its fertile highlands, should produce corn, coffee, wheat, and sisal for export to England. To that end, it created plantations for white settlers by moving the Masai and Kikuyu tribes from their lands and into reservations.

Providing cheap labor for the white settlers, however, turned out to be a problem. The Kikuyu and Masai peoples were self-sufficient and saw no need to work for money. Thus, to meet the need of white settlers from Britain and South Africa for cheap labor, the colonial administration had to adopt measures to undermine native economic independence and to force the local people to depend on a paid labor market for their needs.

First, the colonials instituted a hut tax that had to be paid in cash. Thus the natives would have to earn money to stay out of jail. Next, officials reduced the size of the reservations so that there was not enough land to meet the needs of the tribe. They also taxed the few commodities used by Africans, which raised prices. Finally, they instituted a passbook system and required tribal leaders to produce a quota of workers or be replaced. While the twenty thousand whites in Kenya received full government services and assistance, the four million blacks were neglected.

Not surprisingly the black population decreased from 4 million to 2.4 million in the first two decades of the twentieth century. Many whites expected that the blacks would simply die off. "As Kenya's colonial commissioner commented in 1904, after he had pushed the Masai and many other tribes further back into preserves, 'There can be no doubt that the Masai and many other tribes must go under. It is a prospect which I view with equanimity and a clear conscience.'"[20] When a secret society of the Kikuyu called the Mau Mau rebelled and attacked white-owned farms in the 1950s, brutally killing perhaps a hundred whites and 1,800 of their African supporters, the British retaliated with a vengeful campaign marked by shocking atrocities that annihilated over a hundred thousand Kikuyu.[21]

In dozens of other ways the colonial system skewed the development of the colonies. For example, the capital cities in colonies often were not established in the best place to administer the country, but in the spot that gave easiest access to the outside world. Thus, twenty-eight African capitals are in port cities, while those in Chad, Niger, and Mali are all in the extreme southwest corner of these vast countries.[22] The plantations produced cash crops for export—sugar in the Caribbean, coffee in Brazil, tea in Sri Lanka—instead of subsistence crops for local consumption—corn, beans, or rice. The frequent result was a local economy skewed to cash export that was dependent on the "mother" country and vulnerable to the fluctuations of the international market, while local people often went hungry.[23] Economic dependency and underdevelopment are two of the legacies of colonialism. It can be said that the colonial powers created the Two-Thirds World.

The church, by now Protestant and Catholic, continued to play an ambivalent role in the process of colonization. Missionaries were certainly sincere in their belief that they were bringing a saving truth to peoples who had not heard the gospel, that they were saving souls.[24] The idea that Europeans were bringing Christianity and civilization to primitive cultures and heathen peoples was used to justify European expansion and colonial domination. In hindsight, this appears to be a smokescreen for a pattern of exploitation that is directly contrary to the gospel. But there were surely many people who sincerely thought they were doing what was right. Anglican Archbishop Desmond Tutu, who won the Nobel Peace Prize for his nonviolent resistance to apartheid in South Africa, reflects on the connection between Christianity and colonization from the African perspective: "They used to say that the missionaries came to Africa and they had the Bible and we had the land. And then they said, 'Let us pray.' And when we opened our eyes, we had the Bible and they had the land!"[25] Although having the Bible may be a good thing, using the Bible to steal the land and dominate the people is diametrically opposed to the Bible's teaching.

Education soon became a primary activity of the missionaries, but this too was ambivalent, if not insidious. "The colonial education system was geared to building a class of unimaginative but obedient administrators and concentrated on Westernizing the most able of the indigenous people."[26] Education communicated the so-called superior values of the colonial masters to the elite among the indigenous people and created a cadre of dutiful bureaucrats to carry out the ruler's orders.[27] This fostered a "colonial mentality," that is, a cultural inferiority complex that becomes a self-fulfilling prophecy. An exploited people comes to internalize the stereotypical characteristics born of the prejudices of their exploiters. The result is a dependence that is rooted not only in economic and social structures but in a psychic sense of inferiority. It is no wonder, then, that when Mahatma Gandhi, aware of events like the British maiming of Bengali weavers and the massacre at Jallianwalla Bagh,[28] was asked by a British reporter what he thought of Western civilization, he replied, "I think it would be a good idea." The deleterious effects of colonialism were not only economic and social but also cultural and psychological. Colonialism was an assault on human dignity, perpetuated by Western Christians. Colonial peoples have experienced this and generally understand this history, but colonial powers often manage to deny or rationalize or forget what happened. This history calls for repentance and reparation.

The importance of the history of colonialism for relations among people today was driven home to me by an Irishman I once met on a ferry from France to Ireland. He told me that in his worldwide travels people often mistook his accent to be British, as had I. He said that once he set them straight, people welcomed him with generous hospitality. He could tell that his anecdote had puzzled this naive American, so he explained: "The British have oppressed people all over the globe, but the Irish have never had an empire. Lots of people dislike the British, but they love the Irish, because we have a lot in common with them." I now know the difference between a British and an Irish accent, and the difference it can make.

Phase Three—The United States Emerges as a Neocolonial Power in the Twentieth Century

As the power of Portugal and Spain declined in the first part of the nineteenth century, their colonies in Latin America won their political independence (1808–1826). In the twentieth century the remaining European powers and the emerging powers in Asia spent themselves in two world wars and in efforts to maintain their empires against colonial rebellions. During the twentieth century, and especially in the period after World War II, most colonies in Asia, Africa, and the Caribbean gained their political independence. The economic structures established during colonial rule, however, have allowed the North to continue to exploit the South. This pattern of economic domination, in the absence of direct political rule, is called neocolonialism. The United States emerged as the preeminent neocolonial power in the latter half of the twentieth century.

Because the United States freed itself from colonial rule (1776), one might think it would be in sympathy with anticolonial sentiment, and in solidarity with those trying to shake the shackles of a colonial past. Indeed, in the 1950s, Ho Chi Minh, having read the US Declaration of Independence, wrote to the US president asking for assistance in Vietnam's struggle for independence from French colonial rule. But during the twentieth century, as the European powers declined, the United States stepped in to fill their boots, militarily and economically—as Ho Chi Minh discovered. The United States first supported France and then took France's place on the battlefield in Vietnam in the 1960s.

In 1898, the United States occupied Cuba, Puerto Rico, and the Philippines as part of the spoils from the Spanish-American War (1898). Puerto Rico, some would argue, remains a colony of the United States (it is technically a Commonwealth). In the Philippines, the United States inherited the Filipino rebellion against Spanish colonial rule and crushed it.[29] American textbooks tend to call this episode the Philippine Insurrection. Filipino historians refer to it as the Philippine-American War.

President William McKinley captured the American mindset toward the world at the beginning of the twentieth century in a personal revelation to a group of Protestant missionaries who were visiting him at the White House.

McKinley told the visitors how he had agonized and prayed about what to do with the Philippines. Then late one night it came to him:

> (1) That we could not give them back to Spain—that would be cowardly and dishonorable; (2) that we could not turn them over to France or Germany—our commercial rivals in the Orient—that would be bad business and discreditable; (3) that we could not leave them to themselves—they were unfit for self-government—and they would soon have anarchy and misrule over there worse than Spain's was; and (4) that there was nothing left for us to do but to take them all, and to educate the Filipinos, and uplift and civilize and Christianize them, and by God's grace do the very best we could by them, as our fellow-men for whom Christ also died.[30]

First, of course, the United States had to subdue the Filipinos, already a deeply Catholic people, who were fighting for the very self-government that McKinley thought they were incapable of achieving.

Americans thought of themselves as benevolent colonizers, trying to remake the Philippines in our image through education and a market economy.

> But the U. S. performance in the Philippines was flawed. The Americans coddled the elite while disregarding the appalling plight of the peasants, thus perpetuating a feudal oligarchy [imposed by Spanish colonial rule] that widened the gap between the rich and the poor. They imposed trade patterns that retarded the economic growth of the islands, condemning them to reliance on the United States long after independence. The American monopoly on imports into the Philippines also dampened the development of a native industry. At the same time the unlimited entry of Philippine exports to the United States bound the Archipelago inextricably to the American market. Economically at least, the Filipinos were doomed to remain "little brown brothers" for years—though many, despite their nationalist rhetoric, found security in the role.[31]

Despite American pretensions of a more relaxed attitude and benevolent intentions, American colonialism seems indistinguishable from European colonialism.

With the exception of these three countries that were the spoils of the Spanish-American War, the United States did not have direct colonial relationships. Instead of imposing political control, the United States usurped economic influence and control over former colonies as the power of European countries declined and its own power rose during the twentieth century. This economic influence was backed up by military power. The Philippines clearly illustrates this, but it is hardly a singular case.

Since the Spanish-American War, the United States has intervened militarily in the Caribbean and Central America over twenty times. Early in the twentieth century the United States literally fabricated the country of Panama in order to create a canal for its own use. The most recent US intervention in Panama was in 1989. The United States occupied Haiti from 1915 to 1934, the Dominican Republic from 1916 to 1924, and Nicaragua from 1926 to 1933. The United States intervened in the Dominican Republic in 1965 to prevent a constitutionally elected president, who had been overthrown, from returning to power, and in Haiti in 1994 to return an elected president to power (a better idea). The United States sponsored a rebellion in Nicaragua throughout the 1980s. It has supported brutal despots in Haiti, Nicaragua, Guatemala, the Dominican Republic, and Panama.[32]

The rationale for these interventions has been a mixture of economic and strategic interests. The Caribbean, after all, is perceived by America to be its backyard, as president after president has repeatedly proclaimed in justifying these interventions.[33] The United States brought to these adventures the same condescending domination that characterized its relationship with the Philippines. Americans have been surprised to find that even if we start schools and build roads, people deeply resent being controlled by, or dependent on, others.

America's backyard, according to the Monroe Doctrine of 1823, extends well beyond the Caribbean into South America. In the early years of 1970, Chile, a stable and relatively prosperous democracy, elected a socialist president, Salvador Allende, who won a plurality of votes in a three-way contest. When Allende began to nationalize the copper industry, depriving American companies of their lucrative profits, he was overthrown and killed in a CIA-aided coup that resulted in a military dictatorship under General Augusto Pinochet.[34]

United States influence in Latin America, however, has primarily been economic rather than overtly military. The perpetuation of the economic domination of the Two-Thirds World by the First World after the colonies achieved political independence is simply a new form of colonialism—neocolonialism. The domestic and global structures of injustice usually did not change when Europe ceded or lost direct political control of the colonies. Theologically this systematic injustice is social sin. Global economic inequity, that is, the widening gap between the rich and the poor (the topic of chapter 3), is rooted in the patterns and structures established under colonialism.

THE INDUSTRIAL REVOLUTION

The interplay between colonialism and the Industrial Revolution has already been noted. The wealth amassed from colonialism fueled the Industrial Revolution, which, in turn, further consolidated the power of Europe over the colonies. The point of this section is to try to communicate a sense of how technology has shaped the modern world and of what that means in terms of justice and peace.

When Britain Was the World's Workshop

The Industrial Revolution is a phenomenon of the nineteenth century. It began in Britain and by the end of the century had spread to Europe and the United States. The development of science and the scientific method during the Enlightenment (eighteenth century) prepared the way. Science seeks to understand the way things work; technology applies science to practical problems. The previous three centuries produced an explosion of scientific knowledge and technological advances. Since we are at the crest of this historical wave, we forget how far and how fast the industrialized nations have come. It is important to appreciate the amount and the rate of change that has occurred.

The impact of the Industrial Revolution is dramatized at the St. Fagans National History Museum near Cardiff, Wales. The museum has a row of identical cottages furnished in a typical fashion for a working-class family from 1800 to 1985. Thus, there were seven identical houses in a row. The inside of the house hardly changed from 1800 to 1860. A wooden table and chairs stood on, at first, a dirt floor, then a rough-hewn wooden floor in front of an open fireplace. The family had few and simple possessions. Suddenly, in the second half of the nineteenth century, there was a dramatic change. There appeared curtains and rugs, table settings, a wood-burning stove for heat and cooking, even knick-knacks decorating the room. Life was

> **For Reflection**
>
> William Manchester titled his bestselling book on the Middle Ages and the Renaissance *A World Lit Only by Fire* (Boston: Little, Brown, 1992). No electricity, only candles. No steamships, only sailing ships. No engines, only horsepower. What a very different world that was.
>
> Yet, when traveling in remote areas in the Philippines, I encountered villages "lit only by fire." There are different worlds in our contemporary world.

becoming progressively more refined and more cluttered. By 1985 the house itself hardly seemed adequate for a family. Where does one put the bathroom? Refrigerator? Bedrooms?

Historians now talk of a First Industrial Revolution, primarily in Britain, from 1750 to 1871, and of a New or Second Industrial Revolution throughout the developed world from 1871 to 1960. The development of an industrial economy in nineteenth-century Britain was preceded by social and technological innovations in agriculture that dramatically increased the productivity of the land. A confluence of other social and technological changes seem to have erupted in the Industrial Revolution: the transition from a feudal to a market economy, developments in textile production, improvements in iron and steel manufacture, and the creation of the steam engine. All this led to the rapid transition from crafting by hand to producing by machine, thus multiplying the productivity of labor a hundredfold. In the nineteenth century the gross national product of Great Britain increased by an astounding 400 percent.

The Industrial Revolution increased other things as well: human misery, pollution, and population. An economy based on industry more than agriculture meant the movement of people from rural areas to overcrowded cities, where they worked long hours for low wages in dangerous mills or mines. The industrialists increased their profits by exploiting the labor of children, women, and men. Unemployment was a constant worry in a rapidly changing economy. The cities were ill-prepared to handle the influx of so many people. It is the condition of working people that Charles Dickens would dramatize, Karl Marx would decry, and Pope Leo XIII would address in the first social encyclical, *Rerum Novarum: The Condition of Labor* (1891).[35]

Industry produced more goods, but its byproducts fouled the air and polluted rivers and lakes, harming the health of humans and the habitats of animals and plants. The increase in productivity and wealth came at a terrible cost to the environment.

In the late eighteenth century there was a surge in the population in Europe and even in countries as far removed as the United States and China. The causes of this population boom are not clear. There were improvements in public health and in the food supply and diet, and women were marrying younger. Whatever the exact reasons, there were suddenly many more "have-nots" crowding into major cities and stuffed into rural hovels. This increasing labor force would fuel the Industrial Revolution as much as the coal and the steam it ran on and the steel it produced.

At first, however, the Industrial Revolution produced the prospect of a mismatch between the number of people and the resources of a finite earth to sustain them. In 1798 Thomas Robert Malthus, an English country curate, expressed this concern in his famous *Essay on Population*. Malthus noted that population increased geometrically, like interest on a savings account. If the annual population growth rate is 2 percent, then the population will double every thirty-five years. Britain's population was doubling every twenty-five years. Malthus thought it inconceivable that the productivity of the land could keep pace with this growth in population. He predicted that population would be kept in check only by widespread famine, disease, and/or war. Malthus's pessimism was out of step with the optimism of the intellectuals of his day who were anticipating the perfectibility of humanity and who engaged Malthus in critical debate.[36]

In the nineteenth century Malthus's dire predictions proved to be wrong. Three escape hatches prevented the Malthusian trap from closing on the British people. The first was *emigration*. Between 1815 and 1914 around twenty million Britons left the country and settled in the United States, Canada, Australia, and southern Africa. Nearly half of Britain's population emigrated. The second was the remarkable *improvement in agricultural productivity*. Not only did Britain itself produce considerably more food, it was also able to import food from the lands its subjects were settling. In the nineteenth century the power of the land was able to match the power of population. The third and most significant development was the *Industrial Revolution* with its leap forward in productivity and in wealth. "During the nineteenth century as a whole, the British population grew *fourfold*, whereas the national product grew *fourteenfold*."[37] Human ingenuity, then, was key to avoiding the Malthusian trap.

> Thus, "the power of population" was answered, not so much by "the power in the earth" itself, but by the power of technology—the capacity of the human mind to find new ways of doing things, to invent new devices, to organize production in improved forms, to quicken the pace of moving goods and ideas from one place to another, to stimulate fresh approaches to old problems.[38]

Moreover, the Industrial Revolution led to social changes that decreased population growth. Thus, Britain went through a demographic transition that stabilized population over time.

It is important to note, however, that not every country escaped the Malthusian trap in the nineteenth century. Ireland and India, two countries under British domination, experienced famine. These famines, however, like most famines, were caused more by oppressive political and economic policies rather than by simple Malthusian scarcity. War, in the form of the social turbulence of the French Revolution and the attempt at imperial conquest under Napoleon Bonaparte, served to vent France's population pressures.[39]

In the twenty-first century, Malthus's predictions pose an acute problem. The earth's population continues to explode—six billion in 1999, seven billion in 2011, and around eight billion projected by 2024—and the growth is happening primarily in the developing countries, which lack the wealth and technology to cope with the increase. The escape hatches open to Britain are closing or closed today. In this century Malthus may prove to be right after all. (Chapter 4 will further address this problem.)

Change, more and faster, has characterized the New Industrial Revolution in the twentieth century. Technology, powered by fossil fuels and nuclear energy, produced an astounding array of inventions that have dramatically altered patterns of human life and the arrangements of human society. This radical change continues to be a mixed blessing.

Future Shock: Coping with Rapid Change

People who move into another culture often experience culture shock. Familiar patterns and rituals do not work, and they are unfamiliar with the ones that do. This experience is the basis of Alvin Toffler's notion of future shock.[40] The scope and speed of change can make it difficult for individuals and societies to cope or adjust.

Thomas L. Friedman, a *New York Times* columnist and the author of eight books that function as guides to our changing contemporary world, updates Alvin Toffler for the first fifteen years of the twenty-first century with his book *Thank You for Being Late*. Friedman argues that the exponential growth in computing power that occurred around the year 2007 marks another great leap forward in human history comparable to the invention of the printing press in the fifteenth century and the steam engine in the nineteenth century. On January 9, 2007, Steve Jobs announced that Apple had invented the mobile phone, now rightly called a smartphone—a hand computer. In the same year storage capacity for computing exploded, thanks to a company called Hadoop. Around the same time Facebook became widely available, Twitter started to scale globally, Amazon launched the Kindle, Airbnb was conceived, big data analytics kicked into gear, and Change.org, the social mobilization site, emerged. (Gordon) Moore's law, which states that computational processing power will double roughly every two years, for only slightly greater cost while consuming less power, has held up for more than fifty years and counting. This acceleration in the exponential growth of technology was accompanied by comparable accelerations in climate change, population growth, biodiversity loss, and globalization, making the world hyperconnected and interdependent. These simultaneous accelerations in Moore's law, Mother Nature, and the Market constitute the "age of accelerations" in which we now find ourselves and which is transforming almost every aspect of contemporary life. Although humanity's pace of adaptation has quickened from a generation to ten to fifteen years, that is not good enough; we can't keep up anymore, and we experience future shock.[41]

The Ambivalence of Technology

The title of Friedman's book comes from an offhand comment to a friend whose tardiness allowed him to have a few moments of contemplation. The smartphone in your pocket gives you access to incredible amounts of information. Information, however, is neither knowledge nor wisdom.[42] Data can be false, misleading, or trivial. Privacy goes out the window when our digital footprints are virtually permanent and widely accessible.[43] Dating apps can fine tune our social lives but diminish genuine relationships. It is convenient that our smartphone performs the function of maps, compasses, calendars, address books, calculators, watches, music collections, and libraries. Yet too many of us seem addicted to our gadgets, walking through halls or down sidewalks with ear buds in both ears, staring at our phones, oblivious to our surroundings and to other people. The experience of successive generations can be so different as to make it difficult for parents and children and even siblings to understand one another and communicate. The pace of life tends to accelerate beyond endurance. Mastering the role and place of tempting technology in our life is a spiritual struggle in which our humanity itself is at stake.

Technology not only presents social, psychological, and spiritual challenges but also economic and cultural concerns. The Industrial/Technological Revolution characterizes the world and the experience of most people in the developed countries of the North. It is a basis of their wealth and power. But the experience of the majority of people in the less developed countries of the South seems that of another century, another age. The lack of technology is a basis of their poverty. This gap between the rich and the poor raises profound questions of justice.

Increasingly these questions of justice and economic inequality are looming in the global North as well. The skills a person has developed over a lifetime—a master cobbler or travel agent, for example—may suddenly be useless. Apps like Uber and Airbnb displace taxi drivers and hotels. Machines can improve life through increased productivity and new roles for women, for example, but technology can also create social problems—such as unemployment resulting from computers and robots. Artificial intelligence (AI) is transforming the workplace in the United States and other developed countries. Although sometimes AI can lead to an increase in jobs, it will usually eliminate jobs, mostly lower-paying ones, but also some higher-paying ones. The time of medium-skilled, high-paying jobs is past. The workplace now and in the future will focus on skills, which will require both an evolution in education and lifelong education. Future jobs will be in AI and in areas that AI

> Pope Francis reflects on media and the digital world in his encyclical *Laudato Si': On Care for Our Common Home* (2015), #47:
>
> Furthermore, when media and the digital world become omnipresent, their influence can stop people from learning how to live wisely, to think deeply and to love generously. In this context, the great sages of the past run the risk of going unheard amid the noise and distractions of an information overload. Efforts need to be made to help these media become sources of new cultural progress for humanity and not a threat to our deepest riches. True wisdom, as the fruit of self-examination, dialogue and generous encounter between persons, is not acquired by a mere accumulation of data which eventually leads to overload and confusion, a sort of mental pollution.

does not do well, that require creativity, cross-domain thinking, and people skills. Governments will have a role in developing creative policies that redistribute the wealth to those in need. Some have suggested a Universal Basic Income (UBI) as part of the solution, or people could work fewer hours. The populism that is popping up all over the world, including in the United States, is a harbinger of these challenges. Future shock has a social dimension.[44]

THE PRELUDE TO THE TWENTY-FIRST CENTURY

Colonialism and the Industrial Revolution help us understand the great divide between the North and the South and point to the source of wealth and power in the contemporary world. If we are seeking justice and peace, it is also important to have a sense of recent history.

The Cold War dominated politics and international relations from the end of World War II in 1945 until around 1990, when it abruptly ended. It is also important to note the interplay of democracy and tyranny in many places around the world since 1989 (when the Berlin Wall came down), and the economic and cultural trend that is called globalization. The post–Cold War era is a time in history that is ripe with opportunity to create justice and make peace.

Great Powers and Empire

The Modern Era, from 1500 to the present, can be understood as a competition among states for empire. Indeed, imperialism is nearly synonymous with colonialism, and industrialization enabled a country to gain the economic and military power necessary to join the competition for empire.

As we have seen, from the sixteenth through the nineteenth centuries, the great powers were all European. Each, in turn, tried to dominate the others. Spain was the dominant power at the beginning of the seventeenth century. The Treaty of Westphalia, in 1648, concluded the Thirty Years' War in Europe between the alliance of Spain and Austria versus most of the rest of Europe. Spain's defeat marked the decline of its hegemony and the rise of the power of the Netherlands. The Treaty of Westphalia confirmed the notion of sovereign states engaged in a balance of power relationship with each other. At the beginning of the nineteenth century, France sought to dominate Europe, but Napoleon Bonaparte (1769–1821) was ultimately defeated by an alliance led by Great Britain at the Battle of Waterloo (1815). The nineteenth century was the century of the British Empire.

In the twentieth century two non-European powers—the United States and Japan—entered the competition, and different countries in Europe—Germany, Russia, and Italy—began to jockey for power. The First World War (1914–1918) was a horrific, unnecessary, and nonsensical contest between European alliances led by Britain and Germany. Germany lost after the United

States entered the war in 1917 on the side of Britain. Germany resented the punitive conditions imposed by the Treaty of Versailles in 1919. In Eastern Europe, the Russian Revolution of 1917 enabled Russia to incorporate its neighbors into the Union of Soviet Socialist Republics (USSR) under Russian control. The Soviet Union represented the establishment of a new, more powerful Russian Empire.

In the 1930s, Japan, which had already occupied Taiwan and Korea, conquered China. In Europe, Germany, under the leadership of Adolf Hitler, was gaining ascendancy and gobbling up its neighbors. The German invasion of Poland in 1939 marked the beginning of World War II. Hitler signed a non-aggression pact with Joseph Stalin's Soviet Union, which allowed him to quickly overrun France. Then he double-crossed Stalin and invaded the Soviet Union. After Japan destroyed much of the US Pacific Fleet in a surprise attack on Pearl Harbor in late 1941, the United States entered the war, first against Japan, then against Germany. The Second World War brought the inhumanity of warfare to new lows through the attempted genocide of the Holocaust, the obliteration bombing of enemy cities, and the introduction of nuclear weapons in the destruction of Hiroshima and Nagasaki.[45]

The Cold War

World War II decimated the great powers of Europe and Asia. The United States emerged relatively unscathed and with a robust economy. Of the sixty million deaths in World War II, by far the greatest share was suffered by the Soviet Union. Yet the Soviet army had repulsed the German invasion and by the end of the war controlled Eastern Europe and East Germany. When Winston Churchill (UK), Franklin D. Roosevelt (US), and Stalin (USSR) met at Yalta in 1945, they agreed that Eastern Europe would remain under Soviet influence and that Germany would be split into four sectors, each controlled by one of the allies. Berlin, the German capital, deep within the eastern, Soviet sector, was also divided among the four allies—the United States, Britain, France, and the Soviet Union. Thus, what Churchill called the Iron Curtain, dividing the West from the East, was established in Europe. In the early 1960s the Soviet Union turned Churchill's metaphor into a literal wall that divided West and East Germany and West and East Berlin. West Berlin became a capitalist and democratic island in the midst of Communist East Germany.

The Second World War thus dissolved into the Cold War, a continuous, yet relatively stable, conflict between two superpowers—the United States (the West) versus the Soviet Union (the East)—and between the ideological, political, and economic systems they represented—capitalist democracy versus socialist communism. Each developed a network of alliances—the North Atlantic Treaty Organization (NATO), led by the United States, and the Warsaw Pact, led by the Soviet Union—and struggled to retain Third World clients and to enlarge their spheres of influence. While this was a global struggle between West and East fought on many fronts—Korea, Vietnam, Cuba and Central America, Africa, the Middle East, Afghanistan—the main fault line ran through Europe. The great fear of the West was that the Soviet Union would overrun Western Europe, thus consolidating the whole Eurasian landmass from Siberia to Ireland under a communist Russian Empire. The Soviet Union feared yet another invasion from Western Europe.

The United States adopted a foreign policy of "containment," which sought to halt and oppose Soviet and communist expansion throughout the globe by whatever means possible—military, political, economic, ideological. The Soviet Union joined the fray, trying to contain United States and NATO hegemony wherever and however it could. The two superpowers and their allies engaged in a massive arms race in both conventional and nuclear weapons in service of containment. Thus, anticommunism became the single, overriding goal of US foreign policy during the Cold War. Anticommunism justified gargantuan defense budgets, a massive arsenal of doomsday weapons, wars, proxy wars, interventions, coups, counterinsurgency, foreign aid, and support of anticommunist dictators. While the Cold War led to several wars and civil wars throughout the Third World, it did not result in a direct confrontation between the two superpowers, in part because they were deterred by the threat of "mutually assured destruction" through nuclear weapons.

> Find examples of Soviet and American interventions in the interests of containment during the Cold War. Do they mirror each other?

It is not that these two superpowers and the systems they represent are of equal moral value. Communism is a totalitarian system that denies fundamental human rights and that deserves condemnation and committed opposition. Still, during the Cold War period, *both* sides too frequently practiced the dubious ethic of the end (winning the conflict) justifying the means, *any* means. The single-mindedness of the policy of containment may also have blinded US policy makers to the complexity of global situations and to the ambiguity of their own intentions and actions. Thus the Cold War led to many debates and divisions within the West about the ethics of foreign policy.

The End of the Cold War

After forty-five years of conflict and tension, the Cold War (1945–1990) ended with the collapse of communism in the West, first in Eastern Europe, then in the Soviet Union itself. In 1985 a reform-minded leader, Mikhail Gorbachev, rose to power in the Soviet Union. In 1989, when the Solidarity movement in Poland directly challenged the communist government, the Soviet Union sat back and allowed the government to fall. Soon refugees from Eastern Europe were pouring into Western Europe through gaping holes in the Iron Curtain. On November 12, 1989, Germans from East and West began chipping away the Berlin Wall with sledgehammers, wishing, as one of them quipped, that it had not been Germans who had built that wall. The fall of the Berlin Wall symbolized the collapse of communism in Eastern Europe. Within a year (1990) Germany had formally reunited, and communist governments throughout Eastern Europe had been replaced by fledgling democracies. With the notable exception of Romania and the Bosnian civil war, this "velvet revolution" was accomplished nonviolently.

Gorbachev hoped that domestic reform would save the communist system within the Soviet Union, but he could not hold back the tide of change. By the end of 1991 democracy had swept aside communism in the Soviet Union itself, and the fifteen republics of the USSR were becoming independent. World maps were being revised to include new nations with unfamiliar names such as Belarus, Ukraine, Estonia, Georgia, and Kazakhstan. It was a remarkable transformation.

Analysts differ on why the Cold War suddenly ended. Some argue that the Reagan arms build-up in the 1980s forced the Soviet Union into bankruptcy as it tried to keep pace. Others believe the Soviet system collapsed from economic stagnation and bureaucratic corruption. One thing is clear: communism did not work. In retrospect, Russia was exposed as virtually a Third World economy with a genuinely frightening nuclear weapons capability, a respectable space program, and a large but ineffective military that at first was unable to subdue the rebel province of Chechnya. Russia now has a mixed economy. Market reforms of the 1990s privatized much of Russian industry and agriculture. The state, however, still controls the two driving forces in the economy, the energy and defense-related sectors. Russia appears to be a democracy, but Vladimir Putin has served as either president or prime minister since 1999 and was elected to six-year presidential terms in 2012 and 2018. Putin's increasingly authoritarian and repressive rule means that Russia no longer meets the criteria to be considered an electoral democracy. In 2014, Putin seemed to resurrect Cold War tensions by exploiting a political crisis in neighboring Ukraine in order to annex Crimea and stir up a Russian insurgency in Eastern Ukraine.

THE TWENTY-FIRST CENTURY

The Ebb and Tide of Democracy

The democratization of Eastern Europe and the former Soviet Union was part of a third wave of democracy sweeping the globe from about 1974 through

2006. In the Cold War period most of the countries of South and Central America, for example, were ruled by dictators and characterized by frequent coups, but by 1990 nearly every country in Latin America and the Caribbean was, at least formally, a democracy, with the notable exception of Cuba.[46]

> When the third wave began in 1974, only about 30 percent of the world's independent states met the criteria of electoral democracy—a system in which citizens, through universal suffrage, can choose and replace their leaders in regular, free, fair, and meaningful elections. At that time, there were only about 46 democracies in the world. . . . In the subsequent three decades, democracy had a remarkable global run, as the number of democracies essentially held steady or expanded every year from 1975 until 2007. Nothing like this continuous growth in democracy had ever been seen before in the history of the world. While a number of these new "democracies" were quite illiberal . . . the positive three-decade trend was paralleled by a similarly steady and significant expansion in levels of freedom (political rights and civil liberties, as measured annually by Freedom House).[47]

Around 2006, however, this expansion of freedom and democracy stagnated. Since then the number of electoral democracies has oscillated between 114 and 119 or about 60 percent of the world's states.[48] Is it the beginning of a reversal like that which followed the previous waves of democracy, or is it a pause that allows the consolidation of previous democratic gains? Is democracy in decline?[49]

Whether or not democracy can right itself globally, there is a strong perception that it is ebbing in the second decade of the twenty-first century. For example, the so-called Arab Spring began in Tunisia in December, 2010, and quickly spread to Egypt, Yemen, Bahrain, Libya, and Syria. At first it seemed to offer the promise of moving from entrenched dictators to democracy in some countries of the Middle East and North Africa. Except for Tunisia, where democracy may have gained a tenuous foothold, the hoped-for transition toward democracy failed. Egypt ended up with a new dictator. The authoritarian regime in Bahrain never fell. Yemen and Libya are in political chaos, and the civil war in Syria grinds on with the authoritarian ruler Bashar al-Assad still in power. The Middle East and much of Africa and Asia (India is an especially notable exception) seem immune to democratization and thus to respect for human rights and civil liberties. The authoritarian rule and repression of President Putin in Russia, Xi in China, Duterte in the Philippines, Orban in Hungary, etc. is worrying. This authoritarian resurgence, the failure of many emerging democracies to build effective modern states, and the inadequate economic and political performance of advanced democracies are three good reasons for the perception that democracy is declining (see chapter 6).[50]

Genuine democratization has generally signaled political and social progress. It is the form of government most conducive to the implementation of human rights, the common good, justice, and peace. It demands, however, peoples and leaders committed to those values and principles.

Globalization

The last few years of the twentieth century and the beginning of the twenty-first century have been characterized by "globalization." Much has been written about this phenomenon, but it remains difficult to define. In its most positive sense, it refers to the increasing interdependence of the peoples on earth and to a vision of global harmony and unity. Amazing advances in communications technology have fueled globalization. Capital can be transferred anywhere in the world by the touch of a "send" key, and consumer goods can move rapidly from country to country, continent to continent. Labor can also migrate to where it is needed, but more slowly. Capitalism, with its profit motive, now dominates the world economy. Not surprisingly, this has resulted in winners and losers, progress and pitfalls.

Since the beginning of the Industrial Revolution, there has been a tendency to exploit workers, to concentrate wealth in the hands of a few, to plunder the earth of its natural resources, and to pollute the environment. Transnational corporations now scour the earth in search of the cheapest labor, the laxest environmental regulation, the lowest taxes, and the greatest profit. The poor are often oppressed and the earth polluted in this process. Yet, paradoxically, this process also represents the opportunity for economic progress and a better life for many—as did the Industrial Revolution.

Thus the *Great Recession*, which began in the United States in earnest in September 2008 with the collapse of Lehman Brothers, a Wall Street investment bank, quickly spread to other developed countries, especially in Europe.[51] Although the economies in the developed world were still climbing out of the recession eight years later, especially in regard to labor, this cataclysmic event barely registered in the lives of the poor (see chapter 3).[52]

Globalization also tends to homogenize the diverse cultures of the world into a monoculture dominated by Western values and mores. Religious fundamentalism, an often violent rejection of the modern world, represents a backlash against the experience of powerlessness and cultural fragmentation often produced by globalization.

The end of the Cold War did indeed present the global community with a ripe opportunity to create a world that is more just and that lives in peace. The kingdom of God, however, has not yet come. The gap between the rich and the poor continues to widen. Ethno-nationalist conflict has volcanically risen to the surface all over the globe in places such as Bosnia and Kosovo, East Timor, Rwanda and Burundi, Sri Lanka, Ukraine, and Great Britain. Terrorism has become a terrible tool for the disillusioned and the displaced. Human rights are universally recognized but widely violated. Nuclear weapons still hang over humanity's head like the sword of Damocles, and conventional weapons continue to spread like a plague. Environmental damage may threaten the planet itself and thus all of its inhabitants.

These are some of the obstacles to justice and peace at the beginning of the twenty-first century. Now that we have a sense of how humanity arrived at this promising but precarious point in history, we are ready to address these issues.

STUDY QUESTIONS

1. What injustices in the contemporary world are based in colonialism?

2. Is the United States an imperial power?

3. What justice and peace issues in the contemporary world are rooted in the Industrial/Technological Revolutions?

4. Do smartphones and social media help or hamper personal relationships? Human and spiritual development?

5. How are technology and artificial intelligence changing our world in the "age of accelerations"? What steps should be taken to make these changes contribute to the common good?

6. Does the collapse of communism mean that socialism is not a viable economic system? What problems are there with capitalism?

3

POVERTY, ECONOMIC JUSTICE, AND HUMAN DEVELOPMENT

Blessed are you who are poor, for the kingdom of God is yours. Blessed are you who are now hungry, for you will be satisfied. But woe to you who are rich, for you have received your consolation. Woe to you who are filled now, for you will be hungry. (Luke 6:20–21, 24–25)

Central to the biblical presentation of justice is that the justice of a community is measured by its treatment of the powerless in society. . . . The way society responds to the needs of the poor through its public policies is the litmus test of its justice or injustice.

US Conference of Catholic Bishops,
Economic Justice for All, ##38, 123

If the Kingdom of God is the true human society, it is a fellowship of justice, equality, and love. But it is hard to get riches with justice, to keep them with equality, and to spend them with love.

Walter Rauschenbusch
Christianity and the Social Crisis, 77

Poverty is the bane of humankind. It is not a new problem, but the gap between the rich and the poor is widening and worsening today. This is ironic, tragic, and unjust, because, perhaps for the first time in human history, there is enough wealth on earth to meet the basic needs of every person. Until the misery and degradation of billions of brothers and sisters is alleviated there will be no justice, and there will be no peace.

This chapter explores the gap between the rich and the poor among nations and within nations. It begins by reflection on the meaning of poverty. Then it analyzes the economic gap between the global North and the global South, examines the promise and peril of globalization, and focuses on key issues in the debate about economic development and human development and overcoming poverty: multinational corporations and foreign investment, foreign aid, international trade, debt, and economic inequality. The final section of the chapter explores issues related to poverty and conflict.

THE HUMAN FACE OF POVERTY

In 1990 I traveled widely throughout the Philippines, visiting small Christian communities in urban and rural settings. Experiencing the problems faced by a developing country was a transformative experience. The United States has pockets of poverty in the midst of wealth; many Americans never see the stark conditions in inner cities or the hollows of Appalachia. The Philippines has isolated islands of wealth in a sea of poverty; human destitution is public, omnipresent, and pitiful. It is a different world.

There was a section of Manila called Smokey Mountain. It was the garbage dump, a mountain of refuse adjacent to Manila Bay. At the time of my visit, several thousand people inhabited Smokey Mountain, eking out a living by selling scraps from the dump. The stench was overpowering. This abject poverty, unknown to most Americans, is all too common in the Two-Thirds World.[1]

By and large hungry children are not the ones we sometimes see on TV or in news magazines with distended stomachs and arms and legs like toothpicks, victims of *famine* in Ethiopia or Somalia. Some people do starve to death, but even famine, the extreme of hunger, is usually the result of war or social upheaval along with adverse weather conditions. Such was the case in Ethiopia and Somalia. Most often, however, the poor die of disease after being weakened by *chronic malnutrition*. People are malnourished, not because there is not enough food but because they cannot afford to buy food because of their poverty.

For Reflection

It is difficult for a middle-class American to walk in the sandals of a poor Kenyan or Pakistani or Guatemalan. Economist Robert Heilbroner suggests a thought experiment of transforming a typical suburban American family into a typical family in the Two-Thirds World to convey the point:

"We begin by invading the house of our imaginary American family to strip it of its furniture. Everything goes: beds, chairs, tables, television sets, computers, lamps. We will leave the family with a few old blankets, a kitchen table, a wooden chair. Along with the bureaus go the clothes. . . .

Poverty means that people are not able to meet their own basic needs. Poverty means being hungry and malnourished; drinking unsanitary water; living in crowded, unsafe, inadequate, or no shelter; having no shoes or shirt to wear; being illiterate; having no access to even basic health care, such as immunizations against childhood diseases or treatment for diarrhea. The poor are anxious and fearful, constantly struggling to survive. Poverty means breaking your back for twelve hours in the hot sugar cane fields only to go deeper in debt to the landowner, or sweating over a sewing machine for ten hours and still not being able to afford three simple meals a day. At least two out of every three people on earth live on less than $10 a day.[2] They represent the "Two-Thirds World."

If poverty demeans human dignity and stunts human potential, its antidote is human development. *Development* means changing the whole social system so that every person has the opportunity to fulfill his or her full human potential and live a dignified and productive human life. Development is more than an economic concept; it is a human concept. Three core values are included in the meaning of human development: *sustenance*—the ability to meet basic needs, including food, shelter, health, and security; *self-esteem*—a sense of worth and self-respect; and *freedom*—the ability to participate in significant personal and social choices. Since poverty precludes the attainment of these values, development aims to establish economic conditions and structures conducive to the realization of human potential and dignity. Generally, economic development requires rising per capita incomes, the elimination of extreme poverty, better employment opportunities, and decreasing income inequalities. Therefore, economic growth constitutes the *necessary* but not the *sufficient* condition for development.[3]

"Now we have stripped the house: the bathroom has been dismantled, the running water shut off, the electric wires taken out. Next we take away the house. The family can move to the toolshed. [The cars, of course, exit with the garage]....

"Communications must go next. [No phone. No Internet.] No more newspapers, magazines, books—not that they are missed, since we must take away our family's literacy as well. Instead, in our shantytown we will allow one radio.

"Now government services must go. No mail delivery. No garbage pick-up. No fire protection. No water. No sewers. There is a two-room school, three miles away. There are, of course, no hospitals or doctors nearby...."

Robert Heilbroner, *The Great Ascent: The Struggle for Economic Development in Our Time* (New York: Harper & Row, 1963), 33–35, slightly edited.

Before addressing some of the issues involved in economic development, it is important to understand the economic inequalities that characterize the contemporary world.

THE REGIONS OF THE WORLD, THE TWO-THIRDS WORLD, AND THE GAP BETWEEN THE NORTH AND THE SOUTH

Specialists in international relations often divide the world into nine regions:

1. North America (Canada and the United States)
2. Latin America (Mexico, Central America, the Caribbean, and South America)

3. Europe
4. Russia and the Commonwealth of Independent States (CIS) (the fifteen republics of the former Soviet Union)
5. The Middle East and North Africa (the countries on the southern and eastern shores of the Mediterranean Sea and the Persian Gulf, often referred to as simply the Middle East)
6. Africa (sub-Saharan Africa)
7. South Asia (from Afghanistan through Indonesia)
8. China
9. Japan and the Pacific (including Australia and New Zealand)

These designations will generally be used in this book, but it is important to note that other terms and other divisions are used, especially regarding Asia. East Asia usually refers to China, Korea, and Japan. Southeast Asia refers to the countries from Myanmar (Burma) through Indonesia and the Philippines. South Asia sometimes includes Southeast Asia, and sometimes it does not. These regions are artificial divisions, but they do reflect commonalities of politics, economics, culture, and religion among the countries in the different regions.

In terms of economics, the most important division is between the richer, technologically developed countries of the North—North America, Europe, and Japan and the Pacific—and the poorer, less technologically developed countries of the South—Latin America, Africa, most of the Middle East, and Asia. The North contains about 20 percent of the world's people, but uses 60 percent of its goods and services, leaving the 80 percent of the population in the South with the use of only 40 percent of global resources.[4]

The North has been designated the "First World" and the South has been called the "Third World"—unfortunate and outdated terms. These terms mix the "apples and oranges" of economics and politics. The difference between the countries of the First World and the Third World was primarily economic— wealth vs. poverty, industrial and technological development vs. the lack thereof. The designation "Second World" referred to the Communist countries—the East vs. the West—distinguished more by their politics than their economic development. The Second World is no more. Central and Eastern Europe, Russia, and most of the former republics of the Soviet Union have undergone a political and economic transition. Economically, at least, it has been successful. Most of these countries transitioned from a socialist to a capitalist economy and are now classified as high-income countries.[5] The political transition from totalitarian police states to democracies has varied according to geography. The Central and Eastern European countries are classified as free by the independent watchdog organization Freedom House, and some are now in or applying for the European Union. Russia and most of the countries of the former Soviet Union, however, are classified as not free by Freedom House and have authoritarian governments.[6]

Even before the end of the Cold War, the Third World was a problematic designation. It tended to be a pejorative term, suggesting losers. It is important to remember that the term referred only to economic and technological development and *not* to cultural, spiritual, or human development. India, for example, is one of the world's centers for spiritual development; Filipinos are undoubtedly among the world's most hospitable people. Nor does the term Third World capture the diversity of economic development found in the less industrialized countries. The economies of Niger, Nepal, and Haiti, which are among the poorest in the world, should not be lumped together with those of Algeria, South Korea, and Costa Rica, for example, which are much more economically developed. The First and Third designations also gloss over the history of colonial exploitation that is the background for the current situation. More than a hint of racism lurks within the terms.

It is difficult, however, to find more adequate language for highlighting the global reality that a minority of the countries of the world, with a minority of the world's population, enjoy a high standard of living, while most of the people on earth struggle to meet their most basic needs. The notion of the "Two-Thirds World" at least captures the idea that the poor greatly outnumber the rich. Half of the world's people live on $2.50 a day, and 80 percent on less than $10.00 a day.[7] The use of "North" and "South" points to the reality of richer and poorer countries in a helpful way.

Global wealth is becoming more concentrated. In 2000, the wealthiest 1 percent of the population had 32 percent of global wealth. By 2010, they had 46 percent of global wealth. The super-rich, the wealthiest 0.1 percent, have astonishing riches. In the United States, the share of national wealth among the super-rich increased from 12 percent in 1990 to 19 percent in 2008 (before the Great Recession), and then to 22 percent in 2012.[8] In 2016, Oxfam reported that the world's sixty-two richest people were as wealthy as half of the world's population. By 2017, due to information that poverty in China and India was worse than previously thought, the eight richest people had equivalent wealth to half of the world's population.[9]

MEASURING POVERTY AND DEVELOPMENT

The meaning of abject poverty—its human reality and global prevalence—is almost beyond the comprehension of economically comfortable Americans. Certainly any compassionate and just person, when made aware that nearly a billion brothers and sisters on planet Earth are hungry, will care enough to want to right this wrong. The causes of global poverty, however, are complex and controversial, as are the solutions. Indeed, it is even hard to measure poverty.[10] In order to address the global issue of poverty, it is important to understand some economic terms and the ways that poverty, economic inequality, and development are measured.

The most common measure of poverty is *income analysis*, which is based on the annual *gross domestic product* (GDP)—the value of all goods and services produced within a country's borders; or *gross national product* (GNP)—GDP plus net income from abroad; or *gross national income* (GNI)—GDP plus income paid into the country by other countries for such things as interest and dividends (less similar payments paid out to other countries). When divided by the number of people in the country it yields the *per capita* GDP or GNP or GNI. While per capita GDP (or GNP or GNI) can give some sense of the economic well-being or standard of living of a country's average resident, it does not tell us anything about the distribution of income within the country. If a country has ten people, for example, one of whom is enormously wealthy and the rest destitute, the per capita GDP may look healthy even though most of the people are desperately poor. In countries with a rich elite and a multitude of poor, there is high economic inequality. The *Gini coefficient* (or index) is used to gauge the economic inequality of a nation. It ranges from 0 (exact equality) to 1 (one person owns everything). The higher the Gini coefficient the greater the inequality of wealth and income within a country.[11] Driven by the extraordinary economic growth in China and India, relative global inequality among countries declined from 1975 to 2010. This happened despite a trend toward increasing inequality within countries. However, absolute inequality has been increasing since the 1970s. To illustrate the difference between relative inequality and absolute inequality, let's say in 2000 one person in a country makes $1 a day and another person makes $10 a day. Because of economic growth, by 2016 the first person now makes $8 a day and the second person $80 a day. The relative difference between the two stays the same, with the second person making ten times what the first makes, but the absolute difference has gone from $9 to $72.[12]

Before 1992, the per capita GDP of various countries was compared based on the official exchange rates of the countries' currencies. These market exchange rates, however, may not reflect a currency's true purchasing power in the local context. Thus, since 1992 most economists have begun making the comparison on the basis of *purchasing power parity* (PPP), that is, how much of a common "market basket" of goods and services each currency can purchase locally. In general, PPP comparisons produce slightly lower per capita GDP figures in wealthy countries and higher ones in poorer nations.[13]

A different measure of poverty is a *people centered, basic needs approach,* which is used in the *Human Development Report,* first published in 1990. The United Nations Development Program (UNDP) argued that economic growth, as measured by GDP per capita, was a necessary, but not sufficient, measure of genuine human development. Thus, the UNDP fashioned the *human development index* (HDI) in an attempt to measure a more holistic conception of human development. The HDI combines standard of living (per capita GNI), life expectancy, and educational attainment.[14] In 2015 the HDI ranking of forty-seven countries was more than twenty places higher or lower than their ranking by per capita income. Barbados, for example, ranks fifty-fourth on the HDI but seventy-fourth in per capita GNI, while Oman ranks fifty-second in HDI and thirty-first in per capita GNI. Although Barbados has about a third of the per capita income of Oman, it does just as well in meeting the basic needs of all of its people.[15]

THE MILLENNIUM DEVELOPMENT GOALS AND THE 2030 AGENDA FOR SUSTAINABLE DEVELOPMENT

At the UN's General Assembly meeting in 2000, 189 heads of state, recognizing their collective responsibility for human development, set eight goals for poverty eradication and development, to be achieved by 2015. The Millennium Development Goals (MDG) included, among others: eradicating extreme poverty and hunger; achieving universal primary education; and promoting gender equality and the empowerment of women. Many of the goals had specific targets to monitor progress.

The MDGs were the most successful antipoverty movement in history. As a result, people are living longer; extreme poverty is decreasing every day; fewer people are hungry; more children, especially girls, are in school; the child mortality rate was halved, as was the global maternal mortality ratio; new HIV infections fell by 40 percent; and more people have access to basic social services such as safe drinking water. Nevertheless, the MDG fell short of several of its targets, inequalities persist, and progress has been uneven. Poverty is concentrated, with over 60 percent of those in extreme poverty found in five countries. Disparities between rural and urban areas remain pronounced.[16]

All of the MDGs are connected to poverty. People without access to safe drinking water, for example, are impoverished. The first goal, however, to eradicate extreme poverty and hunger, is perhaps most directly related to this chapter. In 2015, the World Bank revised its definition of extreme poverty (or the International Poverty Line [IPL]) from $1.25 in consumption per day to $1.90. In 1990 there were about two billion people, or 37 percent of the world's population, in extreme poverty; and in 2015 that number had decreased to about 705 million people or less than 10 percent of global population. Thus, on average, the number of people living in extreme poverty had decreased by 137,000 per day in the twenty-five years from 1990 to 2015.[17] Thus the MDG exceeded the target of halving the proportion of people living in extreme poverty by 2015.

This story is certainly good news,[18] and it is real; but it also needs to be put in context. Poverty has declined rapidly in Asia, especially China and India, but it has also risen in thirty developing countries, mostly in Africa. China's extreme poverty rate plummeted from 66.5 percent in 1990 to 1.9 percent in 2013, and in South Asia the extreme poverty rate fell from 44.6 percent to 15 percent. There is, however, some statistical sleight of hand in the figures on the reduction of poverty. The focus on the proportion of people in poverty, rather than absolute numbers, makes population growth an asset rather than a liability in the story. Often population growth can offset the gains from economic growth. The focus on "extreme poverty" as defined by the World Bank's IPL (now $1.90 in consumption a day) enhances the poverty reduction figures and obscures the everyday reality of poverty. A person living on $1.90 a day anywhere in the world is truly destitute, but half of the world's population lives on less than $2.50 a day and 80 percent on less than $10 a day. Such people and families are certainly struggling to meet their basic needs—they are poor. Hunger affects one of every nine persons on earth, and one of every three is malnourished. People are hungry and malnourished primarily because they are poor and cannot afford to purchase food. Poverty is also on the rise in developed countries, where an estimated 300 million people lived in poverty in 2012.[19]

As the United Nations met in September 2015 to assess the successes and shortcomings of the Millennium Development Goals, world leaders were already in the process of taking the next step—the *2030 Agenda for Sustainable Development*. At that meeting of the UN General Assembly, world leaders committed themselves to an even more ambitious agenda for creating a world where every person can flourish in healthy communities on a sustainable earth. They approved seventeen Sustainable Development Goals to be met by 2030, with 169 specific targets. These are the seventeen goals:

Sustainable Development Goals for 2030

Goal 1　　End poverty in all its forms everywhere.

Goal 2　　End hunger, achieve food security and improved nutrition, and promote sustainable agriculture.

Goal 3　　Ensure healthy lives and promote well-being at all ages.

Goal 4　　Ensure inclusive and equitable quality education and promote lifelong learning opportunities for all.

Goal 5　　Achieve gender equality and empower all women and girls.

Goal 6　　Ensure availability and sustainable management of water and sanitation for all.

Goal 7　　Ensure access to affordable, reliable, sustainable, and modern energy for all.

Goal 8　　Promote sustained, inclusive, and sustainable economic growth; full and productive employment; and decent work for all.

Goal 9　　Build resilient infrastructure, promote inclusive and sustainable industrialization, and foster innovation.

Goal 10　Reduce inequality within and among countries.

Goal 11   Make cities and human settlements inclusive, safe, resilient, and sustainable.

Goal 12   Ensure sustainable consumption and production patterns.

Goal 13   Take urgent action to combat climate change and its impacts.

Goal 14   Conserve and sustainably use the oceans, seas, and marine resources for sustainable development.

Goal 15   Protect, restore, and promote sustainable use of terrestrial ecosystems, sustainably manage forests, combat desertification, and halt and reverse land degradation, and halt biodiversity loss.

Goal 16   Promote peaceful and inclusive societies for sustainable development, provide access to justice for all, and build effective, accountable and inclusive institutions at all levels.

Goal 17   Strengthen the means of implementation and revitalize the global partnership for sustainable development.[20]

These seventeen goals (more than twice the number of the MDGs) can be read as either visionary or as idealistic pieties, depending on your perspective, until you remember that there are 169 specific targets accompanying them. Then you wonder whether this vision is realistic and feasible. The first Sustainable Development Goal seems to respond to the criticism above about the narrowness of the focus on extreme poverty in the MDGs. The first two of the targets for this goal to end poverty in all its forms everywhere pledge to eradicate extreme poverty by 2030 and to reduce by at least half the proportion of people of all ages living in poverty in all of its dimensions according to national definitions. While this will not fulfill the stated goal, it seems possible and realistic.

The Sustainable Development Goals for 2030 articulate a comprehensive vision of human development, and the exhaustive list of 169 targets grounds this vision in specific policies to fulfill the goals. There is no doubt that the 2030 Agenda for Sustainable Development will need to be followed by a 2045 Agenda, but if the MDGs are a revealing precedent, the global community will make significant progress in diminishing poverty and enhancing human development thanks to this challenging vision and the struggle to implement it.

GLOBALIZATION: PROMISE AND PERIL

In the second chapter we saw how the tremendous productivity of the Industrial Revolution (along with colonialism) allowed Britain (and then other countries) to attain remarkable economic growth. From about 1850 to 1920, the world experienced a first period of globalization. Since the end of the Cold War in 1989, the world has been experiencing a second period of economic integration or globalization.[21] It is once again, as Charles Dickens says in the opening line of *A Tale of Two Cities* (1859), the best of times and the worst of times.

Most mainstream economists posit that there can be no economic development without sustained economic growth, that is, unless a nation's economy registers a growth in GDP year after year.[22] Otherwise the population shares scarcity and will generally experience unemployment and declining income. Globalization, ushered in by the age of the worldwide web, offers the promise of tremendous productivity and economic growth, but it can be a brutal process when it is focused only on profit and not on people. If it is to be good news for human flourishing, and especially for the poor, global capitalism will need to be managed so that economic growth is inclusively distributed and benefits everyone. The poor need globalization that wears a human face.[23]

The collapse of communism in the Soviet empire seemed to end the economic debate between state socialism and free-market capitalism. The centrally planned economy offered by the communist version of socialism did not work. Some version of capitalism or a mixed economy with Democratic Socialism seemed to be the only viable alternatives left on the horizon. Capitalism offers a productive economic system that can generate the income necessary for economic development.[24] The challenge is to manage this new system to benefit the Two-Thirds World and to find a healthy balance between economic growth and the common good.

Globalization is integrating the world into one global market. It is facilitated by new communication technology—computers, the internet, smartphones, and media networks. Capital roams the earth at lightning speed, to the tune of over $1.5 trillion a day in foreign-exchange trading.[25] In 2014 global trade in merchandise and services amounted to almost $24 trillion, up from $13 trillion in 2005.[26] Long-distance transportation has become more efficient, and shipping costs have been reduced, in part because what is transported has often become lighter. Global trade is benefiting consumers and the producers who are most competitive. Labor too is migrating, but at a slower pace than capital, and in the face of many more restrictions. Many migrants are refugees from war or criminal violence, and some are "economic" migrants seeking to leave a troubled state and find opportunity for a better life.[27] Their labor, unskilled and skilled, can make a contribution to their new home.

Thomas L. Friedman, a foreign correspondent and columnist for the *New York Times*, likens a country's entrance into the global market to putting on a "Golden Straitjacket." This means a country must adapt to the following free market rules:

> making the private sector the primary engine of its economic growth, maintaining a low rate of inflation and price stability, shrinking the size of its state bureaucracy, maintaining as close to a balanced budget as

possible, if not a surplus, eliminating and lowering tariffs on imported goods, removing restrictions on foreign investment, getting rid of quotas and domestic monopolies, increasing exports, privatizing state-owned industries and utilities, deregulating capital markets, making its currency convertible, opening its industries, stock, and bond markets to direct foreign ownership and investment, deregulating its economy to promote as much domestic competition as possible, eliminating government corruption, subsidies and kickbacks as much as possible, opening its banking and telecommunications systems to private ownership and competition, and allowing its citizens to choose from an array of competing pension options and foreign-run pension and mutual funds. When you stitch all these pieces together you have the Golden Straitjacket.[28]

As a result of these policies a country's economy generally grows and its average income increases, but its politics shrink in that there is little choice but to abide by these rules or capital will flee the country.[29] The economic success of several countries in Asia beginning in the mid-1990s illustrates how golden these policies can be.

While globalization generally produces economic growth, it also has negative consequences. Capitalism tends to concentrate wealth and to widen the gap between the rich and the poor; globalization has not delivered universally shared prosperity. Productivity has increased, but that has not always translated into higher wages, and the pay gap between highly skilled and unskilled workers has increased considerably. While the global middle class has increased in numbers, the middle class in developed countries is in jeopardy, with stagnant wages and reductions in social services. This has fueled the rise in populist politics and autocratic leaders discussed in chapter 6. While the rich have gotten richer, the middle class in developed countries has been left behind.[30] Globalization is often accompanied by the spread of Western and American values and products, symbolized by the Golden Arches of McDonalds or the influence of Western music and fashion. Many decry this loss of local identity, practices, and values. Increasing productivity also uses up the earth's resources and pollutes the atmosphere, the land, and rivers, lakes, and oceans. The fast and greedy world of globalization seems to be leaving the poor and middle class behind,[31] homogenizing culture, and speeding up environmental destruction and climate change. Thus, it is not surprising that there has been a backlash against globalization in the name of the poor and middle class, of cultural diversity, and of the earth itself.

Global capitalism, however, offers the productivity that seems necessary, but not sufficient, for overcoming poverty. A free market, however, does not mean an unregulated market. It is important to manage the system so that it meets the basic needs of all people, respects local cultures, enhances participation in society, conserves the earth and its resources, and produces sustainable growth. The goal is to leave no one behind, "to ensure that globalization works for people—not just for profits."[32]

Besides this practical debate about the benefits and liabilities of a form of global capitalism that might be called market fundamentalism and a defense of a more humane and managed capitalism, there is a theological and moral objection to capitalism. In *The Problem of Wealth*, Elizabeth Hinson-Hasty, a theological ethicist, argues that capitalism is incompatible with Christian faith and tradition because it is based in a self-centered understanding of human identity rather than the relational and communal identity at the heart of the Christian faith. The Christian metaphor of God as a communal Trinity indicates that God's very nature is relational; humanity is created in God's relational image. Thus, Christians are fundamentally relational and communal, embracing the values of reciprocity, cooperation/collaboration, interdependence, solidarity, sustainability, inclusion, and accountability to "the commons" or for the common good. Capitalism inevitably results in hyperindividualism and market idolatry, in the concentration of power and privilege in an elite, and in greed, exploitation, and corruption.[33]

OVERCOMING POVERTY

If globalization is going to work for the poor, what must be done? There are several issues that need to be addressed in response to this question: investment, foreign aid, trade, debt, and equity.

Multinational Corporations and Foreign Direct Investment

In order to enter the globalization expressway to economic growth, developing countries often need an infusion of capital. Multinational corporations (MNCs) are one source of this investment.

MNCs are centrally organized but produce and sell their goods in many countries. Many of them are based in high-income, developed countries, but some are now appearing in the Newly Industrialized Countries (NICs), such as Samsung and Hyundai in South Korea, and some in developing countries, like Pemex in Mexico. Whatever its national origin, a MNC seeks to maximize its own interests and those of its shareholders rather than the interests of any country or of the poor. Although MNCs are not in the development business, their investment of capital, technology, and management skills, which can create jobs and foreign exchange for developing countries, can contribute to economic development. The question is: whose interests does such private foreign investment serve?

MNCs are central actors in the globalization of the world economy. They are not the pawns of any state, rich or poor, but independent actors, influenced by a global market that they in large part create and manipulate, and from which they profit. The global economy has become fiercely competitive and unforgiving of inefficiency; it can seem to transcend the control of even the most powerful governments or corporations.

In truth, however, the economy is a human reality, not one that transcends human control. The economy is a system established by human choices, which should serve human needs and which can be changed by human decisions.[34]

Corporations are also human realities. If their boards of directors and managers single-mindedly seek the maximization of profit without a thought for their workers, the environment, or the communities in which they are located, then that is a choice rather than the nature of a corporation. A corporation can also choose to seek a fair profit for its owners, to pay a fair wage to its workers, not harm the environment, and contribute constructively to the community. The tensions implied in these choices become particularly acute when powerful MNCs operate in poor countries.

One issue is the sheer wealth and power of MNCs in comparison with that of developing countries. In a ranking of countries and corporations according to the size of their annual product in 2017, sixty-nine of the top one hundred are corporations and only thirty-one are countries.[35] Thus, countries in the Two-Thirds World are often at a disadvantage in negotiating with an MNC for needed investment and jobs. This is especially so if the MNC is subcontracting with a foreign-owned factory in a free enterprise zone in a developing country. If, for example, the cost of labor rises in Indonesia, or if Indonesia raises taxes or strengthens regulations such as its minimum wage or environmental or safety laws, a company, such as Nike, can move its operations to Vietnam. Nike simply terminates one contract, for example, with a Taiwanese-owned factory in Indonesia, and enters into another contract, with a Korean-owned factory in Vietnam.[36] Workers, communities, and even governments are often at the mercy of MNCs.

Too often the end result of this global economic system of investment and trade is not the economic development of poor countries but a net transfer of more wealth from the South to the North. In 2012, for example, developing countries received a total of $1.3 trillion in aid, investment, and income from abroad. About $3.3 trillion, however, flowed from them to the global North. In the years 1980–2012, the net outflow from the global South to the North adds up to $16.3 trillion. This transfer of wealth primarily results from *interest payments* on debt ($4.2 trillion since 1980), which enriches big banks and dwarfs foreign aid during that period; *profits* from foreign investments in developing countries; and, most significantly, unrecorded and often fraudulent *capital flight*, most of which takes place through the international trade system by MNCs.[37]

MNCs argue that they invest large amounts of capital in developing countries and bring sophisticated technology and management skills, which creates jobs, produces goods and services, and increases economic growth. Critics contend that the MNCs *control* capital and technology, introduce inappropriate technology (tractors instead of tillers), manipulate markets, exploit workers, crush cultures through advertising (for example, infant formula instead of breast milk, Coca-Cola instead of water), and in the end take the profits home.[38] The critics call this neocolonialism. The challenge is to make sure MNC investment in the global South results in genuine human development, not exploitation.

As usual the issues here are complex and controversial. Critics of the MNCs contend that they make exorbitant profits in the Two-Thirds World by *exploiting vulnerable workers*. The 4,825 garment factories in Bangladesh, for example, employ 3.5 million workers. The garment industry produces goods for export, principally to Europe and North America, and accounts for 80 percent of Bangladesh's total export revenue. Most garment workers, 85 percent of whom are women, make little more than the minimum wage, which the government in Bangladesh raised from approximately $20 to $33 a *month* in 2010. A living wage in Bangladesh, enough to provide a family with food, shelter, and education, has been calculated as at least $60 a month. These workers are not earning a subsistence wage, much less a just or living wage, as called for in Catholic social teaching.[39]

Bangladeshi factory workers face appalling conditions typical of sweatshops. Many work fourteen hour days, seven days a week, in cramped and hazardous workplaces. Since 1990, there have been fifty major factory fires that killed more than four hundred workers and injured thousands. In April 2013 the Rana Plaza building in an industrial suburb of Dhaka collapsed, killing 1,127 people.[40] Sexual harassment and discrimination are rampant. Although workers have a legal right to organize, in practice union organizers and unions are not tolerated.[41]

Investigations of Samsung's production facilities in Vietnam reveal "a vulnerable, mostly female workforce that may be sacrificing its neurologic and reproductive health in digitized Dickensian workshops that make cutting edge smartphones." Unseen toxins can be hazardous to health, and the stress from overwork can be crippling.[42]

As bad as the pay and the conditions are, many workers find them preferable to the agricultural work that may be the only alternative for these women and men. Furthermore, not all facilities fit the stereotype of a dreadful sweatshop. Some pay more than the minimum wage, are clean and safe, and even subsidize meals, housing, health care, and transportation for their workers. Export factories are the first stage of industrialization and sometimes improve.[43]

The issue of *child labor* in developing countries is also controversial. Worldwide, one in six children aged five to seventeen, nearly 250 million in all, are engaged in work that the International Labor Organization (ILO) thinks should be abolished. Over eight million children are involved in appalling sorts of work, including forced labor, warfare, prostitution, pornography, and other illicit activities.[44] Who could countenance the practice of ten-year-olds working ten-hour days sewing soccer balls in Pakistan or rugs in India?[45] But what about a fourteen-year-old girl working six hours a day in an apparel factory in Honduras? Education for the majority of Hondurans ends with the sixth grade. Honduran law allows fourteen-year-olds to work six-hour days with permission from their parents. If teenagers are not allowed to work in the factories, they will not be in school, but rather seeking more demanding work for even less pay in the fields or doing domestic work.[46] In many parts of the world teen labor is different from child labor. Responses to child labor include compulsory schooling, monitoring compliance with the laws already established in developing countries, and, of course, saving children from the worst forms of labor that result in irreversible psychological or physical damage. An education is key to human flourishing and the development of a healthy community.

In response to the controversy about sweatshops in the 1990s, President Clinton (1993–2001) established the White House Apparel Industry Partnership, a task force that included representatives of labor unions, human rights groups, and industry powerhouses, to develop a Workplace Code of Conduct. Not surprisingly, the task proved to be difficult and contentious. In November 1998, the task force announced an accord in which apparel makers who signed the Code of Conduct pledged to provide abuse-free factories, hire workers at least fifteen years old, limit the workweek to sixty hours, pay at least the local minimum wage, and protect the right of workers to organize. The Fair Labor Association (FLA) was established to monitor the code.

However, many of the apparel unions, such as UNITE, and the Interfaith Center for Corporate Responsibility, rejected the agreement because of two issues: the credibility of the FLA to monitor it and the definition of a living wage. Because the local minimum wage is not even a subsistence wage in countries such as Indonesia and Haiti, labor and human rights representatives argued unsuccessfully that companies should commit themselves to pay a wage that could provide the basic needs for a family. Apparel companies and retailers insisted that a "living wage" is too difficult to define and too expensive.[47]

At the beginning of the new century the antisweatshop campaign secured a firm foothold on many US campuses through United Students Against Sweatshops (USAS). This student organization successfully lobbied administrations at many American universities to guarantee that university-logo garments and merchandise, a $2.5 billion industry in 1999, were not produced in sweatshops. USAS established the Worker Rights Consortium (WRC) to monitor compliance with codes of conduct. In August 2017, the USAS successfully pressured Nike to allow the WRC to monitor its subcontracted garment factories.[48]

Although the efforts of the Apparel Industry Partnership and USAS give some reason for hope, ending exploitative sweatshop labor is an uphill battle. A daunting problem is the size and mobility of the industry. In 2016, the store-based US apparels industry was valued at approximately $292 billion;[49] sub-contracting allows the industry to quickly move production from country to country. It is nearly impossible to monitor such a sizeable and slippery system. The essential keys to justice are "tough government enforcement of workers' rights and labor standards, and high levels of unionization."[50] Yet governments are more likely to side with MNCs than their workers.

Unfortunately, since the turn of the century, antisweatshop activism has significantly diminished, even though the suffering of workers continues. The USAS remains active but does not get much attention. One reason for this lack of protest may be the continued decline of the labor movement in the United States, which was a catalyst and support for antisweatshop activism. Another reason may be the lower profile of some clothing stores, such as Forever 21, in comparison to Gap and Nike in the 1990s. The different economic context is another factor. The 1990s were a time of economic expansion, while now the United States and the global economy are still recuperating from the Great Recession, and morally righteous shopping is less affordable. Finally "haul videos" and the social media culture around fashion may encourage young people to buy cheap clothes in bulk without a moral second thought.[51]

The exploitation of the worker has been a social justice issue since the beginning of the Industrial Revolution, and it continues to be a major concern as MNCs comb the earth in search of cheaper labor and higher profits.

Foreign Aid

Another form of investment in developing countries consists of foreign aid or assistance from one government to another. Some Americans are skeptical about foreign aid because they think the United States should take care of its own poor and address its own social problems before helping others. This view is in tension with the theological understanding that humanity is the family of God, brothers and sisters to one another, and that each person has an unearned value from being created in the image and likeness of God. According to this perspective, a hungry child from Chad, China, or Colombia should elicit the same concern as a hungry American child. In justice, all deserve an opportunity to develop their full human potential. Indeed, the greater need of brothers and sisters in the Two-Thirds World may invoke a greater responsibility from the more affluent in the human community. Moreover, as we have seen, there is at least an indirect connection between the wealth of the few and the poverty of the many on planet Earth. Our obligation to respond to the needs of the poor should be rooted more in justice and solidarity than in charity.

Foreign aid also fits with America's perception of itself as generous. As the world's wealthiest country, surely the United States can afford to assist the neediest. Indeed, in a May 2017 opinion poll, 81 percent of Americans supported humanitarian assistance, and two-thirds supported development assistance and assistance for global health. Aid tied to strategic purposes, however, received only lukewarm support. Thus President Trump's attempt to slash spending on humanitarian and development aid by over 25 percent in his 2018 fiscal year budget proposal, while maintaining funding for aid tied to US strategic interests, is the opposite of public opinion. While many Americans agree with President Trump that the United States has overreached in foreign affairs, there is solid public support for the United States making a measured contribution to promoting economic development around the world and to alleviating human suffering.[52]

Nevertheless, over 50 percent of Americans think the United States spends too much on foreign aid. This view, however, is based on a wildly incorrect perception of US spending on foreign assistance. When asked what percentage of the federal budget was designated for foreign aid, the median answer was 20 percent. In fact foreign aid (or official development assistance [ODA]) is consistently less than 1 percent of the federal budget, or $35 billion in 2017.[53]

In fact, the United States is not especially generous in its foreign assistance. In 2017 the United States gave the eighth lowest percentage of its GNI (0.18 percent) to foreign aid of the twenty-nine Organization for Economic Cooperation and Development (OECD) countries. Since the United States has the world's largest economy, it gave the largest gross amount of foreign aid—$35 billion. In the mid-1990s the United States was not even giving the largest gross amount of foreign aid. Japan was consistently giving more than the United States, even though its economy was about half the size, and in 1995 the United States was in fourth place, behind Japan, France, and Germany.[54] In 1970 the UN General Assembly agreed on a goal for development assistance of 0.7 percent of a country's GNI. In 2017, only five of the twenty-nine OECD countries (Sweden, Luxembourg, Norway, Denmark, and the United Kingdom) met or exceeded that goal, and only six of the rest gave 0.4 percent of their GNP. According to official data collected by the OECD Development Assistance Committee (DAC), total ODA reached a new high in 2016 of $142.6 billion. Compare this with world military spending in 2016 of $1.6 trillion.[55]

Russia and China are not in the OECD and thus are not included in the comparisons above. In 2016 Russia's ODA was $1 billion or 0.08 percent of its GNI. Recipients of Russian foreign aid are mostly countries in the Commonwealth of Independent States (the former Soviet Union) and Syria, Serbia, and Guinea.[56]

China is not very forthcoming about its foreign aid. In 2013 it is estimated that China gave about $5 billion in foreign assistance. Africa is a major recipient of China's assistance. Between 2000 and 2012, China funded 1,665 projects in fifty-one African countries, which comprised 69 percent of its aid projects. China's giving and lending seems indifferent to the governance structure of the recipient country. China is motivated by a convergence of the interests (need) of the recipient and China's foreign policy interests. Not included in these figures are President Xi Jinping's "One Road, One Belt" initiative, begun in 2013, which had invested an estimated $1 trillion, primarily in infrastructure projects abroad, by 2017. Critics charge that this massive program amounts to debt traps for vulnerable countries, as it did for Sri Lanka. China repeatedly gave loans to Sri Lanka, at the request of its president, Mahinda Rajapaksa, for a port project that feasibility studies showed would fail. When it did fail, China took over the territory in Sri Lanka as collection of the debt. Thus, China seems to be using foreign assistance in the neocolonial fashion that has characterized the West.[57]

Like most donor states the United States uses bilateral (from one government to another) foreign aid in political bargaining with recipient countries. For example, when Pakistan developed a nuclear weapons program in the late 1980s, the United States terminated its sizeable flow of foreign aid to Pakistan. Aid was restored when Pakistan supported US military action in neighboring Afghanistan in 2001. A US law requires that food aid sent to Africa be produced by US agriculture and shipped in US vessels. If instead the United States bought food grown in Africa, it would save money, get aid to hungry people faster, and support African farmers. Efforts to rescind the law have been successfully opposed by the so-called Iron Triangle of food aid—US agribusiness, US shipping companies, and US charities, all of which profit from the current system. US charities, including CARE and Catholic Charities, fund a significant fraction of their budget by selling grain they ship to Africa from the United States. Similar conditions are usually written into foreign aid agreements for industrial goods (tractors, etc.) and military armaments. Competitive bidding might result in getting less expensive tractors, if tractors are what the recipient really needs. Although much bilateral foreign aid today is in grants, some of it is in loans that contribute to the indebtedness of poor countries.[58] Every college student knows the difference between a grant and a loan.

Perhaps the least controversial and least politically motivated form of foreign assistance is *disaster relief* in response to natural disasters such as earthquakes, flooding, etc. The deadly earthquake in Haiti in 2010 illustrates that international disaster relief can be complex and difficult in both the emergency and the reconstruction phases of assistance. Initial relief efforts were chaotic and poorly coordinated, with people dying while planes with supplies were stacked up over the small airport unable to land. Eight years later, despite billions of dollars in official and private funds pledged, Haiti is still struggling to get back on its feet.[59] On September 20, 2017, Maria, a category 4 hurricane, devastated Puerto Rico, a territory of the United States. Both the initial response and the long-term response were disorganized and inadequate. By the end of January 2018 an estimated 450,000 people still did not have electricity or necessary supplies.[60] When such tragedies strike people who are already poor the effect can be overwhelming.

Foreign aid has too often fallen victim to corruption or been used for inappropriate, ostentatious, unwise, or even harmful projects. During the Cold War, when the political purpose of aid was to oppose Communism, the United States turned a blind eye to corruption, waste, and human rights abuses of recipients. Now the war on terrorism is again tempting the United States in this direction. Enriching and arming dictators might create allies, but this is often at the cost of moral principles and integrity, and the greater suffering of the poor.

It is perhaps unrealistic, and maybe unwise, to think foreign aid should be blind to the interests of a nation's foreign policy, but surely its primary purpose should be humanitarian—to empower the poorest through assisting them in meeting their basic needs and in flourishing as human beings?[61]

International Trade

Among those concerned for the economic development of the Two-Thirds World, there has been an energetic debate about trade policy. Some have argued for *inward-looking development policies* (called "import substitution") that attempt to build indigenous industries and technologies appropriate for a country's resources through high tariffs and import quotas that protect domestic production. Others have fostered *outward-looking development policies* (called "export promotion") that welcome foreign investment and encourage free trade in the global marketplace.[62]

A kind of compromise view tries to fit the arguments of both free-trade and protectionist models to the specific economic and political realities of diverse nations in the global South that may be at different stages of development. It is important to attend to the specific situation of a developing country, but also to realize that fluctuations in the world economy can have a decisive impact on the success of a particular development strategy. An expanding world economy, for example, can assist an export-oriented policy, while a global recession can stifle it, as happened in 2008–2009. Thus, the economic decisions taken by developed countries can have a significant, sometimes devastating, impact on developing economies.

The global reality of economic development in the twenty-five years from 1990 to 2015, however, clearly skews the debate regarding a developing country's economic development strategy toward an export-oriented policy. The levels of human development have increased in every region of the world in the period 1990–2015. In that period the aggregate HDI for the least developed countries increased by 46 percent, and for low human development countries by 40 percent. The global extreme poverty rate ($1.90 a day) fell from 35 percent in 1990 to an estimated 11 percent in 2013. The decrease in extreme poverty has been especially remarkable in East Asia, where it fell from 60 percent in 1990 to 3.5 percent in 2013, and in South Asia, where it fell from 45 percent to 15 percent. This is due primarily to the stunning economic development in China and India in this period, with China's annual economic growth averaging more than 10 percent year after year, and India's exceeding 7 percent from 1996 to 2008. Both of these countries sold off their unprofitable state-owned industries (China beginning in 1976 with the death of Mao, and India in the 1990s triggered by the 1991 collapse of its major trading partner, the Soviet Union), and focused on export-oriented economic development. In the 1980s and early 1990s the NICs of East Asia—South Korea, Taiwan, Hong Kong, and Singapore (the "four tigers" or the "four dragons")—also successfully adopted an export-oriented development policy. The Great Recession of 2008–2009 did make China and indeed all global economies glance inward for some stability, but a decade later most nations have recovered; and many developing countries actually recovered more quickly.[63] Thus, while it is true that what works for one developing country may not work for another due to a variety of factors, such as resources, governance, leadership, etc., the notable economic development success stories are countries that have adopted an outward-looking, export-oriented economic policy.[64]

Trade is vitally important for economic development because it can produce wealth which can decrease poverty. Developing countries received 24 percent of their GDP from trade (their exports) in 2017. In comparison, their income from foreign investment was about 2.5 percent of their GDP and from foreign aid about 0.5 percent. Global trade, however, is a game that is often rigged against developing countries through trade barriers and subsidies.[65]

Often tariffs are higher for processed products than for raw materials (higher for shirts than for cotton, for example), which adversely affects the terms of trade between developed and developing countries (there is more profit in shirts than in cotton) and hampers their efforts at industrialization. The agricultural subsidies, for example, paid to farmers in OECD countries and seven other countries, including China, were opposed by farmers in the global South as unfair and harmful to their development. This was a perennial sticking point in World Trade Organization (WTO) negotiations until the industrialized West finally agreed in 2016 to phase out farm subsidies over two years. Eliminating trade barriers and subsidies in developed countries that inhibit imports from developing countries is an urgent priority and a way to greatly accelerate development.[66]

Perhaps the North should move beyond free trade with the South toward trade arrangements that give a *preference to developing countries* that need assistance in becoming more competitive and whose egalitarian domestic policies indicate that economic growth will likely mean genuine development for the poor. The General System of Preferences (GSP) allowed by the WTO makes such preferential trade for developing countries possible.[67] Either free trade or preferential trade will necessitate assistance programs for displaced workers in developed countries.[68]

Free trade agreements (FTAs) aim to reduce or eliminate trade barriers, such as tariffs and quotas among the countries freely bound by the agreement. For example, the *North American Free Trade Agreement* (NAFTA) bound Canada, Mexico, and the United States together in a free trade arrangement that gradually reduced import/export tariffs between them, in most cases, to zero. NAFTA was also a precedent for including labor and environmental protections into FTAs.[69] Trade talks among these three North American countries resulted in a new FTA called the United States–Mexico–Canada Agreement (USMCA) on October 1, 2018.[70] Because free trade is generally beneficial, FTAs are usually good for their member states.

The WTO is a global, multilateral intergovernmental organization (IGO) that fosters, monitors, and adjudicates international trade. The WTO has limited powers of enforcement. By August 2016, 164 countries, including all the world's major trading states, were members. The WTO framework is based on the principles of reciprocity and nondiscrimination applied to the "most-favored nation" (MFN) concept. Thus trade restrictions imposed on a most-favored trading partner by a WTO member must be extended equally to all WTO members.[71]

There can be winners and losers as a result of free trade, which can be ruthlessly competitive, but most mainstream economists think that the benefits far outweigh the costs. Some even argue that countries should practice free trade even if other countries do not, and the freer, the better—trade barriers are a bad idea.[72] Regulation is necessary to protect the vulnerable, but free trade can be a powerful engine for economic growth.

The Debt Crises

Debt is a daunting obstacle to economic development for many countries in the Two-Thirds World. The 1982 *debt crisis*, when Brazil, Mexico, and other countries threatened to default on their loans, began in the 1970s. During the Cold War the United States and the Soviet Union made loans to the newly independent countries in the global South that may have been ill-advised economically, in an attempt to buy their political allegiance. Then in 1973 the Organization of Petroleum Exporting Countries (OPEC) dramatically increased the price of oil, caused a crisis, and made huge profits, which they deposited in Western banks. Awash in petrodollars, the banks eagerly lent billions of dollars to developing countries at low, but adjustable or floating, interest rates.

Borrowing capital can be sensible, even advisable, when the money is invested productively, such as in building industry and infrastructure, because the profit can be used to repay the loan. Unfortunately, huge chunks disappeared because of graft and corruption by the ruling elites, as happened in the Philippines where President Ferdinand Marcos (ruled 1965–1986) and his cronies stole over $5 billion. Some of the debt was incurred to pay for oil, which had become very expensive after 1973. Thus the Arab sheiks had their petrodollars returned to them to be loaned again. Perhaps 20 percent of developing countries' debt was used to purchase weapons.[73] Note that the poor generally did not benefit from these loans, nor did the poor participate in the decisions about whether to borrow or how to spend the money because most developing countries were not democracies in the 1970s.

Then, in the 1980s, interest rates increased dramatically. During the Reagan administration, the United States lowered taxes and increased military spending by borrowing heavily, which sent international interest rates skyrocketing. Interest rates doubled and tripled, pushing interest payments beyond the means of developing countries. At the same time, prices for raw materials (commodities) plummeted, leaving poor countries with even less income to service their debt. Thus, Brazil and Mexico considered defaulting on their loans, in effect declaring bankruptcy, and threatening the stability of the global financial system.

Commercial banks, in conjunction with First-World governments, scrambled to renegotiate loans to prevent default. Several years of this process alleviated the immediate debt crisis. The commercial banks, which were seriously overextended, reduced their investment in developing countries and placed themselves on surer financial footing. Most First-World banks became sound and secure. Developing countries, however, remain seriously indebted to commercial banks, developed countries, and to the World Bank and the International Monetary Fund (IMF). Between 1982 and 1990 the poor nations of the Two-Thirds World transferred $418 billion into the coffers of First-World banks.[74]

By the mid-1990s, in the forty-one heavily indebted poor countries (HIPCs), which owed some $170 billion to foreign creditors, half of their 600 million people lived in extreme poverty (less than a dollar a day).[75] This stark reality sparked antipoverty activists to create an international antidebt campaign called Jubilee 2000. Inspired by the Jubilee principle articulated in Leviticus 15, which calls for the releasing of debt every fifty years, Jubilee 2000 pressed for the forgiveness of debts to mark the new millennium.

The antidebt campaign resulted in the World Bank and the IMF launching the HIPC initiative in 1996. These programs aimed to reduce the overall debt burden of the forty-one most heavily indebted poor countries to a sustainable level, if the countries recorded several years of sound economic policy. In 1999 the HIPC initiative was accelerated and made more generous. In 2006 the G8 countries agreed to additional debt relief for countries that had completed the HIPC program through a scheme called the Multilateral Debt Relief Initiative (MDRI). By 2018, thirty-six countries—thirty of them in Africa—had received the full amount of debt relief for which they were eligible, a total of over $120 billion.[76]

Despite three rounds of debt cancellation for heavily indebted poor countries in 2016 the external debt of the 122 developing countries amounted to $6.878 trillion or between 26 and 30 percent of their GNI. The annual debt service for developing countries is $916 billion.[77] This is money that cannot be used for constructive investment or for social services for their people.

It was important to ensure that debt relief would not simply benefit the incompetent, corrupt, authoritarian governments that racked up the debts in the first place. Thus, in order to qualify for the HIPC initiative a country has to develop a totally transparent "poverty reduction strategy" showing how it will use the savings from debt reduction to reduce poverty. As a result, nutrition programs, primary education, and basic health care expenditures increased, by a factor of three in some cases. Many of these countries are "failed states" in need of considerable remedial assistance to become functional. The HIPC program has proved demonstrably helpful to many of these desperate nations. Not only has the burden of external debt been reduced, but many countries have developed healthier economic practices focused on the poor and marginal.[78]

In 2010–2012 debt problems surfaced in the eurozone of the European Union. Some of the poorer EU countries—Portugal, Spain, Ireland, but especially Greece—struggled with heavy indebtedness. In a 2011 bailout agreement, bankers holding Greek debt accepted fifty cents on the dollar. Even so, long-suffering Greeks expressed anger in the streets and the ballot box toward the budget cuts required to meet the conditions of the bailout.[79]

The Jubilee Debt Campaign has pointed out that developing countries' debt payments increased by 45 percent between 2014 and 2016, attaining the highest level since 2007. Low interest rates have quadrupled loans to low and middle income countries from 2008 to 2016, but now interest rates are slowly increasing. Falling commodity prices and the rising value of the US dollar have contributed to this looming debt crisis. External debt payments across the 122 developing countries have increased from 6.7 percent of government revenue in 2014 to 9.7 percent in 2016. Banks may again be engaging in risky lending.[80]

The words of the "Our Father"—"And forgive us our debts, as we also have forgiven our debtors" (Matt 6:12)—call Christians to an important ideal, but one that is difficult to practice in a way that effectively liberates the poor. Forgiving and relieving debt are essential ingredients in reducing poverty, but unless carried out in combination with good economic policies, soundly administered, debt relief is unlikely to benefit the poor. Perhaps "lead us not into temptation" is fitting for the banks that are tempted to make questionable loans.

Economic Inequity and Human Development

Thus far this chapter has focused primarily on the gap between the North and South. Unfortunately, globalization often results in a "winner takes all" competition that can concentrate wealth at the top and leave the poor worse off and full of resentment.[81] A rising tide may lift all boats, but economic growth is not always like a rising tide. It is often more like a jungle where the fittest eats all the others. If economic growth is going to result in human development, it is essential that the poor be its beneficiaries.

Achieving economic growth is not easy for developing countries in a competitive global economy. The system is stacked against them. Steps such as the reduction or forgiveness of debt, MNCs' compliance with international codes of conduct, reformed development assistance, and preferential trade can enable poor countries to achieve economic growth. But economic growth, though essential, is only half the battle. International or external economic reforms must be coupled with domestic or internal reforms focused on the poor. Indeed, without attention to equity in the distribution of goods and services, economic growth itself cannot be sustained.[82]

Equality (roughly equal incomes throughout a society) is not the goal of development, but equity (fair distribution) seems essential for genuine human development. The goal is to meet the basic needs of everyone in a society so that each person has the opportunity to flourish and to participate in and contribute to the community. The aim is not to bring down the rich so much as to remove the crippling obstacle of poverty so that everyone has enough. While wealth may be an obstacle to spiritual growth, as the gospel clearly indicates,[83] it is not, in itself, an obstacle to economic development. Increasing inequity in income, however, is an indication that economic growth is not benefiting the poor or enhancing the common good.

A rich elite ruling over an impoverished majority is a legacy of colonialism in most developing countries. Latin America has the world's most unequal distribution of income. In Latin America the wealth of the thirty-two richest people in the region is equivalent to that of the 300 million poorest people. Latin America also has the most unequal distribution of land in the world. The largest 1 percent of farms in Latin America occupy more land than the other 99 percent of farms. Colombia is the most extreme case where the largest 0.4 percent of farms occupy 68 percent of productive land. The countries of Latin America and other regions of the Two-Thirds World are characterized by enclaves of the wealthy elite living in a sea of poverty.[84]

Global income inequality, although stable at the moment, remains very high.[85] In 2016 the top 1 percent captured 20.4 percent of global income, while the bottom 50 percent received 9.7 percent of global income. In the period 1980–2016 the bottom 50 percent of the global population received 12 percent of income growth, and the top 1 percent appropriated 27 percent of income growth.[86]

The publication of Thomas Piketty's *Capital in the Twenty-First Century* in 2014 highlighted inequality in the public policy debate. Based on historical data, Piketty concluded that the return on capital is always higher than economic growth. Therefore the owners will do better than workers. If there are no regulations or policies aimed at distributing wealth, capitalism will concentrate wealth among the elite.[87]

There is good evidence that there is a correlation between economic growth and income equity (fair distribution). Neither can be sustained without the other; economic growth and human development are mutually reinforcing. This makes sense when one realizes that a growing economy needs more and better-educated workers, and it also needs a larger market—meaning more consumers. It is social spending and fair wages within countries, and fair investment and fair trade among countries that produce these conditions for continued growth. Henry Ford was wise to pay his workers enough so they could afford to buy the cars they were producing; Nike, on the other hand, is not paying its Indonesian workers enough to feed their families, much less buy a pair of sneakers.[88]

Inequity also affects social and political power.[89] There is a link between a large gap between the rich and the poor and political instability, civil conflict, populism, and corruption, both within countries and among countries. Within countries, the rich elite simply buy the politicians who then enact social policies that perpetuate the power of the elite and the marginalization and powerlessness of the poor. Wealth inequity is a threat to democracy itself.[90] Wealthy countries and MNCs neglect or exploit less powerful countries and their people, as we have seen.

Policy actually makes a difference regarding economic inequity. For example, more aggressive redistribution through taxes and direct social subsidies has spared Europe from the acute class disparities to which Americans have grown accustomed. Unequal access to quality education is helping reproduce poverty in the United States generation after generation. In the Two-Thirds World, China's strategy based on low-skilled manufacturing for export, and underpinned by aggressive investment in infrastructure, has proven more effective at raising living standards for the bottom half of the population than India's more inward-looking strategy, which has bestowed the benefits of globalization more on the well-educated middle class.[91]

There *are* clear strategies and policies that governments can pursue to insure that economic growth results in equal opportunity for every child and genuine human development:[92]

1. A political commitment to increasing *job* opportunities and employment that pays a living wage.
2. Social spending that enhances human capabilities, particularly on *education* and *health*.
3. Increasing access to productive assets, especially *land*, financial *credit*, and *technology*. Land reform is key to rural development, which is in turn essential to feeding hungry people and slowing the migration to the cities. The Grameen Bank in Bangladesh, founded by Muhammad Yunus in 1976, demonstrated that small loans to poor women for microenterprises (microcredit) can benefit the poor and make a profit for the bank.[93] There is a strong correlation (0.87) between a country's wealth (per capita GDP) and internet access. Thus, resolving the technology divide is another challenge in closing the gap between the rich and the poor.[94]
4. A focused investment in *women*'s capabilities through education, child care, credit, health care, and employment.[95]
5. A responsible *government* that gives high priority to the needs of all the people and to the common good, and controls corruption.[96]

Thomas Piketty's suggestion for responding to economic inequality is a global tax on capital. Under his plan, in whatever form your wealth exists and wherever it is, it would be taxed at the same rate. This sounds good in theory, but given the difficulty of agreeing on tax policy in any single country, is it feasible that 196 countries could come to agreement?[97]

Economic inequity also raises questions of social and moral responsibility. The richest 1 percent has as much wealth as the rest of the world population combined. The richest nine people have as much wealth as the poorest four billion people—$687 billion. The world's 2,208 billionaires have amassed over $9 trillion.[98] How much is enough in a needy world? In 2010, Warren Buffet and Bill Gates initiated the Giving Pledge, which encourages wealthy people to pledge to give away at least half of their fortunes either while alive or when they die. As of 2018 there are 183 signatories who have pledged over $365 billion. But it is not only billionaires who have more than enough, more than they need. As followers of Jesus who challenged the rich young ruler to sell all his possessions and distribute the money to the poor, and warned that it is easier for a camel to go through the eye of a needle than for a rich person to enter the kingdom of God (Luke 18:18–27), Christians have a responsibility for open-handed generosity and courageous justice. As Gandhi said, "Earth provides enough to satisfy everyone's need, but not everyone's greed."[99]

Practical Solutions to Poverty

Although it may have gotten less media attention than Piketty's book, *Poor Economics: A Radical Rethinking of the Way to Fight Global Poverty* by Abhijit V. Banerjee and Esther Duflo (New York: Public Affairs) was a publishing sensation in development economics in 2011, sparking significant critical discussion and receiving acclaim, including Business Book of the Year from the *Financial Times*, Goldman Sachs, and *The Economist*. It offers practical responses to the concerns of the poor based on observing the lives and choices of the poor themselves, and on evidence of what works and what doesn't.

Both authors are professors at the Massachusetts Institute of Technology. They spent fifteen years looking to the poor as a source of knowledge about the reality of poverty and its alleviation.[100] In 2003 they decided to bring the scientific gold standard for academic research, the randomized controlled trial, to the concrete concerns of the poor. They do not grapple with the big theoretical issues such as "Does financial assistance help or hurt the poor?" but with practical problems such as "Should insecticide-treated bed nets for preventing malaria be given to the poor or should the poor be charged for them?" (Giving them out does not diminish their use [58].) By 2010 they were engaged in over 240 experiments in forty countries. This is a fascinating, accessible, and enlightening book. I simply want to recount some of their observations and the key insights I gleaned from the book.

The authors state that the three I's—*ideology, ignorance, and inertia*—on the part of the experts, aid workers, and policy makers often explain why policies fail and aid does not have the intended effect (16). Ideology can include economic theories and fundamental assumptions about reality. These three I's also influence the choices of the poor in negative ways. "[T]he poor often lack critical pieces of information and believe things that are not true" (268). For example, their uncertainty about the biology and benefits of immunizations, coupled with their reluctance to pay present costs for uncertain and hidden future rewards, often result in not immunizing their children. Information, public policies, and incentives might overcome this ignorance and inertia.

Regarding *hunger*, the book notes that those in extreme poverty are usually undernourished and malnourished (not starving), and nine million children die each year from the effects of chronic malnutrition. The poor tend to eat food that tastes good rather than what will yield the most calories or is most nutritious (23–24). Imagine that! Childhood malnutrition can directly affect the ability of adults to function successfully in the world. Therefore, the authors suggest focusing food subsidies on the unborn and children in the first three years of life (31). This is the wisdom of the perennially underfunded Women, Infants, and Children (WIC) program in the United States. They also suggest fortifying salt with iron and iodine so everyone gets these minerals that are key for healthy development (31–35).

Poor Economics contends that there are lots of "low hanging fruit" in the area of *health*, that is, actions that can save lives and enhance the quality of life that are low cost. These are mostly preventive steps in the area of public health, such as breast feeding (only 40 percent of infants are breast fed), chlorine (which can prevent diarrhea and infectious disease), immunizations, and bed nets (41–42).[101] Research has confirmed that "nudges," small incentives, can motivate people to take advantage of preventive programs such as immunizations (65–68). The health care systems in many developing countries are appalling. The health care workers at government clinics often do not show up for work. Clinics were found to be closed 35–55 percent of the time. Private health care is offered by charlatans and quacks who underdiagnose and overmedicate, and often do more harm than good (50–56).

The Millennium Development Goals focused on enrolling all children in school. In turns out that enrolling is not sufficient for getting an *education* because teachers are absent 20 percent of the time, and even if on campus, they may not be in the classroom (74–75)![102] Many teachers also bring an elitist attitude and low expectations toward their poor students. Parents also shared these low expectations of their children, which become self-fulfilling prophecies (86–92). The good news is that despite the poor quality of education, going to school is still beneficial for the poor. In Indonesia every year of primary school raised adult wages 8 percent. Here too nudges were helpful, including conditional cash transfers. Mexico tried this method of providing subsidies to families *if* the children attended school regularly and the family participated in preventive health care programs. Enrollment increased by 4 percent for boys and 8 percent for girls. Soon developing countries everywhere were offering conditional cash transfers (78–81). Much more progress could be made if the quality of the education improved. Research suggests that focused attention on each student is more beneficial than the credentials of the tutor or teacher in the primary grades (83–86).

Another of Banerjee and Duflo's key lessons is that "[T]he poor bear responsibility for too many aspects of their lives" (269). Risk is an everyday fact of life for the poor, and it is stressful. The poor have to worry about income, food, violence, crime, corruption, and, especially, health. Cataclysmic global events, such as the 2008–2009 Great Recession, barely register in their already fraught lives (134–40). Meanwhile those who are better off have lots of the difficult and beneficial decisions (those with costs today for future benefits) made for them. For example, their water is chlorinated; nutritious food is readily available; they have access to a savings account; they are included in social security and retirement plans (269). Such *public programs*, if universal, would have beneficial results for the poor and for their countries, such as a lowering of the fertility rate and decreasing population growth (127–29).

The benefits of microfinance institutions (MFIs) were alluded to above. The poor can be ingenious small-scale entrepreneurs, but, with few exceptions, their enterprises are tiny and barely profitable (213–22). Although 44 percent of the extremely poor operate such a small business, their dream is not suddenly becoming Bill Gates or Jeff Bezos. They want for themselves and their children *steady employment, with a decent salary*, through a government job or a position in a private firm. It is such jobs, even starting with sweatshop conditions, that begin to have a transformative effect on the lives of the poor (227–34).

Public policies that benefit the poor and the common good are not difficult to enact, but they won't have much impact if they are not properly implemented. For example, the Uganda government decided to give per-student grants to the schools to enhance education through its infrastructure, including teachers. A follow-up study found that only 13 percent of the funds ever reached the schools; half got no funds at all. The money ended up in the pockets of district officials. Good policy, poor implementation. When this corruption was exposed by the press, there was public outrage, which produced change. The key is sorting out the broken *political process* (235–37).[103] Corrupt institutions are often the legacy of colonialism, whose purpose was wealth extraction rather than promoting the common good and human development (238). Bad institutions are persistent and difficult to change. Sometimes there are regime changes, but more often change is incremental and happens at the local level. Procedures for accountability, such as audits and public exposure, can make a difference (244–46). Rules are important, as is who gets to make the rules (248–50, 261–62). India, for example, decided to require that some leadership positions on village councils be reserved for women and minorities, and this has made a difference both in terms of pro-poor policies and in changing attitudes toward women and minorities. Outside nations and corporations can have an impact regarding human rights and accountability if they genuinely care about the poor and vulnerable.

Poor Economics focuses on the practical concerns and choices of the poor and seeks evidence for what can make a positive difference in their lives. This may well be a better starting point for development economics than economic theory. It represents a change in epistemology—toward a concrete, decentralized, local, evidence-based, relational approach, consistent with the subsidiarity and solidarity principles in Catholic social teaching.

For economic justice to be realized and human development to happen for the poor there have to be changes both in the global economic system, within the countries of the Two-Thirds World, in local communities, and within the hearts and minds of the earth's citizens.

POVERTY AND CONFLICT

Finally, an observation that is perhaps obvious, but that needs to be stated: poverty is an important cause of revolutions, wars, and violence; and war results in poverty. There is an interrelationship between poverty and conflict.[104]

During the Cold War most conflicts and revolutions in the Two-Thirds World were viewed by the United States and the Soviet Union through the prism of the East–West conflict, as a struggle between communism and democratic capitalism. Very often, once the ideological shell was stripped away, these conflicts represented a struggle by a poor majority of people for justice and a better life. In many of the conflicts and revolutions in Latin America during the 1960s through the 1990s, a crucial element was the struggle of the poor for justice. This was true in Nicaragua, El Salvador, and Guatemala, in Haiti, Jamaica, and the Dominican Republic, in Chile, Brazil, and Colombia. Poverty was also an important ingredient in the struggle against apartheid in South Africa, the people power revolution in the Philippines, the troubles in Northern Ireland, the overthrow of the shah of Iran, and the Palestinian conflict with Israel. Poverty and oppression are seedbeds for revolution.

Poverty is in itself a violence against human dignity, and it sometimes leads the poor to violently respond to their desperate situations. A violent revolution by the poor generally begets a disproportionately violent response by the army or the government to protect the status quo. Poverty can result in a spiral of violence.[105]

The destructiveness of violence and war results in poverty. War creates refugees, people who leave their homes and often their homeland to escape the violence. Refugees leave behind their belongings and resources and become instantly impoverished. War destroys cities, homes, schools, hospitals, crops, offices, and factories. War perversely reverses the corporal works of mercy, creating conditions in which people's basic needs are not met. Crops are defoliated and people go hungry. Reservoirs are contaminated and people go thirsty. Homes are destroyed and people are without shelter or clothing. People are injured and sickness is sown. Prisoners are taken. Sometimes the dead remain unburied.[106] Economic growth and human development are clearly impossible under conditions of war and violence.

The majority of the people on earth live in poverty, struggling to meet their basic needs and fulfill their God-given potential. This reality is a tremendous obstacle to the dream of creating a just and peaceful world order. It is even more of a scandal because it need not be. The poverty of the many exists in sharp contrast with affluence of the few. The parables of the Rich Fool (Luke 12:13–21), the Rich Man and Lazarus (Luke 16:19–31), and the Great Feast (Luke 14:15–24) stand as a warning to contemporary Christians who are comfortable with their riches in a hungry world. God invites humanity to a great banquet, but everyone must be included at the table.

STUDY QUESTIONS

1. Have you experienced or observed poverty? What does poverty do to the human spirit?

2. When Jesus says, "Blessed are the poor in spirit, for theirs is the kingdom of heaven" (Matt 5:3), what does he mean?

3. Why are the countries of the global North rich and the countries of the global South poor?

4. Is globalization good news or bad news for the poor? What steps can be taken to make globalization work to benefit the poor?

5. When multinational corporations move into developing countries, are they a blessing or a curse for the poor? What can be done to make their presence a blessing?

6. Is the United States generous with foreign aid? Should US foreign aid be increased? What, if any, conditions should be placed on foreign aid?

7. Do you think that peace on earth can coexist with global poverty?

4

CLIMATE CHANGE, RESOURCE DEPLETION, AND ENVIRONMENTAL DESTRUCTION

Then God said to Noah and to his sons with him: "As for me, I am establishing my covenant with you and your descendants after you, and with every living creature that is with you, the birds, the domestic animals, and every animal of the earth with you, as many as came out of the ark." (Gen 9:8–10)

Modern Society will find no solution to the ecological problem unless it takes a serious look at its lifestyle. In many parts of the world, society is given to instant gratification and consumerism while remaining indifferent to the damage which they cause. . . . Simplicity, moderation and discipline, as well as a spirit of sacrifice, must become part of everyday life, lest all suffer the negative consequences of the careless habits of a few.

Pope John Paul II
"Peace with God the Creator; Peace with All of Creation" (1990), #13
Message for World Day of Peace, January 1, 1990

On a warm Saturday morning in the spring of 1974, shortly after the celebration of the fourth Earth Day, I was walking along 56th Street in New York City. A black Lincoln Town Car, with four big men in black suits and white shirts, windows rolled down, passed me going in the same direction. As the car slowed to stop at a red light, the man riding "shotgun" threw a big Styrofoam coffee cup out of the window. It fell at the feet of a young woman who was walking toward me. She picked up the cup, walked over to the stopped car, and threw it back in the window onto the lap of the astonished litterer, with the firm admonition, "New Yahk is not your gahbage can." Then she proceeded calmly down the sidewalk.

In some ways this story can function as a parable about environmental issues. I do not know what effect the woman's action had on the occupants of the car, but she certainly raised my consciousness and changed my behavior. I admired her conviction and her courage. Indeed the earth is not our garbage can, and we humans have got to take responsibility for our waste and encourage others to do so as well.

Yet environmental issues are complicated and insidious. If the man throws the cup into a garbage can, the city is cleaner and more pleasant. The cup, however, still has to be disposed of by being buried in a landfill or burned in an incinerator. Polystyrene, the technical name for Styrofoam, is nonbiodegradable, difficult and costly to recycle. If incinerated, it produces greenhouse gases and pollutes the atmosphere. It is a petroleum-based material, and it takes energy to produce the cup. The chemicals used in production are hazardous to human health. Environmental responsibility may mean not buying or producing the cup in the first place. But are there realistic alternatives for having our morning coffee on the run? Maybe it is our fast-food lifestyle that is the root problem. Yet the modern economy depends on that lifestyle. Even a brief reflection on a simple Styrofoam cup raises radical questions and seemingly intractable problems.

Here is the conundrum that humanity faces regarding environmental and economic justice. The earth's ecosystems are wondrously diverse and resilient, with a capacity to create and maintain life in countless forms. But the planet itself is finite, and the balance of its ecosystems is fragile. The human species has been so successful in reproducing and in consuming that we are radically altering the ecosystems on which all life depends. The sheer number of humans is leaving a deep impression on planet Earth. At the same time, as we have already noted, in order for humans to survive and flourish, in order to have economic and human development, economic growth seems necessary.[1] Indeed, as we shall see, economic development seems to be an essential ingredient in stopping the runaway growth of the human population. But economic growth, through increased industrial productivity, presently requires large quantities of fossil fuels and other resources. This depletes the earth's resources and heats up the atmosphere, like an engine running faster and faster. How does society meet the needs of the eight billion people now alive, the majority of whom are poor, without compromising the prospects of future generations, especially through global warming? Economic growth seems essential, but the use of fossil fuels to provide the energy for increased productivity is changing the climate in disastrous ways. This chapter will address the issues packed into this dilemma.

VALUES AND CONCEPTS

The three interrelated levels of analysis (situation/information, interpretation/evaluation, and response/action) are involved in this examination of ecological problems. Science provides significant, albeit ambiguous, information, which further complicates the politics of environmental justice. Humanity's relationship with nature raises complex ethical and conceptual questions as well.

Christianity has been accused of being the culprit in the ecological crisis through its conception of human dominion over the earth and its creatures.[2] "God blessed them, saying: 'Be fertile and multiply; fill the earth and subdue it. Have dominion over the fish of the sea, the birds of the air, and all the living things that move on the earth.'"[3] This anthropocentric (human-centered) perspective encourages the exploitation of the earth, and Western cultures have done just that.

In response, many Christian theologians, while acknowledging a history of abuse, have interpreted the creation stories in terms of stewardship,[4] or more recently, companionship,[5] rather than dominion.[6] Other theologians, such as Thomas Berry, have moved toward an earth-centered perspective, drawing on sources outside the Christian tradition.[7] Philosophers have had their own version of this debate in the clash between "deep ecology,"[8] with its ecocentric approach, and the mainstream environmental movement, which calls for human responsibility toward the earth in the interests of humanity.[9]

It is not the purpose of this chapter to enter into this important discussion in detail, but, of course, values and perspectives are the foundation of any analysis. Environmental issues are theological, philosophical, and ethical, as well as scientific, technological, economic, and political in nature. Neither a *biocentrism* that asserts the equal value of a person and a fly nor an *anthropocentrism* that assigns only instrumental value to the natural world makes much sense. A *theocentric* vision that sees the universe and the earth as created by God who calls humanity into right relationship with God, one another, and all of creation seems at once more biblical and more realistic. Humanity is neither above, nor over against, nor below creation. We are earthlings, embedded in creation, and in relationship with the natural world. All of God's creation is good and valuable in itself; all of creation stands before God in profound poverty as creatures; and all of creation is a sacrament of God's goodness and creative power. In responding to the needs of the poor and in respecting the value of earth, humanity is seeking a right relationship with God, one another, and the natural world. "Right relationship" is what God has created us for and called us to.[10]

THE ANTHROPOCENE EPOCH

The universe began about 13.7 billion years ago with the Big Bang. Our planet formed about 4.6 billion years ago, and life emerged on earth about a billion years later. Humanity (*Homo sapiens*) evolved in Africa about 200,000 years ago during the Pleistocene epoch. As early as 125,000 years ago humans reached the Middle East, then seemed to retreat back to Africa. About 75,000 years ago modern humans again began to migrate out of Africa, first to the Middle East, then to Asia, Australia, Europe, and eventually to North America and beyond. The Pleistocene was characterized by a cooler climate and the ebb and flow of ice ages. The Holocene epoch began 11,700 years ago with the end of the last ice age and the emergence of a stable, warm climate. Humans developed agriculture by the early Holocene, and what we know as civilization and recorded history have taken place entirely in the Holocene. If we were to imagine the universe story as fourteen bound volumes, each representing a billion years, the Holocene would be the last sentence, on the last page, of the last volume.[11]

Both the evolution and extinction of the earth's whole collection of species generally happen gradually, thus maintaining the earth's biodiversity over geologic time. For example, the background extinction rate for mammals is about one species every seven hundred years, and for amphibians about one species every one thousand years. During the last 540 million years (the Phanerozoic Eon), however, there have been five big extinction events, and many smaller extinction events, each with different, sometimes mysterious, causes. The most catastrophic extinction event, the "great dying," happened 252 million years ago near the end of the Permian period. It involved the conflagration of huge deposits of carbon-rich rocks (coal) and spectacular gas explosions. Ninety percent of life in the ocean and 75 percent of life on land was extinguished. Humanity is now releasing carbon into the atmosphere at ten times the rate as happened in the End-Permian extinction event.[12] The last big extinction event, which killed off all the dinosaurs and wiped out three-fourths of all species on earth, was about sixty-six million years ago, near the end of the Cretaceous period of the Mesozoic era.[13] Some smaller extinction events, such as that of large land mammals (mammoths and their cousins, the mastodons, longhorned bison, saber-toothed cats, giant ground sloths, etc.) and including the Neanderthals (*Homo neanderthalensis*), near the end of the Pleistocene epoch, appear to *correlate* with the arrival of humans on different continents.[14]

Today humans are dominating the earth. The human population has exploded from one billion in 1825 to more than eight billion in 2025. The biotic community is going through what can be persuasively argued is a sixth mass extinction event, and this one is *caused* by humans. By 2050, it is estimated that global warming alone will have committed a minimum of 10 percent and more likely 24 percent or more of all species toward extinction.[15] Human action is changing the chemistry of the atmosphere and of the oceans; rearranging earth's flora and fauna, often with devastating results; depleting forests, fisheries, and fresh water; damming and diverting rivers; replacing natural vegetation with agricultural monocultures; constructing sprawling megacities; removing mountaintops and fracking deep underground; consuming natural resources at an astounding rate; and polluting the air, water, and land with toxins and greenhouse gases. These changes are so widespread, so rapid, and so ecologically devastating that geologists are seriously considering whether we have entered a new geologic epoch defined by humanity's dominant impact on the earth's ecosystems—the Anthropocene (from the Greek *anthropos*, meaning human).[16]

Theologian Thomas Berry (1914–2009) says that the "great work" of our age is to respond morally and constructively to the new reality represented by the Anthropocene:

> The Great Work now, as we move into a new millennium [or a new epoch], is to carry out the transition from a period of human devastation of the Earth to a period when humans could be present to the planet in a mutually beneficial manner.... Such a transition has no historical parallel since the geobiological transition that took place 67 million years ago when the period of the dinosaurs was terminated and a new biological age begun.[17]

Berry calls this emergent period when humans would be present to the earth in a mutually enhancing manner the Ecozoic era.[18]

CONSEQUENCES OF GLOBAL WARMING AND CLIMATE CHANGE

The previous section suggests that human activity is disrupting the natural world so profoundly that we have entered into a new geological epoch—the Anthropocene. The Intergovernmental Panel on Climate Change (IPCC), a group of more than 1,500 scientists assembled from sixty nations by the United Nations, said in their Fifth Assessment Report in 2013: "Warming of the climate system is unequivocal, and since the 1950s, many of the observed changes are unprecedented over decades to millennia. The atmosphere and ocean have warmed, the amounts of snow and ice have diminished, sea level has risen, and the concentrations of greenhouse gases have increased."[19] Global warming is the most serious ecological challenge facing humanity because disrupting the climate affects everything. Nearly all other environmental issues are tied to or worsened by global warming, the causes of which have been well documented.[20] What, then, are the consequences of global warming?

Overview

Without substantial efforts to curb the rise in the emissions of carbon dioxide, the global average temperature is projected to rise by a third of a degree Celsius or more every ten years, or three or more degrees in a century. Thus the projection is that the average surface temperature of earth will increase an additional 1.5 to 4.5 degrees C by the end of the twenty-first century, depending on the policies adopted in the coming years. For a sense of perspective, there is only a difference of five or six degrees Celsius between the coldest part of an ice age and the warm period between ice ages.[21] "Based on well-established evidence, about 97 percent of climate scientists have concluded that human-caused climate change is happening."[22] In August 2000, the North Pole melted, a phenomenon that probably has not occurred for fifty million years and certainly has never been seen before by humans.[23] The hottest year since records began in 1880 was 2016, topping 2015, and the ten hottest years have all been since 2003, except for 1998. In 2016, the amount of carbon dioxide in the atmosphere climbed to its highest level in 800,000 years, sea-surface temperatures and global sea level were the highest on record, the sea ice extent in the Antarctic was at a record low, and it was the fortieth consecutive year (since 1977) that average annual global temperature was above the long-term average.[24] There is no doubt that greenhouse gases are accumulating in the atmosphere, and it is clear that earth is already warming and experiencing the consequences.[25]

The impact of climate change will vary considerably from place to place. There will be some winners, but more losers. For example, in Siberia, Scandinavia, and northern Canada, warmer temperatures may lengthen the growing season and allow the cultivation of different crops.[26] In general, the poor will suffer more from global warm-

---

Pope Francis on Climate Change

The climate is a common good, belonging to all and meant for all. At the global level, it is a complex system linked to many of the essential conditions for human life. A very solid scientific consensus indicates that we are presently witnessing a disturbing warming of the climatic system. In recent decades this warming has been accompanied by a constant rise in the sea level and, it would appear, by an increase of extreme weather events, even if a scientifically determinable cause cannot be assigned to each particular phenomenon. Humanity is called to recognize the need for changes of lifestyle, production and consumption, in order to combat this warming or at least the human causes which produce or aggravate it. . . .

If present trends continue, this century may well witness extraordinary climate change and an unprecedented destruction of ecosystems, with serious consequences for all of us. . . .

Climate change is a global problem with grave implications: environmental, social, economic, political, and for the distribution of goods. It represents one of the principal challenges facing humanity in our day. Its worst impact will probably be felt by developing countries in coming decades.

Pope Francis, *Laudato Si': On Care for Our Common Home*, ##23, 24, 25.

ing than the rich, because the poor do not have the resources to adapt to the changes, and because the people in some of the hardest hit regions, such as Bangladesh and sub-Saharan Africa, are already poor.[27]

Global warming exacerbates most of the environmental problems that humans are causing and/or facing on earth. Thus, we will explore these environmental and ecological issues, giving attention to the impact of global warming, as well as to the issue itself. We will consider the following topics: extreme weather events; melting ice and rising sea levels; ocean acidification; factory farming; and deforestation and biodiversity.

Extreme Weather Events

There is a difference between weather and climate. Weather is what happens in a particular locale day to day. Climate refers to long-term trends and patterns in the weather over continents or the planet. Weather is naturally variable and often unpredictable. Climate is more stable and is measured in decades, centuries, millennia, and epochs. The natural variability of the weather is like rolling climate dice. Some winters are warm; some are cold, but over time they average out. The enhanced greenhouse effect induced by human activity is loading the dice. There will still be variability in the weather, but we can expect the average (or the norm) to be hotter. For example, in the 1950s record highs and record lows were nearly even (52 record highs and 48 record lows). Between 2000 and 2009 there were twice as many record-high temperatures (291,000) as record-low temperatures (142,420). The warming climate loaded the dice.[28] As a result we can also expect more extreme weather events, such as storms, floods, heat waves, droughts, and wildfires.

In the two decades 1995 through (August) 2015, weather-related disasters killed 606,000 people; left 4.1 billion people injured, homeless, or in need of emergency treatment; and cost more than $1.9 trillion.[29] There were an average of 335 weather-related disasters (which killed ten or more people) every year over these two decades, twice the rate in the previous ten years. Weather-related disasters affected developed and developing countries, with the United States and China reporting the most events, but the poor are most harmed by such disasters.

For example, there has been an increase in intense *heat waves* across the globe, such as in 2017, when major heat waves hit many places, including the southwest and northwest United States, central and southern Europe, and Pakistan. Studies indicate that under the worst case scenario such conditions could represent a normal summer in 2050 and a cool summer in 2100.[30] Hotter summers are becoming the new norm in the Northern Hemisphere.[31]

In the Western United States, *forest fires* are becoming more frequent, stronger, and burning longer. Scientists think that increased dryness or "fuel aridity" accounts for this and that climate change is responsible for 55 percent of increased aridity from 1979 to 2015. Forest fires, of course, release carbon dioxide, which exacerbates climate change.[32]

Droughts are not new to California, but the period extending from fall 2011 through 2015 has been the driest since record keeping began in 1895. The California agriculture that provides the country with nuts, fruits, and vegetables uses 80 percent of the state's water for irrigation. Heat and drought also result in more frequent and intense wildfires. Drought is expected to increase in the temperate zone (that is, mid-latitudes between roughly 25 and 65 degrees north and south) and in the areas around the equator.[33] Drought, like all extreme weather events, tends to hurt the poor the most. The countries in the Horn of Africa, especially Kenya, Somalia, and Ethiopia, have experienced four extreme droughts since the turn of the century. Climate change is adding famine to the suffering of the poor in these areas.[34]

Warmer air holds more water. In a warmer world average precipitation increases, and the hydrological cycle becomes more intense, resulting in heavy downpours, more intense thunderstorms, and more frequent and worse *floods*. During the first five days of October 2015, there were three events worldwide that exemplify the flooding caused by heavy rainstorms: after two weeks of constant rain in Santa Catarina Pinula, a suburb of Guatemala City, a mudslide buried the 125 houses in the El Cambray II settlement, killing over 450 people. Torrential rains hammered a twenty-mile stretch of the French Riviera, causing flash floods that killed at least twenty people.[35] "Mind-boggling rain amounts," including twenty-four inches of rain in a suburb of Charleston, caused "biblical flooding" in the southeast United States, especially in South Carolina. Based on historical weather data, this was considered to be a "1-in-a-1,000-year" rain event, meaning that there was a 0.1 percent chance of it happening. It was the sixth such event in the United States since 2010. The death toll was at least fourteen, and the damage was estimated to be more than $1 billion.[36] Computer models predict an even greater risk of severe storms in the eastern and central United States after about 2040.[37]

Hurricanes, cyclones, and typhoons are all the same weather phenomenon—a tropical storm with sustained winds of seventy-four miles per hour or greater—but different regions use different terms. In the Atlantic and Northeast Pacific such storms are called hurricanes; in the Northwest Pacific, typhoons; and in the South Pacific and Indian Ocean, cyclones. These violent, rotating storms get their energy from the heat of the ocean water. Thus, it is expected that as the oceans heat up there will be more and more intense cyclones, although neither observations nor projections have as yet confirmed this expectation.[38]

Nonetheless, these storms have been deadly and destructive. Hurricane Katrina devastated New Orleans in 2005; "Superstorm" Sandy (the largest ever Atlantic hurricane) wreaked havoc from Cuba to Maine in 2012; and Typhoon Haiyan, one of the strongest ever recorded, killed more than 6,300 people and left another eleven million homeless in the Philippines in 2013. Hurricanes Florence and Michael devastated the North Carolina coast and the Florida panhandle in 2018.

A compounding problem for the environment and climate change is that these storms cause deforestation. For example, Hurricane Katrina destroyed or damaged an estimated 320 million trees across the Gulf coast, containing about 100 million tons of carbon. The toll from Hurricane Maria, which struck Puerto Rico in September 2017, was twenty-three to thirty-one million trees.[39]

Given the natural variability of the weather, it is impossible to say that a particular flood or hurricane was either caused by or made worse by global warming, just as it is impossible to say that a person's lung cancer was caused by smoking or by radiation from nuclear testing. What can be said is that global warming is loading the dice of weather variability, and more and worse incidences of extreme weather can be expected.[40]

Melting Ice and Rising Sea Levels

Since half of humanity inhabits coastal zones around the world, and some of the lowest lying areas are the most fertile and most densely populated, sea level is extremely important. Average sea level is projected to rise about twenty centimeters (cm, about eight inches) by 2030 and one meter (about three feet) by 2100.[41]

Perhaps one of the clearest signs of the reality of global warming is the increased seasonal melting of the sea ice in the Arctic. Many scientists expect the Arctic to become ice free in the summer by the end of this century or sooner. Because Arctic ice is floating on the sea, like ice in a glass of water, its melting does not raise sea levels. It does threaten polar bears and other animals who depend on the ice for their livelihood. Since ice reflects the sun's rays, and open sea absorbs the sun's rays, the melting of the Arctic creates a feedback loop that exacerbates global warming. It also opens up shipping lanes and creates the possibility of drilling for oil and harvesting other Arctic resources, which in turn can create political conflict among the nations with a stake in the Arctic region.[42]

Another negative feedback loop is connected to the warming of the land in the sub-Arctic, such as in Alaska. Just a few feet from the surface but going to a depth of tens or even hundreds of feet down is permafrost, organic matter that died and froze before it could decompose. As the permafrost thaws microbes will convert some of it to carbon dioxide or methane and release it into the atmosphere, where it will cause more warming. Global permafrost is thought to contain about twice as much carbon as is currently in the atmosphere, enough to contribute as much as 1.7 degrees F to global warming over several centuries.[43]

In Greenland, where the surface melting of ice is now widespread when the

Arctic temperature is especially warm, another vicious cycle is taking place: the soot from forest fires elsewhere in the world coats some of the ice in Greenland, causing it to absorb more heat and warm faster. As it melts, the ice gets darker, having the same effect.

The greatest amount of the earth's ice is in East Antarctica, which is generally high and cold and least likely to melt. Some scientists, however, have concluded that the melting of a large section of the mighty ice sheet in West Antarctica has begun, and may now be irreversible in coming centuries. This melting is due to strong winds, tied to global warming, which are pulling warmer waters from the depths to the surface. In yet another feedback loop, the more melting, the more energy for greater winds to stir up the ocean waters.[44]

At present, the great ice sheets of Greenland and Antarctica are roughly stable. This is the basis of the projection of only up to a meter (about three feet) rise in sea level by 2100. This might not seem like much, but it is extremely problematic for the billions of people living on the coast. Furthermore, some scientific research suggests that the melting of these great ice sheets could begin sooner, causing a rise in sea level of five or six feet by 2100. If the Thwaites Glacier in West Antarctica should melt faster than anticipated, as some scientists fear, it could add around eleven feet to the three-feet rise in sea levels expected this century.[45]

The earth's *river deltas* are especially vulnerable to rising seas.[46] *Bangladesh* is a striking example of the plight of developing countries and of the poorest people, facing the consequences of a problem they did not create. Bangladesh produces just 0.3 percent of the emissions driving climate change. With a total population is about 160 million people, it is one of the most densely populated countries in the world, and many Bangladeshis live on the country's low-lying, flat delta, made up of the confluence of 230 rivers and streams. The saltwater of the rising seas intrudes into the rivers, making the water brackish and poisoning the fields. Because its rivers are so polluted, Bangladesh pumps groundwater for its drinking supplies. Thus, as the sea is rising, its cities are sinking, compounding the problem of flooding. The storm surge and flooding from almost annual cyclones typically wash away the mud and bamboo huts of the poor and leave them with nothing. It is projected that by 2050 rising sea levels will inundate 17 percent of the land and create fifty million Bangladeshi environmental refugees. Given that rich countries are primarily responsible for polluting the atmosphere, should they compensate the poor countries such as Bangladesh who suffer the consequences? Should they be willing to take in environmental refugees?

Rising seas and higher storm surges are also a problem for developed countries, but they have more resources to adapt to the situation. In the densely populated Netherlands, for example, more than half of the landmass consists of coastal lowlands that are below present sea level. Over many years the Netherlands, often working with natural forces, has built up a system of dykes and coastal dunes that should protect it from the sea at least through the twenty-first century. A similar system has been recommended for the Norfolk coast in eastern England and may be something the east coast of the United States should consider.[47]

A global rise in sea levels of three feet would mean storm surges of more than six feet on the East Coast of the United States, putting Boston, Providence, Philadelphia, New York, Baltimore, and Norfolk, Virginia, in jeopardy. Miami is built on top of porous limestone, making its infrastructure especially vulnerable to rising seawater.[48]

Low-lying island groups that are barely above sea level will first have their fresh water and soil contaminated by seawater, making their homes uninhabitable; then many will disappear altogether. These are the prospects for island nations such as the Maldives in the Indian Ocean, Kiribati and Tuvalu in the South Pacific, and the Marshall Islands in the North Pacific.[49]

Algae blooms, some of them toxic, are getting worse and more widespread, exacerbated by the warming water, heat waves, and extreme weather associated with global warming. They are appearing in fresh water and marine coastal waters, from Lake Superior and Lake Erie, to the "red tide" in the waters off southwestern Florida, to the West Coast.[50]

A final impact of sea level rise is on areas where few people live—*wetlands and mangrove swamps*. Coastal swamps and marshes are vital to biodiversity and to overall world ecology. For example, these wetlands account for over two-thirds of the fish caught for human consumption, and many birds and animals depend on them for part of their life cycle. Because of a variety of human activities, coastal wetlands are already being lost at a rate of 0.5–1.5 percent a year. Sea level rise will increase this loss. Economic development and its attendant land reclamation and pollution also threaten wetlands and coasts.[51]

Ocean Acidification

The build-up of carbon dioxide in the atmosphere is changing the chemistry of the oceans. There is a constant exchange of gases between the atmosphere and the oceans. The increase of carbon dioxide in the atmosphere has meant that the oceans, a carbon sink, are absorbing more CO_2. As Elizabeth Kolbert notes, "Under what's known as a 'business as usual' emissions scenario, surface ocean pH will fall to 8.0 by the middle of this century, and it will drop to 7.8 by the century's end. At that point, the oceans will be 150 percent more acidic than they were at the start of the industrial revolution."[52]

About one-third of the carbon dioxide that humans have pumped into the air since the beginning of the industrial revolution has been absorbed by the oceans—an amazing 150 billion metric tons. It is not only the scale, however, that is significant, but the speed of this transfer, which is probably unprecedented in the history of earth. This is happening in decades rather than millennia. The speed of ocean acidification gives marine life no chance to adapt through evolution.[53]

The likely result of ocean acidification is a substantial reduction of marine biodiversity. Scientists think that ocean acidification played a role in at least two and perhaps three of the big five mass extinctions in the distant past, as well as in other lesser extinction events. Thus, ocean acidification is sometimes called global warming's "equally evil twin." Some species will proliferate because of the elevated carbon dioxide levels, but that growth, of toxic algae, for example, or plant species, may not be good for ecosystems as a whole. Many other species will perish. Acidification is especially hard on a group of creatures known as calcifiers, which build a shell or external skeleton or internal scaffolding out of the mineral calcium carbonate. Coral reefs, one of the wonders of the sea, depend in part on calcification, and are likely to deteriorate into rubble by 2100.[54]

Factory Farming

This section will focus on livestock production, an aspect of industrial agriculture.[55] Livestock production refers to farming to produce meat (chicken, turkey, pork, beef, lamb, etc.) and food products associated with animals (eggs, milk, etc.). In developed countries such as the United States, and increasingly in less developed countries, this is now done through factory farming, or in "Concentrated Animal Feeding Operations" (CAFOs). This industrial method of adding meat and animal products to the human diet raises questions related to its treatment of animals and its environmental/ecological consequences.

> In tropical and subtropical seas, we find coral reefs comparable to the great forests on dry land, for they shelter approximately a million species, including fish, crabs, molluscs, sponges and algae. Many of the world's coral reefs are already barren or in a state of constant decline. "Who turned the wonderworld of the seas into underwater cemeteries bereft of color and life?" This phenomenon is due largely to pollution which reaches the sea as the result of deforestation, agricultural monocultures, industrial waste and destructive fishing methods, especially those using cyanide and dynamite. It is aggravated by the rise in temperature of the oceans. All of this helps us to see that every intervention in nature can have consequences which are not immediately evident, and that certain ways of exploiting resources prove costly in terms of degradation which ultimately reaches the ocean bed itself.
>
> Pope Francis, *Laudato Si': On Care for Our Common Home*, #41.

At factory farms, animals are crammed into large warehouses, often in cages or pens, never experiencing the earth or sun, and unable to partake in their natural and social behaviors. Pigs can't wallow in the mud, root for food, build nests, or interact with their mothers when young. Caged chickens don't have room to spread their wings, much less establish a pecking order. Unsurprisingly, animals so unnaturally stressed become deranged. Since chickens will peck each other to death in such conditions, their extremely sensitive beaks are clipped or cauterized with no anesthesia. Broiler chickens (raised for meat) are bred to gain the most weight as quickly as possible. Since their anatomy is not designed for so much weight this compounds their suffering. At about the age of six weeks they are slaughtered in a "killing line." They are hung upside down, dipped in electrified water (which paralyzes them, but does not render them unconscious); their throats are slit, and they are dumped into scalding water. Because the killing line zips along at a speed of about one hundred birds a minute, some of their throats are missed, and they are boiled alive. Such conditions are not aberrations, but typical of factory farms. The treatment of nearly all the animals that produce the meat, eggs, and milk that humans consume raises moral issues.

> The livestock sector emerges as one of the top two or three most significant contributors to the most serious environmental problems, at every scale from local to global. . . . [I]t should be a major policy focus when dealing with problems of land degradation, climate change and air pollution, water shortage and water pollution and loss of biodiversity.[56]

Global production of meat and milk are projected to double from 2000 to 2050. The focus here will be on land degradation and climate change.

Through grazing (26 percent) and feedcrop production (33 percent), livestock accounts for 70 percent of all agricultural use of land and 30 percent of the ice-free terrestrial surface of earth. Expansion of livestock production is a key factor in deforestation, especially in Latin America, where rain forests are being cleared for pastures and feedcrop farming. This makes no sense because it creates a desert. The emerald beauty of a rainforest is only skin deep. The luxuriant vegetation and canopy of 200-feet-tall trees is supported by the constant decay of its moist ground surface. When the vegetation and trees are cleared, the soil stops being replenished and quickly becomes barren. After only six or seven years it is worthless for agriculture or grazing.[57] Thus, such deforestation is the worst of both worlds: it is economically shortsighted and ecologically devastating by increasing the carbon dioxide in the atmosphere and exacerbating climate change. Deforestation also destroys habitat and is a major contributor to loss of biodiversity.

"The livestock sector is a major player [in climate change], responsible for 18 percent of greenhouse gas emissions measured in CO2 equivalent. This is a higher share than transport."[58] Much of this contribution is through methane produced by enteric fermentation by ruminants (cows and sheep) and through nitrous oxide from manure. Livestock also account for nearly two-thirds of ammonia emissions, which make significant contributions to acid rain and the acidification of ecosystems. Livestock in the United States produces much more sewage than the human population.

Besides the issue of the treatment of animals and the significant contribution to deforestation, land degradation, water use and pollution, wastes, climate change, and biodiversity loss, there are *social problems* associated with factory farms, including their impact on rural communities and workers.[59] CAFOs undermine small livestock farmers in *rural areas* and create a stomach-turning stench in the neighborhood.[60] *Working conditions* in factory farms and slaughterhouses are dangerous and dehumanizing. The air in CAFOs is smelly and toxic, and the work is as uncomfortable and stressful for humans, as the conditions are for the animals. Lots of blood, terrified animals, sharp tools, and an extremely fast killing and processing line make meatpacking the US occupation with the highest injury rate and the highest turnover rate. Workers are often undocumented immigrants who can't risk speaking up for their rights.

The Food and Agriculture Organization of the United Nations (FAO-UN) limits its analysis of livestock production to the environmental consequences. It argues that industrial livestock production has a major impact on the environment and climate change and that this sector affords an opportunity to limit environmental harm at reasonable cost. The FAO's suggested remedies include regulations on the scale, inputs, and wastes associated with CAFOs, the elimination of subsidies that perversely encourage environmental harm, and, most importantly, achieving greater efficiency through pricing the use of natural resources (such as land, water, waste sinks) so as to account for the full economic and environmental cost, including all externalities.[61]

> Research and stage a class discussion on a moral response to factory farming.

If, however, the ethical analysis of factory farms includes not only their significant impact on the environment and climate change, but also the cruel treatment of animals, the dehumanization of workers, and its inefficiency (on average it takes about six pounds of grain protein to produce one pound of meat protein under CAFO conditions), then a more radical solution presents itself. A strong philosophical and theological case can be made that it is wrong to consume meat (and dairy products and eggs) produced in factory farms. Indeed, given industrial farming's significant contribution to climate change, one of the best ways to reduce your personal carbon footprint is to eat less meat, or, better, become a vegetarian.[62]

Deforestation, Forest Degradation, and Loss of Biodiversity

Deforestation means that forested land changes to a nonforest use, such as a pasture or a farm; *forest degradation* is the decrease in tree density in land that remains a forest. Trees, and thus forests, are carbon sinks because they take in carbon dioxide from the atmosphere and release oxygen through the process of photosynthesis. When wood is burned or decomposes, it releases the trapped carbon dioxide back into the atmosphere. Deforestation has been responsible for about 10 percent of annual carbon emissions. In the period 2011–2015, however, global deforestation rates declined by 50 percent in comparison with the decade 2001–2010 (good news!). In the period 2011–2015 data from forest degradation was included in the FAO-UN Global Forest Resources Assessment (FRA) for the first time, and it was discovered that forest degradation contributes about 25 percent to the carbon emissions from trees. Thus, global deforestation rates are declining, while global forest degradation continues to increase, partially offsetting each other. Nevertheless, global carbon emissions from deforestation and forest degradation decreased by 25 percent during the period of 2011–2015, from an average of 3.9 to 2.9 gigatons (billion tons) per year.[63]

The contribution of expanding agriculture and livestock production to deforestation, especially in tropical forests of the global South, is mentioned above. Logging or commercial harvesting of wood, legally or illegally, is another major cause of deforestation. A randomized trial, which is rare in the field of environmental policy, conducted in the tropical forests of western Uganda, demonstrated that paying owners not to cut down their trees works and is a cost-effective way of slowing climate change.[64]

Forests are ecologically valuable as conservators of soil and water resources by absorbing fresh water and preventing soil erosion and flooding, and as carbon sinks. Perhaps the greatest ecological tragedy of deforestation, however, is the *loss of biodiversity,* or the depletion of species of insects, plants, and animals.

Most people are now familiar with the notion of endangered species. The danger, of course, comes from humankind, sometimes through direct killing, as with buffalo in the American West and overfishing, but more often indirectly, through the alteration or destruction of habitats, as with coral reefs. But when humans destroy huge swathes of tropical forest, we are terminating thousands of species whose existence will never be known to us.

Tropical forests cover only 7 percent of the earth's surface, but they house perhaps 80 percent of all the species on the planet.[65] Harvard biologist E. O. Wilson tells of finding on one tree in Peru as many species of ants as exist in the whole of the British Isles.[66] The prodigious variety of species means that many species are adapted to a particular niche and found nowhere else. A particular species of tree, for example, may attract specific insects which in turn attract certain birds. One characteristic of these micro-ecosystems may be temperature. When the temperature goes up because of global warming (which is happening at an astonishing rate of change in geological terms) the tree cannot easily go a bit higher up the mountain in order to adjust. When loggers or agriculturalists destroy the trees in this micro-ecosystem many other species vanish along with them.[67]

Species naturally evolve and sometimes disappear. Human activity, however, through global warming and ocean acidification, in polluting the atmosphere and waters, and in transforming land use through urban sprawl and clearing tropical forests, is extinguishing species at a rate up to a thousand times faster than the natural pace of evolution. It is estimated that one of every twenty species on the planet could be eradicated by 2060.[68] In doing this we are vastly diminishing the genetic heritage of earth, and we are hurting the interests of humanity itself. Nearly 25 percent of the pharmaceuticals used in the United States today, for example, contain ingredients originally derived from wild plants.[69] Who knows what miracle cures are going up in smoke today? Both economically and ecologically it would make much more sense to harvest carefully the economic, genetic, and biological fruits of tropical forests, rather than to destroy them.[70] In response to the rapid losses that are happening, scientists all over the earth are building repositories of everything from seeds to mammal milk to frozen cells of endangered species to ice cores in the hope of saving this heritage for a postapocalypse world.[71]

> **Loss of Biodiversity**
>
> It is not enough, however, to think of different species merely as potential "resources" to be exploited, while overlooking the fact that they have value in themselves. Each year sees the disappearance of thousands of plant and animal species which we will never know, which our children will never see, because they have been lost forever. The great majority become extinct for reasons related to human activity. Because of us, thousands of species will no longer give glory to God by their very existence, nor convey their message to us. We have no such right.
>
> Pope Francis, *Laudato Si'* #33; see ##32–42, and ##82–88.

E. O. Wilson argues that saving the earth's living environment, including all its species and all the ecosystems they compose, is essential to saving earth's physical environment. "The only way to save upward of 90 percent of the rest of life [from extinction] is to vastly increase the area of refuges, from their current 15 percent of land and 3 percent of the sea to half of the land and half of the sea." This plan has been demonstrated to be feasible by putting together large and small fragments around the world to remain relatively natural without uprooting the people living there.[72]

RESPONDING TO GLOBAL WARMING

The UN Paris Agreement

On December 12, 2015, representatives of 195 nations reached consensus on a landmark accord to lower greenhouse gas emissions to help stave off global warming.[73] The Paris Agreement was accomplished at the twenty-first meeting of the United Nations Framework Convention on Climate Change (UN FCCC). Just six years previous, in December 2009, the climate change summit in Copenhagen had collapsed in acrimonious discord, especially between developed and developing countries—yet another failure of the nations of the world to take seriously the reality of global warming. Yet in Paris nearly all nations made voluntary, legally binding, significant commitments to reduce their greenhouse gas emissions and to meet every five years to assess and strengthen those commitments.

Two important factors made this agreement possible. The first was that the reality of climate change became even clearer. The 2013–14 Report of the Intergovernmental Panel on Climate Change (IPCC) gave extensive scientific documentation of the seriousness and reality of climate change and of its anthropogenic basis. Furthermore, people in all corners of the earth were beginning to experience the consequences of climate change through melting glaciers, rising seas, heat waves, floods, extreme storms, droughts and water shortages.

Second, the attitudes and policies of the two biggest standoffs, the United States and China, shifted remarkably. Historically the United States has contributed the most to greenhouse gas emissions and the least to leadership on climate change. President Obama, however, took global warming seriously and issued an executive order in 2014 that set stringent new Environmental Protection Agency (EPA) regulations designed to slash carbon emissions from US coal-fired power plants. At the same time, China, which had surpassed the United States in greenhouse emissions in 2006 and now emitted twice as much carbon annually, was facing air pollution in its major cities that made it impossible to see, much less breathe. In November 2014 in Beijing, President Obama and Chinese President Xi Jinping announced that the world's two largest and most polluting economies would jointly pursue plans to reduce greenhouse gas emissions. This breakthrough encouraged developed and developing countries to join in. Thus nearly all (186) the 195 nations present at the Paris climate summit came with publicly announced emission reduction plans for the next ten or fifteen years.

The success of the Paris Agreement depends on global peer pressure (since there are no penalties for noncompliance) and on the continued commitment and action of future governments. In the case of the United States, that commitment has been seriously undermined by the election of Republican Donald J. Trump as president in November 2016. Republicans, most of whom are skeptical about human-caused climate change, despite the overwhelming scientific consensus in that regard, also had majorities in both the House of Representatives and the Senate.

On June 1, 2017, President Trump capped off a series of anti-environmental actions by officially withdrawing the United States from the Paris Agreement. Prior to this withdrawal, President Trump issued an executive order that would nullify President Obama's clean power strategy to shut down hundreds of old coal-fired power plants and freeze the construction of new ones. He also decided to roll back Obama administration goals for fuel efficiency standards for cars,[74] ordered a review of a rule requiring that existing oil and gas well operators provide information about methane emissions, proposed a budget that would end funding for climate-related scientific programs, and issued another executive order aimed at opening up protected waters in the Atlantic and Arctic Oceans to offshore drilling. In withdrawing from the Paris accord President Trump has effectively ceded American leadership in the international campaign to curb global warming and made it clear that the United States government has no intention of meeting its Paris commitment to cut its emissions about 26 percent from 2005 levels by 2025.[75] It may well be, however, that the actions of consumers, corporations, cities, and states will in fact reduce US emissions enough to meet the initial Paris commitment despite federal opposition.[76] The final communique at the conclusion of the July 2017 Group of 20 (G–20) summit meeting in Hamburg, Germany, affirmed the Paris Agreement as "irreversible," and included a detailed policy blueprint outlining how nineteen of the countries would meet their goals, in an explicit break with President Trump.[77]

Given the political will, the implementation of the commitments made at Paris would take the world about halfway to the arbitrary, but meaningful, goal of keeping global warming to 2 degrees C (3.6 degrees F), which represents a carbon level of about 450 ppm. Since we are already at 400 ppm and the earth has warmed 0.6 degree C, there is obviously an urgency to reducing greenhouse gas emissions and achieving a zero carbon economy. It is even more urgent if the parties to the Paris Agreement pursue efforts to limit the temperature increase to 1.5 degrees C above pre-industrial levels, that is, decrease carbon concentrations in the atmosphere to 350 ppm.[78] What steps, actions, policies can accomplish this?

A Strategy to Avoid Catastrophic Climate Change

The difficulty of reducing emissions is compounded by the need for more energy for economic development to reduce poverty and for a growing global population. A strategy for achieving this will require *individual* commitment and sacrifice and, more importantly, *structural change* through public policy and actions by investors, business, and industry, especially in the energy, transport, and agricultural sectors. For example, if I choose to replace the incandescent bulbs in my house with energy-saving LED bulbs, I will lower my carbon footprint if the energy source for my electricity is a coal-fired power plant. If my energy source is renewable solar energy or wind power, my action reduces energy consumption, but has no direct effect on carbon emissions.

The energy source for electricity is much more significant than the kind of bulb in lighting fixtures. What then are some of the structural changes needed to stabilize global warming and avoid some of the worst consequences of climate change?

1. Reducing tropical deforestation can make a large contribution to slowing the increase of carbon in the atmosphere. Planting trees (afforestation and reforestation) can sequester carbon out of the atmosphere and can be especially beneficial in this century as the world focuses on reducing the atmospheric concentration of carbon.[79] Soil is also a carbon sink. Regenerative agriculture, as opposed to an industrial model for agriculture, can be a factor in mitigating climate change and restoring the health and productivity of the land.[80]

2. Reducing methane emissions. Methane has a shorter lifetime in the atmosphere (twelve years) than carbon (100–200 years); it is responsible for about 15 percent of global warming. Curtailing deforestation will cut methane emissions from biomass burning. Methane production from landfill sites could be reduced if more waste were recycled or incinerated for energy generation, and if landfills collected the methane either for flaring or (better) energy generation. Carbon dioxide is a by-product of burning wastes or methane, but it is a less potent greenhouse gas. Reducing leakage from natural gas pipelines and from fracking and other aspects of petrochemical production is a cost effective way of reducing methane emissions. Finally, better management could reduce methane emissions from sources associated with agriculture, by adjustments in the diet of cattle or attention to the details of rice cultivation.[81] Individuals can facilitate changes in agriculture by eating less meat, especially beef and lamb. Opting for a vegetarian or vegan diet may be one of the best ways to reduce one's carbon footprint.

3. Energy conservation. In a fossil fuel economy, the less energy used, the less fossil fuel burned. Energy efficiency and conservation are important steps in reducing carbon emissions and for transitioning to a nonfossil-fuel economy. This requires a new attitude, a different mindset, especially in developed economies. It also requires changes in public policy to encourage and reflect a change in attitude. For example, sport utility vehicles (SUVs) now account for over half of the vehicles bought in the United States and one out of three sold globally. SUVs are counted as small trucks and therefore do not have to meet the same fuel and emissions standards as sedans (cars). Public policy focused on energy efficiency would require SUVs to meet the same emission standards as cars. It would also increase the tax on gasoline and use the revenue for environmental subsidies.[82] Standards for housing construction should require sufficient insulation and energy-efficient windows. All appliances should meet high standards of energy efficiency.[83] It is up to individuals, however, to choose to buy fuel efficient vehicles and appliances.

4. Eliminate fossil fuels as a source of energy. The burning of fossil fuels (coal, oil, and natural gas) accounts for about 80 percent of carbon dioxide emissions from anthropogenic sources.[84] Meeting or exceeding the goal of keeping global warming below 2 degrees C (3.6 degrees F) will require eliminating the burning of fossil fuels by 2100.[85]

The five biggest oil companies made over $1 trillion in profit in the first decade of the twenty-first century. Much of the huge profits in fossil fuels are the result of a historical accident. The fossil-fuel industry was allowed to dump its carbon wastes for free because the world did not realize how harmful this pollution was. Thus, *putting a price on carbon pollution* (internalizing these externalities) through a tax on carbon and/or a cap-and-trade approach would enlist the market in the fight against global warming by raising the cost and reducing the value of fossil fuels.[86] The fossil-fuel industry has and will resist this, but the enlightened will of citizens can prevail. The campaign at many universities to divest from fossil-fuel stocks is a step in this direction, and even the financial sector is beginning to see that divestment from fossil-fuel companies is not only moral, but prudent, in a warming world.[87]

> Brainstorm ideas and policies for saving energy and promoting energy efficiency.

The United States is not the only country struggling to eliminate fossil fuels in the production of energy. In 2017, there were over 1,600 coal plants planned or under construction in sixty-two countries. The new plants would expand the world's coal-fired power capacity, the dirtiest form of energy production, by 43 percent. Chinese corporations were behind 700 of these new plants in China and around the world, and India's National Thermal Power Corporation is the world's single largest coal-plant developer.[88] Even Norway, which hopes that only electric cars will be sold in the country by 2025, is one of the world's biggest oil producers, almost all of it for export. In 2017, the emissions from Norway's oil exports will be ten times its domestic carbon emissions. A weakness of the Paris climate agreement is that countries are assessed only on their domestic emissions, not their impact on the planet as a whole.[89]

On the positive side, Britain and France have pledged to end the sale of gas and diesel cars by 2040. Norway and India have expressed the desire to do the same, and ten other countries have set targets for electric cars. Volvo has announced that it will make only electric cars as of 2019. General Motors and Ford announced plans for several new all-electric models by 2023 and envision an all-electric future. Tesla shook up the industry with the success of its first mass-market electric model. This switch to electric in transportation is motivated by global warming, by the harm to health of pollution, and by regulatory pressure. Of course, progress depends on whether electricity is produced by fossil fuels or by clean energy.[90]

Eliminating fossil fuels in energy production will be a challenge indeed, one that begins with a change in attitude that results in curtailing the power of the fossil fuel industry.

5. Develop and implement appropriate nonfossil-fuel energy sources. The CO_2 emissions from natural gas are 25 percent less than from oil and 40 percent less than coal. Thus, in the transition from a fossil fuel economy, *switching to natural gas* might yield substantial savings in carbon emissions.[91] Also in this transition period *carbon capture and storage* (CCS) technology could reduce carbon emissions. CCS technology, however, requires further research and development to be made feasible and affordable.[92]

Nuclear energy is carbon free, and it could be an alternative energy source to fossil fuels.[93] Nuclear power, however, is saddled with another set of environmental and economic problems. The mining of uranium is water intensive and endangers the health of workers. The accident at Three Mile Island in Pennsylvania in 1979, the uncontained meltdown at Chernobyl in Ukraine in 1986, and the 2011 Fukushima disaster in Japan demonstrate the safety issues from the operation of nuclear power plants. High doses of radiation can cause death, and lower doses can result in cancer and genetic defects. Nuclear power plants produce 400 to 500 pounds of plutonium and other highly radioactive wastes a year. Plutonium is extremely carcinogenic, and it has a half-life of 24,400 years, which means it lasts virtually forever.[94] There is as yet no approved facility or means to store the 80,000 tons of spent nuclear fuel already in existence in the United States. Finland, however, is implementing a well-thought-out plan to entomb about 6,000 tons of spent reactor fuel in granite bedrock at the Onkalo repository on Olkiluoto Island.[95] Still, the safe storage of such toxic and corrosive substances for tens of thousands of years may be an impossible assignment for fallible human beings in an ecosystem in flux.[96] To make matters worse, plutonium can also be enriched for use in nuclear weapons.

Although nuclear power accounts for 20 percent of the electricity consumed in the United States (and more in countries such as France and Japan), cheap natural gas is making it even more unprofitable and accelerating pressure to close reactors.[97] Decommissioning a nuclear power plant, which has a working life of perhaps fifty years, is expected to cost twice as much as it did to build the plant.[98] It is for economic reasons, then, that no new plants had been ordered in the United States since 1978 until the Watts Bar Unit 2 nuclear plant in Spring City, Tennessee, began operation in 2016. The only ongoing construction is on two reactors at the Vogtle nuclear power plant in Georgia, which is pressing ahead despite facing delays and overruns. There are fourth generation nuclear power plants in development with more advanced reactors that promise to be safer, less expensive, and produce less radioactive wastes.[99] Given the threat of global warming, whether to invest in more nuclear energy is a necessary and urgent public policy discussion.

A variety of *renewable energy* sources are available; nearly all of them depend on the power of the sun, directly or indirectly. The earth receives as much energy from the sun in forty minutes as we consume in a whole year. If we can harness this energy efficiently and economically, it will provide for all our needs.[100]

Hydropower is the oldest form of renewable energy, and it now generates about 18 percent of the world's electricity. Some hydroelectricity schemes are very large, such as the Three Gorges Dam in China, the Itaipu Dam on the borders of Brazil and Paraguay, and the Grand Coulee Dam on the Columbia River and Hoover Dam on the Colorado River in the United States. Hydropower is a primary reason that Latin America has the world's cleanest electricity.[101] There is untapped hydroelectric capacity, much of it in Africa, Asia, and Latin America, that could double or triple the output from hydropower. Large dams, however, have significant social repercussions, such as the displacement of people from the reservoir site, and environmental consequences, such as loss of land, impact on species, and sedimentation of the river. Small hydroelectric schemes that can generate energy for a farm or a village at a modest cost are increasing and have much potential.[102]

Biomass energy. In much of the developing world, the population lives "off-grid" in areas with no access to modern energy. Nearly two billion people rely on *traditional biomass* (firewood, dried dung, rice husks, etc.) for cooking and heating. About 10 percent of world energy is produced by traditional biomass. Often open fires are used, which are inefficient and which also cause serious illness from indoor pollution. The use of a vented stove can increase the efficiency of burning biomass from 5 percent to 20–50 percent, depending on the sophistication of the stove, and at least disperse the pollution outside. *Modern biomass*, which contributes to the production of commercial energy, can take several forms. One is to incinerate the garbage produced by modern society (about a half ton per person annually in developed countries) to generate energy rather than let it rot in landfills. Modern technology enables this to be done with negligible air pollution. Wet wastes (sewage sludge, farm slurries, and manure) can yield biogas (mostly methane) with the help of an anaerobic digester and be used to produce energy. Crops can be grown as fuel. This use of land, however, should not compete with food crops or contribute to deforestation. The ideal fuel crop should have high yields with low energy inputs (fertilizer, crop management, transportation, irrigation). Willow and elephant grass (*Miscanthus*), which can be grown on poor land only marginally useful for agriculture, meet these requirements. Since the 1970s, Brazil has been producing ethanol from sugar cane for use as fuel in transport. Ethanol burns cleaner and produces less carbon than gasoline. Burning biomass releases CO_2 into the atmosphere, but it is renewable energy because the process of photosynthesis captures carbon when it is grown again. Whether or not biomass is burned for energy, CO_2 will be released as it decomposes.[103]

The use of *wind energy,* produced by ever larger turbines, has grown quickly since the turn of the century, generating over 2 percent of world energy by 2012, at a cost competitive with fossil fuels. Modern wind generators are not as elegant as nineteenth-century windmills, but they are much more efficient. Besides the eyesore issue, the nature of the wind means that wind generators are intermittent in operation. This is less of an issue when wind generators are contributing to a larger electricity grid that employs diverse power sources. Offshore wind farms can remove the turbines from sight and sometimes find more steady winds. By 2050, it is projected that wind will be generating about 12 percent of the world's electricity.[104]

Solar energy. The simplest way to use the sun's energy is to turn it into heat. Solar water heaters and stoves are easily constructed. Buildings can use passive solar design or more actively employ the radiation from the sun. Solar power can be concentrated through mirrors or photovoltaic (PV) solar cells to generate electricity. At present neither is economically competitive with fossil fuels or wind energy for large-scale electricity provision, although the cost is declining. More research to improve the efficiency of solar power and efforts to develop economies of scale will reduce the cost. Still, solar energy is versatile and can now beneficially supplement other energy sources. To meet the 2 degree C global warming goal it is hoped that solar energy will be generating about 26 percent of the world's energy by 2050.[105]

Other renewable energy sources available in particular regions would include geothermal energy from deep underground and the energy of the tides, currents, or waves in the ocean. Geothermal energy is important in Iceland, where conditions make it easier to tap. The movements of the ocean are difficult to exploit, but have the potential to make important contributions as a regional energy source. Fuel cells could efficiently convert hydrogen and oxygen directly into electricity. Future research and development may make fuel cells feasible. It may also be possible to harness safely the virtually limitless power of nuclear fusion in the future.[106]

6. Geoengineering the climate. Some suggest a technological solution to global warming, such as cooling the planet by shooting aerosols into the stratosphere or whitening clouds to reflect sunlight back into space.[107] There are practical, political, and philosophical issues with such technological solutions.

On a practical level are such proposals feasible? Can humanity begin to control the climate on a massive scale? What will be the consequences, foreseen and unforeseen, of such manipulation of nature? Might such a solution go too far and result in a frozen planet, for example? Will such solutions cause unforeseen problems worse than global warming? We know that the climate of earth is extremely complicated and that we do not fully understand it.

The politics and ethics of such a proposal might be at least as difficult as the science and technology. How could global agreement on the deployment of a technology that would have different impacts on different countries be achieved? Who would decide? Would the United States, for example, agree to a technology that cooled the atmosphere but also created a desert in the prairie states? If the technology seemed to work, would it be unethical not to use it, given the disproportionate effects of climate change on the poorest nations? How would the international community address geopolitical frictions resulting from this technology?

Finally, some, noting that technology has gotten the earth community into this mess, wonder if more technology is a proper solution. Wouldn't this simply be another example of human hubris with inevitable tragic consequences?

Despite these issues, given that humanity has in fact altered earth's climate and the seriousness of the consequences of global warming, perhaps there is a need to invest in *research* (as distinguished from implementation) on ways to cool the planet and the potential side effects of geoengineering proposals. Since humanity has in fact unintentionally embarked on a large-scale geophysical experiment in global warming, perhaps geoengineering research makes sense. Has humanity, however, ever developed a technology that we haven't used?

The Cost of Transitioning to a Zero Carbon Economy

A reasonable ethical and economic principle is that the polluter should pay the environmental costs of carbon emissions.[108] At present, many countries subsidize fossil fuels. Worldwide, these subsidies to the fossil-fuel industry amount to an average of more than $10 per ton of carbon dioxide. In the interests of slowing global warming and because an industry as profitable as fossil fuels does not need government support, these subsidies should be removed immediately. Instead, governments should subsidize energy conservation and carbon-free energy.[109] These two steps would make carbon-free and renewable energy even more economically competitive with fossil fuels. Third, as mentioned above, a price should be imposed on carbon pollution through a carbon tax or similar mechanism (e.g., tradable permits for carbon pollution). These fiscal measures should be applied in the electricity sector and on solid, liquid, and gaseous fuels used for houses, industry, business, and transport. A fourth step is to adequately fund research and development aimed at technological innovation to facilitate this transition to a zero carbon economy.[110] It is predicted that decarbonizing the energy system through 2050 will cost an additional $44 trillion. This will be offset by $115 trillion in fuel savings, in addition to saving the costs associated with avoided climate change.[111] Technologies should be generously transferred to developing countries to enable them to use the most appropriate and efficient energy technologies for their economic development. The 2015 Paris Agreement strongly urges the rich countries to spend a $100 billion a year to help poorer countries avoid and adapt to the effects of climate change.[112]

The Deep Decarbonization Pathways Project (DDPP) is perhaps the most serious effort to develop a detailed road map for a zero carbon economy. It has enlisted teams from sixteen countries that account for the large majority of emissions, including the United States and China, to devise strategies and plans. Its analysts use conservative assumptions and realistically presume that developed countries will not make big changes in their lifestyles and developing countries will strive for higher standards of living. Its overall plan is consistent with the first five points covered in the strategy above. The DDPP cautions that governments should begin with the long-term goal and work back from there, and that an overreliance on natural gas, a current temptation, is a dead end. It also suggests that achieving the zero emissions goal will require the entire economy, including transportation, to be electrified as much as possible.[113]

There are many ways for individuals to reduce their carbon footprint: drive fewer miles, eat less meat, avoid plane trips, buy an electric or hybrid car, install solar panels. In the end, however, it may be the exercise of one's citizenship to enact policies that will result in a zero carbon economy that is most important.[114] Lobby the federal government and support the efforts of businesses and local and state government to adopt far-sighted, enlightened environmental and economic policies.[115]

POPULATION GROWTH

Today global population reached a record high, and tomorrow it will break the record once again. Most of the history of the human species has been a struggle to survive, to multiply and fill the earth. It took all of human history to reach a population of one billion (around 1825), but only 100 years to add a second billion people. Fifty years later, in 1975, global population had doubled again to four billion, and in fifty more years, in 2025, the population is expected to double again to at least eight billion people.[116] Humanity has recently been very successful at multiplying and filling the earth. Human flourishing now depends on stabilizing the human population.

To understand population growth it is important to grasp the concept of *exponential growth*. Exponential growth happens when a quantity continuously increases by a constant percentage over a given period of time—when, for example, a population grows by 2 percent annually. This is the principle behind compound interest on a savings account. At a growth rate of 1 percent a year, a quantity, such as population or savings, will double in seventy years. The doubling time at a 2 percent rate of growth is thirty-five years. The global population growth rate peaked sometime in the 1960s at 2.1 percent. In 2005 world population was growing at an annual rate of 1.24 percent; by 2015 it dropped to 1.18 percent. At that rate about 83 million people (the equivalent of the population of Germany) are being added to the global population every year, more than 200,000 every day. The world population is projected to reach 8 billion by 2025, and to increase to 9.7 billion in 2050 and 11.2 billion by 2100.[117] Even a low rate of exponential growth of a population within a finite ecosystem cannot continue indefinitely without negative consequences. Either the birth rate will have to decrease or the death rate will increase.[118]

Another way of viewing demographic trends is through the fertility rate, which refers to the average number of children a woman would have in her lifetime on the basis of fertility rates in a given year. A fertility rate of 2.1 means that each couple is replacing itself, and population growth has stabilized. This does not mean, however, that population growth will level off immediately. There is a "demographic momentum" that increases population for some time before it finally levels off because the population has many people in their reproductive years. In other words, although each woman is having fewer children, there are more women having children. Worldwide, the fertility rate was 2.51 in the period 2010–2015, and steadily declining. In developed regions it was 1.67 in that period, but in less developed regions, the fertility rate was 2.65.[119]

There are regional differences in the growth of population. Well over 90 percent of the growth is occurring in the Two-Thirds World. In 2015,

> Sixty per cent of the global population live[d] in Asia (4.4 billion), 16 per cent in Africa (1.2 billion), 10 per cent in Europe (738 million), 9 per cent in Latin America and the Caribbean (634 million), and the remaining 5 per cent in Northern America (358 million) and Oceania (39 million). China (1.4 billion) and India (1.3 billion) remain the two countries with the largest populations, representing 19 and 18 per cent of the world's population, respectively.[120]

The populations of Russia, Japan, and Europe are declining, and the population of most developed countries is stable or projected to decline. An exception is the United States, whose population continues to grow at a receding rate of about 0.75 percent (boosted in part by immigration). This means that the number of Americans will increase from 322 million in 2015 to about 388 million in 2050. While the increase in the US population is not especially significant in terms of the sheer numbers of global growth, an increase in the number of Americans is bad news for the planet's ecosystem and natural resources. "According to one calculation, the average American baby represents twice the environmental damage of a Swedish child, three times that of an Italian, thirteen times that of a Brazilian, thirty-five times that of an Indian, and 280 (!) times that of a Chadian or Haitian because its level of consumption throughout its life will be so much greater."[121] The per capita energy consumption of an American is roughly twice that of a German or a Brit, nearly five times that of a Chinese, ten times that of a Colombian, fifteen times that of an Indian, more than twenty times that of a Filipino, and a hundred times that of an Afghan or Haitian.[122]

Thus, Pope Francis is partially correct when he says, "To blame population growth instead of extreme and selective consumerism on the part of some, is one way of refusing to face the issues. It is an attempt to legitimize the present model of distribution, where a minority believes that it has the right to consume in a way which can never be universalized, since the planet could not even contain the waste products of such consumption."[123] Consumerism is indeed the primary cause of the ecological crisis, more than population growth per se. Still *the role of population growth in perpetuating poverty* by effectively cancelling out the benefits of economic growth must be acknowledged.[124] Some of the highest population growth is happening in the forty-eight least developed countries, thirty-three of which are projected to triple their populations, and ten of which (all in Africa) are expected to have a five-fold population increase by the end of the century. After pointing this out, the United Nations observes, "The concentration of population growth in the poorest countries will make it harder for those governments to eradicate poverty and inequality, combat hunger and malnutrition, expand education enrollment and health systems, improve the provision of basic services and implement other elements of a sustainable development agenda to ensure that no-one is left behind."[125] Proliferating populations contribute heavily to stresses on both social systems and the ecosystem. The economy has to create ever more jobs and wealth to meet the needs of ever more people. To do this, the economy must use more energy and more resources, which depletes the goods of the earth and produces more pollution (in a fossil-fuel economy).

Among the greatest challenges of our era is figuring out how to feed the 9.7 billion people projected to occupy the earth by 2050, while also advancing rural development, reducing the agricultural emissions that cause global warming, and protecting valuable ecosystems, land, and fresh water. To accomplish this the world will have to produce 70 percent more food calories by 2050 than it did in 2006.[126] About 800 million persons are hungry and chronically malnourished. Thus far, however, hunger seems to be caused by poverty and the maldistribution of resources, not by scarcity. So far, food production has increased even faster than population.[127]

In order to continue this trend, there are several steps that can be taken:

- Halve the 25 percent of food that is lost or wasted.
- Shift to diets with less meat, and especially less beef.
- Reduce population growth by achieving replacement level fertility, especially in sub-Saharan Africa.
- Boost crop yields, especially in sub-Saharan Africa, through better land and water management and more efficient agriculture.
- Increase the productivity of aquaculture.[128]

These steps can produce more food, advance rural development, reduce agricultural emissions, and protect ecosystems.

Overcrowding can be another problem associated with population growth. The population density (people per square kilometer) of Asia (142) is four times that of Europe (33) or the United States (35).[129] North America has well over two acres of arable land to support each inhabitant, but Asia has little more than a third of an acre per person.[130] Already over half of the world's population lives in cities that occupy only about 4 percent of earth's land, and this concentration of people in urban areas is expected to increase in the near future. For example, despite somewhat successful efforts to curb population growth, Bangladesh, one of the most densely populated territories on earth, will see its population density rise to 1,553 people per square kilometer by 2050.

As natural environments deteriorate from overuse, people *migrate* from rural areas to overcrowded cities and from the global South to the North.[131] While *urbanization* tends to lower fertility rates in the long run, the influx of people is overwhelming the capacity of cities to provide basic social services, such as housing, sanitation, water, education, health care, and work. In 2014 there were twenty-eight megacities with over ten million inhabitants, most of them in the Two-Thirds World. By 2030 there will likely be forty-one megacities. It is projected that 6.4 billion people will inhabit urban areas by 2050.[132] Mexico City, for instance, which could have a population of nearly forty million by 2034, already faces air pollution that is a grave threat to human health, as does Delhi in India and Beijing in China, among others.[133]

Keys to stabilizing population are economic development and education, especially focused on girls and women, and ready access to family planning services and contraceptives. Population growth occurs when the birth rates exceed the death rates in a society. The process of economic development results in a fairly universal pattern known as the "demographic transition." First, death rates fall mostly owing to public health measures, such as better sanitation and diet, and immunization against diseases. As a result, the population increases. Later, birth rates fall because people become more educated, more secure, more urbanized, and women's status in society rises. It then becomes reasonable to have fewer children, and population stabilizes. Great Britain went through this demographic transition with the Industrial Revolution. Other developed countries have followed the pattern.[134]

Agrarian people are acculturated to having large families because children are assets: their labor contributes to the family, and they provide security in the parents' old age. The high infant mortality rate associated with poverty also motivates people to have more children. Having many children, then, makes sense for the rural poor. To make it more reasonable to have fewer children, economic development is necessary.[135] Thus, economic development seems to be the ordinary way to move through a demographic transition and stabilize population.

Thus we enter into an ecological and economic conundrum: economic growth is necessary (but not sufficient) for economic development, which is, in turn, necessary for stabilizing population growth. But economic growth, at least initially, tends to boost population growth. And, as we have seen, population growth can make economic growth very difficult to accomplish. Furthermore, industrialization (presently an important ingredient in economic growth) depletes resources and damages the environment, especially in a fossil-fuel economy. Yet economic development seems necessary to stabilize population growth, lest the human population exceed the carrying capacity of earth.

It should be noted that some developing countries have been successful in lowering the rate of population growth through aggressive government-sponsored family planning.[136] Thailand's population growth was cut from 3.2 percent to 1.6 percent in only fifteen years, in part through the efforts of Mechai Viravaidya, a dynamic and creative former government economist who has promoted various methods of contraception. Over 70 percent of couples in Thailand practice family planning.[137] Bangladesh lowered the fertility rate from 7 to 4.5 through the efforts of family-planning workers. In 1993, 45 percent of couples practiced family planning, while only 6 percent did so in 1974.[138] Zimbabwe has used a similar program to slow the growth of its population "from catastrophic to merely dreadful."[139] China reduced its fertility rate from 6 to 2.5 in a single decade (the 1970s) through what many consider a Draconian policy of "one child per couple," a policy rescinded by China in 2015.[140] India had mixed success with a less coercive approach. This success was followed by a period (1995–2007) when international financial support for voluntary family planning fell by more than half. Happily both international and private support (the Gates Foundation, for example) are now increasing.[141]

Religion and culture interact with population policy in complex ways. Included in the mix are cultural understandings of gender roles and of the status of women. The Catholic Church's well-known opposition to artificial methods of birth control is based on a controversial interpretation of natural law philosophy, rather than in a directly pronatalist (supporting birth) position. In practice, however, it results in church opposition to most family-planning programs. Many Catholic theologians, however, have questioned the wisdom of the Catholic Church's position.[142] This critique is based on an alternative interpretation of natural law and on the need to stabilize population growth.

Conservative Muslim clerics often oppose efforts at contraception as well, although the teaching of the Qur'an on birth control is ambiguous at best. In Iran, for example, the politically influential Muslim religious leaders now officially approve of birth control. An educational session on birth control is required in Iran in order to get a marriage license, and condoms, pills, and sterilization are free.[143]

Most religious teachings were developed in a time and in a context in which procreation was essential for survival. Past cultural norms were logically pronatalist. Today the situation is quite different. Stabilizing population growth may be necessary for future human flourishing and for the good of creation.

Economic development remains the primary way to accomplish the demographic transition. It is also clear, however, that aggressive government programs that make available a variety of contraceptive methods and provide education and incentives for family planning can lower the population growth rate. In particular, "If there is a single key to population control in developing countries, experts agree, it lies in improving the social status of women."[144] Population control is not a mystery; it is a difficult cultural, economic, and political task. In essence it requires alleviating poverty and raising the standard of living. A gradually declining population is a welcome side effect of efforts to directly improve people's (and especially women's) lives through greater access to health care and improved education.[145]

SUSTAINABLE DEVELOPMENT

"Sustainable development" has been suggested as a way through the conundrum posed by the apparently contradictory goals and consequences of economics and ecology. Economic development seems required, but not sufficient, to overcome poverty and allow for greater human development. Economic development also seems essential to stabilize the worrisome growth of human population. Mainstream economics has considered economic growth essential for economic development. Economic growth, however, usually entails industrialization, which depletes resources and increases energy use. In a fossil-fuel economy this results in greenhouse gas emissions that lead to global warming and climate change and other environmental and health problems. The goals of economic development to overcome poverty and of reduction of greenhouse gas emissions in order to stave off climate change seem in direct conflict with one another. Efforts to conquer poverty usually harm ecosystems, which will eventually impoverish us all.[146]

A Native American proverb expresses the vision and values necessary for sustainability: We do not inherit the earth from our parents; we *borrow* it from our grandchildren. Thus, sustainable development means economic development that meets the needs of the present generation in a way that does not compromise the needs of future generations.[147] This is a laudable concept that is readily understood, but difficult to put into practice. Indeed, one wonders if sustainable development is an oxymoron. This dilemma might be resolved with a two-pronged strategy: the zero carbon energy strategy developed above, and a focus on economic equity or an economics of enough rather than economic growth per se. In this way the needs of everyone in the present generation, especially the poor, might be met in a way that does not compromise the needs of future generations or the health of the environment.

A realistic and affordable framework for achieving a zero carbon economy by 2100 was presented above. That framework also accounts for economic development in response to poverty and for population growth. Economic growth will require more energy, but that energy will be produced from sources other than fossil fuels and used more efficiently. Thus economic growth need not contribute to global warming and climate change. There is evidence that economic growth is already being decoupled from carbon emissions.[148]

Moreover, instead of concentrating on economic growth as a strategy for alleviating poverty, perhaps the focus should be on increasing economic equity.[149] This improvement in the quality of life of the poor could be had with relatively little sacrifice by people in developed nations. There is enough wealth in the world to alleviate poverty without huge strides in economic growth, but wealth needs to be creatively and generously distributed to those who need it. A focus on economic equity and the fair distribution of goods, with less pressure for economic growth, may be the ticket to a future that offers quality of life to everyone.

It would be ecologically disastrous for the Two-Thirds World to reach the standard of living of the developed North in a fossil-fuel economy, a lifestyle that is already altering the earth's ecosystem on a magnitude similar to that of being struck by a devastating asteroid. Sustainable development, if taken seriously, means a new way of thinking and a different way of living for the North.[150]

Human flourishing includes the satisfaction of basic needs, intellectual challenge, creative expression, meaningful activity, healthy relationships, supportive community, and spiritual growth. Perhaps there are already more than enough goods for a meaningful and satisfying human life for all. Less might be spiritually better for the global North; and it would surely be beneficial for the earth, and, if the excess is properly redistributed, liberating for the poor and for the rich. Pope Francis is correct when he says, "The same mindset which stands in the way of making radical decisions to reverse the trend of global warming also stands in the way of achieving the goal of eliminating poverty."[151] He is referring to an attitude that defines success in terms of consumption and that develops an economic system based on greed and profit rather than the common good.

Sustainable development is a radical idea that is more rhetoric than reality in today's public policy discussions.[152] There is a need for political, religious, and moral leaders who embody and proclaim these values and this vision. The words of Pope John Paul II, quoted at the beginning of this chapter, are challenging indeed. What if affluent Christians took seriously the call to simplicity, moderation, discipline, and a spirit of sacrifice? That would indeed be good news both for the poor and for the earth.

WASTE DISPOSAL

Highly radioactive wastes are so toxic and dangerous that they pose thus far unresolved disposal problems. The disposal of other toxic chemicals is similarly costly and difficult, and the disposal of more ordinary refuse is complex and controversial.

It is conservatively estimated that world nations produce 440 million tons of *hazardous or toxic wastes* each year, that is, wastes that are dangerous or potentially harmful to human health or the environment. Toxic wastes are usually produced by industry or commerce, but also come from residential use, agriculture, the military, medical facilities, and light industries, such as dry cleaners.

The 1989 Basel Convention on the Control of Transboundary Movements of Hazardous Wastes and Their Disposal (Basel Convention) and the 1995 Basel Ban Amendment made all toxic waste exports from Organization of Economic Cooperation and Development (OECD), that is, most developed countries, to non-OECD countries (developing countries), even for recycling, illegal. The United States, the largest producer of toxic wastes, has ratified neither the Basel Convention nor the Basel Amendment.[153]

The United States has two laws pertaining to hazardous wastes both under the purview of the US Environmental Protection Agency (EPA).[154] The 1976 Toxic Substances Control Act attempts to regulate toxic chemicals. However, many chemicals were grandfathered in when the law was passed, and industry has no obligation to test or certify chemicals as safe before they are put on the market. Chemical companies spend vast sums on lobbying Congress (over $100,000 per member in 2015) to effectively block serious oversight. Almost none of the chemicals we encounter daily has been tested for safety, and it is nearly impossible to get the EPA to regulate chemicals that experience and data suggest are hazardous.[155] The Superfund Act (1980, 1986) authorized and funded the EPA to locate toxic waste sites and to force the responsible parties to clean them up. As of February 2016, there were 1,323 toxic waste sites on the Superfund's National Priorities List, and 391 such sites had been deleted from the list as no longer hazardous. Neither of these acts is especially effective in protecting the health and safety of Americans from hazardous industrial chemicals in the atmosphere, water, or land.

There are several problems with cleaning up toxic waste. It is expensive and dangerous; there are few effective methods of disposal; and each has its own environmental and economic drawbacks. Burning toxic waste liberates the toxins and pollutes the air, which in turn pollutes waterways, land, and enters the food chain. Which chemicals are toxic and how dangerous they are (for example, how carcinogenic) are often not known. Incinerators are a huge capital investment (around $500 million) and create few jobs. They are usually built in poor and/or minority neighborhoods, violating the principle of environmental justice. Burying toxic waste in landfills almost always contaminates groundwater, and it also pollutes the air.[156]

Clearly, it is a good idea to reduce the production of toxic chemicals, even if that might add to the cost of products. Industries should be required to certify that chemicals are safe prior to their use, to properly dispose of toxic wastes, and to clean up past messes. International agreements now prohibit dumping toxic and nuclear wastes at sea, and the global norm expressed in the Basel Convention prohibits the export of toxic wastes, a practice exploitative of developing countries.

Garbage or "municipal solid waste" (MSW) is another problem. MSW includes household, office, and retail wastes, but excludes industrial, hazard-

---

Bottled Water and Plastics

One can imagine situations where bottled water can be temporarily helpful—in natural disasters or in places where safe drinking water is hard to come by. But in the developed world, where safe drinking water comes out of the nearest tap, bottled water is an environmental disaster. It takes seventeen million barrels of crude oil to manufacture the 1.5 million pounds of nonbiodegradable plastic bottles annually, and another eighteen million barrels of oil to transport it—equivalent to a full day's worth of America's total oil consumption. Only 13 percent of the sixty million water bottles discarded by Americans every day are recycled. Scientists estimate that about eight million metric tons of nonbiodegradable plastic end up in the ocean every year, adding to the 100 million tons of plastic already floating there. Bottled water is a fetishized commodity, emblematic of a culture of conspicuous consumption, which the earth cannot afford.

ous, and construction wastes. Garbage includes waste such as durable goods (furniture, tires), nondurable goods (newspapers, plastic bottles), containers and packaging (milk cartons, cardboard boxes), and compostable wastes such as food and yard waste.[157]

The consumer society in the United States is a throwaway society. Americans generate about 50 percent more garbage per person than other Western economies with similar standards of living. About 63.5 percent of MSW is dumped in landfills; 29 percent is either recycled or composted; and 7.5 percent is sent to Waste to Energy Facilities.[158]

The goals of MSW management are to dispose of it in a way that reduces greenhouse gas emissions and other environmental impacts, that does not harm human health, and that is as economical as possible.

Source reduction, that is reducing the amount of garbage generated, with the ideal being zero waste, is the most effective way to meet these goals. Packaging and containers make up 30 percent of the MSW produced in the United States; durable goods constitute about 20 percent; nondurable goods about 25 percent, and biodegradable yard trimmings and food scraps about 25 percent. Producers should bear extended responsibility for the goods they make and the packaging of those products. If businesses were held responsible in this way, they would have an incentive to minimize the volume of packaging material, thus reducing their costs as well as their wastes. Corporations would also be motivated to produce goods that last, and are reparable, reusable, and recyclable, contrary to the planned obsolescence business model that is the current norm. Individuals should bear the primary responsibility for compostable waste, such as yard trimmings and food waste, either by composting it themselves or through local taxes that pay for it to be collected and composted.[159] Consumers can exercise environmental responsibility by, for example, purchasing efficiently packaged materials, buying in bulk, frequenting consignment shops or reuse centers, bringing their own shopping bags, recharging batteries, and choosing reusable plates, cups, and silverware rather than disposable. They can also throw away less, remove their names from junk mail lists, shop differently, start a compost pile, and recycle. (Shopping online may increase waste from packaging, unless it is recycled.) A separate tax or charge for local waste disposal can drive home its cost and motivate consumers to be environmentally responsible.[160] Anything business, consumers, and government can do to reduce the amount of petroleum-based plastic produced seems especially worthwhile.

In 2011 about twenty million more tons of trash was recycled (rather than dumped in landfills) than in 2008.[161] *Recycling* is usually much more expensive than using landfills. The environmental benefits of recycling come primarily from reducing the need to manufacture new products—less mining, logging, and drilling—and from reducing greenhouse gas emissions. About 90 percent of these benefits come from recycling paper, cardboard, and metals, such as aluminum, because these materials more efficiently reduce carbon dioxide in the atmosphere.[162] Recycling plastic is also fairly efficient in reducing carbon dioxide, and it is good for both land and water ecosystems. Over 70 percent of Americans are served by curbside recycling programs. Americans recycle about 35 percent of their municipal waste, about average for a developed country, while Germans recycle 65 percent, South Koreans 59 percent, and Turks only 1 percent.[163]

Waste to Energy (WTE) *Facilities* commonly either incinerate garbage or use biodigesters to create methane from biogenic waste (paper, food, yard waste), which is then burned to create heat and energy. The biodigester approach offers more environmental promise. Burning methane emits carbon dioxide, but methane is a much more powerful greenhouse gas than CO2. As mentioned above, waste incineration can create a variety of toxic air pollutants, and it also produces toxic ash.[164]

Although the number of US *landfills* has steadily decreased, the total capacity has increased. Some cities in the Northeast, where landfills tend to be scarce, ship their garbage to landfills in the South and Midwest. This arrangement, which might grate at first (take care of your own garbage!), can be beneficial to all concerned. Cities get rid of their refuse, and rural areas and distant regions benefit by the creation of jobs and the expansion of their tax base. Moreover, federal regulations require that new landfills be lined with clay and plastic, equipped with drainage and gas-collection pipes, covered daily, and regularly monitored. Modern landfills are safer than their predecessors, but they still leach hazardous material into the groundwater and the air.[165] Although landfills were the third largest source of US anthropogenic methane emissions, accounting for about 1.7 percent of total greenhouse gas emissions in 2013, over 64 percent of landfill-generated methane is captured and combusted into CO2 through flaring or (better) electricity production. Landfill gas, however, is dirty gas, and burning it releases other toxic pollutants as well.[166]

Waste disposal, like other environmental issues, benefits from a combination of supportive public policy, enlightened commerce, and committed citizens. In the long run, however, nature itself, where there is little waste, should become the model for humanity. We must become conscious of producing less waste (in the way we package consumer goods, for example), of creating products that can be repaired and recycled (for example, sneakers with biodegradable soles), and of recycling the materials produced. For example, eco-industrial parks already exist where one company's waste becomes another's resource, where the sulfur dioxide scrubbed from a power plant's smokestacks becomes a raw material for a wallboard company.[167] This approach is not only good for the environment but generally reduces costs and improves efficiency. It requires, however, not only technological innovation and creativity, but a new attitude, a new way of thinking. Zero waste is the ideal we should strive for.

ENVIRONMENT, CONFLICT, AND SECURITY[168]

There is a reciprocal connection between war and the environment. War and the preparation for war destroy the environment and deplete natural resources. Competition for vital resources and environmental scarcity can be contributing contexts for conflict and war, resulting in "resource wars." Both of these phenomena are complex.

War and the Environment

One obvious link between war and the environment is that war is terribly destructive of earth and nature.[169] Burning crops, defoliating fields, and poisoning water have long been common practices in warfare. If we want to protect the environment, we should cultivate peace.

The *way war is fought* often multiplies its environmental effects. Since insurgents try to melt into the population like fish in a lake, the counterinsurgency philosophy of the United States was to "drain the lake." In Vietnam this meant destroying villages and herding the people into centers, and defoliating and poisoning the countryside with Agent Orange so that it could not hide nor support the Vietcong. Both people and the land continue to suffer the effects of these hazardous chemicals. Chemical weapons programs have created a plethora of toxic wastes, which complicates the conversion of military sites to civilian use.[170] In the 1991 Persian Gulf War, retreating Iraqi forces spilled large amounts of Kuwaiti oil into the Persian Gulf and blew up hundreds of Kuwaiti oil wells, leaving them burning.[171] The use of "weapons of long-term destruction"—land mines, cluster bombs, and depleted uranium shells— can render vast tracts of land unsafe and unproductive, and continue to kill and maim civilians long after the war is over. Environmental cleanup after war is expensive, dangerous, and sometimes impossible.[172]

Preparation for war also pollutes the earth, consumes excessive amounts of energy, depletes natural resources, and produces as much as 10 percent of global carbon emissions annually. The manufacture and above-ground testing of nuclear weapons have dispersed radioactive materials locally, regionally, and globally. It is difficult to directly link this exposure to higher incidences of cancer or disease, but studies have suggested a correlation.[173]

The Department of Defense is the United States' largest consumer of fossil fuels with emissions comparable to a country such as Denmark. When a modern army is deployed its carbon footprint is enormous.[174] In the first four months of the 2011 intervention in Libya, for example, NATO flew about 12,000 sorties. Each mission lasts about four hours at an estimated cost of $40,000 per hour.[175]

A nuclear war would be the greatest environmental disaster imaginable. Indeed, the resulting nuclear winter might leave earth a barren, uninhabitable wasteland.[176] Thus Pope Benedict XVI calls for "progressive disarmament and a world free of nuclear weapons, whose presence alone threatens the life of the planet and the ongoing integral development of the present generation and of generations to come."[177] War is an ecological catastrophe.[178]

The Environment and War

War destroys the environment and depletes natural resources. *Competition over vital resources and environmental scarcity*, on the other hand, can contribute to conflict and result in "resource wars."[179] Neither Pope Francis nor Benedict XVI uses this term, but they do refer to the need to address conflict over resources such as energy and water.[180] There is a complex connection between resource depletion and environmental degradation, on the one hand, and conflict and war on the other.

First, competition over *vital, nonrenewable* resources, such as oil, can contribute to conflict. Access of developed nations to Middle East oil contributed to the motivation to fight both the 1991 Persian Gulf War and the war in Iraq in 2003. In this "econocentric approach" to foreign policy, the military plays an important role by protecting supplies of vital energy resources. Thus, the United States has engaged in joint military training exercises with Kazakhstan and Uzbekistan in the Caspian Sea region, which is now thought to have perhaps the second largest reserves of oil in the world.[181]

It is rare for the scarcity of *renewable* resources to be a direct cause of a major *interstate* war. The possible exception might be a conflict over water, but even here only a narrow set of circumstances seems to contribute to war between nations. There must be a genuine conflict over a river (or other body of water), with a history of antagonism between the countries, and the downstream country must be much stronger militarily than the upstream country.[182] There are a number of conflicts between countries over the control of water: India and Bangladesh contest the Ganges River; Turkey and Syria the Euphrates River; Israel, Lebanon, Syria, and Jordan draw on the Jordan River; and Israel and the Palestinians dispute the aquifer under the West Bank. Only in the case of the Nile River, however, would it seem all these conditions might be met. Egypt is stronger militarily than its upstream neighbors, Sudan and Ethiopia, and Egypt has threatened several times that it will go to war to ensure an adequate supply of water from the Nile River. Countries have found themselves nose to nose over fishing rights and other resource issues as well, but seldom has this led directly to interstate warfare.[183] Indeed, although more than 250 major river systems are shared by two or more countries, cooperation over shared water resources is common.[184]

Scarcities of renewable resources, however, can contribute to *intrastate or regional* conflict and violence.[185] "Scarcities of critical environmental resources—in particular cropland, freshwater, and forests—are contributing to mass violence in several areas of the world. While these "environmental scarcities" do not cause wars between countries, they do sometimes sharply aggravate stresses within countries, helping stimulate ethnic clashes, urban unrest, and insurgencies. . . . Policymakers and citizens in the West ignore these pressures at their peril."[186]

Experts in the field of "warfare ecology" identify three sources of environmental scarcity:

- Resource depletion and degradation, which decreases the *supply* of a resource
- Population growth and/or increased consumption, which boosts *demand* for a resource
- "Structural scarcity," which results from an imbalance in the *distribution* of a resource

Structural scarcity is most often the result of the wealthy and powerful taking resources from the poor and weak. Today's structural scarcity often has roots in colonialism, when a powerful elite appropriated the land and other resources. It is often reenforced by the institutions and policies of global capitalism, which dictate, for example, that land be used to grow cash crops for global trade and profit, rather than subsistence crops for local use. These three sources of environmental scarcity interact in pernicious ways to result in the ecological marginalization of the poor, but the "resource capture" (the taking of resources by the powerful) associated with structural scarcity almost always plays a role.[187]

Environmental scarcity leads to social disruptions that can contribute to conflicts. Expanding populations, for example, can cause deforestation, soil degradation, and water depletion, all of which can decrease agricultural production. Food scarcity can then contribute to conflict among different ethnic groups (as in Sudan) over land and water. "Environmental scarcity is never a determining or sole cause of larger migrations, poverty, or violence; it always joins with other economic, political, and cultural factors to produce its effects."[188] Few conflicts justify a single-issue label such as "environmental conflict." Rather, environmental stress should most often be viewed as a symptom that something has gone wrong, usually economically and/or politically.[189]

Poverty and environmental scarcity can often become a downward spiral, each creating more of the other. In Haiti, for example, the poor have deforested the land in order to produce charcoal. Now they are poorer because there are no more trees for charcoal, and the rain has washed away the topsoil, decreasing food production.

Environmental scarcity can be an important factor in migration from one country to another or from the countryside to overstretched cities. Both Pope Francis and Pope Benedict express concern for these environmental refugees.[190] Migrants and refugees often generate social tension and/or ethnic conflict, which can spark violence. Migration can also become a downward spiral, creating more environmental scarcity. The rate and scope of environmental scarcity as a source of conflict is likely to increase.[191]

Resources can also fuel conflict. In Sierra Leone, for example, diamonds not only triggered a brutal civil war but produced the wealth necessary to purchase the armaments to continue it. Diamonds were also a factor in the protracted civil war in Angola, and they have contributed to violence in Zimbabwe. Minerals are key to the conflict in the Democratic Republic of Congo. Precious stones and timber fueled fighting in Cambodia; oil profits paid for the civil wars in Sudan and Colombia; and opium funded the civil war in Afghanistan.[192]

One result of the growing awareness that environmental scarcity and social and economic deprivations are sources of conflict has been a *"greening of U.S. diplomacy."*[193] In trying to anticipate the global crises of tomorrow, American intelligence agencies are paying much closer attention to phenomena such as the water hyacinths choking Lake Victoria, droughts in Somalia or Senegal, overcrowding in Chinese cities, and the AIDS epidemic in East Africa.

War and the preparation for war destroy the environment and deplete natural resources. The cost of war diverts finances from sustainable development, in effect harming both the poor and future generations. Resource wars illustrate the complex relationship among competition for vital resources, environmental scarcity, and violent conflict. The demand for vital nonrenewable resources, such as oil, may well contribute to interstate warfare. The scarcity of renewable resources, such as land, forests, and water, exacerbates social, economic, political, and cultural tensions and contributes to intrastate conflict and violence. There are, then, important links between war and the environment and between peacemaking and protecting creation.

The principles of Catholic social teaching connect justice, peace, and environmental responsibility. Pope Benedict is correct when he says, if you want to cultivate peace, protect creation. He could also say if you want to protect creation, cultivate peace.

STUDY QUESTIONS

1. Do you think that earth has moved from the climatic sweet spot of the Holocene epoch into a new geologic epoch where humanity is dominating nature, the "Anthropocene"? Why or why not? If yes, what are the implications of this evolution?

2. Do you think that the growth of the human population is approaching the carrying capacity of the earth? What proposals would you suggest for responding to population growth?

3. Pope Francis calls Christians to work for justice for the poor and to protect creation. Is sustainable development an oxymoron or a realistic possibility?

4. Is it possible for humanity to emulate nature and eliminate waste? How do you implement the slogan "reduce, reuse, and recycle"?

5. Name some places where you think resource competition and environmental issues have played a part in conflict. How should US foreign policy take "environmental security" into account?

5

HUMAN RIGHTS

So God created humankind in his image, in the image of God he created them; male and female he created them. (Gen 1:27)

Any human society, if it is to be well-ordered and productive, must lay down as a foundation this principle, namely, that every human being is a person; that is, his nature is endowed with intelligence and free will. Indeed, precisely because he is a person he has rights and obligations flowing directly and simultaneously from his nature. And these rights and obligations are universal and inviolable, so they cannot in any way be surrendered.
Pope John XXIII, Pacem in Terris (1963), #9

Throughout history, humans have oppressed one another. On the basis of some accident, such as race, color, ethnicity, birth, nationality, gender, sexual orientation, age, class, caste, or religion, people's humanity has been violated. Oppression and discrimination can take many forms—slavery, imprisonment, torture, violence, impoverishment, exclusion, humiliation—but at its heart is dehumanization. The full humanity of the victim is denied, and, paradoxically, the oppressor becomes less human through the denial. Too often, citizens have been persecuted by the state with the blessings of religion. Prejudice and discrimination are not new, but in the last sixty years the human community has begun to name this oppression as a violation of human rights and, at least in theory, to condemn these practices. Unfortunately, violations of human rights continue to plague our world; but there has been some progress, and there is the necessity of more.

Tyranny tolerates little dissent. During the Cold War, dissidents in Communist countries feared the midnight knock on the door by the secret police that would result in imprisonment in a work camp or "psychiatric hospital." China, North Korea, and Cuba continue to imprison people critical of Communist rule. Dictators everywhere arrest, torture, and often execute those who protest their oppression. In El Salvador during the late 1970s and 1980s paramilitary death squads would snatch those who took the side of the poor, torture and kill them. When Archbishop Óscar Romero began to advocate for the poor and to criticize the military in El Salvador, he was assassinated while saying Mass on March 24, 1980. Later that year four American churchwomen and, in 1989, six Jesuit priests and two laywomen added their blood to the tens of thousands of Salvadoran peasants slaughtered there. Similar events took place in other countries in Latin America, such as Argentina, Chile, and Guatemala, and elsewhere. In Sierra Leone, one of the "failed states" in West Africa, sadistic rebels terrorized the population by randomly cutting off both hands of their victims or by burning people alive.[1] Before Abu Ghraib in Iraq became known for American torture, it was the torture chamber used by Saddam Hussein.

Not all violations of human rights involve death squads, torture, maiming, or imprisonment. Some involve "routine" discrimination: being denied an education or job because of one's race or gender, or being refused housing because of one's sexual orientation. In addition, poverty is an immense obstacle to the flourishing of the human spirit. The United States, with its tradition of racism, its record of support for military dictatorships, and as one of the few Western nations that

The Nobel Peace Prize has been awarded to several individuals who have been activists and advocates for human rights, including Martin Luther King Jr., the American civil rights leader (1964); Mairead Corrigan and Betty Williams, two women from Belfast, Northern Ireland, who sought a dialogue between Protestants and Catholics (1976); Mother Teresa of Calcutta, for her work among the poor (1979); Adolfo Perez Esquivel, for resisting the repression of Argentina's military dictatorship (1980); Lech Walesa, the leader of the Polish trade union Solidarity (1983); Bishop Desmond Tutu, the South African anti-apartheid leader (1984); Holocaust survivor and witness Elie Wiesel (1986); exiled Tibetan leader His Holiness the Dalai Lama (1989); Nelson Mandela and F. W. de Klerk, for their leadership in ending apartheid in South Africa (1993); Shirin Ebadi, the founder of the Defenders of Human Rights Center in Iran (2003); Liu Xiaobo, professor of literature and political prisoner in China (2010); Tawakkol Karman (along with two other women), a Yemeni journalist, politician, and human rights activist (2011); Kailash Satyarthi, an Indian critic of child labor and advocate of children's rights, along with Malala Yousafzai, a Pakistani proponent of female education (2014); and Dr. Denis Mukwege and Nadia Murad, for their efforts to end the use of sexual violence as a weapon of war (2018).

It would be interesting to choose one of these Nobel laureates and research his or her life.

practices capital punishment, is hardly immune to the charge of human rights violations. In some places the repression has stopped or lessened, but in others it continues. This chapter will explore the struggle for human rights in all its complexity.

HISTORY AND CONTEXT

Before World War II, human rights were viewed as a local and national matter and not a topic for international relations. The horror of the Holocaust and the attempt at the Nuremberg trials to hold German army officers accountable gave international validity to human rights concerns.

The United Nations has played an important role in setting the standards for human rights. On December 10, 1948, the newly formed United Nations issued its Universal Declaration of Human Rights. No country voted against the declaration, although some abstained—the USSR and its allies because there was not enough emphasis on social and economic rights, South Africa because of race, and Saudi Arabia because of religious and gender issues.[2] Because the declaration did not have the binding force of a treaty, the United Nations developed the International Covenant on Economic, Social, and Cultural Rights and the International Covenant on Civil and Political Rights.[3] Together these three documents are often referred to as the International Bill of Human Rights. They summarize the minimum social and political guarantees internationally recognized as necessary for a life of dignity in the contemporary world. Table 5.1 lists the human rights that have been recognized by the community of nations.[4]

The United Nations has also released several other conventions on particular aspects of human rights: on the Elimination of All Forms of Racial Discrimination (1965); on the Suppression and Punishment of the Crime of Apartheid (1973); on the Elimination of Discrimination against Women (1979); against Torture and Other Cruel, Inhuman, or Degrading Treatment or Punishment (1984); and on the Rights of the Child (1989). Although none of these conventions has enjoyed universal ratification, they have an average 88 percent ratification rate, and together they have established clear norms regarding human rights.[5] The United Nations has also issued a (nonbinding) Declaration on the Right to Development (1986).

The doctrine of national sovereignty has made the United Nations less effective in redressing violations of human rights. States reserve the right to interpret and implement international human rights norms.[6] The UN Human Rights Council replaced the Commission on Human Rights in 2006, and it is the world's most prominent forum for protesting infractions of human rights by states. Although the council is constrained by being composed of states elected by the UN General Assembly without regard for their human rights

Table 5.1
INTERNATIONALLY RECOGNIZED HUMAN RIGHTS
The International Bill of Human Rights recognizes the rights to:

Equality of rights without discrimination (D1, D2, E2, E3, C2, C3; P30, 44, 48, 65, 86, 89)
Life (D3, C6; P11)
Liberty and security of person (D3, C9; P11)
Protection against slavery (D4, C8)
Protection against torture and cruel and inhuman punishment (D5, C7)
Recognition as a person before the law (D6, C16; P27; "juridical protection of [human] rights")
Equal protection of the law (D7, C14, C26; P69)
Access to legal remedies for rights violations (D8, C2)
Protection against arbitrary arrest or detention (D9, C9)
Hearing before an independent and impartial judiciary (D10, C14)
Presumption of innocence (D11, C14)
Protection against ex post facto laws (D11, C15)
Protection of privacy, family, and home (D12, C17)
Freedom of movement and residence (D13, C12; P25)
Seek asylum from persecution (D14; P103–8)
Nationality (D15)
Marry and found a family (D16, E10, C23; P15)
Own property (D17; P21)
Freedom of thought, conscience, and religion (D18, C18; P12, 14)
Freedom of opinion, expression, and the press (D19, C19; P12)
Freedom of assembly and association (D20, C21, C22; P23)
Political participation (D21, C25; P26, 73, 146)
Social security (D22, E9; P11, 63–64)
Work, under favorable conditions (D23, E6, E7; P18, 19)
Free trade unions (D23, E8, C22)
Rest and leisure (D24, E7)
Food, clothing, and housing (D25, E11; P11)
Health care and social services (D25, E12; P11)
Special protections for children (D25, E10, C24)
Education (D26, E13, E14; P13)
Participation in cultural life (D27, E15; P12, 13, 64)
A social and international order needed to realize rights (D28; P60–63, 75–77, 139, 141)
Self-determination (E1, C1; P42, 43, 94)
Humane treatment when detained or imprisoned (C10)
Protection against debtor's prison (C11)
Protection against arbitrary expulsion of aliens (C13; P103–8)
Protection of minority culture (C27; P56, 94–97)
[Assistance in development (P121–25)]

Note: This list includes all rights that are enumerated in two of the three documents of the International Bill of Human Rights or have a full article in one document. The source of each right is indicated in parentheses, by document and article number. D = Universal Declaration of Human Rights; E = International Covenant on Economic, Social, and Cultural Rights; C = International Covenant on Civil and Political Rights.

Source: Jack Donnelly, *International Human Rights* 4th ed. (Boulder, CO: Westview Press, 2013), 7. The author has cross-referenced Donnelly's list with Pope John XXIII's *Pacem in Terris* (Peace on Earth, abbreviated P in the list) in David J. O'Brien and Thomas A. Shannon, eds., *Catholic Social Thought: The Documentary Heritage* (Maryknoll, NY: Orbis Books, 1992, 2010). Numbers refer to paragraphs in the document.

record, it regularly does work of real value. It is a largely impartial forum for the consensual development of new international human rights norms, and it engages in limited monitoring of the human rights records of states. Since it has no enforcement authority, the council operates on an information-advocacy model of human rights implementation. The UN Office of the High Commissioner for Human rights (OHCHR) personifies this approach. Three women who have served as high commissioners have turned the office into a major force for human rights: Mary Robinson of Ireland (1997–2002), Louise Arbour of Canada (2004–2008), and Navanethem (Navi) Pillay (2008–2014) of South Africa. Many of the conventions regarding aspects of human rights or separate multilateral human rights treaties also have implementation or monitoring committees, but they all depend on the cooperation of states. While these monitoring and implementation mechanisms are admittedly weak, the awareness and behavior of some governments have been changed, and victims have been aided.[7]

The creation of the International Criminal Court (ICC) on July 1, 2002, was a new attempt to put more bite into the protection of human rights. The ICC will bring criminal cases against individuals accused of genocide, crimes against humanity, and war crimes. It is housed at The Hague in the Netherlands, where the International Court of Justice, which rules on civil disputes between nations, already resides. The impetus for the ICC was the atrocities committed in the Bosnian War (1992–1995) and the genocide in Rwanda in 1994. The first day of the court's existence coincided with the renewal of the UN peacekeeping mandate in Bosnia. The United States threatened to withdraw its troops from that peacekeeping mission unless given blanket immunity by the court. Although President Clinton signed the treaty establishing the ICC, Congress refused to ratify it, and the Bush administration was strongly opposed to the new court, fearing that US troops could be vulnerable to politically motivated prosecutions. Neither Russia nor China has joined the ICC, but European nations have adamantly advocated for it and were vociferously critical of Washington's actions, which seemed to jeopardize UN peacekeeping operations all over the world.[8] Although the Obama administration worked with the ICC on matters it deemed in the nation's interest, it made no effort to formally join the court, nor has the Trump administration.

The Cold War twisted the principled concern for human rights into a weapon in the ideological battle between the East (the Soviet Union and the Warsaw Pact nations) and the West (the United States and NATO). The West focused its rhetoric on civil and political rights, such as freedom of the press and the right to peacefully assemble and protest, decrying the failure of Communist countries to honor these rights. The East emphasized social and economic rights, such as employment, housing, and health care, disparaging the condition of the underclass in the United States. Peoples in the Two-Thirds World, meanwhile, were struggling toward self-determination in a global context that forced them to choose sides.

The Cold War period (1945–1989) was an era when violations of human rights were routine and ubiquitous, and, paradoxically, it was the time when the concept of human rights became established and accepted, and even extensively monitored.[9] The United Nations, as we have seen, was largely responsible for establishing human rights as an international norm. Nongovernmental organizations (NGOs), such as Amnesty International and Human Rights Watch, built sterling reputations for impartially investigating human rights transgressions and accurately reporting their findings.

There was plenty of work for these NGOs to do. Communist countries were totalitarian societies. Two-thirds of the world was desperately poor, and those countries, with few exceptions, were ruled by brutal dictators or repressive militaries. Many of those countries were in a state of civil war characterized by guerrilla insurgencies and military counterinsurgencies. Innocent civilians were often caught in the middle, violated by both sides. While the world was coming to conceptual clarity that it is wrong to violate a person's human rights, such abuse was pervasive.

Happily, since about 1986, there has been some progress regarding civil and political rights. In Asia, the "People Power" revolution deposed the conjugal dictatorship of Ferdinand and Imelda Marcos in the Philippines, while South Korea and then Taiwan moved toward representative government. Pakistan and Bangladesh held free elections with peaceful transfers of power, although both countries continue to struggle with honoring civil and political rights. Except for Cuba, elected governments hold office in every country in the Western Hemisphere, although the democratic credentials of some, such as Venezuela, remain suspect. The political imprisonment, torture, and disappearances that were commonplace in Latin America in the 1980s have abated.[10] Africa too has been touched by this wave of liberalization, although much more lightly. The enfranchisement of the black majority in South Africa is the most startling story of partial success, but other countries, such as Benin, Ghana, Namibia, and Botswana, have become electoral democracies. "In a number of countries where we take democracy for granted, such as South Africa, we should not. In fact, there is not a single country on the African continent where democracy is firmly consolidated and secure—the way it is, for example, in such third-wave democracies as South Korea, Poland, and Chile."[11] Thus, Africa and the Middle East (except for Israel) remain human rights backwaters, as do such Asian countries as China, North Korea, Vietnam, and Myanmar (Burma).

The "Velvet Revolution" (1989–1991) converted Eastern Europe and the former Soviet Empire from police states into fledgling democracies, many of which, notably Russia, have fallen flat. In the former Czechoslovakia, for example, a commission charged with investigating over 150,000 informants of the old secret police paid scant attention to due process. Merely turning the tables does not represent genuine progress toward respect for human rights. Indeed, *the treatment of the guilty and the despised is the litmus test of human rights in a society.*[12] The 1994 division of Czechoslovakia into the Czech Republic and Slovakia was due, in part, to concerns about the fair treatment of minorities. The transition toward human rights has been neither smooth nor successful in many of these formerly Communist countries. Old habits and ingrained prejudices are difficult to change.

THE UNITED STATES

The Cold War Period

While there is no comparison between the human rights records of the United States and the former Soviet Union, Washington's actions during the Cold War were problematic regarding human rights. US foreign policy during this period submerged human rights concerns in order to combat the threat of communism. Thus, the United States showered oppressive and corrupt anti-Communist dictators with economic assistance and military aid throughout the Cold War. The United States supported, for example, the Shah in Iran, Marcos in the Philippines, Somoza in Nicaragua, Duvalier in Haiti, Stroessner in Paraguay, and Mobutu in Zaire (now the Democratic Republic of the Congo). None of these men shied away from imprisoning opponents, torture, or murder. There are even disturbing examples of US efforts to overthrow freely elected governments: in Guatemala in 1954, Chile in 1973, and Nicaragua after 1984, for example. The Soviet record was equally appalling, backing, for example, the Mengistu regime in Ethiopia, among the most barbaric on record.[13] The difference is that the United States is supposed to be committed to the principles of freedom and justice.

There were nuances of difference among the American administrations during the Cold War, but anticommunism was the cornerstone of US foreign policy. President Jimmy Carter (1976–1980) did give human rights an important role, but global realities often compromised his administration's practice of this principle. Ronald Reagan (1980–1988) campaigned against the Carter human rights policy and on behalf of a single-minded focus on overcoming communism, and once elected he acted on these values. Congress, however, gradually reasserted human rights as a foreign policy consideration during the 1980s.

The end of the Cold War could mean a more prominent place for human rights as an international interest, and, as we have seen, there has been some decrease in global political repression. There is a tension, however, between the doctrine of national sovereignty and the principle of human rights. The economic benefits of trade also impinge on legitimate concerns about violations of human rights. China's repression of political protestors in Tiananmen Square in 1989 stands as a symbol of human rights abuse in the post–Cold War world, yet no American administration has given more than lip service in protest against China's ongoing human rights violations. Ideology no longer justifies allowing repression, but sovereignty and economics continue to be obstacles to substantive international action on behalf of human rights.

The Soviet Union's criticisms of the US *domestic* record on social and economic rights during the Cold War were generally dismissed, but they contained more than a grain of truth. In the late 1980s, for example, the case could be made that Cuba's health care system was better than America's in meeting the basic needs of their *entire* population. Homelessness in one of the richest nations on earth is a moral outrage. The United States seems to be afflicted with a certain blindness, perhaps born of self-righteousness, to its domestic failures in the area of human rights: "The United States, however, is said to suffer from, for example, police brutality, civil rights problems, or a health care crisis, which are spoken of as if they are qualitatively different from torture, racial discrimination, or denial of the right to health care."[14] The history of slavery and segregation and the near genocide of the indigenous peoples should certainly caution Americans about feelings of self-satisfaction regarding human rights, and urge on us a genuine watchfulness and the reality of the need for reform.

Torture and the "War on Terror"

In response to the "war on terror" declared by President George W. Bush (2001–2009) after the 9/11 attacks, the United States wrongfully and illegally violated human rights by engaging in torture and reneging on civil rights such as the protection against arbitrary arrest and detention, access to a fair trial, and the right to privacy.

On December 9, 2014, Senator Dianne Feinstein (D-CA) released the 524-page executive summary of the Senate Intelligence Committee's investigation of the Central Intelligence Agency's (CIA) interrogation program in the years after 9/11. The report confirmed what was already known—the US government illegally detained and cruelly tortured prisoners and lied about it to Congress and the world.[15] The CIA torture program included sites for secret detention and extraordinary renditions all over the world.[16] According to the torture report, at least 26 of the 119 known CIA prisoners were wrongfully detained. The Senate report sheds new light on the brutality of the techniques used on prisoners, including "rectal feeding" and waterboarding. It also discusses in detail twenty case studies rebutting CIA claims that its "enhanced interrogation techniques" ever provided useful information. *Torture is ineffective, immoral, and illegal.* Why, then, did the United States engage in torture?

The short answer is, of course, fear. The shocking attacks on the World Trade Center and the Pentagon that claimed three thousand innocent victims on September 11, 2001, effectively terrorized the United States. For many Americans these events seemed to justify whatever means necessary to prevent another attack. A moral and rational response to terrorism, however, recognizes that it is wrong to ensure our safety by compromising our foundational values and principles, by losing our soul. We ought not combat terrorism by becoming terrorists. The practice of torture is a form of terrorism.[17]

The *immorality* of torture may seem intuitively obvious, yet the ethics of torture is complex and controversial. Catholic theologian John Perry insightfully begins his ethical analysis of torture with "moral phenomenology," that is, descriptive accounts of torture.[18] Waterboarding, for example, was one of the "enhanced interrogation techniques" used by the CIA on high-value terror suspects. The victim is gagged and strapped to an inclined board with his feet higher than his head. The person's head is covered with a cloth, and water is repeatedly poured over it, stimulating the gag reflex and giving the experience of drowning. Khalid Shaikh Mohammed, the 9/11 mastermind, was subjected to waterboarding 183 times. This is certainly torture, and it is appalling.

Torture is wrong, first, because it violates the intrinsic dignity of the human person who is created in the image of God.[19] Torture is intentional brutality aimed at destroying the identity and sense of meaning and purpose of the victim. Torture often results in chronic injury and pain, but even when it doesn't, it leaves irreparable psychological damage by undermining the mutual trust essential for communal life.[20]

Second, torture diminishes the character of any nation that employs it.[21] The Bush administration's practice of torture has stained the reputation of the United States and facilitated the recruitment process of Muslim extremist groups. American torture endangers US prisoners of war or detainees.

Third, torture violates the vulnerable and defenseless; it is an abuse of power, aimed at inducing fear through domination.[22]

Fourth, torture degrades and dehumanizes the torturer.[23] There is no honor in torturing another human being, no courage required. Torture is hands-on; it is interpersonal. Whether or not the torturer experiences guilt for his or her actions,[24] this sort of power and domination debases the human spirit and destroys human community.

Finally, Christians should be especially sensitive to the evil of torture in that Jesus was tortured to death by being humiliated, scourged, and crucified.[25] "The pictures of Abu Ghraib should remind us that whatever we do to the least of these detainees, we do to Christ."[26]

"In the post–World War II period, torture has been declared universally and unconditionally *illegal* in international law through the Geneva Conventions (1949), the UN Universal Declaration on Human Rights (1948), and the UN

Convention against Torture and Other Cruel, Inhumane or Degrading Treatment or Punishment (1984, ratified by the United States in 1994).[27] The Eighth Amendment of the US Constitution prohibits cruel and unusual punishment, and the US Torture Statute (1994) codifies the Convention against Torture and establishes torture as a federal crime. Thus, torture is clearly prohibited in the United States."[28] Andrew McCarthy, a commentator who wants to search for loopholes in the murky language of international treaties and ultimately to justify torture in extreme circumstances, concludes, "Let me spell it out. It is illegal in the United States, under any circumstances, to torture anyone— even unlawful combatant terrorists who may have information about ongoing plots that, if revealed, could save thousands of lives. Period."[29] Torture is a crime without a defense.[30] Again it needs to be said that it is the treatment of the guilty and despised that is the litmus test of human rights in a society. In the aftermath of September 11, the United States failed that test.

Since torture is ineffective, immoral, and illegal, and since the Senate torture report documents the policy and practice of torture during the Bush administration (2001–2009), why haven't those who authorized it and those who did it been prosecuted? Holding those responsible for this official government program would help ensure that this never happens again, and it would aid in regaining America's moral credibility.[31]

International law, Christian ethics, and Catholic social teaching[32] now prohibit torture universally, unconditionally, and absolutely. During this period, the theological community decried US participation in torture in both religious periodicals and academic journals.[33] Church leaders, however, were rather quiet. The only direct statement by a church body (that I am aware of) is the *Resolution on Human Rights in a Time of Terrorism and Torture* approved by the 217th General Assembly of the Presbyterian Church USA in 2006. This statement is a model of the sort of teaching that Christians should expect from church leaders. Officially, the Catholic Church and the churches in general were not much of a counterweight to the Bush administration's torture policy. Clear and frequent statements of the church's opposition to torture and its rationale could have influenced public opinion and public policy.[34]

The National Religious Campaign Against Torture (NRCAT, nrcat.org) was launched in early 2006 to stand against torture, abuse of detainees, and the erosion of due process of law in the United States. NRCAT released a statement signed by American religious leaders, including Bishop William Skylstad, president of the US Conference of Catholic Bishops, on November 2, 2006. The statement reads:

> Torture violates the basic dignity of the human person that all religions hold dear. It degrades everyone involved—policymakers, perpetrators, and victims. It contradicts our nation's most cherished values. Any policies that permit torture and inhumane treatment are shocking and

morally intolerable. Nothing less is at stake than the soul of our nation. What does it signify if torture is condemned in word but allowed in deed? Let America abolish torture now—without exception.

All people and organizations are invited to sign the statement. NRCAT offers everyone in the body of Christ a way to stand for human dignity and community, and to oppose torture and abuse.

Torture is morally outrageous. Silence and complicity are not the right responses. Where were the protests and the prophetic denunciations? The people of God, leaders and laity, should speak out to stop the repugnant practice of torture and abuse.

Under the aegis of preventing terrorism, the United States also suspended some civil liberties, especially the right to privacy. The Patriot Act in October 2001 lifted some restrictions on the snooping powers of US intelligence agencies. We now know that the result has been the de facto cancellation of the right to privacy in the United States. Documents leaked in June 2013 by Edward Snowden, a former National Security Agency (NSA) subcontractor, revealed the truly Orwellian practices of the NSA in spying on the daily lives of Americans and beyond. Those documents disclose that the NSA can collect information from hundreds of millions of people around the globe, that it has circumvented or cracked much of the encryption that protects sensitive data on the internet, that it has broken into the communications links of major data centers across the globe, and that, according to its own records, it has broken privacy laws or exceeded its authority thousands of times a year.[35] Congress has done nothing to rein in the NSA or other intelligence gathering agencies or to protect the privacy of American citizens in response to these revelations.

THE MEANING OF HUMAN RIGHTS

Human rights make strong claims. "Right" is not a word to be thrown around loosely. If a person has a right, then the community and other persons have a duty to respect and fulfill that right. Because a right confers an obligation on the community, it is not surprising that various societies have contested the foundation, meaning, and scope of human rights.

During the Cold War, each of the three "worlds" was said to emphasize a different aspect of human rights. The First World stressed civil and political rights and the right to private property. The Second World gave priority to social, economic, and cultural rights as prerequisites to civil and political rights. The Third World also emphasized social, economic, and cultural rights, as well as the right to self-determination and the right to development.[36] These, however, are self-serving, ideological distinctions that have little basis in any sound theory of rights. *All* of these rights are affirmed in the International Bill of Human Rights (Table 5.1) based on UN documents, and all of them require respect and satisfaction if human beings are to flourish.

There is a remarkable parallel between the formulation of human rights by the United Nations and that found in contemporary Catholic social teaching. The clearest expression of the meaning and scope of human rights in Catholic thought is in the encyclical of Pope John XXIII titled *Peace on Earth*. It was written in 1963 while the Second Vatican Council was underway. Pope John's list of human rights closely parallels that of the UN Universal Declaration of Human Rights (see Table 5.1). The convening of the United Nations (1948) and of the Second Vatican Council (1962–1965) both produced transnational bodies with a focus on issues of justice and peace in a pluralistic world: "The need to find consensus on a normative basis for international justice and peace without suppressing the legitimate differences within regions and social systems led both bodies to a human rights focus."[37] Human rights have become the moral framework within which a society should be ordered. There can be many legitimate ways of organizing a government and a society, but all of them should recognize and respect human rights.[38]

Human rights are entitlements or claims that a person has simply because one is human. Such rights are held equally by all human beings, and they are inalienable. Human rights are rooted, then, in a theory of human nature. Various philosophical systems provide stronger or weaker foundations for a concept of human rights.[39] The dignity of the human person, realized in community, is the foundation of Catholic social thought and its theory of human rights.[40] Thus, the Catholic conception of human rights is personalistic *and* communitarian, not individualistic, as some Enlightenment philosophers would have it.[41] The theological foundations of human dignity and human rights are based on the creation of all people in the image of God, the trinitarian concept of God,[42] redemption by Jesus Christ, and the call to a transcendent destiny. The Christian tradition provides a solid foundation for a theory of human rights. The concept of human rights, however, finds healthy roots in all of the major religious traditions.[43]

Constructive human rights *policies* should focus on establishing a full set of social rights for the protection of human dignity. The full set of social rights would include the following: the rights to food, clothing, shelter, health care, and rest; the right to political participation; the rights to nationality and to migrate; the rights of assembly and association; the rights to work, to adequate working conditions, and to a just wage; the right to found a family or live singly; the rights to freedom of expression, to education, and to religious expression.[44]

Theologian David Hollenbach proposes three principles to guide the development of human rights policies designed to overcome the marginalization of the poor, minorities, and the oppressed:

1. The needs of the poor take priority over the wants of the rich.
2. The freedom of the dominated takes priority over the liberty of the power-ful.
3. The participation of marginalized groups takes priority over the preserva-tion of an order which excludes them.[45]

These principles are helpful yardsticks for measuring the impact of legislative or policy proposals on human rights and for assessing foreign policy. They also highlight the value of human rights as moral norms in a pluralistic world, and they expose the fundamental questions that human rights standards can raise in every sort of political and economic system.

CULTURAL RELATIVISM

The United Nations called its Declaration of Human Rights "Universal," that is, applicable to and binding on all nations and people. The claim of universal human rights, however, is controversial in a pluralistic world. Some nations have claimed that the International Bill of Human Rights, with its affirmation of equal rights for women, for example, is too Western in its conception and articulation. On the other hand, American conservatives have been reluctant to affirm some of the social, economic, and cultural rights, such as the right to work or the right to health care. Thoroughgoing relativists would deny the theoretical possibility of universal norms, noting the sometimes radical differ-ences among cultures.

In arguing in favor of universal norms regarding human rights, it is not nec-essary to take an extreme or absolutist position. Not every value is absolute; indeed, there may be conflicts among and exceptions to universal norms. The fact of cultural relativism, however, does not mean that whatever a particular culture sanctions is right. There may well be universal norms that adhere to human beings as human and that transcend and critique culture.

In sorting out the tension between universal standards and the different practices of various cultures, it can be helpful to distinguish three levels of spec-ification regarding human rights.[46] The first level is the *concept* of a human right, such as the right to work. This general statement of principle admits to little cultural variability. Second, there is the *interpretation* of the principle. A guar-anteed job or unemployment insurance might be two legitimate interpretations of the right to work. Finally, there may be many different ways to *implement* an interpretation of a right. A government might employ a large percentage of the population in a wide network of civil service jobs, or it might stimulate the economy to provide ample employment opportunities for its people.

The right to political participation might be interpreted as the right to vote; voting itself can take place in a two-party system or a multiparty system, for individual candidates or for slates of candidates, or through direct referenda.

But a one-party system that really admits of no choice may violate the right to political participation.

While standards of modesty for women and men may legitimately vary according to culture and context, it would seem, however, that the rights to equality of treatment without discrimination and to education would require every society to offer equal opportunities for education to women and men.

If the norms regarding human rights are not universal, then they offer little moral guidance for a pluralistic world.[47] While sensitivity is certainly called for in addressing clashes between cultural values, caution should not be equated with indifference or inaction. Even if we are not entitled to impose our values on others, we are responsible for owning our values, witnessing to them, and acting on them. Practices such as female infanticide, apartheid, anti-Semitism, slavery, human trafficking, sexual exploitation of children, female genital mutilation, and torture deserve neither respect nor tolerance.[48]

DISCRIMINATION AGAINST WOMEN

Women are oppressed and subjugated everywhere in the world. Patriarchy and sexism are characteristic of every society and culture on earth. Indeed, only recently has feminism (a belief in the equality of the sexes) meaningfully challenged patriarchy (the institutionalized belief that men are superior to women and should control and dominate them). Although some nations have made significant progress toward the goal of gender equality, no society has reached that goal. Indeed, Pulitzer Prize–winning journalists Nicholas Kristof and Sheryl WuDunn "believe that in this century the paramount moral challenge will be the struggle for gender equality around the world."[49]

Throughout the world, equal rights for women are denied in nearly every aspect of life. Wherever people are oppressed, women suffer more, first as members of the oppressed group and then as women. This section will examine discrimination against women and its effects with regard to economic structures, political participation, health, violence against women, education, and progress toward honoring the rights of women.

Economic Exploitation and Wage Discrimination

Women are paid less for comparable work and are discriminated against in opportunities for employment and promotion. In the thirty-four countries in the Organization for Economic Cooperation and Development (OECD), girls are doing as well as or better than boys in education, but women still earned 14 percent less on average than men in 2017, down from 20 percent in 2000. Although the gender wage gap exists in all countries, it varies considerably, from 1.8 percent in Costa Rica to 9.4 percent in Hungary and Poland, to 18.2 percent in the United States, 24.5 percent in Japan, and 34.6 percent in South

Korea. Earnings tend to rise in line with people's level of education, but across all countries and all levels of education, women earn less than men, and that gap actually increases with more education. On average about 18 percent of workers in OECD countries are low paid, but the rate for women is 25 percent, while that for men is 14 percent. Men even make more than women in traditionally female occupations, such as nursing and education.[50]

The *Global Gender Gap Report 2016*, published by the World Economic Forum, measures the relative gaps between women and men in education, health, economic opportunity, and political power in 144 of the world's countries. In 2016 the gender gap regarding economic opportunity slipped to 59 percent, the lowest score since 2008. The World Economic Forum calculates that it will take 171 years (i.e., in 2186) before women earn as much as men.

It is no accident that sweatshops in Latin America and Asia employ mostly women: they can be paid less and are more vulnerable to exploitation. When people are hungry, it is often the custom for the men and boys to eat first, and for the girls and women to eat what is left over. The "feminization of poverty," that is, the higher incidence of poverty among women and among households headed by women, is a reality in both developed and developing countries.[51] Thus, educating and empowering women are keys to overcoming poverty.

In less developed countries, the life of a poor peasant woman is one of unending menial labor: gathering wood for cooking, hauling water, washing clothes by hand, preparing food from scratch, and working the fields, while caring for perhaps a half-dozen children.[52] In industrial countries, some of the drudgery has been eliminated from household duties by appliances such as washing machines and vacuum cleaners, but many women have jobs and then go home to their "second shift" of cooking, cleaning, and child care.

Political Participation

It was only in 1920 that women in the United States received the right to vote. Political participation is still restricted for women, either through law or common practice, in many countries. In 2016 the gender gap in political power between men and women was 23 percent and slowly but steadily rising.[53] The global average for female parliamentary representation in 2016 was 22.8 percent. Women have attained the top leadership post in more than seventy countries, including Israel, the Philippines, Pakistan, Norway, Bangladesh, Argentina, Sri Lanka, New Zealand, Liberia, Ukraine, Denmark, Jamaica, Iceland, Chile, Malawi, South Korea, Brazil, Germany, Australia, and Great Britain, so that a female head of government is now less rare.[54] In most countries women do not enjoy the full protection of the law. "More than 170 countries—about 90 percent—still have laws that end up denying women and girls the same rights and protections enjoyed by their male counterparts."[55]

Domestic Life

In many countries of the world, women do not fare any better at home than in public life. In many cultures, women remain subject to the rule of their father or husband and can be forced to marry the man chosen by their father. Throughout much of the world, the dependency of women on men and the inferiority of women to men is socially constructed and institutionalized, so much so that it seems natural to women and men. Indeed, women are often complicit in the oppression of women: women routinely manage brothels in poor countries, ensure that their daughter's genitals are cut, feed sons before daughters, even beat their daughters-in-law.[56] Such attitudes and practices, deeply embedded in culture, are very difficult to change.

Health Care

Nicholas Kristof, a *New York Times* columnist, related the story of Prudence Lemokouno, a twenty-four-year-old mother of three who went into labor in remote Cameroon, West Africa, to illustrate the woeful lack of health care for women. After three days she was taken by motorcycle to a hospital seventy-five miles away where Kristof encountered her and her desperate husband, Alain Awona. Her undelivered baby was already dead, and Prudence would soon die without an emergency Caesarean section. The hospital at first wanted $100, but the presence of foreign journalists persuaded the lone doctor to take the $20 that the family had. After Kristof and a companion donated blood and chipped in more money, they waited six hours to discover that the doctor had vanished for the night. The next day the doctor did the operation, but by then the infection in Prudence's ruptured uterus was untreatable, and she died horribly three days later. The year was 2006. Prudence died because she was a poor female in a rural area of a developing country—among the most overlooked and disposable people in the world. "In much of the world, the most dangerous thing a woman can do is become pregnant."[57]

According to the World Health Organization, about 830 women die every day from pregnancy or childbirth complications, nearly all of them (99 percent) in developing countries. Young adolescents, whose bodies are not fully mature, face a higher risk of complications. Between 1990 and 2015, the global maternal mortality rate (the number of maternal deaths per 100,000 births) dropped by 44 percent. Nevertheless in 2015, an estimated 303,000 women died during and following childbirth. In the United States maternal death in childbirth is much higher than in other developed countries, about five times higher than in Britain, for example.[58]

Maternal mortality is only the tip of the iceberg in relation to maternal morbidity—the injuries and health problems that result from pregnancy and childbirth. For every woman who dies during childbirth, twenty or thirty others experience lingering problems from the process.[59] Among the most common and worst injuries in the developing world are fistulas and tears caused by unsafe abortions or obstructed birth, such as experienced by Prudence Lemokouno in the case above. Fistulas result in incontinence of bladder and/ or bowels, which results in the social ostracization of the woman because of the stench. Thus, fistulas are a physical, emotional, and social problem for millions of women in poor countries. Before C-sections were developed in Western medicine, fistulas were common everywhere. Most of the time, fistulas can be repaired with surgery. Most poor women, however, do not have access to places such as the Addis Ababa Fistula Hospital in Ethiopia, run by Catherine Hamlin, a transplanted Australian gynecologist. Skilled care before, during, and after childbirth can save the lives and safeguard the well-being of women and their newborn babies. The persistence of maternal mortality and morbidity is due to the marginalization of women in the developing world; women are viewed as expendable commodities.[60]

This is the context for assessing the actions of President Trump and the Republican Congress in cutting off health care for women from organizations that have any connection to abortion. One of Mr. Trump's first actions was to impose the "global gag rule," ending funding to overseas health aid groups with any connection to abortion, including counseling that mentions it as an option. This is expected from Republican administrations, but it results in excruciating suffering and death to impoverished women who rely on such aid programs for health care. Then President Trump cut off all US funding for the United Nations Population Fund (UNFPA) because some Republicans incorrectly think the fund colludes with the Chinese government on forced abortions. In reality, the fund works for women's reproductive health and safe childbirth and has nothing to do with abortions. Moreover, in 1992 the fund persuaded China to switch to a more effective IUD, thus averting a half-million abortions a year, and over the years preventing twelve million abortions in China. The birth control provided by the UNFPA averted more than 3.7 million abortions in 2016. Is the Trump/Republican policy truly pro-life?[61]

Violence

Perhaps the most shocking problem faced by women is their everyday experience of violence and the threat of violence. In every country, across all classes, women are beaten by their husbands and fathers; assaulted and raped by relatives, acquaintances, and strangers; and harassed and intimidated on the street, in school, at work, and at leisure.

Millions of girls and women are trafficked into sexual slavery or forced labor every year.[62] Thousands of others are victims of honor killings.[63] *Rape* is ubiquitous as a tool to control women. In countries such as Ethiopia, girls are kidnapped and raped so that they will marry the one who kidnapped her in order to save her family from public shame.[64]

Mukhtar Mai grew up in a peasant family in rural Pakistan. In July 2002, her thirteen-year-old younger brother, Shakur, was kidnapped and gang-raped by boys from a higher-status clan, the Mastoi. After doing this, the Mastoi became anxious that they might be punished. So they held on to Shakur and covered up their crime by accusing him of having sex with a Mastoi girl. When the village tribal assembly held a meeting to deal with this accusation of illicit sex, Mukhtar attended on behalf of her family to apologize and try to resolve the conflict. The tribal council decided that an apology would not be enough and sentenced Mukhtar to be gang-raped to punish Shakur and their family. Four men carried out the sentence and sent Mukhtar staggering home half naked before a jeering crowd. Once home Mukhtar prepared to do what any Pakistani peasant woman would do in this situation—kill herself to cleanse herself and her family of the shame. Her parents, however, kept watch over her and prevented her suicide. Then a local Muslim leader heroically spoke out on her behalf at Friday prayers. As Mukhtar reflected on her experience, her attitude morphed from humiliation to rage. She decided to report the rape and demand prosecution. Sur-

> On March 19, 2015, Farkhunda Malikzada, a twenty-seven-year-old Islamic law student, visited a famous religious shrine in Kabul, the capital of Afghanistan, to bring clothing for the needy. She was aghast to see illiterate mullahs selling good-luck charms to visitors, and decided to return the next day to speak out against this superstitious and un-Islamic behavior. She preached for hours in the courtyard and managed to dissuade many people from buying the trinkets. Then one of the shrine attendants, Zain-ul-Din, loudly accused Farkhunda of being an infidel who had burned the Qur'an. A mob of hundreds of men quickly gathered, surrounded Farkhunda, railed against her, savagely beat and kicked her, ran over her with a car, and burned her body. The incident was captured on numerous cell-phone videos, and her accuser and dozens of her assailants were arrested and tried. At first considered a pariah, Farkhunda has now been acclaimed a female religious martyr killed by ignorant and exploitative men.
>
> Joseph Goldstein, "From Pariah to Martyr after Death in Kabul," *New York Times*, March 30, 2015, A6.

prisingly, the police arrested her attackers. When President Perez Musharaf heard about the case, he sent her the equivalent of $8,300 in compensation. Instead of taking the money for herself, Mukhtar decided to invest in what her village needed most—a school. Mukhtar's story has received worldwide attention, and she has become a champion for education and for female victims of violence.[65]

Long-standing laws that allowed rapists to avoid prosecution if they married their victims have been repealed in most countries—in Uruguay in 2006 and France in 1994, for example—but not so much in the Middle East. Such laws were built around patriarchal attitudes that link a family's honor directly to women's chastity. Now women's rights groups are advocating the repeal of marry-your-rapist laws through provocative public awareness campaigns in Middle East counties, such as Lebanon, Jordan, Bahrain, and Morocco.

In many US states, exceptions to the minimum age for marriage allow rapists to marry their teenage victims. Twenty states do not set any minimum statutory age for marriage, which allows child marriage. Changing such laws is a step toward changing such patriarchal beliefs and violent realities and affirming the dignity of women.[66]

Muslim women were systematically raped by Serbian soldiers in Bosnia, as were Tutsi women during the slaughter by the Hutu in Rwanda in the 1990s. In the first decade of the twenty-first century, the epicenter for rape as a weapon of war moved to three African countries: the Democratic Republic of Congo (DRC), Liberia, and the Darfur region of Sudan. In the next decade, rape has been a defining horror of the war in northeastern Nigeria between the Boko Haram terrorist group and Nigerian forces. The United Nations estimates that Boko Haram has violated at least seven thousand women and girls. Then Nigerian security forces continue the sexual exploitation of these victims in refugee camps. Major-General Patrick Cammaert, former commander of UN peacekeeping forces in the eastern Congo, says that groups at war use rape as a weapon because it destroys communities totally. He added, "It has probably become more dangerous to be a woman than a soldier in armed conflict."[67] As a result, the UN Security Council unanimously passed Resolution 1820 in 2008, affirming rape as a weapon of war and a war crime. This has not stopped the so-called Islamic State, or ISIS, from enslaving and systematically raping girls and women of the Yazidi religious minority group in Iraq, a practice they believe is condoned and encouraged by the Qur'an. Nor has it hindered the security forces in Myanmar from systematically raping Rohingya women and girls to facilitate a policy of ethnic cleansing.[68]

The ubiquity of *sexual harassment and sexual assault* in the United States and throughout the world became apparent in October 2017, when the *New York Times* reported that dozens of women, including actress Ashley Judd, had been sexually harassed and assaulted by movie producer Harvey Weinstein.[69] When actress Alyssa Milano tweeted that any woman who had been sexually harassed or sexually assaulted should respond "Me Too," over 66,000 women responded, stimulating a tidal wave of stories, conversations, and accusations. When Milano became aware that Tarana Burke had started a "Me Too" organization in 2006 to give victims of sexual violence, especially the marginalized, a voice and to work to stop it, she gave Burke and the organization credit on national TV. Since then the egregious mistreatment of women (primarily) in every workplace and setting from Hollywood, to restaurants, to the home, to politics, to education has become clear, and women are effectively speaking out and struggling to redress the power imbalance that is the foundation of sexual harassment and sexual assault. Suddenly the rules of the game have changed. This sexual violence is not random; it is aimed at women as women, and meant to frighten and control them. It amounts to "sexual terrorism," a system perpetuated by men for the domination of women. This coercive patriarchy is unfortunately found in the Hebrew Scriptures, in what Scripture scholar Phyllis Trible labels "texts of terror."[70]

One of the most abhorrent customs related to gender violence and men's inordinate desire to control female sexuality is the practice of *female genital cutting* (FGC). Female genital mutilation is practiced by a wide variety of ethnic groups, whether their religion is Christian, Muslim, or Traditional, in a band of thirty countries concentrated in north-central Africa, from Egypt and Somalia to Senegal and the Ivory Coast. It is estimated that 200 million women have undergone this centuries-old practice, and each year about three million more girls endure the procedure. Female genital cutting is declining worldwide but at a pace slower than population growth.[71]

One form of the procedure involves the removal of the clitoris and sometimes some of the labial tissue. In some countries, such as Somalia, Ethiopia, and Sudan, infibulation, a more severe form of genital mutilation, is practiced. The clitoris and all of the woman's external genitalia are removed and the wound is sewn shut until she is married, leaving a small hole for urination and menstruation. In some places genital cutting is done on girls aged four to ten; among other peoples it is a ritual of adolescence. It is done, usually without anesthesia, by local excisors, midwives, barbers, or relatives using a razor blade or crude knife, or sometimes now by medical practitioners. Female genital mutilation diminishes or eliminates a woman's ability to experience sexual pleasure. Besides the physical and psychological trauma of the procedure itself and its primary consequence, the cutting can result in severe bleeding, problems urinating, and even death. Long-term results include cysts, infections, infertility, as well as complications in childbirth and increased risk of newborn deaths. There are no health benefits for girls or women from this procedure. Female genital cutting is mutilation.[72]

The purpose of the cutting, according to a local excisor in the Ivory Coast, is to ensure a woman's fidelity to her husband and her family. A woman's role in life is to care for her children, keep house, and cook. If she has not been cut she might be distracted by her own sexual pleasure.[73] Many people who practice genital cutting believe that a woman will be sexually aggressive, even promiscuous, without the procedure. As an Egyptian farmer explained, "If a woman is more passive it is in her interest, it is in her father's interest and in her husband's interest."[74] Clearly FGC serves the goals of patriarchy. In some cultures female genital cutting is a prerequisite for marriage.

That was the case among the Maasai people in Kenya and Tanzania. Indeed, the ritual of cutting was foundational to how Maasai society was organized and functioned. Then eight-year-old Nice Leng'ete, who had hidden to escape being cut two years in a row, persuaded her grandfather to allow her to decide for herself whether she would be cut. Her grandfather was an elder, and thus could not be overruled, but the community still ostracized her. Because Nice had not been cut, she was not forced into an early marriage, and she became the first girl in her village to go to high school. When some of the other girls admired her uniform, she explained that she had an opportunity to continue her education because she had refused the cut. Soon some of them showed up at her house fleeing the ceremony just as she had. She helped them and had to go into hiding to avoid being beaten by the village's young men. Ms. Leng'ete then decided to try to bargain with the elders as she had bargained with her grandfather. After a painstaking four-year process of slowly educating the young men about HIV, adolescent development, sexuality and health, and finally the consequences of FGC, who then persuaded the elders, and so on, she persuaded the village that everyone would be healthier and wealthier if girls stayed in school, married later, and gave birth without the complications cutting can create. She and the elders created a ceremony that did not involve cutting to mark girls becoming women. Ms. Leng'ete became the first woman to address the council of ruling elders of the Maasai people. In 2014 the ruling elders formally abandoned female genital cutting.[75]

FGC has been illegal in Kenya since 2011. Twenty-four African countries ban FGC, as well as twelve developed countries with migrant populations from countries that practice FGC, including the United States.[76] The campaign against this horrific practice, however, has learned that legal prohibition and Western condemnation do not change centuries-old cultural practices. Effective approaches are similar to what Nice Leng'ete developed among the Maasai. They build an Africa-style consensus, which is rooted in the culture and the particular context, based on respectful, inclusive dialogue and a comprehensive educational program that eventually explores the dangers and drawbacks associated with female genital cutting.[77] This comprehensive, dialogic, prolonged, inclusive, educational approach offers hope not only for eliminating FGC but perhaps for curtailing honor killings and other forms of violence against women.

Education

Throughout the world, women have historically been excluded from educational opportunities, a trend that persists but has improved.[78] Globally, 781 million adults and 126 million youth (aged fifteen to twenty-four) lack basic literacy skills, and more than 60 percent of them are women. In 2012, enrollment in primary education for girls and boys in developing regions reached 90 percent, up from 82 percent in 1999.[79] Girls, however, still lag behind by about 5 percent. Secondary school enrollments have shown improvement, but fewer countries are near gender parity than for primary education. In higher education, global gender disparities now favor women except in sub-Saharan Africa and southern and western Asia.[80]

When women are educated, good things happen for women, families, and society. For example, both women and their babies are less likely to die in childbirth. Women marry later and have fewer children. Educated mothers take better care of their children and are more likely to send them to school. Education can narrow pay gaps between men and women and make it more likely that women are employed. The more education, the better the results. Education is key to empowering women.

Progress

The plight of women remains bleak, but it is in fact improving. The *Human Development Report* (HDR) devised its *gender-related development index* (GDI) in 1995. The GDI adjusted three factors in its human development index (HDI)—life expectancy, educational attainment, and income—for gender inequality. In the HDRs between the years 1995 and 2009, there was a high degree of correlation between a nation's HDI and its GDI, with the top fifteen countries generally the same in both categories. In 2009, when the GDI was temporarily discontinued, the top thirty-one countries had a GDI above .900 (with a score of 1 signifying gender equality).

The *Human Development Report 1996* drew several conclusions from the GDI rankings: (1) no society treats its women as well as its men; (2) the pursuit of gender equality is not necessarily associated with high growth in income, and it can be pursued at all levels of income; and (3) progress in gender equality can be attained by nations characterized by different political ideologies, economic conditions, cultures, and stages of development.[81] The key to progress toward gender equality seems to be the will to succeed, that is, an awareness that sexist discrimination exists, that it is wrong and needs to change, followed by the removal of restrictions on women and targeted social programs on women's behalf.

This point was partially confirmed in 2014, when the gender development index (GDI) was reintroduced. The correlation between a country's HDI and GDI no longer held. The highest score (1.000) was by Slovakia, which ranked 37 in HDI. Venezuela (.999) (HDI 67) and Argentina (1.001) (HDI 49) tied for second in GDI. Hungary (.998) (HDI 43) was fourth; Norway (.997) (HDI 1) was fifth, and the United States (.995) (HDI 5) was seventh. This lack of correlation was not because high HDI countries were performing poorly in gender equality, but because so many countries were doing so much better. The top 110 countries had a GDI score of .900 or better. In thirteen countries the ratio of female to male HDI was greater than 1, that is, women score higher in these development indicators (life expectancy, educational attainment, and income) than men. In part, this is because nearly everywhere in the world women's life expectancy is higher than that of men, but the higher scores indicate that many countries have improved in educating women and paying them more equitably.

Since all the world's major religions developed in patriarchal cultures, sexism is often found in religious texts and fostered by religious practices. In every religious tradition today, however, feminist theologians and scholars argue that patriarchy and sexism are not intrinsic to religious beliefs or tenets.[82] Violence and discrimination against women are among the most pervasive problems facing the global community. Women's rights must be recognized as human rights everywhere in the world.[83] The dignity and equality of women need to be tenaciously promoted through education, public policy, and law.

RACE, CASTE, AND RELIGION

Discrimination can also be based on race, caste, or ethnicity. Ethnic conflict has become such a problem in the post–Cold War world that it will be addressed in the following chapter. This section will focus on the denial of human rights based on race and include attention to caste and religion.

Race and Racism

Race is a social construct. Theologically there is one human family with God as our common creator; we are all brothers and sisters to one another. This theological affirmation of solidarity and community is confirmed by science. Biologically and psychologically the human species is more alike than different, and the differences among individuals of a given race are far greater than the differences among races. There are different blood types, but they are found throughout the human species. Any female human being can theoretically procreate with any other male human being. Tissue type and size, not race, are the obstacles to organ transplantation. Genetically there is only the human race, and all humans trace their origin to Africa.[84] Race is a social fabrication in the service of power that uses physical characteristics, primarily skin color, to distinguish one group of human beings from another. This differentiation that has no scientific or theological basis has led to much conflict, injustice, and suffering.

Racism, therefore, is the problem. Racism consists in a *belief* that one racial group is inherently superior to another racial group. In the twentieth century much attention has been paid to white racism—the attitude of superiority and supremacy of whites toward peoples of color—and justly so, since the European colonizers brought an insufferable belief in their innate superiority to their conquest of the world.[85] Racism is not the sole preserve of whites, but white racism has a particularly sordid modern history.

Indigenous Peoples

The Europeans who settled the United States developed a belief in "manifest destiny"—that they were a people chosen by God to rule this land, which had been given to them by God—to justify taking the land inhabited by the indigenous people and slaughtering the Native Americans. Dee Brown tells this story from the Indian perspective in his bestselling book, *Bury My Heart at Wounded Knee.*[86] It is a story of broken promises and savage massacres.

One example of the violence wrought is the massacre at Sand Creek in Colorado on November 29, 1864. Cheyenne and Arapaho Indians had camped at Sand Creek, about forty miles from Fort Lyon, with the assurance that they were safe from attack. Major Anthony, the commander of Fort Lyon, had even encouraged the warriors to hunt buffalo to feed the tribe. Most of the men were away from the camp, when seven hundred US cavalrymen under the command of Colonel John Chivington descended on the camp at sunrise, firing randomly at the Indians. Chief Black Kettle came out of his lodge and raised an American flag and a white flag of surrender on a long lodge pole. He called to his people not to be afraid, that the soldiers wouldn't hurt them. As hundreds of women and children gathered under Black Kettle's American flag, the soldiers opened fire from two sides of the camp. The cavalry indiscriminately slaughtered men, women, and children. Most of the dead Indians were scalped by the soldiers and many were mutilated. Although lack of discipline, drunkenness, cowardice, and poor marksmanship allowed many Indians to escape, when the shooting ended 105 Indian women and children and twenty-eight men were dead. Most had been unarmed and had offered no resistance. Of the forty-seven casualties among the soldiers, most were the result of their careless firing on one another.[87] This is sadly characteristic of the way the West was won.

Those Native Americans who still live on reservations experience the highest rate of poverty and the shortest life span of any group of Americans. A few tribes, such as the Mashantucket Pequot and the Mohegan in Connecticut, have exploited loopholes in the law to open casinos that have been financially successful. Native peoples have been victims of white racism in the United States and, as we saw in the section on colonialism in the second chapter, throughout the world.

Slavery, Segregation, and White Supremacy/Privilege

Racism in the Americas is also rooted in the colonial trade in African slaves. As many as nine million Africans were captured and shipped to the New

World prior to 1863, nearly half of them to the southern United States.[88] Many died from the horrid conditions on slave ships. When they arrived, they were bought and sold like cattle. Their labor was key to the plantation system in the southern United States, the Caribbean, and South America. African slaves were beaten, tortured, and raped by their white masters. Families were broken apart, and living conditions were abominable. "In popular memory—in white memory—the plantations of the antebellum south were like a necklace of country clubs strewn across the land. In reality, they were a chain of work camps in which four million were imprisoned. Their inhabitants, slaves, were very much survivors, in the Holocaust sense of that word."[89] In the movie *Roots*, a captured runaway slave is given the choice between castration and having his foot cut off. Slaves were totally stripped of their dignity as human beings, terrorized, and exploited.

In the United States, the system of slavery was officially abolished (1863) during the Civil War (1861–1865). The brief era of Reconstruction (1865–1877) that followed the Civil War was an opening for genuine progress for former slaves and the South. The Republican-dominated Congress of 1867 enacted laws and constitutional amendments that gave former slaves the right to vote and hold office and empowered the federal government to protect the principle of equal rights. Within a decade, however, the federal government withdrew its troops from the South and abandoned black citizens to the resurgence of white supremacy.[90]

This was accomplished, first, through vagrancy laws that resulted in the incarceration of thousands of blacks, along with an enormous market for convict leasing, which made prisoners to be literally "slaves of the state" and forced laborers for plantations and corporations throughout the South. Second, through "Jim Crow" segregation laws (laws promulgated at the state and local level to enforce segregation) that "disenfranchised blacks and discriminated against them in virtually every sphere of life, lending sanction to a racial ostracism that extended to schools, churches, housing, jobs, restrooms, hotels, restaurants, hospitals, orphanages, prisons, funeral homes, morgues, and cemeteries."[91] And lastly through a highly successful terrorism campaign by the Ku Klux Klan. In the spring of 1922, for example, in Kirvin, Texas, near Dallas, three black men, two of them almost certainly innocent, were accused of killing a white woman, and, while hundreds of spectators looked on, they were castrated, stabbed, beaten, tied to a plow and set afire. A report on the history of racial terror lynchings and killings released by the Equal Justice Initiative in Montgomery, Alabama, chronicles 3,959 victims in twelve Southern states from 1877 to 1950. Many of these victims were murdered not for crimes but for minor transgressions of the racial hierarchy, such as talking back to whites. The report includes a map of where these terrorist acts happened, and Bryan Stevenson, the founder and director of the organization, plans to erect plaques commemorating each lynching. Mr. Stevenson has also been the impetus behind the Legacy Museum and the National Memorial for Peace and Justice, both in Montgomery, Alabama. The memorial bears the names of more than 4,400 victims of terror killings inscribed on 800 steel pillars representing the counties in the twelve Southern states where the lynchings occurred.[92]

The Jim Crow system of segregation lasted for nearly a hundred years. Blacks in the South were kept separate from whites. Blacks received an inadequate education, were excluded from better-paying jobs, denied the vote, confined to substandard housing with few public services, and systematically excluded from positions of leadership and power. After the Great Depression, in the waning days of Jim Crow, African Americans, especially in the South, were excluded from the New Deal initiatives in social policy—the minimum wage, union rights, Social Security, and even the G.I. Bill—that created the modern white middle class.[93]

The civil rights movement in the United States began gathering steam in the 1950s. It was fueled by the Supreme Court decision (1954) in the case of *Brown v. Board of Education,* which overturned the "separate but equal" doctrine of the *Plessy v. Ferguson* decision (1896) by declaring separate educational systems inherently unequal and contrary to the Fourteenth Amendment to the Constitution. The civil rights movement resisted the system of segregation in the courts and in the streets. Widespread nonviolent protests throughout the South were punctuated by the Montgomery Bus Boycott (1955–1956), the Birmingham Desegregation Campaign (Spring, 1963), and the March on Washington on August 28, 1963. This decade of resistance, led by the Reverend Dr. Martin Luther King Jr. and others, resulted in the Civil Rights Act of 1964, which prohibited segregated public facilities in the United States. Since voting rights were the weakest aspect of the new law, the summer of 1964 saw an invasion of black and white students into the South to work on voter registration. In January and February of 1965 King's Southern Christian Leadership Conference (SCLC) collaborated with the Student Nonviolent Coordinating Committee (SNCC), led by John Lewis and Hosea Williams, on gradually escalating demonstrations focused on voting rights in Selma, Alabama. In early March, the Selma Campaign decided to march from Selma to Montgomery, the state capital. This work led to the Voting Rights Act of 1965, which de facto enfranchised blacks in America.[94]

In June 2013, however, in *Shelby County v. Holder,* the Supreme Court invalidated one of the provisions of the Voting Rights Act that involved a process called preclearance. This required states with a long history of racial discrimination in voting to get approval from the federal government for any changes to their voting laws. The Supreme Court argued that this provision was outdated and no longer necessary. Critics of the decision contend that ever-evolving racially discriminatory voting practices continue unabated.[95]

Slavery and the system of segregation have been abolished in the United States, but racism and its effects persist. Progress has been made, but intermarriage and genuinely integrated neighborhoods, schools, and churches remain rare, while discrimination, direct and systemic, is still too common. Despite the election of Barack Obama as president of the United States in 2008 and again in 2012, America has not become a "postracial" or colorblind society.[96] At present, the United States is a multiracial society rather than a truly integrated community. America's history of white racism will not be easy to transform.

Racism is a *belief* in racial superiority. Since racial superiority is believed rather than factual, it tends to be immune to evidence to the contrary and selective in reflecting on experience. In the United States (and perhaps Western societies in general), racism functions as a *culture*, that is, a set of shared beliefs, values, and assumptions that inform the way of life of a community. A culture of racism undergirds the economic, social, and political disparities experienced by different racial groups. The culture of racism forms the perspective and shapes the identity, consciousness, and behavior of American society. Thus, much of white racism happens on an unconscious level rather than that of blatant bigotry. The purpose and result of this culture of racism are to justify and protect white privilege, entitlement, and social dominance. White privilege is the direct result, the flip side, of racial injustice. It refers to the reality that whites have advantages not shared by people of color, ranging from employment opportunities and living wherever they can afford to shopping without suspicion and ease in hailing a cab. Racism persists because although most white Americans are consciously in favor of racial equality and interpersonal decency, they are unconsciously committed to structural inequality in order to maintain social, economic, and political dominance—white privilege.[97]

The New Jim Crow

It should come as no surprise, then, that just as a culture of racism replaced slavery with segregation a New Jim Crow has emerged in the wake of the civil rights movement. Since it is no longer socially acceptable to explicitly use race as a justification for racial injustice, we now use our criminal justice system to label people of color "criminals" and then legally engage in all the practices supposedly left behind. "We have not ended racial caste in America, we have merely redesigned it."[98]

Even in the midst of the civil rights movement, Southern conservatives began calling for a restoration of "law and order" in response to the civil disobedience of protestors and urban riots, such as those that swept the nation following the assassination of Martin Luther King Jr. in 1968. The riots fueled the argument that civil rights for blacks resulted in rampant crime. President

Ronald Reagan's War on Drugs (1982), coupled with the crack cocaine crisis in inner-city neighborhoods (which the CIA used to help fund its covert war in Nicaragua), resulted in the mass incarceration of poor people of color. Although studies show that people of all colors use and sell illegal drugs at similar rates, it was black and brown people who swelled the prison population from 300,000 to more than two million in less than thirty years. In major cities, as many as 80 percent of young African men now have criminal records. Once locked up, men and women are locked out of mainstream society and social mobility. Once a person has the stigma of "felon," all the Jim Crow forms of discrimination kick in: discrimination in employment and housing, denial of the right to vote,[99] denial of educational opportunities, exclusion from jury service, ineligibility for receiving public housing, welfare assistance, and other public benefits. Mass incarceration is, metaphorically, the New Jim Crow, the third manifestation of a racial caste system in the United States. As with slavery and segregation, it will take a major social movement to dismantle this new American caste system.

One aspect of the New Jim Crow, the routine incidences of white police officers killing unarmed African American men and women with impunity, may prove the midwife of a mass movement of resistance based on the principle "Black Lives Matter."[100] The impetus of this movement was the protests in response to the shooting of Michael Brown in Ferguson, Missouri (near St. Louis), August 9, 2014. This was not the first such incident to garner national attention. For example, Rodney King was beaten by Los Angeles police officers in 1991; Abner Louima brutalized in Brooklyn in 1997; Amadou Diallo killed by four New York City police officers in 1999; Sean Bell shot in Queens in 2006; Oscar Grant shot in Oakland in 2009; and Trayvon Martin killed in Sanford, Florida, in 2012. This pattern, however, was repeated ad nauseam beginning in the latter half of 2014: Eric Garner on Staten Island; Ezell Ford in Los Angeles; Akai Gurley in Brooklyn; twelve-year-old Tamir Rice in Cleveland; Rumain Brisbon in Phoenix; Anthony Hill in Decatur, Georgia; Tony Robinson in Madison, Wisconsin; Walter Scott in North Charleston, South Carolina; Freddie Gray in Baltimore; Samuel Dubose in Cincinnati; Laquan McDonald in Chicago; Alton Sterling in Baton Rouge, Louisiana; Philando Castile in St. Paul, Minnesota; Sylville Smith in Milwaukee; Darnell Thomas Wicker in Louisville; Paul O'Neal in Chicago; Terence Crutcher in Tulsa, Oklahoma; Deborah Danner in the Bronx; fifteen-year-old Jordan Edwards in Balch Springs, Texas; Genevive Dawes in Dallas; Stephon Clark in Sacramento; Antwon Rose II in East Pittsburgh; and, witnessing to Native American Women's Lives Matter, Loreal Tsingine in Winslow, Arizona.[101] In July 2015, Sandra Bland committed suicide in jail after being held for three days. She was arrested for "assaulting a public servant" after being pulled over for failing to signal a lane change.[102]

Often police officers are not charged or prosecuted for taking black lives, and when they are, juries rarely convict them in criminal court. This is true even when apparently incriminating videos, from officer body-cams or bystanders, are available. Why is this so? On one level, videos can be ambiguous and interpreted from a variety of perspectives, and juries can still be persuaded by the officers' testimony that they feared for their lives.[103] On a deeper level, the culture of racism in America has always blamed black victims for the violence of slavery, segregation, lynching, riots, and now police killing of unarmed African Americans. Racism results in the killings and in exonerating the killers.[104]

Obviously these are not isolated incidents. They illustrate the disposability of African American lives, just as mass incarceration demonstrates the economic abandonment of African Americans in the global economy.[105] Can we dismantle the culture of racism and white privilege in the United States?

South Africa—Apartheid

South Africa's system of apartheid (separateness in the Afrikaner language) provides another particularly egregious example of white racism. This system of state-enforced segregation, which was the last bastion of colonial white supremacy in Africa, allowed a white minority—only 18 percent of a population of over forty million—to keep strict control of the black majority. Apartheid guaranteed 87 percent of the land and 75 percent of the income to the white minority. Blacks were legally allowed to live only in one of twelve *bantustans* (so-called homelands), and were required to have a special permit to live and work in the other 87 percent of the country. Blacks were required to carry a valid passbook with them at all times or be imprisoned. Public facilities, schools, and residences were strictly segregated. Blacks had no civil or political standing in the Republic of South Africa. Resisting the system of apartheid could result in arrest, detention, torture, and death. Nelson Mandela (1918–2013), the first black president of a reformed South Africa (1994–1999), spent nearly forty years of his life in prison for resisting apartheid, then was awarded the Nobel Peace Prize (with F. W. de Klerk) for dismantling this system of segregation.[106]

The formal system of apartheid in South Africa collapsed in 1994 because of courageous resistance from blacks and because of economic, social, and political sanctions imposed by the world community. As in the United States, the legal system of apartheid has been abolished, but racism and its effects, including black poverty and white privilege, persist.

Global Racism, Prejudice, and Discrimination

Unfortunately, racism, prejudice, and discrimination are universal temptations. Some examples:

- While Europe has long been split by ethnic conflict, racial tensions were less noticeable until recently. Now racism is rearing its ugly head in response to the immigration of people of color.
- Because of the slave trade, Brazil has the largest African population outside of Africa. Color consciousness and a social preference for light-skinned persons has resulted in a subtle pattern of discrimination that has relegated blacks to the bottom of the economic order.
- Only 1 percent of Peru's population is black, but they are employed almost exclusively in menial jobs, such as pallbearers and doormen, where their skin color is thought to add prestige. The country's indigenous majority suffers much of the same racism at the hands of the Hispanic elite, but hostilities born of colonial history keep indigenous people and blacks from uniting against discrimination. In fact they often discriminate against each other.
- In Central and East Africa, black Africans treated the descendants of Indian immigrants with harsh discrimination in the years after independence. The discrimination was clearest in Uganda, where the dictator Idi Amin expelled all Indians from the country (1972) and confiscated their property.[107]

Race and ethnicity are responsible for too much of the violence and suffering in the world.

Caste

Caste refers to prejudice and discrimination based on one's birth family. It means that one's position in life is largely determined by one's birth family. It is similar to class, which is an economic distinction between groups of people, but it is even more insidious in that caste implies little possibility of improving one's lot in life. It is a kind of predestination. In India's Hindu culture, people are born into one of four main castes and multiple subcastes. About 15 percent of India's population, however, is born outside of a caste, into a fifth caste called the Untouchables or Dalits. These people were considered unclean, and they were relegated into the lowest occupations—waste removal, disposing of dead animals, or working with leather. They were made to live on the margins of the village or city and were excluded from temples and public facilities. Mahatma Gandhi called the Untouchables *Harijans*, the children of God, and he vigorously campaigned for their inclusion into society. India's constitution completely outlaws the exclusion of Dalits, making the observance of caste a crime. Specific laws forbid discrimination and set up affirmative action programs for the Dalits. The laws, however, are hard to enforce and implementation has been slow.[108]

While the plight of the Dalits in India is perhaps the clearest example of discrimination based on caste, it is practiced in more subtle forms in many other societies. Too often caste and class can largely determine one's fate in life.

Religion

Freedom of religion is an important declaration in the International Bill of Rights, a right that is unfortunately too often violated. It was only with Pope John XXIII and especially the Second Vatican Council document *Declaration on Religious Freedom* (*Dignitatis Humanae*, 1965) that the Catholic Church affirmed religious freedom, but the church is now a strong advocate for this cause.[109]

Religious intolerance often results in discrimination and persecution. Anti-Semitism is widespread in Europe and in much of the world. It found its most horrific expression in the Holocaust during World War II, and unfortunately it continues to the present.[110] Since September 11, 2001, anti-Muslim sentiment, or Islamophobia, the fear of and consequent discrimination against Muslims, has increased in the West.[111] Christians are being persecuted by Muslims in the Middle East and North Africa and by radical Hindus in India,[112] where Muslims and Hindus engage in sporadic bloodbaths against each other. Such intolerance and persecution should give way to mutual respect and interfaith dialogue in order to respect the best in all religious traditions.

Discrimination against the LGBT Community

Many religions and cultures have condemned homosexuality, and, as a result, homosexuals have been marginalized and persecuted. Discrimination against the LGBT (lesbian, gay, bisexual, and transgender) community, including verbal and physical abuse (so-called gay bashing), is widespread. There is good reason today to confess this discrimination as sordid and sinful, to repent, and to recognize the human dignity and human rights of homosexuals. LGBT rights, however, are not explicitly protected in international human rights law. The International Bill of Rights has been developed by consensus, and there is no global consensus opposing discrimination against gender and sexual minorities and affirming LGBT rights. There is no reason that advocates of LGBT rights should not campaign on their behalf, but their moral claims to justice and human rights are not yet universally recognized. Because this book is "a Christian primer," this brief discussion will focus on the church and its teaching about and treatment of homosexuals.

Until the emergence of psychology in the twentieth century, sex acts between people of the same sex were thought to be unnatural. Now, however, we know that a certain percentage of the population is sexually attracted to persons of the same sex. This idea of sexual orientation or sexual preference, like the term "homosexual" itself, is relatively new. One's sexual orientation, whether heterosexual, homosexual, or bisexual, is experienced as a given, not a choice. This new understanding necessitates a rethinking of the traditional condemnation of homosexuals.

The Catholic Church and many Protestant denominations have responded by distinguishing between homosexuals, that is, *persons* who prefer the same sex, and homosexual *acts* of genital expression. Homosexuals are not condemned, but homosexual acts are still considered sinful. While many theologians and some denominations would go further and accept both homosexuals and homosexual acts in a committed relationship, even this official distinction between person and act calls into question any discrimination or persecution against homosexuals. Even if one considers a person's lifestyle immoral (e.g., too materialistic or sexually unfaithful), that does not justify violence against that person or discrimination in employment, housing, education, or other opportunities enjoyed by every citizen. Disrespect for and discrimination against homosexuals is wrong, and it should be made illegal in order to offer protection for rights long denied.

Human rights, as articulated in the International Bill of Rights, are rooted in the dignity of persons created in the image of God, a dignity realized in community. A guarantee of human rights is the minimal obligation of any state worthy of allegiance, and human rights are important standards for guiding the international obligations of states and foreign policy. The ultimate litmus test of human rights in any society is how the guilty and despised are treated.

STUDY QUESTIONS

1. How would you explain the paradox that while human rights are increasingly recognized in theory, they continue to be violated in practice?

2. Should human rights be a cornerstone of US foreign policy? What would be the implications of a principled human rights foreign policy for trade policy?

3. Is the idea of "rights" being taken too far in US society today? What *are* the rights of human beings?

4. Discuss the cultural practice of female genital cutting. Is this a legitimate cultural practice or a violation of human rights? When are practices relative to a particular culture? Are there universal human rights whose violation can never be justified?

5. Discuss the inequality between men and women, globally and in US society. Does religion reinforce this inequality?

6. Is the United States a society deeply divided along racial lines? How can the culture of racism and white privilege be dismantled?

7. Discuss examples of homophobia you may witness in everyday life.

6

CONFLICT, WAR, AND PEACE

One of the most disturbing threats to peace in the post–Cold War world has been the spread of conflicts rooted in national, ethnic, racial, and religious differences. . . . Precisely because of their intractable and explosive nature, ethnic conflicts can be resolved only through political dialogue and negotiation. War and violence are unacceptable means for resolving ethnic conflicts; they serve only to exacerbate them. Nor are political solutions alone sufficient. Also needed is the commitment to reconciliation that is at the heart of the Christian and other religious traditions. For religious believers can imagine what some would dismiss as unrealistic: that even the most intense hatreds can be overcome by love, that free human beings can break historic cycles of violence and injustice, and that deeply divided people can learn to live together in peace.

US Conference of Catholic Bishops
The Harvest of Justice Is Sown in Peace (1993)

No peace without justice, no justice without forgiveness.

Pope John Paul II
Message for World Day of Peace, January 1, 2002

The twentieth century was surely among the bloodiest in a bloody history, with two world wars, wars of independence, wars to contain or spread communism under the umbrella of the Cold War, and numerous revolutions and civil wars.[1] The last decade of the century was characterized by an eruption of ethno-nationalist conflict in places such as Bosnia and Rwanda. In the early years of the twenty-first century, ethno-nationalist conflict has subsided somewhat, only to be supplanted by the emergence of power struggles and by terrorism. The multiple causes of conflict make the resolution of conflict and the prevention of war especially complicated at this moment in history.

Conflict is inevitable. Nearly everyone agrees that war is the worst way to respond to conflict, but many will also argue that it is sometimes necessary. Conflict results from a clash of interests and/or ideas. Fortunately, most of the time conflict between states or within a state can be resolved without violence.

The pacifist or nonviolent strand within the Christian tradition contends that war can never be morally justified, that war is always wrong. In the fifth century, when the Holy Roman Empire was faced with a barbarian invasion, St. Augustine baptized the Greek and Roman concept of a "just" war into the Christian tradition. Augustine taught that war could be a rule-governed exception in which the state could depart from Jesus's command to love our enemies. If fought for a just cause, under legitimate authority, and with the right attitude, war could be morally justified.

The idea of just war has developed through Christian history, becoming what might be called a "justified war tradition." Woven through the tapestry of Christian tradition has been a minor thread of Christian nonviolence.[2] Today some theologians are developing a third paradigm for the moral analysis of conflict called "just peacemaking," which aims to emphasize God's call to be peacemakers in a realistic and practical way.[3] War itself has mutated dramatically in contemporary times. Can modern war still be morally justified?[4] To respond to that question we need to examine modern warfare as well as the resources for analyzing war and peace within the Christian tradition.

This chapter will explore the landscape of global conflict[5] as we make our way through the twenty-first century, highlighting some areas where war or peace is breaking out. Major themes of the chapter will be ethno-nationalist conflict, humanitarian intervention, and a moral response to terrorism.

ETHNO-NATIONALIST CONFLICT

The decade of the 1990s may well be remembered as ushering in an era of ethno-nationalist conflict. When the Cold War ended, many people expected a period of peace and prosperity to follow. One analyst even proclaimed "the end of history."[6] History, however, did not move into a peaceful reign of democratic capitalism, but degenerated into a morass of ethnic conflict. The international community found itself torn between the principles of national sovereignty, territorial integrity, and nonintervention on the one hand, and the principles of self-determination and human rights on the other, and struggled to find a response. Ethnic conflict, in its many apparitions, which resulted in gross violations of human rights, remains a serious barrier to peace in the contemporary world.

Although ethnic conflict is as old as human history, nationalism gives it a new shade. Clans and tribes have always fought one another over territory or resources, or sometimes simply because of fear of people outside of their own group. Peoples have united to form empires by conquering other peoples. The idea of a sovereign state, however, is relatively recent, and the principle of self-determination that decrees that nations should be states is even newer.

Americans tend to have difficulty understanding ethno-nationalist conflict. Because the European colonizers nearly annihilated the indigenous people in North America and because the United States has been settled by wave after wave of immigrants, the United States has always been a multi-ethnic society. Most large American cities have the remnants of "Little Italy," "Germantown," or "Chinatown" sections, but today that often designates a cluster of good ethnic restaurants rather than a genuinely ethnic enclave. There is much debate about whether America is truly a melting pot, but while there are surely ethnic and especially racial tensions and conflicts, the American reality is quite different from that of most countries in the world. Since every ethnic group has come here at some point to establish a new home, no ethnic group in the United States (except the remaining indigenous people) can claim that this is their ancestral home. In most other countries several competing ethnic groups do make that claim. Thus, to understand the power of ethno-nationalism in other countries, Americans often have to disregard their own experience.

When Nations Want to Become States

Ethnicity is difficult to define, with no strictly objective criteria essential for its existence. Rather, ethnicity is subjective, a conviction of commonality. Groups of people can distinguish themselves from other groups by characteristics such as language, religion, social customs, physical appearance, region of residence, or by a combination of these features.[7] In a way, ethnic groups are "psychological communities" whose members share a persisting sense of common interest and identity that is based on some combination of shared historical experience and valued cultural traits.[8] When an ethnic group becomes politicized and begins to claim a certain territory as its homeland, it becomes a "nation."[9]

Technically, there is a difference between a nation and a state and between nationalism and patriotism, although the terms are often used interchangeably. Properly speaking, "nation" refers to a group of people who believe they share a common ancestry, or to the largest human grouping predicated on a myth of common ancestry. It is close to the notion of a fully extended family.[10] There is no need for the belief in a common ancestry to be factual or historical. Indeed, as Walker Connor, an expert on ethnicity and nationalism, says, "the myth of common and exclusive descent can overcome a battery of contrary fact."[11] In another place, Connor puts it this way, "It is not chronological or factual history that is the key to the nation, but sentient or felt history. All that is required for the existence of a nation is that the members share an intuitive conviction of the group's separate origin and evolution."[12] Thus, the existence of a nation—a people—is subjective, subconscious, and sometimes even sentimental in nature. It is based on blood and belonging. It is a phenomenon of the masses, not a proclamation of an elite.[13] Nationalism, then, is the love and loyalty one feels for one's nation or people.

An important aspect of nationalism is the sense of a homeland. There are a few primarily immigrant societies, such as the United States, Argentina, and Australia, but most of the land masses of the world are divided into ethnic homelands: a Scotland (land of the Scots), Poland, Finland, Zululand, Kazakhstan (*stan* means "land of"), Afghanistan, and the like. Nations have a strong attachment to a place—where they feel they originated, where their ancestors are buried, where their blood has been spilled. Again, this perception need not, and often will not, accord with historical fact, but that in no way diminishes a people's attachment to the "land of their forebears." Since a nation feels a sense of primal ownership for a place, its people view others, even those who may have lived there for centuries, as aliens or outsiders in their homeland.[14] Nationalism, then, when stirred by some change or current event, comes to mean the reclamation of a people's homeland by ejecting aliens who have taken up residence there. In the period from 1991 to 1995, in the villages of the Krajina section of Croatia and in much of Bosnia, this meant literally the elimination and expulsion of one's neighbors.[15]

A "state," on the other hand, is a legal and political entity, a government that exercises control over a defined territory.[16] Contemporary states are recognized as sovereign, both internally and externally. States exercise control over the people within their territory, and they interact autonomously with one another, signing treaties, joining organizations, setting trade policies, and the like. The love and loyalty one feels for one's country or state is properly called patriotism.

Thus, one may correctly refer to British patriotism, but to Scottish, Welsh, or English nationalism; to Canadian patriotism, but to Quebecois nationalism; to Belgian patriotism, but Flemish nationalism, and so on. The difficulty is that in a world of perhaps 5,000 nations (since there are at least that many linguistic groups), there are only around 195 states. Of those states, only about fifteen, such as Japan, Iceland, and Portugal, are ethnically homogeneous, or genuine nation-states. Thus, more than 90 percent of all states are ethnically heterogeneous, that is, they are comprised of more than one significant ethnic group. In 40 percent of these states, there are five or more significant ethnic groups, and in nearly one-third, the largest ethnic group is not even a majority (e.g., Kazakhstan). The state of Nigeria contains more than one hundred different ethnic groups (as did the former Soviet Union).[17]

Many ethnic groups coexist amicably within a single state, as do Swedes who live in Finland, for example. Others become assimilated into multi-ethnic societies. But when an ethnic group begins to coalesce to take political action because of its swelling sense of identity or because of its victimization through discrimination, the resulting conflict can threaten to rip apart a state. The principle of national self-determination, which says that nations or peoples should be autonomous and free to control their own destiny, can wreak havoc in multinational states.[18]

Ethno-national conflict does not always lead to violence or civil war. Since the end of the Cold War, for example, Czechoslovakia has amicably split into the Czech Republic and Slovakia. The breakup of the Soviet Union into its fifteen constituent republics created fifteen new states by political fiat rather than by war. Most of these new states, however, face their own internal ethnic conflicts, and these have not always been peacefully resolved, as the war in Chechnya illustrated.

When ethno-national conflict does become violent, the struggle is often protracted and brutal. States do not readily cede territory or authority, and ethnic groups who have power do not easily accede to the demands of a minority or the oppressed. Thus, fighting can linger for decades, as it did in Northern Ireland, Sudan, and Sri Lanka. Ethnic conflict is often motivated by hatred of the other group. This polarizes the conflict, and the out-group is often dehumanized and stripped of all human rights. Atrocities by one group provoke atrocities by the other group, resulting in a destructive spiral of violence. Any restraints called for by the rules and conventions of war fall by the wayside. Genocide—killing members of a group because of their ethnicity with the intent to destroy in whole or in part the ethnic group itself—becomes the logic of much ethnic warfare.[19] Because such conflicts are not only about politics or economics but are filled with cultural and personal animosity, they tend to be extremely difficult to resolve.[20] The trust necessary for negotiation and conflict resolution is often absent.

Contemporary ethnic conflict is often part of the heritage of history. The Balkans marked the dividing line between the Roman Empire in the West and the Ottoman and Russian empires in the East. Thus, division and conflict in Bosnia go back nearly a millennium. Not surprisingly, colonialism is key to many of the ethnic conflicts in the Two-Thirds World. The European powers arbitrarily divided up Africa among themselves at the Congress of Berlin in 1884, drawing boundaries on a map with little regard for ethno-national territories. Colonialism has had devastating and lasting effects on the world's indigenous peoples. "Conquered peoples seek to regain their lost autonomy; indigenous peoples ask for restoration of their traditional lands; immigrant workers and the descendants of slaves demand full equality."[21]

Research regarding ethno-nationalist conflict has established some principles or practices for managing conflict in divided societies.[22] According to Ted Robert Gurr, the five principles or practices for managing communal conflict in divided societies include: the recognition and protection of individual and collective rights of racial, ethnic, and religious minorities (a human rights regime); building institutions that promote pluralism, participation, and power sharing (democratization); negotiations aimed at providing regional autonomy and promoting institutions that protect collective interests within states (autonomy solutions for self-determination disputes); engagement by international and regional organizations aimed at preventing and containing violence and at making and keeping peace (international and regional peace building and peace keeping); and international and regional armed intervention to stop gross violations of human rights and to ensure regional security and stability (humanitarian intervention and responsibility to protect).[23] Although in fact ethnic conflict has declined since the turn of the century,[24] it is also true that some ethnic or national self-determination conflicts have endured and seem intractable. Sumantra Bose argues that key factors in such protracted disputes are their ideological nature and the existential fears of the communities engaged in them.[25]

Contemporary ethnic conflict is not inevitable. Although imperial conquest and colonial rule provide a historical backdrop, past divisions or discrimination does not necessarily lead to present conflict. Nor can ethnic conflict simply be ascribed to human nature. Human beings are capable of transcending the social psychology of in-group/out-group violence. While belonging to a community of like-minded persons is important for healthy human development (both identity and relationships), it does not follow that other communities must be hated and fought. Ethnic conflict, although all too common, is neither historically inevitable nor biologically determined.

Christian Ethics and the Idolatry of Nationalism

Christian theology and ethics can provide a critical perspective for evaluating ethnic conflict and nationalism. In the Christian framework the particular and the universal are not in opposition to each other; the Christian tradition affirms both.[26] An ethic faithful to the gospel must be universal in scope, extending love to each and every person. Christian love cannot discriminate; it must embrace every person, near and far.

The teachings of Christian tradition are also incarnational and sacramental, particular and practical.[27] Christian love is concrete, and Christian living is essentially relational and communal. The church is universal, but it is also local—incarnated in the lives of those who gather together to hear the story, share a meal, and become the body of Christ in the world.

Contemporary Catholic social thought has used the virtue and principle of "solidarity" to try to capture the concrete, communal, and universal nature of the Christian faith. "[Solidarity] is not a feeling of vague compassion or shallow distress at the misfortunes of so many people, both near and far. On the contrary, it is a firm and persevering determination to commit oneself to the common good; that is to say, to the good of all and of each individual, because we are all really responsible for all."[28]

In light of this framework, patriotism and nationalism can be good, but neither is an absolute good. When loyalty and love for country or nation become absolute and fanatical, they become idolatrous and are harmful. Love of country or nation is good and valuable. It is a source of identity and of relationships and community that create special duties and obligations, just as the special relationships of marriage, parenthood, and friendship create special responsibilities. But neither patriotism nor nationalism should be an ultimate or primary loyalty, exercising unquestioned authority in our lives. State or nation can become an idol, and that sort of allegiance should be resisted and rejected. Loyalty to one's country or people must be balanced by other commitments, both more intimate and more universal. Ethno-nationalism seems more prone to absolutism and idolatry than patriotism.[29]

A commitment to human rights can reconcile loyalty to a particular state or nation with a global ethic that encourages a universal love. Love of country or nation can no more justify hatred of foreigners than friendship can legitimize despising those with whom one is not acquainted. A country's sovereignty is, then, also a real but relative value; sovereignty is relative to respecting the human rights of every person in the human family.[30] In given circumstances, human rights claims can override the principle of territorial sovereignty and nonintervention. The theory of human rights points to minimal requirements for right relationships with one another in a just society. Protecting human rights is a helpful way to articulate what it means to reverence the dignity of the human person and to embrace all of humanity as family.

Ethical analysis suggests that communal or group rights should be recognized in international law. Thus far, the declarations and covenants promulgated by the United Nations focus on individual rights and the rights of states. Formal international recognition of the rights and responsibilities of ethnic groups or communities within states, the rights of "nations,"[31] would help to balance the needs of individuals versus those of the common good.

Religion seems to be an important factor in many ethnic conflicts: between Catholics and Protestants in Northern Ireland, Jewish Israelis and Muslim Palestinians, Buddhist Sinhala and Hindu Tamils in Sri Lanka, and among Catholic Croats, Orthodox Serbs, and Bosnian Muslims. Religion is one of the features that can distinguish one ethnic group from another. Since religion pertains to core values, it can inflate the intensity and intractability of ethnic conflict.[32] Religious belief can even be used to legitimate intolerance toward another ethnic group.[33] Most analysts, however, have concluded that while religious divisions can be a contributing factor, religion itself is seldom the root cause, main motivation, or principal reason for ethnic conflict.[34]

While it may be true that religion is usually not central to ethnic conflict, the use of religion to inflame nationalism remains troubling. Most religious traditions profess universal love, forgiveness, and reconciliation. Ethno-nationalism often preaches hatred, revenge, and division. How is it that religion can be coopted to espouse hatred and violence? Why isn't religion a powerful force for forgiveness, reconciliation, and peace in Bosnia, the Middle East, or Sri Lanka? The American Catholic bishops deserve to be heard and heeded when they proclaim:

> Every child murdered, every woman raped, every town "cleansed," every hatred uttered in the name of religion is a crime against God and a scandal for religious believers. Religious violence and nationalism deny what we profess in faith: We are all created in the image of the same God and destined for the same eternal salvation. "[N]o Christian can knowingly foster or support structures and attitudes that unjustly divide individuals or groups."[35]

Religion can be and has been a source of courage, forgiveness, and reconciliation in places of ethnic conflict, yet the shadow side of religion remains troubling.[36]

THE GLOBAL LANDSCAPE OF CONFLICT AND WAR

It is impossible to predict when conflict will erupt into war. It is clear, however, that our world continues to be a violent and divided place. This section will attempt to sketch the global landscape of conflict and war in the first quarter of the twentieth-first century.

The Middle East

Israelis/Palestinians

In the Middle East, the Israeli Jews and the Palestinians, who are Arab and mostly Muslim, both claim the small territory on the eastern edge of the Mediterranean Sea as their homeland. The roots of both claims go back centuries—to the Hebrew Scriptures in the case of the Jews and to the first and seventh centuries of the Common Era for the Palestinians.

The more immediate claims go back to the first and second world wars. During World War I the desperate (and duplicitous) British promised the Palestinians their independence in the Hussein-McMahon Correspondence (1915–1916), while promising Jews a homeland in Palestine in the Balfour Declaration (1917), in exchange for support for the British cause against Germany.[37] After World War II, displaced Jews who had survived the Holocaust poured into Palestine fired by the Zionist dream of a homeland; then in late 1947, the newly formed United Nations voted to partition Palestine. By spring 1948, Israel declared itself a state.[38] The five surrounding Arab states—Lebanon, Syria, Jordan, Iraq, and Egypt—vehemently refused to recognize Israel and immediately mounted a half-hearted attack that failed.[39]

The creation of Israel in 1948 provided a homeland and place of refuge for Jews who had been victims of anti-Semitism, which had manifested itself in the horror of the Holocaust. At the same time it displaced the Arab people who had been living in Palestine for well over a millennium. As a result of the partition and the 1948 war, many Palestinians fled the region or were displaced by the Israeli army and settled in refugee camps on the West Bank of the Jordan River or in the Gaza Strip. The surrounding Arab countries attacked Israel in 1967 and again in 1973 and were soundly defeated both times. In 1967 Israel took control of the whole of Palestine, occupying both the West Bank and the Gaza Strip. UN Resolution 242 called on Israel to withdraw to its pre-1967 borders, but Israel has refused to do so to protect its own security.

The pendulum has swung between peace and war, hope and despair, several times since 1973, but the conflict has thus far proven impossible to resolve. A chronology of some major events follows:

- In 1979 US president Jimmy Carter brokered a peace agreement between Egypt's Anwar Sadat and Israel's Menachem Begin at Camp David that has continued to hold, even through the unrest in Egypt resulting from the 2011 Arab Spring.
- In late 1987 the first intifada, a Palestinian uprising characterized by strikes, protests, riots, and Palestinian teenagers throwing stones at Israeli tanks and soldiers, began and persisted for three years. Israel responded with increasing violence and repression.
- In 1993 negotiations took place in Oslo, Norway, resulting in a resolution for increasing Palestinian autonomy that was signed at the White House by Israeli Prime Minister (PM) Yitzhak Rabin and Palestinian Liberation Organization (PLO) chairman Yasser Arafat.[40]
- The 1993 Oslo Accord established the Palestinian Authority (PA) to govern Gaza and the West Bank and eventually evolve into the state of Palestine. Fatah won the majority of seats in the Palestinian Legislative Council (PLC) and the presidency of the PA in elections held in 1996. In the Oslo Accords the Fatah-led PLO recognized the state of Israel and renounced terrorism.
- Hamas, a radical Islamic group that is committed to the destruction of Israel, rejected the Oslo Accords and boycotted the 1996 election.
- In the summer of 2000, President Clinton called Yasser Arafat and Israeli PM Ehud Barak to a meeting at Camp David, to try to complete the Oslo process, but an agreement could not be reached.[41]
- A month later, a visit by Israeli politician and former defense minister Ariel Sharon to the Muslim holy site, the Al-Aqsa Mosque on Temple Mount

in Jerusalem, sparked a second Palestinian intifada and some of the worst violence in the conflict. Palestinian suicide bombers blew up buses, restaurants, and shopping centers in Israel, and in response to each attack the Israeli security forces escalated the level of violence and repression in the West Bank and the Gaza Strip.[42]

- In 2003, Israel decided to build a separation barrier in the West Bank, composed of fences and a concrete wall, similar to the one constructed in Gaza in 1994.

- The second, or Al-Aqsa, intifada lost momentum with Israel's announced unilateral disengagement with the Gaza Strip in June 2004, and Arafat's death in November. Palestinian president Mahmoud Abbas and Israeli PM Ariel Sharon signed a formal cease fire in February 2005. These years of ferocious violence of the second intifada (2000–2005) can be explained by the deepening of the Israeli occupation during the Oslo years (1993–2000) in defiance of Palestinian expectations of greater freedom, the preparation of both sides for war, and the intransigence of both sides after violence broke out.[43]

- In early January 2006, PM Ariel Sharon had a stroke that left him incapacitated (he died in January 2014). In March, Ehud Olmert was elected Israeli prime minister.

- When a second election for leadership of the Palestinian Authority was held on January 25, 2006, Hamas won the majority of seats in the PLC, shocking Israel, the United States, and Fatah. Israel immediately declared that it would refuse to negotiate with a terrorist organization dedicated to its destruction.[44] Fatah's leader Mahmoud Abbas, refused to yield control of the PA to Hamas, which led to a violent struggle (an estimated six hundred Palestinians were killed) between Fatah and Hamas in the Palestinian territories. By mid-2007 Hamas had established control of Gaza, and Fatah remained in control of the West Bank. Fatah and Hamas have been unsuccessfully seeking a unified government since this event, and no further elections have been held.[45]

Gaza is a twenty-five-mile-long and six-mile-wide strip of land on the Mediterranean coast of Israel that served as a Palestinian refugee camp after the 1967 War. Israel disengaged from Gaza in mid-August 2005, under orders from PM Sharon, removing the 8,500 Jewish settlers, destroying their homes, and withdrawing all Israeli Defense Forces (IDF). Israel maintained control of the coastline, the airspace, and the borders, aided by the security barrier already in place. When Hamas gained control of the Gaza Strip in June 2007, Israel closed the borders and blockaded Gaza, effectively imprisoning the 1.8 million Palestinians living there.[46]

Since then, Israel has launched three major military interventions into Gaza (December 27, 2008–January 18, 2009; November 14–22, 2012; and July

8–August 26, 2014). These wars follow a pattern. Hamas smuggles weapons into Gaza, fires rockets into southern Israel, and stages cross-border attacks, through elaborate tunnels. Israel responds with air bombardment and ground troops, destroying homes, buildings, and infrastructure in Gaza associated with Hamas. Because of Israeli military superiority, Palestinian casualties are always much greater than those of Israelis. Approximately 3,800 Palestinians have been killed in these conflicts, half of whom have been civilians, and over 300,000 Palestinians have been dislocated. Seventy-eight IDF soldiers have been killed and twelve Israeli civilians.

Both Israel and Hamas have been accused of war crimes in these conflicts. In launching 4,881 unguided rockets into civilian areas of Israel in the 2014 conflict (and in previous conflicts), Hamas is intentionally indiscriminate (yet largely ineffective) in its conduct. In its more than six thousand airstrikes in the 2014 conflict, Israel claimed its targets were military, albeit placed in civilian areas by Hamas. The disproportionate Palestinian casualties, 50 percent of whom are civilian, suggest callous indifference and indiscriminate conduct by Israel as well.[47]

Having served as prime minister from 1996 to 1999, Benjamin "Bibi" Netanyahu was reelected PM in March 2009 and continued to lead Israel in 2018. Thus he came back into office shortly after the first Israel–Gaza War and ordered the other two Gaza military interventions. He presided over Israel during both terms of the Obama administration and well into Trump's presidency.

President Obama's second secretary of state, John Kerry, began to mediate a nine-month period of peace talks between Israel and the Palestinian Authority in August 2013. On April 24, 2014, shortly before the nine-month deadline, Israel pulled out of the negotiations. Blame for the failure of these negotiations can be shared among the participants. Key to the demise of the negotiations, however, was Israel's relentless construction of settlements in the West Bank—the supposed state of Palestine in a two-state solution.[48] The tension between Israel and the Palestinians erupted into the third and longest Israel–Gaza War on July 8, 2014.

In mid-September, 2016, the Obama administration finalized a $38 billion military aid package for Israel over the next ten years, the largest of its kind in over six decades of US military support for Israel. Thus, despite tensions with PM Netanyahu that focused on Israel's continuous expansion of Jewish settlements in the West Bank and East Jerusalem, the United States was hardly abandoning its ally.[49]

Still, after the November election of President Trump, who seemed enamored of Netanyahu and uncritical of Israel's settlement expansion, the Obama administration made clear what it thought was at stake through two actions: abstaining in a vote on UN Security Resolution 2334, which condemned Israel's settlement construction,[50] and a blunt speech by outgoing secretary of state John Kerry expressing the Obama administration's deep concern that Israel's persistent expansion of unlawful Jewish settlements in the West Bank and East Jerusalem is making a two-state solution with the Palestinians impossible and undermining Israel's future as a Jewish and democratic state.[51]

There are 2.8 million Palestinians living in the West Bank. There are over 400,000 Jewish settlers scattered throughout the West Bank and another 208,000 in East Jerusalem. More than 100,000 of these settlers were added from 2009 to 2017, that is, during the administrations of Obama in the United States and Netanyahu in Israel. The goal of the settler movement and apparently of Netanyahu's Likud party is the creation of "Greater Israel," that is, the Israel of biblical times, which stretched from the Mediterranean to the Jordan River.[52] This goal is inimical to the two-state solution of two states for two peoples, living next to one another in security and peace. The settlements are statements on the ground that Palestine will not happen. As Secretary Kerry warned in his speech, a one-state solution in which Israel annexes the West Bank and the Gaza Strip faces Israel with a choice of being either a Jewish state or a democracy. Even without the right of return for the now five million Palestinians who fled during the 1948 Arab–Israeli war, insisted upon by the Palestinians and rejected by Israel, the higher birth rate of Palestinians would eventually make Jews a minority in Israel. If Israel treated Palestinians as second-class citizens without voting rights and the full gamut of human rights, Israel would no longer be a democracy.[53]

To a great extent, these issues have been settled by subsequent moves by the Trump and Netanyahu administrations in 2018. First, President Trump fulfilled his campaign promise to move the US embassy to Jerusalem and recognize Jerusalem as the capital of Israel. The US embassy was officially opened in Jerusalem on May 14, 2018, the seventieth anniversary of the state of Israel. This move, deeply offensive to Palestinians, removed the United States from any pretense of being an unbiased arbiter between Israel and the Palestinians.[54] Second, on July 19, PM Netanyahu's governing coalition enacted a law that declared Israel the "Nation-State of the Jewish People," effectively demoting Arabs and other minority people in the country to second-class citizens. The law has the weight of a constitutional amendment and omits any mention of democracy or equality. Israel is no longer an inclusive democracy. This removes the one-state solution from any serious Palestinian consideration.[55] The status quo of Israeli occupation of the West Bank and blockade of the Gaza Strip is oppressive, unjust, and contrary to UN resolutions, but it seems poised to continue.

In a broader sense, efforts to resolve this conflict have failed because the interests and goals of the two sides are diametrically opposed. Israel wants a Jewish state that is a safe homeland for Jews who are repeatedly victimized by anti-Semitism and that is secure from attacks by its Arab neighbors. Palestinians do not recognize Israel's right to exist on land confiscated from them. They want their land back, and they want an independent Palestine with contiguous borders and free access so that some five million Palestinian refugees can return if they wish. Both sides claimed Jerusalem as their capital. Most outside analysts point to the creation of two independent states—Israel and Palestine—as the solution, but this obvious, albeit complex, step fails to satisfy the more extreme interests of either side. It is currently dead in the water.

Iraq

Several other conflicts in the Middle East require attention. In August 1990, Iraq invaded and occupied its small, oil-rich neighbor, Kuwait. Saddam Hussein, Iraq's tyrannical leader, had economic and historical reasons for invading Kuwait. Iraq had borrowed money from Kuwait to wage a war against Iran in the 1980s, and Saddam thought this debt should be forgiven in light of Iraqi suffering for the Sunni Muslim cause in that war. There was also a dispute about oil wells on the Iraq–Kuwait border. Kuwait had been split off from Iraq at the end of the colonial period in an attempt to limit Iraq's power in the region. Thus Iraq was reclaiming territory it considered its own and asserting its hegemony in the region. The Iraqi occupation of Kuwait was violent and brutal.

None of these reasons justified the Iraqi invasion in the eyes of the rest of the world, which became gravely concerned at the prospect of Saddam Hussein gaining increasing control of the world's oil supply. President George H. W. Bush (1989–1993) was able to assemble a US-led coalition, under the auspices of the United Nations and with the approval of the US Congress, to reverse the first cross-border aggression of the post–Cold War world. The coalition that fought the Persian Gulf War in early 1991 was supported by all the major powers and by nearly every country in the Middle East. After several weeks of intense bombing of Iraqi troops, allied ground troops liberated Kuwait from a devastated and traumatized Iraqi army. Having accomplished the war's objective, the Bush administration stopped short of marching into Baghdad and overthrowing Saddam Hussein.

The cease-fire agreement required Iraq to destroy its chemical and biological weapons and its nuclear weapons program; it also imposed economic sanctions on Iraq until UN weapons inspectors certified that these weapons had been eliminated. The weapons inspectors found that Iraq's nuclear weapons program was more advanced than most experts thought, and they supervised its destruction and that of much of Iraq's cache of biological and chemical weapons. Iraq, however, never fully cooperated with this process, and Saddam Hussein became increasingly resistant to weapons inspections. In 1998 he finally barred the UN inspection teams from Iraq, claiming that the inspectors were spies and that their invasive inspections were disrespectful of Iraqi sovereignty. Meanwhile, the economic sanctions, coupled with the callous irresponsibility of Saddam's regime, were creating a humanitarian tragedy in Iraq. In the period from 1990 to 1997 it is likely that the economic sanctions contributed to the deaths of about 500,000 Iraqis, with nearly two-thirds of them children.[56]

After the Persian Gulf War (August 2, 1990–February 28, 1991), the United States also created two "no-fly zones" in northern and southern Iraq to protect the Kurdish minority in the north and the Shiite majority in the south. American (and some British) warplanes patrolling these no-fly zones regularly returned fire when threatened by Iraqi air defenses.[57] Thus, there was continuous low-intensity conflict in Iraqi airspace for over a decade.

On October 7, 2001, the United States, with the assistance of the British and the promise of future NATO support, launched airstrikes against al-Qaeda (who were responsible for the terrorist attacks on September 11, 2001) and Taliban forces in Afghanistan in support of the Northern Alliance and ethnic Pushtun anti-Taliban forces there. Although the United States sent ground troops to assist, most of the combat was between the Taliban and its Afghan opponents. By early December the Taliban had been removed from power and an interim government under Hamid Karzai had been established.[58]

In the summer of 2002, President George W. Bush (2001–2009) and members of his administration began asserting that Saddam Hussein was developing nuclear weapons, possessed chemical and biological weapons, and supported terrorists, including al-Qaeda, thus linking Iraq to 9/11. These assertions were based on faulty intelligence from unreliable sources. Because of the alleged threat that the Iraqi regime posed to the security and interests of the United States, President Bush called for "regime change" in Iraq and asserted that the United States could mount a preemptive attack on Iraq to prevent Saddam Hussein from acquiring nuclear weapons or initiating another terrorist attack, perhaps with weapons of mass destruction. The Bush administration was interpreting intelligence in light of its goal of deposing Saddam Hussein and establishing an Arab democracy in Iraq—unilaterally if necessary.[59]

Most of America's allies from the Persian Gulf War, with the exception of Prime Minister Tony Blair of Great Britain, opposed the idea of a preemptive strike on Iraq. There was negligible evidence that Iraq supported al-Qaeda, in part because its radical Muslim political philosophy and Saddam Hussein's secular state viewed each other as enemies.[60] In fact there was no connection between Iraq and 9/11. No one thought that Iraq had a nuclear weapon or missiles capable of striking the United States, and there was little convincing evidence that Saddam was developing a nuclear weapon. Saddam Hussein was an oppressive dictator who wished to exercise hegemony in the region, but why wouldn't he be deterred from using weapons of mass destruction by the threat of his own destruction? Indeed wouldn't an attack aimed at his demise encourage him to use any chemical and biological weapons he might have? While a modern democracy in Iraq might be a good idea, bringing it about would be a difficult task, probably requiring a long occupation, as President Bush Sr. had warned after the Gulf War.[61] France, Russia, Germany, and others thought it best to work through the UN Security Council to disarm Iraq through continuing weapons inspections, which were regularly reporting no evidence of a nuclear weapons program or of biological and chemical weapons in Iraq. The Bush administration meanwhile, in the prelude to the November 2002 congressional elections, procured authorization from Congress to attack Iraq if the president decided it was necessary.

President Bush repeated the administration's concerns about Iraq in his January 2003 State of the Union speech, and those charges were reinforced by Secretary of State Colin Powell's now infamous (because it was embarrassingly false and misleading) February 5 speech to the United Nations on Iraq. On March 17, the United States and Great Britain failed to secure a UN resolution authorizing force against Iraq; President Bush nevertheless gave Saddam Hussein forty-eight hours to surrender. On March 20, the United States and Great Britain began the war against Iraq, with airstrikes codenamed "Shock and Awe" that cleared the way for the ground invasion that followed.[62]

By April 9, the Iraqi regime had crumbled, an event symbolized by Iraqi civilians and US troops pulling down the statue of Saddam Hussein in Baghdad's Firdos Square. On May 1, President Bush dramatically flew to the aircraft carrier the USS *Abraham Lincoln*, and prematurely declared "Mission Accomplished," and the end of major combat operations. On May 23, L. Paul Bremer III, the US head of the Coalition Provisional Authority in Iraq, having already purged Saddam's Baathist Party from the government of Iraq, disbanded the Iraqi army and intelligence service. These hundreds of thousands of armed and now unemployed soldiers and government officials would soon coalesce into an organized and armed resistance that would extend the war in Iraq for six more years. On December 14, 2003, Saddam Hussein was captured in a hole near his boyhood home in Tikrit. He was tried, convicted, and executed by hanging on December 30, 2006.[63]

In January 2004, the Bush administration, after an extensive search in Iraq for biological and chemical weapons and for evidence of a nuclear weapons program, admitted that its prewar claims about weapons of mass destruction in Iraq were mistaken. In July of that year, a US bipartisan commission that investigated the 9/11 attacks concluded that there was no collaboration between the Iraqi regime and al-Qaeda and thus no connection between Iraq and the 9/11 terrorist attacks.[64]

In late April of 2004 photographs were released that revealed US soldiers torturing Iraqi captives at Abu Ghraib prison twenty miles west of Baghdad, a site where Saddam Hussein, the so-called butcher of Baghdad, imprisoned, tortured, and slaughtered his perceived political opponents. Torture is universally recognized as immoral, and it is prohibited in US and international law. Thus, the Bush administration added unjust conduct to its equivocal justification for this war.[65]

Saddam Hussein was guilty of crimes against humanity. However, would Americans and their elected representatives have supported a humanitarian intervention to depose Saddam Hussein if that had been the sole justification of this preemptive invasion?

In the fall of 2005, Iraq held a referendum to approve a constitution, then elected a parliament with a Shiite majority that eventually named Nouri al-Maliki prime minister, a politician with close ties to Shiite majority Iran. Despite the appearance of these shoots of democracy, sectarian violence between Sunni and Shiite Muslims in Iraq was also escalating.

In January of 2007, with the situation deteriorating into a civil war, President Bush announced a "surge" of an additional 20,000 American troops into Iraq to train Iraqi forces and fight beside them, raising troop levels to 168,000. Bush also appointed General David Petraeus, a counterinsurgency expert, to command coalition troops in Iraq, and Petraeus implemented a classical counterinsurgency strategy. At the same time, Sunni tribesmen in Anbar Province in western Iraq experienced an "Awakening" that led them to stop fighting against US troops and instead align themselves with US troops to counter other militants, particularly those who had affiliated with al-Qaeda. Also the Shiite cleric Muqtada al-Sadr, whose Mahdi army had been especially effective in the battle against Sunnis, US troops, and the Iraqi army, decided to observe a voluntary cease fire. As a result of the confluence of these four factors, the violence in Iraq subsided enough for President Bush to withdraw some US troops by the end of 2007.

In November 2008, the Iraqi Parliament approved a United States–Iraqi timetable for the gradual withdrawal of US troops by December 31, 2011. In February 2009, newly inaugurated president Barack Obama announced that all US combat troops would be withdrawn by August 31, 2010, and remaining troops would exit Iraq by the end of 2011. These deadlines were met.

During the eight years of the war in Iraq (2003–2011), over a million US troops participated and nearly 4,500 of them died there. Perhaps 500,000 Iraqis were killed. The financial cost of the war is estimated to be in excess of $3 trillion.[66]

The Arab Spring

On December 17, 2010, Mohamed Bouazizi, a Tunisian fruit vendor, set himself on fire to protest government harassment and corruption. His action sparked escalating street protests, at first calling for economic reforms, then for the resignation of Zine el-Abidine Ben Ali, Tunisia's autocratic president who had ruled for twenty-three years. By the end of January 2011 antigovernment protests had spread to several countries in the Middle East, and within a year, long-standing dictatorships in Tunisia (Ben Ali, 1987–2011), Egypt (Hosni Mubarak, 1981–2011), Libya (Muammar al-Qaddafi, 1969–2011), and Yemen (Ali Abdullah Saleh, 1978–2012) had been toppled.

Then this hopeful spring descended into a bleak winter of chaos, anarchy, and violence.[67] A new military dictator, Abdel Fattah al-Sisi, gained power in Egypt, after there was a "second revolution" against Mohammad Morsi of the Islamist Muslim Brotherhood, who became autocratic and uncompromising within a year of barely winning the first presidential election after the Arab Spring protests. Sisi slaughtered a thousand Islamists and imprisoned both Islamists and many of the youthful secular protesters from Tahir Square. Egypt has come full circle back to where it began in 2011, with a brutal dictator supported by military aid from the United States.[68]

In Libya, Qaddafi learned from the results of Arab Spring protests in Tunisia and Egypt and ordered troops to meet the peaceful protesters with truncheons and bullets. The rebels also took up arms, but were no match for Qaddafi's army. Then NATO decided to intervene under the United Nation's "Responsibility to Protect" protocol to prevent crimes against humanity, with air support for the rebels, using American and French planes. The revolutionary forces finally captured and mercilessly killed Qaddafi on October 20, 2011. By the spring of 2012, Libya still had no government and no government services, and in 2018 continued to languish. Libya is not so much a failed state as a country that was never a state, thanks to colonialism and the Qaddafi dictatorship.[69]

There was already a protest camp set up in Change Square, in Sanaa, the capital of united Yemen, organized in part by Tawakkol Karman (who would share the 2011 Nobel Peace Prize), well before the breakout of the Arab Spring. Yemen is the Arab world's poorest country, and these protests were fueled by the hunger, sickness, illiteracy, and hardship of everyday life and by the desire for recognition of human rights and the rule of law of a modern state.[70] In January 2011, the protest camp swelled into a mini-city fed by the hope generated by the Arab Spring, and the focus of the protest became regime change. President Ali Abdullah Saleh responded to the nonviolent protestors with snipers, who killed fifty-two and wounded hundreds. Although Saleh formally resigned in November 2011, the conflict degenerated into armed sectarian strife between the Houthi in the north, who are Shia and supported by Iran, and Sunni Islamists in the more developed south, supported by Saudi Arabia and the UAE. The United States gives the Saudis logistical and intelligence support in this civil war by proxy.[71] The fierce fighting and bombing, and a cholera epidemic, have created a shameful humanitarian crisis. Nearly 10,000 people have been killed, over half of them civilians, and another 50,000 injured. Twenty-two million people, or 75 percent of the population, are in need of humanitarian assistance, and over eight million face starvation.[72]

Arab Spring demonstrations began in Syria on March 15, 2011, and Bashar al-Assad, Syria's brutal dictator, gradually responded to the street protests with arrests and violence. By July, defectors from the military formed the Free Syrian Army (FSA) and rebelled against the regime, beginning a complex civil war that continued with no end in sight in 2018.[73]

Hafez al-Assad became president of Syria through a coup in 1971, and his son, Bashar, succeeded him upon his death in 2000. Syria is perhaps the most religiously and ethnically diverse country in the Arab world. About 70 percent of the population are Sunni Muslim Arabs, and another 10 percent are Kurds, who are also Sunnis. The Assad family are Alawites or Alawi, who comprise only about 12 percent of the population. Syria's other minority religious groups—Christians (10%), Druze (3%), Turkomen, and Ismailis—tended to support the Assad regimes. Sunni Muslims and the Alawites, an eclectic, Shia-related sect, have nurtured a hatred for each other since the fourteenth century. Assad cleverly placed his Alawite kinsmen in key positions in his expanding security state.[74]

The repression of the Assad regimes sparked a desire for democracy and human rights. For example, in 1982, Hafez Assad commanded his army to put down a rebellion by the Islamist Muslim Brotherhood in the city of Hama. Over 20,000 Syrians were massacred, and sections of Hama were flattened. The Assad regimes imprisoned and tortured Islamists and anyone who opposed their rule. Prior to the rebellion, Alawi and moderate Sunni lived together compatibly. Once the Arab Spring protests put Bashar Assad's regime in question, however, sectarian animosity between Sunni Arabs and the Alawi resurfaced.[75]

The Syrian forces opposing the Assad regime were mostly Sunni Muslims of various allegiances and agendas. In the region, Sunni-majority governments, including Turkey, Saudi Arabia, and Qatar, have assisted the rebels, while Shiite-majority Iran and Lebanon's Hezbollah have supported Bashar Assad. Russia directly intervened in the conflict on behalf of the Assad regime beginning in 2015 with air support, but not ground troops. Early on, the United States called for Bashar Assad to step down, and the Obama administration ineffectively armed and trained some opposition Syrian forces, reputedly spending $500 million to train about sixty fighters. The United States has not, however, been directly involved in the struggle to remove Bashar Assad from power.[76]

The Islamic State (or the Islamic State of Iraq and Syria [ISIS]), or the Islamic State of Iraq and the Levant (ISIL, or Da'esh) has its roots in al-Qaeda in Iraq (AQI), established by Abu Musab al-Zarqawi in 2004, in response to the US-led invasion of Iraq and the fall of Saddam Hussein's regime. Following a radical Islamic ideology, AQI played a role in the anti-US insurrection, and in the sectarian conflict between Iraq's Sunni minority and the ruling Shiite majority. In October 2006, after Zarqawi was killed in a US airstrike, AQI, under the new leadership of Abu Omar al-Baghdadi, changed its name to Islamic State in Iraq, and in 2013 clearly split with al-Qaeda, and became engaged in the civil war in Syria. Bashar Assad's alliance with Iran and Hezbollah played into the Islamic State's sectarian narrative of conflict between Sunni and Shia (and all other religious groups).

In 2014, the Islamic State established its "capital" in Raqqa and took control of the oil-rich city of Deir Az Zor in Syria. Then ISIS invaded Iraq, taking Falluja and Mosul, Iraq's second largest city. Tens of thousands of US-trained Iraqi security forces fled from an attack by about 1,500 lightly armed Islamic State fighters, leaving their sophisticated US weapons and equipment to be gathered up by the Islamic State militia. By January 2015, ISIS controlled territory in eastern Syria and western Iraq comparable to the size of Great Britain, and had an annual income of $1.9 billion, apparently realizing its vision of an Islamic caliphate.[77]

The violence and brutality of the Islamic State was medieval. For example, ISIS released videos of beheading foreign journalists, aid workers, and tourists, and of burning a Jordanian military pilot alive. They carried out a mass execution of five thousand Yazidi in Sinjar, Iraq, and used Yazidi girls and women as sex slaves.[78] They sought to eradicate Christians, Kurds (the Yazidi can be described as the original Kurds), and Shiite Muslims. ISIS sponsored and supported suicide bombings and terrorist attacks all over the world, including Paris, London, New York, and Berlin. They destroyed the ancient Roman ruins in Palmyra, Syria, and other irreplaceable cultural sites.[79]

The rise of the Islamic State further complicated the Syrian civil war. Since the Islamic State was opposed to every other group (including Assad and the Syrian government; Iran, Hezbollah, and Iraqi Shiites; the Kurds; the United States and the West) all of these enemies targeted the Islamic State. In particular the United States, which was conflicted about the Syrian civil war, quickly committed to defeating the Islamic State. The United States supplied air support and weapons for the ground troops of the peshmerga (the well-trained fighting force of the Kurds), the regrouped Iraqi army, and Iranian (Shiite) troops. The United States conducted over 13,300 airstrikes in Iraq and 11,200 in Syria. Although Russia intervened in Syria primarily in support of the Assad regime, it is also flew sorties targeting the Islamic State. Taking back the territory captured by the Islamic State was a grueling three-year slog, involving street-by-street fighting, significant casualties, displaced populations, and massive destruction in cities and towns. Mosul, Falluja, and eastern Iraq, then Deir Az Zor, Raqqa, Manbij, and western Syria were rid of the Islamic State by the end of 2017.[80] ISIS no longer controlled a "state," or could claim to have started a caliphate, but the traditional idea of an Islamic state or the dream of a Muslim homeland had been revitalized and exerted a fresh appeal, especially among alienated young Muslims.[81]

Turkey also fought against the Islamic State along its border with Syria. In early 2018, with ISIS in tatters, Turkey sent troops into northwestern Syria to dislodge Syrian Kurds from the area around the city of Afrin. Turkey has long outlawed the Kurdistan Workers' Party (the PKK), a separatist group considered terrorists by the West. The United States, however, has armed a Syrian Kurdish militia, the People's Protection Units (YPG), who comprise the backbone of the multi-ethnic Syrian Democratic Forces (SDF), and relied on them in the fight against ISIS in Syria. Nearby, US special operations troops are garrisoned outside of Manbij. This increased the tension between Turkey and the United States, both members of NATO. Since the Syrian Kurds rushed their troops to resist the onslaught by Turkey, it also stymied the efforts to mop up the Islamic State.[82]

The Kurds have lived in the Caucasus Mountains for some four thousand years. The Kurds are clearly a nation without a state: "The Kurd's identity is based on a number of shared traits: a common homeland and culture, a myth of common origin, a shared faith in Islam, similar languages, and a history of bitter conflict with outsiders."[83] Kurds are a majority or a significant minority in western Turkey, northeastern Iran, northern Iraq (an area with significant oil resources), and northern Syria. Kurdistan, their potential homeland, would be divided among these four states plus a sliver of Armenia. The Kurds have had the misfortune of living at a major intersection or crossroads: of two empires—the Ottoman and the Persian; of three significant peoples—Turks to the northwest, Persians (Iranians) to the east, and Arabs to the south; and of four aggressive nationalisms—Turkish, Syrian, Iraqi, and Iranian.[84] The riptides of these rivalries have resulted in the violent repression of the Kurds and have thwarted their desire for recognition as a nation-state.

The Shiite Muslims who took over Iran in 1979 slaughtered about 50,000 of the Sunni Muslim Kurds.[85] In 1988 Saddam Hussein slaughtered about 200,000 Iraqi Kurds because they had supported Iran in the Iraq–Iran war. The Iraqi army dropped poison gas on the town of Halabja and killed every man, woman, and child (5,000 people).[86] Yet perhaps the worst oppression of the Kurds has occurred in Turkey, where Kurds comprise 23 percent of the population and are a majority in the eastern section. Kurds in Turkey have been forcibly dispersed and brutally repressed, their language has been banned, and they have been slaughtered by the tens of thousands. A 1991 antiterrorism law allowed the imprisonment of anyone speaking on behalf of Kurdish rights.[87] Turkey is adamantly opposed to Kurdish autonomy, as are all five of the countries where Kurds are present.

The tragic history of the Kurds' "bitter conflict with outsiders" helps us to understand why Turkey sent troops into northern Syria even at the risk of a direct military conflict with its ostensible ally, the United States. The tragedy of the Kurds, however, is not only its conflict with outsiders, but the internal conflict among Kurdish clans. In northern Iraq, for example, the Kurdistan Regional Government (KRG), which has considerable autonomy, has been divided by two feuding camps, the Kurdistan Democratic Party (KDP) and the Patriotic Union of Kurdistan (PUK). This schism degenerated into civil war in 1997. This conflict is actually tribal more than political. The KDP is composed of the tribal allies of the Barzanis, who dominate the northern area and wear red-and-white scarves; and the PUK is the Talabani clan, who control the southern area and wear black-and-white scarves. This enduring tribal conflict hampered the response of the peshmerga in the first days of the ISIS advance into the Kurdish area of Iraq, nearly allowing the capture of the KRG capital, Erbil.[88] This is hardly the only tribal conflict among the Kurds in the five countries that would comprise Kurdistan. The Kurds can be their own worst enemy.

The United States has used, then betrayed, the Kurds in the past. In 1975 the CIA supplied weapons for the Kurds to conduct a brutal guerrilla war against Saddam Hussein's regime, while the United States supported Iran in a proxy war against Iraq. When Iraq and Iran abruptly concluded a peace treaty, the United States immediately cut off aid to the Kurds, leaving them exposed in the face of an all-out Iraqi offensive.[89] The Kurdish peshmerga have been key in the defeat of the Islamic State in both Iraq and Syria. The United States joined the chorus of opposition to an Iraqi Kurd referendum on independence for the KRG held on September 25, 2017, which was supported by 92 percent of the Kurds.[90] Iraq punished the KRG for holding the referendum, but eased the restrictions after about six months.[91]

Israel has also been marginally involved in the Syrian civil war. Israel's main concerns are Bashar Assad's alliances with Iran and Hezbollah, both of which have been instrumental in Assad's survival. Because Israel is concerned that Iran will supply Hezbollah, which is based in southern Lebanon, with even more sophisticated weapons, it has conducted air strikes against Hezbollah supply lines and Iranian military sites in Syria. Israel has also targeted ISIS in southern Syria, and supplied arms and support to some facets of the Free Syrian Army rebels. Israel has also facilitated humanitarian aid to wounded Syrians, at times taking them to hospitals in Israel.[92]

The Syrian civil war is perhaps the most discouraging outcome of the 2011 Arab Spring. Like most conflicts in the Middle East it is bewilderingly complex with the potential to generate momentous global conflicts. By 2018, over 465,000 Syrians had been killed, and a million had been injured. Atrocities have been committed by all sides, but the Syrian army, abetted by its pro-Assad allies, bore the brunt of responsibility for indiscriminate warfare with its use of chemical weapons, barrel bombs, and apparent lack of concern for safeguarding civilians. Over twelve million people, about half of the prewar population, have been displaced from their homes, with five million of those becoming refugees.[93] Russia's efforts toward a political settlement of the conflict have been undermined by Bashar Assad's belief that he can win the war.[94]

The Arab Spring began with protests in Tunisia, and Zine el-Abidine Ben Ali, Tunisia's autocratic president, was the first dictator to resign and flee. Because two leaders from political parties opposed to one another, Rached Ghannouchi of the Islamist Ennahda and Beji Caid Essebsi cofounder of the Nidaa Tounes, an anti-Islamist political party, met, developed a relationship, and put the good of the country first, Tunisia has the best chance of becoming a functioning democracy of all the countries affected by the Arab Spring.[95]

Since the army in Tunisia had not been involved in politics, a civilian government emerged which held a fair election for Parliament in October 2011. The moderate Islamist Ennahda party received 41 percent of the vote and formed a government. Unfortunately, Ennahda did not do enough to control the hardline Islamists who were part of its base, and these extremists assassinated two leftist politicians in summer 2013. This led to demonstrations in Tunis, the capital, marked by tension between secularists and Islamists. It looked like Tunisia was following a script similar to Egypt or might be on the brink of a civil war. Rached Ghannouchi, the cofounder and leader of Ennahda, became convinced that the only way to avoid civil war was for Ennahda to resign from power and have new elections, which Ennahda would surely lose. Not surprisingly, his fellow Islamists, having endured decades of persecution and convinced of the rightness of their cause, would find surrendering legitimately attained power to be madness.

Ghannouchi is an Islamist, but one who has rejected the apocalyptic certainty of many of his fellow Islamists and escaped the black or white perspective of a Morsi. He decided to reach out to Begi Caid Essebsi, at age eighty-six Tunisia's elder statesman and among Tunisia's elite, in search of a partner to seek reconciliation for the good of the country. The two met secretly in Paris and agreed to collaborate for the good of the country. When a joint press release was made three days later, both men endured the angry criticism of their respective parties.

Tunisia's business and professional elite began holding "a national dialogue," led by four groups representing labor, business, human rights activists, and the legal profession, which became known as the Quartet. In early October 2013, Ghannouchi was pressured into signing a "road map" by the

Quartet that included Ennahda relinquishing power to a caretaker authority. He was able to convince his party's angry council that signing the road map was necessary to save Tunisia from civil war, that this was a time when the country's good was more important than the party's interests.

The national dialogue facilitated by the Quartet resulted in the Parliament overwhelmingly passing a new constitution in January 2014. (The Quartet was awarded the Nobel Peace Prize in 2015.) The Nidaa Tounes party won a plurality in the 2014 parliamentary elections, with Ennahda coming in second, and Essebsi was elected president in December 2014 for a five-year term.

Civil war was averted, but Tunisia's economy has struggled, which began to undermine its embrace of democracy.[96] Nevertheless, if Tunisia is fortunate enough to have enlightened leadership in the mold of Essebsi and Ghannouci in its future, it may well remain the only success story in terms of democracy and human rights of the Arab Spring.

Thus, the Arab Spring, which began with so much hope, resulted in a change of dictators in Egypt, a failed state in Libya, two devastating civil wars in Syria and Yemen, the rise and fall of the Islamic State, and one fledgling democracy in Tunisia. There were popular protests in some of the monarchies in the region, such as Bahrain and Jordan, but they were either put down or put off, with no change in the status quo. The Middle East remains a cauldron of ethnic, religious, and territorial conflict.

Europe

Northern Ireland

Great Britain ruled Ireland harshly for about eight hundred years (1169–1921). When the Irish Free State, which evolved into the Republic of Ireland, was established in 1921, six of the nine counties of Ulster, those counties where there was a Protestant majority, were partitioned off into Northern Ireland, and remained part of the United Kingdom.[97]

The basic division in Northern Ireland is the native people versus the colonial settlers. "Politically, the natives were nationalists and the settlers unionists; socially, the nationalists were deprived and the unionists privileged; and religiously, the deprived were Catholic and the privileged Protestant."[98] This has always been a conflict about power and privilege, participation and justice. The antagonists happened to be Protestant and Catholic, and thus religion exacerbates the conflict, but it is not primarily a sectarian conflict.

The Protestants in Northern Ireland are descendants of the seventeenth-century colonial settlers. They are loyal (Loyalist) to the union (Unionist) between Northern Ireland and Great Britain. They identify themselves as citizens of Ulster (Ulstermen), the northern region of Ireland. On July 12, the Orange Order (Orangemen) celebrates the victory of William of Orange at the Battle of the Boyne (1690) with marches and bonfires in its neighborhoods and in those of Catholic nationalists as well.[99] The loyalists fly the Union Jack flag of Great Britain and the Red Hand flag of Ulster. Most attend the Church of Ireland (Anglican) or are Presbyterian. About 60 percent (950,000) of Northern Ireland's 1.6 million people are Protestant settlers. Over the years, the Unionist majority developed a system of governance that kept it in a politically and economically superior position.

The Nationalist minority (650,000) in Northern Ireland identifies with the Republic of Ireland and with the Roman Catholic Church. They are Irish and think that Northern Ireland should be reunited with the Republic of Ireland. The majority of them are Nationalist, that is, they favor a legal and constitutional approach to unification. Republicans share the same goal but think that force is necessary to accomplish unification.[100]

The violence of the "troubles" was precipitated by a nonviolent civil rights movement in 1969. In the mid-1960s, Nationalists, inspired by the wave of civil rights agitation in the United States and elsewhere, decided to temporarily table the goal of unification with Ireland in favor of a civil rights movement. They contended that since Northern Ireland belonged to the United Kingdom, they were entitled to their rights as British citizens. These rights included a right for all adults to vote, fair representation in government, legislation barring discrimination in jobs and housing, and freedom from harassment by the police and militia. Nationalist demonstrations for civil rights were met by violent resistance on the part of the Royal Ulster Constabulary (RUC = the police force) and the Unionists, forcing Britain to send in troops to maintain order.[101] The situation quickly degenerated into a cycle of violence between the Irish Republican Army (IRA) and Unionist paramilitary groups, the RUC, and the British army.

After a series of ceasefires and renewed violence that began in 1994, all-party talks mediated by US senator George Mitchell, resulted in a Northern Ireland peace agreement on Good Friday, April 10, 1998, that was then accepted by a referendum. The agreement established a Northern Ireland Assembly that shared power among the Unionist and Nationalist parties. Britain, however, had to suspend the assembly several times rather than have it disintegrate. In March 2007, Ian Paisley's Democratic Unionist party won the assembly elections and eventually yielded to pressure to share power with Sinn Fein, the IRA's political arm, with Paisley serving as first minister and Martin McGuinness as deputy minister.[102]

By the time of the Good Friday Agreement, more than 3,500 people had been killed in the conflict, half of them civilians, and over 35,500 people had been wounded in over 33,350 shootings and 9,760 bombings. Nearly 2 percent of the population of Northern Ireland, roughly half Nationalists and half Unionists, were killed or injured. The equivalent ratio of victims to population in Great Britain in the same period would have meant 100,000 people would have died in political violence, and in the United States there would have been 500,000 fatalities.[103] There is now a new generation of leaders in Northern Ireland, and, although political cooperation is a struggle and peace remains precarious there, no one wants to return to the violence of the past.[104]

Brexit

On June 23, 2016, Great Britain unexpectedly voted to leave the European Union (EU) by a 52 to 48 percent vote. The dynamics involved in Brexit, as it is called, illustrate a trend toward nationalism in Europe and, to a certain extent, globally.[105]

The Brexit vote happened when Britain's Prime Minister (PM) David Cameron, in order to appease an anti-EU faction in his own party, promised a referendum on the EU if the Tories won the election in 2015, and they did. The vote in favor of Brexit was a victory for the more right-wing anti-EU Tory faction, and Cameron's position became untenable. He tendered his resignation the morning after the referendum vote. More quickly than expected, Theresa May, the home secretary, emerged to succeed him on July 13, 2016.

The "Remain" campaign, led by PM David Cameron and most of his cabinet, warned that there would be dire economic consequences for Britain if it left the EU (labeled "Project Fear" by the "Leave" campaign), which unfortunately is becoming true. The Remain campaign, however, never made a positive case for staying in the EU based on the benefits of European integration and international cooperation in an interdependent world. The European Union contributes significantly to peace and prosperity on the site of two world wars in the twentieth century.

Why did people vote to leave the EU? The Leave campaign, led by Boris Johnson, a former mayor of London and now a Tory member of Parliament (MP); Michael Gove, a Tory MP; and Nigel Farage, the leader of the UK Independence Party (UKIP), made three principal arguments: take back control of the country from an unelected bureaucracy centered in Brussels, spend the country's financial contribution to the EU on the UK ("Spend Britain's £350 million weekly contribution to the EU on the National Health Service" was painted on the Leave campaign bus), and take control of immigration from the EU to Britain. (Membership in the EU means that any citizen of an EU country can immigrate to any other EU country and live there with many of the benefits of a citizen. Two million Brits have immigrated to other European countries, and about three million Europeans, many from Eastern European countries, were living and working in the UK.)

Those who voted to leave the EU tended to be white, working class or poor, older, less educated, rural, and northern. Many of these people have seen their prospects diminish in a global economy and as a result of the austerity measures imposed by the Tories in response to the 2008 recession.[106] Immigrants have become scapegoats for their very real struggles with stagnant wages and reduced government services, even though many of them live in areas where there are few immigrants. In fact, immigration almost universally improves a nation's economy. The Remain campaign did not try to argue in favor of immigration, probably because they were aware that identity will trump economics and facts can't compete with feelings, but the case is there to be made. Thus, stopping the flow of immigrants became a key argument for the Leave campaign. There was an element of xenophobia in the Leave campaign. Indeed this ultranationalist or populist perspective is a trend in Europe and globally. Before exploring this wider implication of Brexit, however, let us look at some of the implications and consequences of Brexit for Britain and Europe.

Britain will remain a member of the North Atlantic Treaty Organization (NATO). Brexit, however, throws the integration of Europe that has been developing since World War II into question. There is fear that others in the now twenty-seven-member European Union might exit.

The Brexit vote may challenge the fragile unity of the United Kingdom. Scotland voted 62 percent to remain, and Northern Ireland voted 56 percent to remain, but there has been no move toward an independence referendum in either place. The border between Northern Ireland and the Republic of Ireland is, however, a significant stumbling block for Brexit. Currently there is no passport control or other inspection; people and goods cross the border at will. Tourists might not even know that a border has been crossed until they stop to purchase something (the two nations use different currencies). Establishing border controls once Northern Ireland is no longer in the EU has significant political, economic, and cultural ramifications.[107]

Brexit will be an economic challenge for Britain. In the wake of the vote to leave, the British pound fell to a thirty-year low, sending oil and food prices up, and hurting Britain's poor straightaway. London has been a global and European financial center, but businesses and banks are relocating out of fear of tariffs and import/export obstacles, and Britain is losing thousands of well-paid jobs. Brexit has also stimulated a "Brexodus" of Europeans working in Britain because of uncertainty about their status. This has caused a crisis in the National Health Service, factories, and farms which cannot find workers.[108] EU-supported building projects (many of them in areas that voted heavily to leave) have been suspended, consumer spending plunged, and housing values have fallen. Britain's recovery from the 2008 recession had been weak, and Brexit will not help.

On March 29, 2017, Mrs. May formally began the two-year process of withdrawing the UK from the EU. The Brexit negotiations opened on June 19, 2017, with PM May and the Tories in a weaker position for the negotiations, having lost their majority in the House of Commons in a snap June election called by Mrs. May. In early December, Britain agreed to pay the EU about 39 billion pounds ($52 billion) for its outstanding financial commitments, a hefty sum, but less than it might have been.[109] A major issue is negotiating trade arrangements between the UK and the EU.[110]

Regarding trade, a "hard Brexit" means a clean economic break between Britain and the EU. This position prioritizes controlling immigration from Europe over economic concerns. This would mean that Britain would have to negotiate a trade agreement with the EU, and with every other country in the world, since it would no longer be included in the EU's trade agreements. This seems to be the basic position of Mrs. May's Conservative government, although they want an exception granted by the EU regarding the Northern Ireland border. This would also be the effect of reaching no deal with the EU by the March 29, 2019, deadline.[111]

"Soft Brexit" means pursuing one of two options that maintain an economic relationship with the EU. The first is remaining in the EU Customs Union, which establishes a free trade area for goods in Europe and negotiates a common tariff on goods coming from outside Europe. This would ease the border concerns regarding Northern Ireland, but would not allow Britain to enter into trade agreements with other countries. It includes only the trade of goods (about 20 percent of the economy) and does not apply to financial and other services, which account for about 80 percent of Britain's economy. The second option is to retain membership in the European Single (or Common) Market, which guarantees the free movement of goods, capital, services, and labor. This would prioritize economic integration over the issue of immigration in that Britain would still be committed to the free movement of people, to the jurisdiction of the European Court of Justice, and to the EU's trade rules. Over 50 percent of voters opted for parties, including Labour, that argued for a form of soft Brexit in the June 2017 election. Many Conservatives also favor a form of soft Brexit, and the business sector leans toward staying in the European Single Market.

Theresa May, whose hold on the office of prime minister is tenuous, faces a conundrum in devising a strategy for Brexit negotiations. The referendum and the election highlight the divisions in British society between young and old, urban and rural, south and north, digital and industrial, cosmopolitan and nationalistic, Scottish and English. No matter which Brexit path she chooses, she will alienate a large part of the nation and many in her own party. Besides dealing with Brexit, both she and her European counterparts will have to deal with a destabilizing Russia, a disruptive America, a surge of migrants and refugees, rising seas and heat waves, and an uncertain economy. Britain and Europe face challenging times.

European and Global Ultranationalism and Populism
Now to return to the idea that Brexit exemplifies an ultranationalist or populist trend in Europe and globally. Donald Trump, unlike most other politicians in

the United States, applauded Brexit in June 2016. Indeed, Mr. Trump appealed to those Americans who have much in common with Leave voters in Britain, including scapegoating immigrants for their problems and xenophobia. It is interesting that Bernie Sanders, the left-leaning Democratic presidential candidate (like the socialist leaning Labour leader Jeremy Corbyn in Britain) also appealed to Americans who have suffered from the inequity resulting from globalization and Republican small government policies. The difference is that Senator Sanders does not simplistically blame immigrants and foster bigotry. This brand of populism or ultranationalism that Mr. Trump tapped into ("Make America Great Again") has risen again in Europe and throughout the world.

Every year Freedom House publishes a comprehensive report on the state of freedom and democracy in the world. *Freedom in the World 2018* is subtitled *Democracy in Crisis*.[112] For the twelfth consecutive year, democracy and its core principles, such as human rights, free and fair elections, freedom of the press, rights of minorities, and the rule of law, experienced setbacks in many countries. Prior to 2006 the trend had been in the direction of greater democratization, but since then, 113 countries have seen a net decline in freedom and human rights, compared to sixty-two that have seen a net improvement. Beginning in 2017, the United States, under the leadership of President Trump, has retreated from its role as advocate for human rights and champion of democracy amid a decline in its own civil liberties.[113] Israel remains a genuine democracy, but Benjamin Netanyahu, in his fourth term as prime minister, is a friend, and perhaps mentor, of the new wave of right-wing, populist, autocratic leaders.[114]

President Vladimir Putin, who has ruled Russia since 2000 and was re-elected to another six-year term in March of 2018, serves as an exemplar for autocrats, especially in Europe, and as chief disrupter of democratic institutions. Putin has suppressed any political opposition and enriched himself and his friends with the practice of crony capitalism. He annexed Crimea from Ukraine in 2014. He has intervened in Syria's brutal civil war, giving air support to its dictator, Bashar al-Assad. He is accused of orchestrating assassinations of exiled former intelligence operatives in Britain. He has meddled in elections in the United States and Europe. His steadfast adherence to the principle of power and disdain for democracy has won him the admiration of fellow despots and would-be autocrats. "Vladimir Putin is a criminal president who poses a clear and present danger to democratic society."[115]

The xenophobic, populist surge that seemed to threaten Western Europe in 2017 crested with ultranationalist parties in parliaments, but not actually in government, except in Austria, where Sebastian Kurz served as chancellor, and in Italy.[116] Populists of various hues were in evidence in the complex results of Italy's election in early March 2018. While there was certainly a backlash against immigration, Italians seemed more angry and disheartened by the economic marginalization of certain regions, the persistence of corruption and organized crime, ineffective politicians, and long-term economic decline. Both the populist Five Star Movement and the right-wing League, the two parties with the most votes, are in the coalition government that was eventually formed.[117]

The four countries of Central Europe—Poland, Hungary, the Czech Republic, and Slovakia—however, all have populist leaders of varying stripes, who worry the leaders of the liberal democracies of Western Europe. Populism is difficult to define, and not necessarily negative, but what is troubling about the populists governing in Central Europe is their xenophobia, expressed through anti-immigration policies, especially aimed at Muslims, and their tendency toward authoritarianism, which undermines democratic institutions, civil liberties, human rights, and the rule of law. These characteristics can be seen all too clearly in the indirect rule of Polish leader Jarosław Kaczyński,[118] and Prime Minister Viktor Orban in Hungary.[119] Things are more unsettled and complex in the Czech Republic and Slovakia.[120] The anti-immigrant xenophobia that has gotten votes for these governing parties is not based in experience, in that the number of migrants and refugees coming in to these four Central European countries has been negligible. It has been shown that the actual experience of settling refugees generally increases tolerance, whereas a political rhetoric of fear has the opposite effect.[121]

The rise of ultranationalist, populist autocrats goes well beyond Europe. In China, the legislature formally amended the constitution to abolish term limits for the president in March 2018, allowing Xi Jinping, who had been president for only one five-year term to rule for life. Mr. Xi was also Communist Party chief and military commission chairman.[122]

China, the world's second largest economy, is a police state with little regard for human rights. It is increasing its influence through aid to developing countries, such as Cambodia, where Hun Sen, lord prime minister and supreme military commander, has ruled for thirty-three years. China is responsible for one-third of Cambodia's foreign investment and for military aid that can help Hun Sen tighten his grip on power.[123] President Xi's "One Belt, One Road" economic development initiative is linking Asia, Europe, and Africa by lending billions to countries there to develop transportation infrastructure (such as railroads, roads, ports, etc.) and other development projects. This creative initiative that includes an educational and cultural component is both impressive in its scale and troubling. While China may well be offering a new model of economic development, this project may also be a new form of colonial control.[124]

President Rodrigo Duterte of the Philippines has empowered the police to kill thousands of Filipinos without due process in an antidrug campaign. Duterte's rule is increasingly autocratic. Malaysians became so enraged by the corruption of Prime Minister Najib Razak, whose administration is reputed to have stolen $3.5 billion from a government fund, that for the first time since independence they voted out the governing party. They replaced Mr. Najib with a ninety-two-year-old former prime minister (1981–2003), Mahathir Mohamed, whose administration had itself been autocratic, but who now promised to clean up the corruption and enforce the rule of law.[125] In April 2017, Turkey's president Recep Tayyip Erdogan declared himself the winner of a referendum that gave him sweeping powers to make law by decree, abolished the office of prime minister and Turkey's parliamentary system, and loosened term limits on the president. In a close vote that took place in a government-created atmosphere of fear and intimidation, Turkey's democracy was effectively replaced by a dictatorship.[126] In Egypt, President Abdel Fattah al-Sisi, the recipient of generous US military aid, sidelined all his opponents, then drafted Moussa Moustapha Moussa, one of Sisi's most ardent supporters, to run so the March 2018 election would not be a one-horse race. President Trump has praised Putin, Xi, Duterte, Erdogan, and Sisi, and has raised no concern about their disdain for democracy and human rights. The United States, especially during the Cold War, has a sad history of selectively embracing (anti-Communist) despots.[127] The erosion of democracy and human rights and the rise of xenophobic and authoritarian populism are worrying trends.

Populism, that is, standing on the side of people who have been left behind or exploited by a hi-tech, globalized economy can be a progressive and patriotic (and successful) political position. Populism need not be xenophobic nor authoritarian. There is an "inclusive populism" that is based on policies and programs aimed at economic justice, rather than a rhetoric of fear and exclusion. This would be a way to "Make America (and the world) Great Again" that is consistent with the founding principles and values of the United States and of Catholic social teaching, such as the dignity of work and of workers, welcoming the stranger, human rights and civil liberties, and economic justice and equity.[128]

In May 2018, a group of twenty-three church leaders, academics, and progressives of faith issued a kind of epistle to the church (and society) titled "Reclaiming Jesus: A Confession of Faith in a Time of Crisis" that was formulated at a retreat on Ash Wednesday. "What we believe leads us to what we must reject," the statement says, laying out six core beliefs and the conclusions that follow. Three of propositions are especially pertinent to the rise of populist, xenophobic, and autocratic politicians. The third proposition says, "We strongly deplore the growing attacks on immigrants and refugees, who are being made into cultural and political targets, and we need to remind our churches that God makes the treatment of the 'strangers' among us a test of faith (Lev 19:33–34)." Proposition five states, "We believe that Christ's way of leadership is servanthood, not domination. . . . Therefore we reject any moves toward autocratic political leadership and authoritarian rule." These threaten democracy and the common good and must be resisted. Finally, in proposition six, the signers argue that the universality of our churches leads us to "reject xenophobic or ethnic nationalism that places one nation over others as a political goal." The signers are a racially diverse and ecumenical group of American Christians, including presiding bishop and primate of the Episcopal Church Michael B. Curry, scripture scholar Walter Brueggemann, spiritual writer Fr. Richard Rohr, Sojourners founder Rev. Jim Wallis (who was a principal drafter of the document), and Rev. Dr. Sharon Watkins, director of the National Council of Churches' Truth and Racial Justice Initiative. This statement reminds Christians of the values we hold and of their implications in our time.[129]

Ukraine and Crimea

In 1991 Ukraine became independent again a year after the Soviet Union collapsed. Crimea, a peninsula jutting into the Black Sea, was first seized by the Russian Empire in 1783 during the rule of Catherine the Great. It was given as a "gift" by Soviet leader Nikita Khrushchev to Ukraine (then part of the USSR) in 1954. The Crimean port of Sevastopol was the base for the Soviet Black Sea naval fleet, from which it had access to the Mediterranean Sea. When Ukraine became independent, the Black Sea naval fleet was divided between Russia and Ukraine.[130]

In 2010, pro-Russian Victor Yanukovych succeeded pro-Western Victor Yushchenko as president of Ukraine. In November of 2013, President Yanukovych rejected a far-reaching accord with the European Union in favor of stronger ties to Russia. His decision frustrated the aspirations of millions of Ukrainians for integration with Europe, and protestors occupied Independence Square, known as Maidan, in central Kiev for months. The peaceful protests eventually became violent, and in the forty-eight hours between February 18 and 20, 2014, eighty-eight people were killed, some by police snipers. The next day, President Yanukovych fled, and later the Parliament voted to remove him from power.

President Putin took this opportunity to send Russian security forces (called "little green men" because of their unlabeled green uniforms) to occupy Crimea and annex it back into Russia. On March 16, a referendum was held, and 97 percent of Crimean voters backed joining Russia. The West condemned this as a sham and imposed economic sanctions on Russia. Ukraine claimed that its territorial sovereignty had been illegally violated by Russia. Although the Crimea has come under the influence of many countries in the region, there is a history of Russian control, and 58 percent of the population is Russian. Moscow aggressively proceeded with the "Russification" of Crimea— flying the Russian flag, using the Russian ruble as the currency, arranging a dozen flights from Moscow without border checks, and making investments in Crimea. A key question will be the treatment of minorities in Crimea, the Ukrainians who are 24 percent of the population, and especially the Tatars, an ethnic Turkic group who have long lived in Crimea but who were expelled by Stalin for allegedly supporting the Nazis and returned after the breakup of the Soviet Union in numbers large enough to constitute 12 percent of the population. A bad sign with regard to human rights is that in 2015 Russia made it a crime to question its claim on Crimea.

Although the annexation of Crimea was bloodless, pro-Russian rebels have fought a simmering war against the Ukrainian army in eastern Ukraine, where nearly 40 percent of the population is ethnic Russian. Since April 2014, over 10,000 people have been killed in eastern Ukraine and twice that many wounded, at least 20 percent of whom have been civilians. Over a million others have been displaced from their homes.[131]

Asia

Kashmir

One of the most dangerous places in the landscape of global conflict is the Indian state commonly called Kashmir (technically Jammu and Kashmir). When India and Pakistan were partitioned in 1947 at the end of British colonial rule, the Hindu ruler of Muslim-majority (65 percent) Kashmir chose to join India. India and Pakistan immediately went to war over Kashmir, and Pakistan gained control of part of the territory. This ethnic and territorial dispute has continued ever since, with India and Pakistan fighting major wars over Kashmir in 1947 and 1965, and a more limited war in 1999. India has more than 250,000 troops stationed in the region, and at least 47,000 people had been killed in the conflict. It is especially dangerous because both India and Pakistan possess nuclear weapons and the missiles to deliver them, and both have threatened to do so if attacked.[132]

Kashmir is a difficult conflict to resolve, in part because for both India and Pakistan it represents a founding principle of the nation. Pakistan considers itself a homeland for Muslims in Southeast Asia, and the Muslims, who are the majority in Kashmir, resent being ruled by "infidels." On the other hand, India proclaims itself a secular, multicultural state and fears that ceding Kashmir would set a precedent for other ethnic minorities within its borders.[133] India accuses Pakistan of supporting Islamic terrorists in attacks against India, and Pakistan accuses India's army of human rights abuses in Kashmir. This is another seemingly intractable and increasingly brutal ethno-nationalist conflict, but one being contested against the backdrop of nuclear weapons.

China

Since at least 1949, when Mao Zedong (1893–1976), the chairman of the Chinese Communist Party, became the founding leader of the People's

Republic of China, the Communist rulers of China have been authoritarian. We have seen that the current president, Xi Jinping, has centered that authority in himself for the foreseeable future. He has been aided in taking control by a sophisticated program of domestic surveillance and intimidation that has eradicated public dissent.[134] The military massacre of students demonstrating for democracy in central Beijing's Tiananmen Square in 1989 is another example of the Chinese Communist Party's disdain for civil and human rights. The repression of two ethnic minorities in designated autonomous regions of China, the Buddhist Tibetans in Tibet, and the Muslim Uighurs in Xinjiang Province, are demonstrations of further violations of human rights. In both cases leaders (such as Tibet's Dalai Lama) have been exiled, hundreds of thousands of resistors killed or imprisoned, and the local population overwhelmed by an intentional relocation of Han Chinese, China's majority ethnic group. China is a human rights black hole.[135]

There are two territorial disputes involving China that are worth briefly discussing: Taiwan and the South China Sea.

On December 2, 2016, then-president-elect Donald Trump accepted a congratulatory phone call from President Tsai Ing-wen of Taiwan that caused a good deal of consternation. No American leader had spoken with a Taiwanese leader since 1979. Was this an indication that the Trump administration intended to upend the United States' intentionally ambiguous, but reliable, "One China" policy?

When Mao's Communist revolutionaries defeated China's Nationalist government in 1949, the Nationalists, under Chiang Kai-shek (1887–1975), retreated to the Chinese island of Taiwan and set up a government in exile— the Republic of China. Both sides, the Communist People's Republic of China and the Republic of China (Taiwan), continued to claim all of China. This dispute became a global Cold War issue because the Soviet Union and the Warsaw Pact recognized the People's Republic as the legitimate government, and the United States and NATO recognized Taiwan. The Taiwan government occupied China's UN Security Council seat until 1971. In the 1970s the United States gradually accepted the reality of China and switched its recognition from Taiwan to Beijing's government in 1979. In 1992 both the People's Republic and the Republic agreed that there is only one China consisting of the mainland and Taiwan, but agreed to disagree about which government is legitimate. This forces all other states to choose one China. The United States' particular "One China" policy has three goals: to nurture constructive relations with Beijing, the world's second largest economy; to protect and arm Taiwan, which is a successful democracy; and to prevent war between the two countries.[136] After some typical bluster from President Trump about the phone call, his administration has basically honored this delicate balance.[137]

During the Obama administration's second term (2013–2017), China began inflating its claims and increasing its presence in the South China Sea. It physically increased the size of islands that it claimed, even creating new islands out of reefs, in order to anchor ports, military installations, and airstrips, especially in the Spratly Islands and on Scarborough Shoal. The South China Sea carries $5 trillion in annual trade, is the site of rich fisheries, and the repository of eleven billion barrels of untapped oil and 190 trillion cubic feet of natural gas. The sea's various coastal countries—China, Vietnam, Malaysia, Brunei, Taiwan, Indonesia, and the Philippines—clash with one another in claiming its islands and resources. In July 2016, the Permanent Court of Arbitration in The Hague ruled in favor of the Philippines on nearly every count in a case it brought against China. Although China has signed the UN Convention on the Law of the Sea, it refused to accept the court's authority.

In response to these provocations by China, the United States has engaged in a perilous game of chicken by exercising its right to freedom of navigation through exclusive economic zones (EEZs) in the sea and reassuring its Asian allies in the region. This mix of pressure and diplomacy seems a sound US strategy.[138]

Myanmar (Burma)

Genocide is not a word tossed around lightly in the foreign affairs/international studies arena. However, scholars at the US Holocaust Memorial Museum and Yale University, the United Nations human rights chief, Zeid Ra'ad al-Hussein, as well as a UN Fact Finding Mission on Myanmar and *New York Times* columnist Nicholas Kristof have said that Myanmar's treatment of the Muslim ethnic minority Rohingya people may well qualify as genocide. Genocide is the intentional and systematic attempt to exterminate a people or nation. The global community has a moral obligation to prevent and address genocide.[139]

Burma gained its independence from British colonial rule in 1948. In 1962 an oppressive military junta took control of the country. The junta changed the name of the country to Myanmar in 1989. The next year the opposition National League for Democracy (NLD) won an overwhelming victory in elections, but the military leaders ignored the results. Aung San Suu Kyi, the daughter of Aung San, who is generally recognized as the Father of the Nation for his role in gaining the independence of Burma, led the NLD. The military dictatorship placed her under house arrest from 1989 to 1995, then again from 2000 to 2002, and finally from May 2003 to November 2010. In 1991 Aung San Suu Kyi received the Nobel Peace Prize for her nonviolent opposition to the military's oppression and her advocacy of democracy. In 2011, Thein Sein was selected as president by the legislature, and he gradually instituted a series of reforms that culminated in an election in 2015 won by the opposition NLD. The constitution forbad Aung San Suu Kyi from being president because her late husband and children are British, but she was given the title "State Counselor" and in effect rules the country, although she does not control the army. The United States encouraged Myanmar's journey toward democracy with a mixture of sanctions and diplomacy.[140]

The population of Myanmar is about fifty-four million. The majority ethnic group are the Burman (Bamar) at 68 percent. The population is 88 percent Buddhist and 4 percent Muslim. The government of Myanmar formally recognizes 135 indigenous ethnic groups, but the Rohingya are not on the list. Other ethnic groups, such as the Shan and the Karen, who are largely Christian, have clashed with the army, with both sides accused of atrocities;[141] but the treatment of the Rohingya is exceptional. The government does not recognize them as citizens and falsely characterizes them as recent immigrants ("Bengali terrorists") from Bangladesh. The one million Rohingya have lived for generations in Rakhine, Myanmar's poorest state. They have their own language and culture, and practice a form of Sunni Islam.

The Arakan Rohingya Salvation Army (ARSA) has occasionally attacked police posts, as they did again in August 2017, killing twelve officers. In every case the response of the security forces might be described as merciless revenge. In the assault on the village of Tula Toli, for example, the army separated the men and boys from the women and girls. They shot all the males and made a bonfire of their corpses. Then they herded the women and girls into huts. They slit the throats of babies, infants, children, and women or chopped them on the head with machetes. They raped the girls and women. Then they set fire to the huts. Human Rights Watch used satellite images to document that some 345 villages were burned to the ground in similar fashion. An estimated 10,000 Rohingya were killed, and over 700,000 have fled into Bangladesh, an impoverished country that does not want them and is unable to accommodate them. Neither these refugees nor the Rohingya who remain in Rakhine are receiving adequate nutrition, access to health care, or education. The army's rampage was genocide in slow motion.[142]

In her public statements Aung San Suu Kyi echoes the prejudice and hatred against the Rohingya of many of her fellow citizens. She is an apologist for the ethnic cleansing (exclusion) of the Rohingya and complicit in their brutal persecution. Her government prosecuted two Reuters reporters who dared report on the army's crimes against humanity. The US Holocaust Memorial Museum has rescinded the Elie Wiesel Human Rights award that she received in 2012, and some have suggested that the Nobel Committee should do the same.[143]

International law imposes an obligation on the global community to take steps to address genocide, and every nation has a moral responsibility to respond to such crimes against humanity as the mass murder of Rohingya civilians, systematic rape, and ethnic cleansing. First, the United States, working with our allies and with the United Nations, should support efforts to properly investigate such human rights violations. Second, the perpetrators of such crimes against humanity should be prosecuted and punished for these atrocities. Third, the United States should lead the global community in providing humanitarian assistance to the Rohingya, both in Rakhine and in Bangladesh. Fourth, any military aid to Myanmar should be stopped and prohibited. Fifth, economic sanctions should be imposed on Myanmar. Finally, the United States should lead efforts to resolve ethnic strife throughout Myanmar, including implementing the recommendations of former UN secretary general Kofi Annan's Advisory Commission on Rakhine State and grant citizenship to the Rohingya people.[144]

Africa

The continent of Africa is rife with ethnic conflict, sectarian struggles, wars over resources, and failed states. From south to north, west to east, fighting burns or simmers in Africa.[145] Dictatorship and corruption are the norm, and poverty is ubiquitous. This section will look at some of the particular conflicts within or among countries, then examine some of the broader themes related to violent conflict in Africa.

Central Africa

On April 6, 1994, Rwanda's Hutu government unleashed the bloodiest hundred days in the second half of the twentieth century. At least 500,000 Tutsi (and their sympathizers) were slaughtered, mostly with machetes. This massacre is rightly regarded as an act of genocide.[146] The world was aghast when a river of their bloated bodies emptied into Lake Kivu. Nearly 100,000 Hutu and Tutsi have also been killed in neighboring Burundi, where a Tutsi government butchered Hutu, sparking a civil war from 1994 to 2005.[147] This complex conflict between the Hutu and Tutsi peoples in Rwanda and Burundi was rooted in the colonial history of the region and was motivated by politics, the scarcity of resources, and ethnic enmity.[148]

Once the massacre began in Rwanda, the Rwandan Patriotic Front (RPF), comprised of well-trained Tutsi exiles in the region under the leadership of Paul Kagame, invaded Rwanda and rapidly advanced across the country, stopped the genocide, and gained control of Rwanda. Although there were some reprisals against the defeated Hutus, the RPF showed restraint and discipline and set up an inclusive government in Rwanda.

The international community, and especially the West with its colonial stakes in Central Africa, failed miserably in responding to the crisis in Rwanda. Although the United Nations worked for a peace agreement prior to April 1994, it abandoned hundreds of thousands of Rwandans to genocidal slaughter when that process broke down.

The RFP leader, Paul Kagame, has led Rwanda since 1994. He has had reasonable success in developing the economy of Rwanda, but he is an authoritarian leader who does not tolerate opposition.[149] A similar situation has played out in Burundi, where President Pierre Nkurunziza, whose rule has been increasingly repressive, is poised to stay in power indefinitely.[150]

Soon the conflict in Rwanda spilled over into Zaire. In May of 1997, the central government of Zaire, under longtime dictator Mobutu Sese Seko (ruled 1965–1997), was overthrown without much of a fight by a revolutionary army under Laurent Kabila, who renamed the country the Democratic Republic of Congo (DRC). Although rich in resources, especially minerals, the DRC is among the world's poorest countries. It is the second largest country in Africa, has a population of diverse and divided ethnic groups, and contains little infrastructure for transportation or communication and no system of education or government services worth noting. When Laurent Kabila was assassinated in the capital of Kinshasa in January 2001, armies supported by several of Congo's neighbors, as well as various independent militias, were active in the country, creating what has been called "Africa's world war" and much civilian suffering. By the time the fighting came to a halt in 2003 over six million people had died from the violence or because of disease and malnutrition. Militia continued to clash in the east, where a United Nations force assisted in keeping the peace.[151]

Mr. Kabila's inexperienced son, Joseph, succeeded him. He was elected president in 2006 and again in 2011. When his second and final term in office ended in December 2016, he refused to hold elections. Despite an agreement brokered by the Catholic Church that called for elections late in 2017, Joseph Kabila remained in power until elections in December 2018.[152]

The Greater Horn of Africa (i.e., the Countries in Northeast Sub-Saharan Africa)

Sudan has been entangled in civil war since its independence from Britain and Egypt in 1956. The northern part of Sudan, including the capital, Khartoum, consists of Muslim Arabs (70 percent), who are often nomadic herders. The north politically and economically dominated the Christian and animist black Africans of the south who tended to be farmers. Competition for scarce land, water, and resources in a warming climate exacerbated the conflict. Various militia formed in the south and rebelled against the government of President Omar al-Bashir (1989–) which was based in the north.[153]

This north–south, Arab–African conflict first played out as genocide by the government in the Darfur region of western Sudan, an area the size of Spain, with an estimated seven million people. When two rebel groups, the Sudanese Liberation Movement (SLM) and the Justice and Equality Movement (JEM) became active in Darfur in 2003, the government armed and funded their traditional rivals, the Janjaweed ("Devils on Horseback"), an Arab militia, to systematically destroy and displace Darfurians. A typical attack on a Darfuri village began with bombing by the Sudanese Air Force followed by a raid by the Janjaweed on horses and camels. Everyone in the village was either murdered or fled. Women and children were raped and enslaved, livestock were stolen, and anything of value was looted. Wells and water supplies were contaminated, and the village was burned to the ground. Although the International Criminal Court (ICC) in The Hague issued two arrest warrants for President Bashir in 2009 for crimes against humanity and 2010 for genocide, this genocide continued. It is estimated that over 480,000 Darfuri have been killed and over 2.8 million have been displaced.[154]

Two prolonged periods of civil war between northern and southern Sudan (1955–1972 and 1983–2005), during which an estimated 2.5 million people, mostly civilians, died from the fighting and starvation, finally concluded with a Comprehensive Peace Agreement in January 2005. South Sudan was granted a six-year period of autonomy, which led to a 2011 referendum in which 98 percent voted for secession, and South Sudan became the world's newest state on July 9, 2011. The United States supported this process with diplomacy and billions in aid. The process of building a new state has been impeded, however, by ethnic conflict, continuing disagreements with the north over oil and the border region of Abyei, and a power struggle between President Salva Kiir, a member of the majority Dinka people (36 percent), and his former vice president, Riek Machar, a Nuer (16 percent; there are eighteen other ethnic groups in South Sudan). The result of this civil warfare is increased poverty; four million people uprooted from their homes, half external refugees, and half internally displaced; atrocities, such as rape, castration, child warriors, and burned villages; and now famine is moving in to South Sudan. The United States has called on the UN Security Council to impose an arms embargo, and UN peacekeepers have been deployed to South Sudan to assist with nation-building efforts and civilian protection.[155]

In 1960 Italian Somaliland and British Somaliland became independent, merged, and formed the United Republic of Somalia. Mohamed Siad Barre took power in a coup in 1969. He declared Somalia a socialist state, nationalized most of the economy, and allied with the Soviet Union in the Cold War until 1978, when he switched to the US side. Barre was ousted in 1991, the victim of warfare among southern Somalia's clans. Although ethnically homogenous (85 percent Somali), southern Somalia remains embroiled in the chaos of clan conflict and the resulting anarchy. In 1991 the northern clans in the former British protectorate unilaterally declared an independent Republic of Somaliland. Although not recognized by any other state, this entity has remained stable and continued efforts at establishing a functioning constitutional democracy. Its neighboring region, Puntland, declared itself autonomous in 1998.[156]

In 1992 US troops arrived in Somalia as part of a United Nations humanitarian mission to alleviate famine conditions and restrain the havoc resulting from the clan-based civil war. In the Battle of Mogadishu, on October 3 and 4, 1993, initiated by the downing of a US Black Hawk helicopter, 19 US Rangers and between 1,500 and 3,000 Somalis were killed.[157] When the United Nations withdrew in 1995, after suffering significant casualties, order still had not been restored, and that continued to be true in 2018, despite interventions by its neighbors, Ethiopia and Kenya, and by the African Union. From 2008 through 2012 pirates operating out of Somalia severely disrupted the busy shipping lanes off the coast. Somalia has a mostly informal economy. Such anarchy and pervasive armed conflict is conducive to poverty. Famine is also appearing again in Somalia.

Ethiopia, Africa's oldest independent country, is the home of the ancient Ethiopian Orthodox Church and has Africa's second largest population of 105 million ethnically diverse people. Its ancient monarchy ended only in 1974 when Emperor Haile Selassie was overthrown in a military coup. In 1991 the Ethiopian People's Revolutionary Democratic Front deposed the dictator Colonel Mengistu (1937–2013), and in 1993 Ethiopia regained its independence through a referendum.

Eritrea was an Italian colony from 1889 to 1941, then administered by Britain from 1941 to 1952 when the United Nations made it an autonomous region of Ethiopia. In 1962 Ethiopia annexed Eritrea as one of its provinces. This sparked a thirty-year war of independence that ended in 1991 with a victory by the Eritrean People's Liberation Front over the Ethiopian army. Eritreans gained their independence through a 1993 referendum, which was the last time there was a meaningful vote. Isaias Afwerki has been president since 1993. He is also chairman of the National Assembly, giving him control of both the executive and legislative branches of government. President Isaias has militarized society by making conscription mandatory and possibly indefinite. He is a repressive despot.

Ethiopia and Eritrea fought another full-scale war over a disputed border from 1998 to 2000 in which an estimated 100,000 people were killed. A UN peacekeeping operation monitored a twenty-five-kilometer-wide Temporary Security Zone, and in 2003 an Eritrea–Ethiopia Boundary Commission (EEBC) was established to demarcate the border based on colonial treaties and international law. The EEBC's 2007 ruling basically agreed with Eritrea's claims, but Ethiopia refused to accept it, leaving troops from both countries dug in at the disputed border. In February 2018, however, Hailemariam Desalegn resigned as prime minister of Ethiopia in the face of popular protests. After being nominated by the ruling coalition, the Parliament elected Abiy Ahmed prime minister. Mr. Abiy decided in June to fully accept and implement the 2000 peace deal with Eritrea. On July 8, 2018, Prime Minster Abiy visited Eritrea, met with President Isaias, and the two leaders made peace between the two countries.[158] Thus ended a senseless war.

Lake Chad Basin

The Lake Chad Basin region is comprised of Nigeria, Chad, Niger, and Cameroon. Nigeria is the most populous country and the largest oil producer in Africa, but due to inequity and corruption most Nigerians are poor. Its elections have been getting freer and fairer. In 2015, Muhammadu Buhari, a former military dictator, defeated Goodluck Jonathan to become president.

Niger, Cameroon, and Chad are among the poorest countries in the world. Paul Biya has been president of Cameroon since 1982. Chad and Niger suffered a series of coups and rebellions, but Idriss Deby became ruler of Chad in 1990, and Issafou Mahamadou has been president of Niger since 2011.

These four neighboring countries face many similar problems, two of which stand out: the violence perpetrated by the Islamist extremist group Boko Haram and by the counterinsurgency campaign against it, and the environmental impact of global warming, which exacerbates both poverty and violence.[159]

Boko Haram was created by the Salafist preaching of Mohamed Yusuf in northern Nigeria, a mostly Muslim area, in 2009. In response to Boko Haram killing some police officers, Yusuf was arrested and summarily executed. He was succeeded by Abubakar Shekau, a master of mayhem; and under his leadership Boko Haram engaged in suicide bombings, village destruction, rape, and kidnappings, first in Nigeria, then spreading to the other countries in the Lake Chad Basin.

In April of 2014 Boko Haram gained international notoriety when they kidnapped 276 girls from the Chibok Secondary school in Nigeria, more than 100 of whom remained in their custody four years later. In the spring of 2015 Boko Haram pledged allegiance to the Islamic State and changed their formal name to Islamic State West African Province (ISWAP). The United States gives military aid to the four countries of the Lake Chad Basin to fight Boko Haram and has special-operations forces stationed there. The United States and France engage in air and drone strikes against Boko Haram in the area. The counterinsurgency campaign by the armies of the four countries often cause as much damage and suffering to their people as does Boko Haram. This conflict has resulted in the deaths of 30,000 people, extensive physical destruction, the displacement of an estimated 2.4 million, and severe food insecurity for 6.6 million. Economic activity, such as farming and fishing, has come to a standstill.

Although it is the terrorist activity of Boko Haram that concerns and engages the United States and the West, the people of the Lake Chad Basin were suffering well before Boko Haram arrived on the scene.[160] Between 1950 and 2000, Lake Chad, once the size of New Jersey, shrank by 95 percent due to global warming. Across the Sahel, the boundary region of the Sahara Desert, the desert is expanding, making water and arable land scarce. As in Sudan, herders and farmers attack one another over land and water. Weapons have flooded the Lake Chad Basin, fueling insurgencies and ethnic conflict. The regimes that replaced those of the rapacious colonial powers have proved just as predatory. Chad, for example, is a weak state with a strong army that is used by President Deby to repress the people and put down any rebellions, as well as fight Boko Haram. The toll of such violence in the period before 2009 rivals that caused by Boko Haram and the counterinsurgency, and, of course, since 2009 the people have had to deal with both sorts of violence. When the West gives military aid to the region's autocrats to fight Islamist extremists, the recipients are also able to further exploit their people, exacerbating the conditions that attract jihadi and insurgents to take up arms in the first place. Violence, poverty, and the suffering of ordinary people only become worse.

West Africa

The United Nations includes sixteen countries in West Africa. Liberia, Africa's oldest republic, was founded by freed American and Caribbean slaves, although 95 percent of the population is native African. The other countries of West Africa were colonized by France, the United Kingdom, or Portugal. The date of independence and colonizing power is in parentheses in this list of countries: Benin (1960 Fr), Burkina Faso (1960 Fr), Cape Verde (1975 P), Ivory Coast (1960 Fr), Gambia (1965 UK), Ghana (1957 UK), Guinea (1958 Fr), Guinea-Bissau (1974 P), Liberia (1847), Mali (1960 Fr), Mauritania (1960 Fr), Niger (1960 Fr), Nigeria (1960 UK), Senegal (1960 Fr), Sierra Leone (1961 UK), and Togo (1960 Fr).

Since independence, most of the countries of West Africa have experienced crushing poverty, violent conflict, coups d'état (Gambia, Niger, Guinea, Guinea-Bissau, and Burkina Faso, for example), dictatorships, and ethnic and religious clashes (Benin, Nigeria, and Mali, for example).[161]

Four of the countries have had brutal and destructive civil wars: Nigeria (the Biafran War from 1966 to 1970);[162] Liberia (the first, 1989–1996, won by American-educated warlord Charles Taylor; the second, 1999–2003, to overthrow Taylor);[163] Sierra Leone (1991–2002, a rebellion by Foday Sankoh's Revolutionary United Front, characterized by brutal guerilla tactics and mutilation, funded by "blood" or "conflict" diamonds);[164] and Ivory Coast (Cote d'Ivoire) (2002–2007, and 2010–2011 over a disputed election between Laurent Gbagbo and Alassane Ouattara).[165] After much chaos and suffering all four of these countries are now functioning democracies.[166]

Most of the population of Mali lives in the southern region. The northern region, however, has been the scene for ethnic conflict, Islamist extremists, and frequent rebellions, especially by the Tuareg people seeking to gain autonomy for the area they call Azawad. Since 2013 nearly 15,000 UN peacekeepers, assembled from countries in the Sahel area around Mali, have been trying to settle this restive region and combat extremism. The United States has built a drone base in neighboring Niger for reconnaissance in this effort.[167]

Ghana, previously called the Gold Coast and historically deeply involved in the slave trade, was the first country in colonial sub-Saharan Africa to claim its independence in 1957 from Britain. Its first forty-five years of independence were characterized by military rule and a succession of coups, all too typical for the region. In 1992, however, a new constitution was developed that created a multiparty democracy. Every four years since, free and fair elections have been held, and three times the president has come from a different party. In 2016, Nana Akufo-Addo, an erudite human rights lawyer, defeated the incumbent, John Mahama, with 53.8 percent of the vote. Ghana is consistently ranked in the top three nations in Africa for freedom of speech and of the press. It is also blessed with natural resources, including cocoa production, gold, and in 2010 offshore oil production began to fuel the economy. Ghana is projected by the World Bank to have one of the world's fastest growing economies in 2018. As a candidate, President Akufo-Addo pledged to have a factory in each of the country's 216 districts, a dam in each village, and free high school education. His challenge is to implement such progressive thinking and to direct this current economic boom into sustainable and equitable development.[168] Peace and political stability can make a real difference for the common good of a nation.

Southern Africa

Called Rhodesia under British colonial rule, Zimbabwe won its lengthy war of independence in 1980. Robert Mugabe ruled Zimbabwe for nearly four decades through brutal repression and cunning manipulation until he was forced to resign by the military in November 2017. In 2000 Mugabe instituted a land reform that seized white-owned farms and gave them to landless blacks with little experience in agriculture. Once the bread basket of the region, Zimbabwe soon could not feed its own people. The economy collapsed. Unemployed and impoverished, many Zimbabweans have left the country in search of a future.[169]

When the Portuguese withdrew from Angola in 1975, the rival groups fighting for independence—the Popular Movement for the Liberation of Angola (MPLA), led by José Eduardo Dos Santos, and the National Union for the Total Independence of Angola (UNITA), led by Jonas Savimbi—turned on each other in a civil war for power that raged for twenty-seven years. When Savimbi was killed in battle in 2002, a ceasefire followed shortly after. It is estimated that 1.5 million people died as a result of the hostilities, and four million were displaced. Land mines have maimed tens of thousands. Dos Santos led the country from 1979 until 2017 when he stepped down from the presidency. He was succeeded by João Lourenço, a former general, who has shown some independence in his early moves as president. Angola is one of Africa's major oil producers, but President Lourenço faces the formidable task of repairing the harm from the civil war and ending the corruption and injustice that has resulted in a rich elite, while 40 percent of the population languishes in poverty.[170]

The population of South Africa is 80.2 percent black African, 8.8 percent "colored" (mixed race), 8.4 percent white, and 2.5 percent Indian/Asian. There are nine major black African tribes and two white tribes—the Dutch or Afrikaners (the British called them "Boers" or farmers), and the British. The whites fought two Anglo-Boer wars (1880–1881 and 1899–1902) against each other before agreeing to rule together over the native peoples in 1910. In 1948 the Afrikaner-dominated National Party (NP) was voted into power by the whites, and formalized the policy of apartheid or separation of the races. Whites and blacks were rigidly segregated from each other, and blacks were exploited and oppressed by whites. The African National Congress (ANC), founded in 1912, led the opposition to apartheid, with campaigns of protest, civil disobedience, and insurgency. ANC leaders, such as Nelson Mandela (1918–2013), were imprisoned, and others were tortured and disappeared. Resistance combined with international pressure, through sanctions, boycotts, and divestment, resulted in the dismantling of the system of apartheid under the leadership of Frederick Willem (F. W.) de Klerk in the early 1990s. Nelson Mandela was released after twenty-seven years in prison and entered into multiparty talks with the government. The first multiracial vote in April 1994 elected Mandela president of South Africa. De Klerk and Mandela won the Nobel Peace Prize in 1993.

The Republic of South Africa is one of Africa's most developed nations, yet it continues to struggle with the vestiges of racial and class divisions, crime and violence, the ravages of HIV/AIDS, and corruption, graft, and greed by its leaders. In 1996 a Truth and Reconciliation Committee under the leadership of Nobel Peace Prize laureate (1984) Archbishop Desmond Tutu, began hearings on crimes committed by the government and by resistance movements during the apartheid period. It concluded that apartheid was a crime against humanity, and that the ANC was also responsible for human rights abuses. The hearings, stories, and forgiveness did begin to heal individuals and the community. Still, the racism that resulted in the apartheid system continues to perpetuate the poverty and exploitation of black South Africans.[171]

The ANC has been in power since 1994. Thabo Mbeki succeeded Mandela in 1999 and was elected again in 2004. In 2008, President Mbeki resigned over allegations that he interfered in a corruption case against his scandal-ridden deputy, Jacob Zuma. Then, when the ANC won the 2009 election, Parliament chose Jacob Zuma as president. Despite constant accusations of corruption, Zuma remained president when the ANC won the 2014 election. In February 2018, President Zuma finally resigned under pressure from the ANC because of corruption charges. The ANC chose Cyril Ramaphosa, a veteran trade unionist and businessman, to succeed Zuma. Since Mr. Ramaphosa had long ago used his ANC connections to become wealthy, it is doubtful that he will drain this swamp. The leaders of the ANC and their cronies have diverted billions of dollars of public funds meant for economic development into their own coffers. Such behavior is hypocritical, truly scandalous, and profoundly harmful.[172]

As we have seen, corrupt leaders are pervasive in Africa. Corruption is not a particularly African problem. It is universal, part of the human condition, but especially tragic in Africa, Latin America, Asia, and the Middle East, the global South.[173] It is correlated with repressive dictatorships, the abuse of human rights, and poverty—conditions ubiquitous in Africa. It is almost impossible for a country and its people to flourish with corrupt, self-serving leadership.[174]

While the conflicts and wars that tear down Africa are about power or territory or resources, they are complicated by the almost total lack of correspondence between nations and states on the continent. The colonial map of Africa paid little attention to ethnic groups, their traditional territories, and their historic animosities. Ethno-nationalist conflict continues to be a major problem in Africa.[175] Religious conflict, particularly between Christians and Muslims, is also fairly common, especially in North and East Africa, where Islamist extremists, such as Boko Haram and Al Shabab, have extended their networks.[176] Population growth and climate change are creating conflicts over diminishing fertile land and water required by increasing numbers of people.[177] These factors, often in combination, make for a continent too often in conflict.

Latin America

Two decades into the twenty-first century, Latin America, while not exactly an oasis of peace in a world of conflict, is calmer than in the thirty years from 1960 to 1990. The incessant coups, succession of military governments and dictators, and revolutions in Central and South America in the twentieth century have almost universally evolved into democratic governments. In 2018 Freedom House ranked all the countries in South America, Central America, and the Caribbean as free or partly free except for Venezuela and Cuba.[178]

Venezuela

In Venezuela, Hugo Chavez, a former military officer whose ill-fated coup attempt in 1992 nevertheless raised the possibility of radical social change among the people, was elected president in 1998 under the banner of the United Socialist Party (PSUV). Chavez pledged to use the country's oil wealth to reduce poverty and inequality. He nationalized hundreds of private businesses and foreign-owned assets including petroleum projects of ExxonMobil and ConocoPhillips and instituted land reform by expropriating millions of acres of land. The poverty rate fell from 50 percent in 1998 to 30 percent in 2012. When Chavez died from cancer in 2013, his chosen successor, Nicolas Maduro, was narrowly elected.

Venezuela has the world's largest proven oil reserves, and petroleum dominates its economy. Unfortunately, the global price of oil, which was funding this social reform, fell from $111 a barrel in 2014 to $27 in 2016. Venezuela's economy collapsed, resulting in a humanitarian crisis in what was once Latin America's richest country.

In 2018, government control of foreign currency exchange and price controls on consumer goods resulted in hyperinflation exceeding 13,000 percent and widespread shortages of food, consumer goods, and medicines. The economy contracted by 12 percent, and Venezuela selectively defaulted on repaying its debt. Frequent protests in the capital, Caracas, were met with escalating government repression.

Politically, Chavez and Maduro were populist leaders who became more and more authoritarian. President Maduro effectively controlled all three branches of government. The opposition, the Democratic Unity Roundtable (MUD), a coalition of centrist, left, and center-right parties, was unsurprisingly internally divided and decided to boycott the May 2018 election "won" by Maduro. Although oil prices began rising in 2018, the state-run petroleum company, PTVSA, was eviscerated by Chavez, and production has steadily declined. Maduro, like Chavez before him, blamed the United States for much of Venezuela's troubles, and the Trump administration responded with negative tweets and economic sanctions. Venezuela has fallen from wealth and democracy to dictatorship and chaos.[179]

Cuba

Cuba has been a communist state since Fidel Castro's (1928–2016) revolutionaries overthrew US-backed dictator Fulgencio Batista (ruled 1933–1959) in 1959. Castro built strong ties with the Soviet Union and received annual subsidies of $4–6 billion until the USSR collapsed in 1990. Although Cuba created a reputable health and education system, it was a totalitarian police state that spied on its people and imprisoned dissenters. The response of the United States was to impose a complete commercial embargo and stringent travel restrictions in order to isolate Cuba economically and diplomatically.

In 2008, Fidel Castro, aging and ill, handed leadership to his younger brother, Raul. As a candidate, Barack Obama expressed an openness to direct diplomacy with Cuba, and as president, Obama eased off the restrictions on remittances and travel. Raul Castro gradually began to liberalize parts of Cuba's state-controlled economy, and the private sector swelled between 2009 and 2013 as a result. Then in December 2014, Obama and Castro surprised the world by announcing that they would pursue the normalization of relations between the two countries. In July 2015, both countries reopened their embassies, and Obama eased travel restrictions, allowing some direct flights from the United States to Cuba and removed Cuba from the list of state sponsors of terrorism. In 2016, President Obama visited Cuba. In a joint statement in January 2017, the United States ended the "wet foot, dry foot" policy, which privileged Cuban immigrants who made it to the United States. It is up to Congress, however, to remove the trade embargo. In April 2018, Raul Castro resigned and chose Miguel Díaz-Canel Bermúdez as president.

Both Democrats and Republicans want Cuba to reform its human rights policies and conduct, but there is disagreement about how to accomplish this goal. Most Democrats and some Republicans support ending the embargo immediately to spur reform. Many Republicans argue that reform must come before economic normalization. There is widespread popular support for normalization in both countries, as well as overwhelming international support. The United Nations has passed a resolution condemning the Cuban embargo for twenty-five consecutive years. President Trump has said sanctions on Cuba will remain until all political prisoners are released and a free and fair election is held. The United States has used the stick approach toward Cuba for nearly sixty years with little effect, perhaps it is time to try the carrot.[180]

Colombia

Colombia appears to have ended a fifty-two-year rebellion. In the late 1960s a number of armed revolutionary groups emerged in Colombia, including the Revolutionary Armed forces of Colombia (FARC), a Marxist group that funded itself through the drug trade. President Juan Manuel Santos (2010–2018), who had been the defense minister in the previous administration, began peace talks with FARC in 2012 that finally yielded a peace accord in September 2016. A month later, the peace accord was narrowly rejected in a national referendum out of concern that it was too lenient on the rebels. A revised peace accord was ratified by Congress in November 2016, and FARC disarmed and joined civil society. At least 220,000 people died in the conflict. President Santos received the Nobel Peace Prize in 2016. Despite its long-standing security issues, Colombia maintains functioning democratic institutions, protects civil liberties, and holds peaceful, transparent elections. Iván Duque Márquez was elected president in August 2018.[181]

Mexico

Mexico has been involved in the drug trade since the 1980s. Mexico now produces all the varieties of illegal drugs, from heroin to ecstasy, as well as serves as a transit site for the drug trade. Over the years, the evolving drug cartels became more powerful than the weak and corrupt local law enforcement. In

2006 the federal government, in partnership with the United States, involved the Mexican military in fighting the criminal drug organizations, and the violence escalated. An estimated 100,000 Mexican soldiers, police officers, criminals, politicians, and civilians had been killed by 2018. Every year this drug-related violence, along with political violence and poverty, has caused thousands of immigrants from Mexico and other Central American countries, such as Guatemala, Honduras, and El Salvador, to attempt to flee through Mexico to the United States. Since 2009, however, Mexican migration to the United States has slowed, and, in fact, more Mexican immigrants have returned to Mexico than have fled to the United States.[182] Since his election in 2012, President Enrique Peña Nieto (2012–2018) redirected the government's strategy toward reinforcing local law enforcement rather than relying on military force. This has decreased homicides but increased kidnappings and extortion. In the United States, an estimated two million people are dependent on opioids, and nearly 60,000 overdosed in 2016. This demand for drugs is a factor in the rise of drug-related crime and violence in Mexico and Central America. Andrés Manuel López Obrador was elected president in July 2018.[183]

Although terrorism is not a major problem in Latin America, criminal violence and violence associated with politics take a toll. Corruption is an irritant and a stumbling block to dealing with the persistent poverty that characterizes the continent.

The United States

Since the war in Korea (1950–1953), which was fought under the auspices of a UN Security Council resolution, the United States has been involved in a number of conflicts, major and minor, all over the globe,[184] some of which have been of dubious legality and justification.

During the Cold War (1945–1990) US interventions were motivated by the policy of containing communism or anticommunism. The wars in Korea and Vietnam (1965–1975) were such interventions, for example, as were interventions in Laos (1953–1975) and Cambodia (1967–1975), and indirect interventions in Nicaragua (1975–1980) and El Salvador (1980). The problem with many of these interventions is that the United States' anticommunist lens blinded decision makers from seeing other realities in the local situation. In Vietnam, for example, Ho Chi Minh, the leader of North Vietnam, although a communist and socialist, was also a nationalist, fighting for the independence of Vietnam from colonial rule, first by the French, then by the Americans, who effectively took the place of the French. The Sandinista revolutionaries in Nicaragua were fighting the oppression of the US-backed regime of Anastasia Somoza (1925–1980), although they too aligned with communism and socialism. The anticommunist lens often put the United States on the wrong side of a just cause. Too often the United States backed repressive dictators as long as they were not communist, such as the Marcos regime in the Philippines, or Somoza in Nicaragua. Admittedly, the moral (and legal) justifications of these Cold War interventions are complicated and controversial.

In the twenty-first century, after the September 11, 2001, attacks on the United States, antiterrorism has become a central motive for US military interventions, primarily in Afghanistan (2001–present) and Iraq (2003–2011), and in places like the Lake Chad Basin in Africa and in opposition to the Islamic State in Iraq and the Middle East. These conflicts, including the dubious justification for the war in Iraq, have already been discussed above. The United States has nearly 200,000 troops deployed abroad in 177 countries.[185] The point here is how often the United States is involved in global conflict, for good or ill.

IS HUMANITARIAN INTERVENTION JUSTIFIED?

Can military intervention solely on behalf of human rights ever be justified? Humanitarian intervention can be defined as "the forceful, direct intervention by one or more states or international organizations in the internal affairs of other states for essentially humanitarian purposes."[186]

Reasons for Skepticism about Humanitarian Intervention

There is nothing new about intervention, but the post–Cold War context poses the question in a fresh way. Both superpowers indulged in interventions during the Cold War—in Korea, Vietnam, Afghanistan, Africa, Central America, and the Caribbean, for example—but for reasons of power politics and national self-interest. In terms of justice, democracy, and peacemaking, most of the Cold War interventions, in hindsight, increased the suffering of ordinary people rather than mitigated it.

Today, tensions such as ethnic conflict, chaos, and anarchy in states where the government appears to have failed, and gross violations of human rights or crimes against humanity raise the issue of military intervention on behalf of human life and human rights, rather than for purposes of national self-interest.[187]

The principles of the sovereignty of states and, therefore, of nonintervention in the internal affairs of a sovereign state stand against the right or the duty to intervene on behalf of human rights. These two principles—sovereignty and nonintervention—have imposed some semblance of order upon an international system with no central government.[188] Sovereign states resent interference in their internal affairs. (How would Americans have reacted if China or France had sent troops to protect civil rights protesters on their march from Selma to Montgomery in 1965?) Such intervention could easily result in escalating regional wars.

A second reason against intervention is the tendency of states to rationalize national self-interest under the cloak of humanitarian rhetoric.[189] Colonial powers always thought of themselves as benevolent, bringing a "higher civilization" to primitive peoples, while taking or exploiting their land, wealth, and resources. Although the United Nations authorized the US-led intervention in Haiti in 1994, the Organization of American States did not support it because of well-founded suspicions of previous US interventions in Latin America.[190]

A third set of concerns about intervention arises from the difficulty of developing a policy for intervention that is clear and consistent, rather than arbitrary and selective. What violations of human rights would justify intervention? Who would authorize it? What would be the feasible goals of humanitarian intervention? Would short-term actions create more severe long-term problems?[191]

Arrayed against these reasons for nonintervention are the very real horrors of genocide in Rwanda, ethnic cleansing in Myanmar, famine caused by the collapse of the state in Somalia, repression by military rulers in Haiti,[192] and pogroms against the Kurds in Iraq and Turkey. Such human suffering cries out to the conscience of the international community.

Christian ethics can be helpful in working through this foreign policy dilemma. First, as discussed above, Christian ethics contends that the sovereignty of the state is a real but relative value. State sovereignty is conditioned from below by human rights and from above by the global common good. Thus, when states grievously abuse the human rights of their citizens, they cannot use sovereignty to silence the concern of others or as immunity for a state to violate its own reason to exist—to foster the common good and protect human rights.[193] Neither sovereignty nor nonintervention are absolute principles, although both carry real moral weight. The challenge, then, is to develop clear ethical criteria for justified military intervention into the internal affairs of states.

The Christian tradition offers two ethical paradigms on war and military intervention—nonviolence (or pacifism) and just-war theory—although it has long been dominated by the just-war position.[194]

Nonviolence/Pacifism

Christians and others who adhere to nonviolence have been perplexed by the question of military intervention for humanitarian purposes. Pacifists oppose warfare in principle. During the Cold War, with every conflict potentially a spark for a nuclear holocaust and with power politics the primary purpose of military interventions, Christian pacifists passionately resisted America's military excursions abroad. But humanitarian interventions in the post–Cold War world have often been motivated by efforts to remedy injustice and alleviate human suffering. When these cherished values are genuinely the purpose of intervention, and when the violence of the armed intervention is expected to be minimal, can a pacifist condone it?

Many pacifists have been able to justify humanitarian interventions, such as those in Somalia, Haiti, and Libya, under the rubric of police actions rather than warfare. Most pacifists are not opposed to all uses of force (although some are), and see the threat of force, or the limited use of force, to be justified by the greater human good that can be accomplished. It is analogous to the force used by the police to protect the community from violent criminals.[195] Although it is true that there can be a real difference between humanitarian armed intervention and aggressive warfare, the willingness to use violence will continue to trouble pacifists. Once violence is justified, the line into just-war thinking has inevitably been crossed.

Just-War Tradition

The criteria developed by the just-war tradition can also offer a framework for justifying humanitarian intervention. The transition from nonviolence to justified force yields the first point in an ethic of intervention: military intervention should be a *last resort*. The just-war tradition has always maintained that war is evil, a rule-governed exception to the presumption in favor of peace. Preventative efforts and nonviolent remedies should be applied before force is justified.[196] Economic sanctions can be effective and should be considered, although these too are fraught with ethical problems. For example, comprehensive economic sanctions can cause hardship and death for civilians, especially children, while leaving the targeted leaders untouched.[197] The last-resort criterion also gives the necessary weight to the principles of sovereignty and nonintervention. "Because of the diversity of states and the dangers of rationalization, the wisdom of Westphalia [regarding respect for the sovereignty of states] should be heeded. Intervention may be necessary, but it should not be made easy."[198] The burden of proof should always rest on those who are in favor of military intervention.

It is the *just-cause* criterion that makes humanitarian intervention tempting. There is a consensus that genocide demands an exception to the nonintervention principle, but how serious and egregious must a violation against human rights be in order to justify intervention? This judgment, no doubt, looks different from the perspective of the victims than from that of the offenders, or of the potential interveners. Theological ethicist Kenneth Himes puts it this way, "While the violation of human rights must be egregious and pervasive so as to grievously affect thousands of individuals, evils such as ethnic cleansing, rampant torture and rape, arbitrary arrests and detentions without trial, mass executions of political opponents, and deliberate targeting of civilian populations in military assaults meet these standards."[199] Just cause, however, is a necessary, but not a sufficient, criterion for intervention.[200]

The just-war tradition insists that war must be declared by a *legitimate authority* based on the idea that only the state can be allowed to authorize the taking of life. Because of the danger of rationalization on the part of individual states, the decision to intervene should ordinarily be authorized by an international organization such as the United Nations and/or a regional security organization. The decision should be multilateral, not unilateral. Given the power differential among states, this does not guarantee probity in judgment, but it does enhance it through procedural restrictions.[201]

The just-war criteria of *right intention* and *the probability of success* are also important as parts of a framework of ethical analysis regarding humanitarian intervention. These criteria focus attention on clearly defining the political goals of the intervention and on the feasibility of effective intervention.

There is no such thing as apolitical military intervention, and it is a dangerous delusion to pretend that political goals can be avoided while offering humanitarian aid. It is also cruel to bring a people back from the brink of death, through famine aid, for example, only to have them continue to suffer from government oppression or social chaos. Thus, it may be that for intervention to be truly humanitarian and just, in many cases it will need to go beyond mere aid or even peacekeeping. It may have to engage in constructive nation-building, that is, in reforming or creating the social and political structures necessary for honoring human rights.[202] This means some sort of ongoing assistance in reorganizing government, disarming military or paramilitary forces, establishing safe enclaves, reestablishing civic peace, supporting negotiated settlements of grievances, punishing the perpetrators of genocide or ethnic cleansing, instituting a judicial system, training and equipping an impartial police force, and so on.[203]

Such goals may require a lengthy commitment of personnel and resources, as in Afghanistan, for example. Such an expanded agenda opens the interveners to the charge of a sort of colonial control over other nations or even of naked imperialism. Yet, to exclude such political goals from intervention is to risk doing more harm than good, or not enough good to bring about permanent change.

This, of course, raises the question of feasibility. If armed interveners must have clearly defined political goals and must be prepared to see the process through to completion, then humanitarian intervention is likely to be rare indeed. By its very nature, humanitarian intervention does not directly serve the national interests of the interveners. Thus, the interveners are placing their soldiers in harm's way, and expending talent and treasure for no direct national benefit. Nor will criminals quickly come to heel nor chaos be easily corrected where havoc is being wreaked. Humanitarian intervention will not always be possible or morally justified, and it will nearly always be difficult to gain popular support for it. Indeed, popular support for the US interventions in Somalia, Haiti, Bosnia, Kosovo, and Libya has been lukewarm or nonexistent. Perhaps, however, this is partly due to the lack of a clearly argued foreign policy on behalf of intervention.[204]

Finally, the just-war tradition requires that the *means* used be proportionate, and that the conduct of the intervention should also be just. The principles of noncombatant immunity and of proportionality have traditionally governed the conduct of warfare. Since the Vietnam debacle, US military strategy has maintained that, in an intervention, massive military power should be brought to bear on an enemy for a short, defined period of time in the pursuit of a clearly defined and limited objective. This strategy seemed to work in the Persian Gulf War (1991), but even there questions of proportionality persist. This hit-and-run strategy poses both moral and political concerns for humanitarian intervention. Massive firepower suggests problems of indiscriminate and/or disproportionate attacks, and quickly withdrawing from the scene precludes the commitment necessary for nation-building activities.[205]

Just Peacemaking

A third paradigm for analyzing the morality of conflict from a Christian perspective has recently been proposed by American Baptist theologian Glen Stassen (1936–2014) and others as a way to break the inertia of the debate between nonviolence and just war and to take seriously the gospel call to peacemaking.[206] The steps or strategies in just peacemaking include confession and repentance, affirmation of common security, transforming initiatives, serious diplomacy aimed at conflict resolution, seeking justice and human rights, and citizen advocacy.[207]

Just peacemaking would emphasize *prevention* of conflict, first of all, by creating a just community and by recognizing and abiding by human rights. Just peacemaking would also urge the use of diplomacy and conflict-resolution strategies and of the techniques of nonviolent direct action before pursuing military intervention as a last resort. Although the just-peacemaking paradigm argues that there is nearly always a realistic and effective alternative to war, it is open to humanitarian intervention. Just peacemaking would encourage nation-building, either through diplomacy or in the aftermath of humanitarian intervention. It believes Christians have a responsibility to *create just community*, which is the only realistic foundation for peace.[208]

Responsibility to Protect

The UN initiative called the Responsibility to Protect (R2P) stresses the responsibility or duty of a state to protect the human rights of its people and to shield them from crimes against humanity. The wider international community shares this responsibility, through the United Nations, and should use diplomatic and peaceful means to protect human rights, and, if those prove inadequate, can use military intervention to defend human rights and stop crimes against humanity.[209]

Humanitarian intervention can be ethically justified, although the need for it must be decided case by case. The just-war tradition provides a framework for the ethical analysis of situations where military intervention is being considered, and just peacemaking proposes practical strategies for preventing and resolving conflict without resort to violence. A Responsibility to Protect gives international backing to a duty for each state to protect its citizens' human rights and prevent crimes against humanity, a responsibility shared by the global community. A public articulation of this framework, these strategies for peacemaking, and the reasons that might justify intervention can be used to build public support for a foreign policy willing to take risks and pay the costs of a just world order.

A MORAL RESPONSE TO TERRORISM

Prior to September 11, 2001, humanitarian intervention was the focus of American analysts in the area of ethics and international relations. The attack by suicidal Islamic terrorists that destroyed the twin towers of the World Trade Center and damaged the Pentagon, killing about 3,000 civilians, refocused US foreign policy on global terrorism.

The response of US president George W. Bush was to declare a global war on terrorism. In his address on September 20, 2001, to a joint session of Congress and to the nation, President Bush said, "We will direct every resource at our command . . . to the destruction and to the defeat of the global terror network. . . . And we will pursue nations that provide aid or safe haven to terrorism. Every nation in every region now has a decision to make: Either you are with us or you are with the terrorists."[210]

The United States demanded that the Taliban, an extremist Muslim group that controlled the government of Afghanistan, apprehend and extradite Osama Bin Laden and other members of al-Qaeda, the terrorist group thought responsible for the attack. When the Taliban did not comply, the United States gave extensive military support to the Northern Alliance in overthrowing the Taliban in Afghanistan.

Terrorism is hardly a new phenomenon. It is probably as old as warfare itself, and it was often used in the twentieth century. The German blitz on London during World War II and the allied firebombing of Dresden and Tokyo could be considered acts of state-sponsored terrorism. Tyrants (whether Communist or anti-Communist during the Cold War) tend to use the military or police to terrorize their subjects through arrest, torture, and disappearances. Often both sides in a conflict accuse the other of terrorism, as has been true in Northern Ireland and Israel versus the Palestinians. The lynching of African Americans were acts of terrorism. On September 11, 2001, the United States experienced a heinous act of terrorism. The incredible horror of the September 11 attack naturally turned terrorism and the response to terrorism into an American preoccupation. What, then, is terrorism, and what is a moral response to terrorism?

President Bush made terrorism synonymous with evil, reinforcing the use of "terrorist" as an epithet. Although terrorism is always wrong, it is a complex phenomenon that is difficult to define. Pope John Paul II called terrorism a "true crime against humanity."[211] Terrorism is a crime (such as the Oklahoma City bombing for which Timothy McVeigh was executed) or a war crime (Palestinian suicide bombers or the allied firebombing of Dresden) because it consciously targets civilians or noncombatants. This makes terrorism always and everywhere wrong, even though the innocence of civilians can be debated (for example, are all Israelis somehow responsible for the occupation of Palestine? Or did all Germans share the responsibility for World War II?). If the moral responsibility to discriminate between civilians and combatants and to direct the violence of warfare only at combatants is lost, then any notion of a morally justified war collapses into a crusade. Terrorism can be perpetrated by a state, by a nation or ethnic group, by a group of dissidents or criminals, even by an individual. Under certain circumstances, state terrorism can be legal.[212]

Terrorism is always unethical and can rightly be condemned. But a moral response to this crime against humanity may depend on who commits it and why. Although I would like to avoid the cliché that one person's terrorist is another person's freedom fighter, there is unfortunately some truth to it.[213] No cause, however just or noble, can justify the use of terrorism. Responding to a terrorist act, however, by redressing the just grievances of an oppressed group or nation may be a better and more effective response than quick reprisals. Not all terrorists, however, are freedom fighters or have even partially just grievances or a just cause. A careful analysis would distinguish, for example, between the Palestinian suicide bombers and those associated with al-Qaeda.

The incessant killing of Israeli civilians by Palestinian suicide bombers that began in the fall of 2000 during the second intifada is a repugnant series of war crimes. It is not surprising that Israel's consistent response was immediate, overwhelming reprisals against the Palestinian groups and areas held responsible. Israel has sent its army to occupy and shut down Palestinian towns, sometimes imposing a total curfew and always restricting the movement of Palestinians. The bomber's family home is often bulldozed to the ground. If found, Palestinians associated with the group responsible, such as Hamas, will be arrested or killed. The Israeli security forces make an effort to be discriminate, but civilians, including children, are too often killed. All Palestinians suffer. Israel's harsh reprisals only fuel more Palestinian hatred and violence, perpetuating a cycle of increasing violence. Perhaps the only way out of this spiral of violence is for Israel to acknowledge the repressive nature of its occupation in the West Bank and control of the Gaza Strip and to redress the just grievances of the Palestinian people.[214] Nonetheless, terrorism is the wrong way to resist Israeli oppression. It is possible that if the Palestinian intifada had picked up the tools of courageous, mass, nonviolent direct action, instead of suicide vests and bombs, Palestinians might be living in their own state today.

In the case of al-Qaeda terrorists, it is unclear what grievances they want redressed and whether their cause is just. Osama Bin Laden and other militant Muslim leaders accused the United States and its allies of engaging in a vast conspiracy "to negate the influence of Islam, undercut the Muslim community, and control the resources of Islamic communities."[215] These extremist Muslims were particularly concerned about the US military presence in Saudi Arabia, where the holy city of Mecca is located, and about the plight of the Palestinians and of Iraq. They are more generally concerned about globalization, secularization, and Western decadence, which they perceive as a threat to the values and success of Islam, and they hold the United States symbolically and practically responsible. Thus the World Islamic Front issued the following *fatwa* (opinion based on the Qur'an) to all Muslims, "The ruling to kill the Americans and their allies—civilians and military—is an individual duty for every Muslim who can do it in any country in which it is possible to do it, in order to liberate the Al-Aqsa Mosque [Jerusalem] and the Holy Mosque [Mecca] from their grip, and in order for their armies to move out of all the lands of Islam, defeated and unable to threaten any Muslim."[216]

Osama Bin Laden was killed by US Navy Seal Team Six in Pakistan on May 2, 2011. Since 2014 the Islamic State (ISIS) has eclipsed the influence of al-Qaeda. The Islamic State is even more rigid and absolutist in its philosophy and more brutal in its tactics, including mass killings, abductions, rapes, beheadings, bombings, and the destruction of ancient sites.[217] ISIS has declared a caliphate, a state based on Sharia law, and demanded allegiance to the ISIS leader, Abu Bakr al-Baghdadi. They wish to protect the true Muslim community from infidels (non-Muslims) and apostates (Muslims who do not agree with them).[218]

The Islamic State and al-Qaeda terrorists are more mass murderers than freedom fighters, and they are attempting to manipulate the Muslim community to accept their extremist interpretation of Islam. They do seem to have struck a chord in the Muslim world, especially with Muslim youth, who feel left behind in a globalized world. Although the United States would do well to critically examine its foreign policy toward the Arab and Islamic world, there is no real hope of placating the World Islamic Front. When terrorists act as criminals, a moral response includes measured retaliation to capture and control them.[219]

The Bush administration's "war on terror" (which President Bush once rightly called a "crusade" before wisely dropping that loaded term) based on an absolutist good (the United States) versus evil (the terrorists and their supporters) perspective is inadequate and unhelpful for a number of reasons.[220]

- It does not allow for any distinction between mass murderers and freedom fighters. While all terrorists are criminals and should be punished, there are situations where reprisals and retaliation will only make things worse. Legitimate grievances should be redressed.
- Once a nation brands its enemy as terrorists there is no incentive for critically examining its own policies, which may have led to the desperation that terrorism often represents.
- The idea that a nation is at war stifles national debate about government policies and tends to lead to the suspension of civil liberties and human rights.
- Unlike most wars, a war on terrorism has neither a clear set of enemies nor the prospect of closure; it cannot be won.[221]

A moral response to terrorism must be more nuanced than is allowed by the metaphors of a "war" or a "crusade against evil."

JUST PEACEMAKING AND TERRORISM

The just-peacemaking paradigm offers ten practices aimed at realistically preventing war and resolving conflict, and implementing these practices could lead to a more holistic approach to preventing and responding to terrorism.[222] One just-peacemaking practice is acknowledgment of wrongdoing (confession) and seeking repentance and forgiveness, which suggests national or communal self-criticism. Al-Qaeda and ISIS have much to confess and repent: they have distorted the teachings of Islam, especially in their indiscriminate attacks on civilians, and their absolutist world analysis is fraught with errors, misinterpretations, and hubris. Although the United States has hardly been anti-Islam, perhaps it too has been absolutist in its approach. The United States also needs to acknowledge, confess, and repent from the torture at Abu Ghraib prison in Iraq, the extraordinary rendition program, which outsourced the torture of suspected terrorists to other countries, and the indefinite detention without trial at Guantanamo Bay prison in Cuba.[223] By torturing suspects and disregarding human rights the United States gave up any moral advantage in the struggle against terrorism and facilitated the recruitment of jihadi in the Islamist cause. The phrase "No peace without justice, no justice without forgiveness" summarizes Pope John Paul II's 2002 World Peace Day message. One wonders if this message of confession, repentance, and forgiveness, proclaimed in the gospel and repeated by the pope, is being heeded by American Christians.

Just peacemaking recognizes that justice is the only sound foundation for peace and that it is essential in preventing terrorism. Thus, two more of its practices are fostering sustainable economic development and advancing democ racy and human rights. If the United States wants to make the world safer, it must make it healthier, more equitable, and more environmentally sound. Policies such as a new "Marshall Plan" aimed at the Arab and Muslim world, free trade accords with Muslim majority countries, and US fiscal responsibility (rather than miserliness, protectionism, and budget deficits) might be more effective in preventing terrorism than increased military action.[224] Respect for human rights is a key ingredient in addressing the unjust conditions that usually breed terrorism.

Along with nonviolent direct action (suggested above for the Palestinians) and cooperative conflict resolution, transforming initiatives are key to a just-peacemaking strategy. These should be constructive policies, even if they carry a reasonable risk, designed to reverse a spiral of violence by enhancing trust between adversaries. For example, given that US support for Israel is a significant irritant to Arab countries and Islamic groups, the United States could pressure Israel to stop its settlements in the West Bank and even channel US economic aid toward buying back Israeli settlements for Palestinians.[225]

A crisis of leadership seems to be behind much conflict today. Hunger for power and greed result in tyranny and oppression, which then beget resistance. Although antagonisms between ethnic groups or nations may have a long history, such enmity is neither natural nor inevitable. Ethnic enmity is invented. National leaders have fanned the flames of ethnic hatred with little regard for the common good or for finding constructive solutions to complex conflicts. Self-serving leadership is often responsible for ethnic conflagrations and the brutal violence that too often characterizes them, or for ideological or religious extremism that rationalizes senseless terrorism. In order to prevent and to resolve conflict, there is no substitute for leaders who have the genuine interests of their people at heart and who are able to recognize that other people also have genuine interests at stake as well. The world needs fewer demagogues and more diplomats.

Key to any just and peaceful arrangement of civil society are the twin values of (1) the *participation* of citizens in decisions that affect their well-being and (2) respect for *human rights*. When people have a real share in the exercise of power by the government, change can usually be accomplished without resort to violence. When human rights are honored, especially the rights of minorities and the marginalized, violent conflict is rare.

Unfortunately, religion has been used to add fuel to the fires of nationalism and extremism, provoking ethnic conflict and terrorism. Mark Juergensmeyer has written about the global phenomenon of religious violence in *Terror in the Mind of God* (published in 2000, before 9/11). Some terrorist acts are secular in motivation, but Juergensmeyer focuses on the many "public acts of violence at the turn of the century for which religion has provided the motivation, the justification, the organization, and the world view" (7). He notes that "every major religious tradition has served as a resource for violent actors, be they Muslim, Christian, Jewish, Hindu, Sikh, or Buddhist, indicating that religion and violence are deeply related" (xi–xii).

Since both religion and nationalism relate to core values, it is understandable that they become intertwined; but when religion legitimizes ethnic nationalism or extremism, religion becomes degraded and distorted. Authentic religion should critique any ideology that inculcates hatred and division or that absolutizes any value other than God.

Religious communities should advocate for conversion, forgiveness, and reconciliation; they should be forces for justice, solidarity, nonviolence, and peace. Religious communities should produce leaders who serve society and work for the common good—such as Gandhi (India), Martin Luther King, Jr. (United States), Bishop Desmond Tutu and Nelson Mandela (South Africa), Dag Hammarskjöld (United Nations), Cory Aquino (Philippines), and Jimmy Carter (United States). And when those in power spew hatred and do violence, religious communities must produce prophets and martyrs, such as Bishop Óscar Romero in El Salvador, and Franz Jaegerstaetter and Dietrich Bonhoeffer in Nazi Germany. Religion should always be a constructive force for justice, equality, reconciliation, and peace in situations of conflict. Unfortunately, religion is not always its best self. Along with Juergensmeyer I say, "My conviction is that the same religion that motivates such potent acts of destruction also carries an enormous capacity for healing, restoration, and hope."[226]

STUDY QUESTIONS

1. Distinguish between a nation and a state. Do you think that every nation should be a state?

2. Is nationalism a danger in the contemporary world? How can nationalism be harnessed as a positive force and be reined in as a negative force? What is your assessment of the global trend toward ultranationalism?

3. What is the basis of the conflict between Israel and the Palestinians? What do you think would be a just resolution of the conflict? What role should the United States play in resolving this conflict?

4. Was the 1991 Persian Gulf War morally justified? Was the 2003 preemptive invasion of Iraq morally justified?

5. What was the Arab Spring? What have been the results of the Arab Spring?

6. Many of the countries of Africa are faced with destitution and violence. Why is this? If you were to design a "Marshall Plan" for Africa, what would it look like?

7. Discuss the moral justification for humanitarian intervention.

8. Discuss a moral response to terrorism.

7

WEAPONS AND DISARMAMENT

Finally, be strong in the Lord and in the strength of his power. Put on the whole armor of God, so that you may be able to stand against the wiles of the devil. . . . Stand therefore and fasten the belt of truth around your waist, and put on the breastplate of righteousness. As shoes for your feet put on whatever will make you ready to proclaim the gospel of peace. With all of these, take the shield of faith, with which you will be able to quench all the flaming arrows of the evil one. Take the helmet of salvation, and the sword of the spirit, which is the word of God. (Eph 6:10–11, 14–17)

We must re-emphasize with all our being, nonetheless, that it is not only nuclear war that must be prevented, but war itself. Therefore with Pope John Paul II we declare:

> *Today, the scale and the horror of modern warfare—whether nuclear of not—makes it totally unacceptable as a means of settling differences between nations. War should belong to the tragic past, to history; it should find no place on humanity's agenda for the future.*

Reason and experience tell us that a continuing upward spiral, even in conventional arms, coupled with an unbridled increase in armed forces, instead of securing true peace will almost certainly be provocative of war.

US Conference of Catholic Bishops
The Challenge of Peace (1986), #219

World security analyst Michael Klare says there is a "deadly convergence" of three trends in the post–Cold War world.[1] One trend is the emergence of ethno-nationalist conflict. The other two trends are the proliferation of weapons of mass destruction (nuclear, chemical, and biological weapons), and the spread of ever-more-sophisticated conventional weapons and delivery systems through the arms trade. These three trends are likely to increase the number and severity of regional conflicts unless the global community takes decisive steps to defuse them. Previous chapters have looked at some of the motives for war in the twenty-first century: empire building and exploitation, poverty and the gap between the rich and the poor, environmental scarcity, violations of human rights, ethno-nationalism, religious extremism, greed, and conflict over land and power. This chapter will explore the issues of nuclear weapons and other weapons of mass destruction, weapons of long-term destruction, targeted killing and drone warfare, cyber warfare, gun safety in the United States, the traffic in conventional arms, and military spending. Weapons are not only the means to conduct war, but are often a contributing cause to war itself.

NUCLEAR MATTERS

The forty-five years of the Cold War (1945–1990) were characterized by a nuclear stalemate between the Union of Soviet Socialist Republics (USSR) and the United States—between the East and the West. The watchword for US foreign policy was "containment." Communism was to be contained and resisted wherever possible. This led the United States into wars in Korea (1950–1953) and in Vietnam (1954–1975), which spilled over into Laos and Cambodia, to keep the nations of Southeast Asia from falling, like dominoes, into communist hands. It also led the United States into military interventions in Latin America (Guatemala, Cuba, Chile, Haiti, Dominican Republic, El Salvador, Nicaragua, etc.) and elsewhere during the 1960s, 1970s, and 1980s.

The two superpowers divided the world into "spheres of influence" and competed with each other for the allegiance of unaligned states. Foreign aid, especially in the form of weapons and military assistance, was a major tactic in this strategy. For example:

- When Anwar Sadat decided to expel the Soviets in 1972 and switch allegiance to the United States, Egypt quickly became the second largest beneficiary, after Israel, of US foreign aid.
- Cuba was heavily subsidized by the Soviet Union in recognition of Fidel Castro's allegiance to communism. Cuba then became a conduit for Soviet aid to rebel armies in Central America and Africa.
- In the 1970s Ethiopia and Somalia, neighbors and combatants over disputed territory, each switched allegiances between the two superpowers. When Marxist guerrillas took control of Ethiopia, that country dropped its close relationship with Washington and turned to Moscow. Somalia, which had forged close links with the Soviet Union, then allied itself with the United States, in 1978. The United States showered Somalia's dictatorship with the weapons used in the early 1990s in civil unrest and against UN and American troops.[2]
- In the 1980s the United States backed rebel armies in the Soviet-allied states of Angola and Nicaragua.

Thus, during the Cold War, the world map was like a chessboard for the superpowers.

The arms race, however, was the major field of competition between the superpowers. Each tried to build bigger, better, and more nuclear weapons than the other. The paradoxical strategic doctrine that made this insane arms race marginally rational was deterrence through "mutually assured destruction" (MAD). MAD meant that both sides would be deterred from using nuclear weapons by the assurance that the victim of a nuclear attack could literally destroy the aggressor in retaliation. The populations of the United States and the Soviet Union were both, in effect, hostages in a situation of nuclear terrorism.

The word *terrorism* is not used lightly here. It is important to remember and appreciate the fear that characterized the Cold War in order to understand the feelings of relief when it ended and the task that still remains. While the fall of communism in Eastern Europe and the former Soviet Union dispelled the political tensions that produced this terror, the weapons themselves still exist. While we no longer live in daily fear that we will suddenly be engulfed in a nuclear firestorm, as long as nuclear weapons exist, this holocaust can still happen.

Lest We Forget: Unimaginable Destruction

The power of nuclear weapons is truly awesome. The blast effect from a one megaton (a million tons of TNT) warhead exploded over a major city would crush and vaporize everything within a one-and-a-half-mile radius. The temperature at the center of the fireball would be eight times hotter than the sun. All human beings within this zone would be immediately incinerated.

A shock front with winds exceeding 600 miles per hour would create a vacuum that would be filled with in-rushing winds of greater than hurricane force. Nearly everything would be destroyed in a three-mile radius from ground zero. Asphalt paving would melt; wood and clothes would spontaneously combust. Trucks would be thrown about like giant Molotov cocktails. Over eight miles from ground zero, winds would reach hurricane force, and most people would suffer second- or third-degree burns from this firestorm. People and animals dozens of miles away who saw the flash from

For Reflection

During the 1950s, Senator Joseph McCarthy stirred anticommunist sentiment in the United States to the point of blacklisting writers, actors, and other celebrities. At the same time, Americans were building bomb shelters and conducting air-raid drills in schools. Those who have no experience of this fear of communism and of nuclear weapons might want to interview someone about the climate in the United States during the Cold War or see films such as *Dr. Strangelove* (1964), *The Front* (1976), *Testament* (1983), *The Day After* (1983), *Good Night and Good Luck* (2005), or *Trumbo* (2015).

the explosion would be blinded or suffer eye damage. Much of the rubble near the blast would be highly radioactive.

Survivors would envy the dead. Many would die slowly from radiation sickness, severe burns, broken bones, and lacerations. Hospitals and health care personnel would be destroyed, disabled, or overwhelmed, as would fire departments, water treatment plants, and food stores. Many of the uninjured would die from epidemics or hunger. Some, no doubt, would commit suicide out of grief or shock. Radioactive particles, pulled into the upper atmosphere by the mushroom cloud, would fall hundreds or thousands of miles away, contaminating milk or food and causing cancer decades later. Survivors of the atomic bomb dropped on Hiroshima in 1945 lived in fear of falling victim to cancer because of their exposure to radiation. The radiation effect of a nuclear bomb is utterly indiscriminate. In a nuclear war, of course, a city could be hit with several warheads. The cumulative effect of a full-scale nuclear war would most likely produce a nuclear winter, lowering the temperature of earth so that little food could be produced.[3]

At the height of the arms race the two superpowers possessed over 50,000 nuclear bombs. Humanity still has the power to undo creation. Jonathan Schell hauntingly reflected on the meaning of this in *The Fate of the Earth*.

> Four and a half billion years ago, the earth was formed. Perhaps a half billion years after that life arose on the planet. For the next four billion years life became more complex, more varied, and more ingenious, until, around a million years ago, it produced mankind [sic]—the most complex and ingenious species of all. Only six or seven thousand years ago—a period that is to the history of the earth as less than a minute is to a year—civilization emerged, enabling us to build up a human world, and to add to the marvels of evolution marvels of our own: marvels of art, of science, of social organization, of spiritual attainment. . . . [A]nd now . . . we hold this entire terrestrial creation hostage to nuclear destruction, threatening to hurl it back into the inanimate darkness from which it came.[4]

These horrific weapons and the policy of deterrence are still with us. It is still possible for "some misguided or deranged human being or faulty computer chip" to launch nuclear warheads. Even worse, nuclear weapons and their delivery systems may be vulnerable to cyberwarfare.[5] It is still possible for the commander of a Trident submarine, with its capacity to deliver over 190 warheads on as many targets, to blackmail the world or to effectively destroy a continent. And as quickly as the political rationale for nuclear terrorism dissolved, it could return, if, for example, the precarious Russian experiment with democracy were to fail.[6] After September 11, there is increasing concern that terrorists might procure a nuclear weapon or create a crude atomic bomb.[7] The weapons themselves, quite apart from the threat or the will to use them, are terrifying.

The end of the Cold War, which has given the world a window of opportunity for nuclear disarmament, ironically saps the motivation to do so. The citizen antinuclear movement that ebbed and flowed in intensity from the 1960s through the 1980s seems to have lost much of its momentum since then. Because it seems less likely today that nuclear weapons will be used, it is difficult to generate much concern about the existence of such destructive power or much debate about the meaning or wisdom of deterrence in such a changed political context. We need to remember the power of these weapons and take advantage of this opportunity to move toward a policy of minimal deterrence as a first step toward living in a nuclear-free world.

Nuclear Proliferation

The nuclear age dawned because of a race, in the midst of World War II, to create an atomic bomb. The United States tested the bomb on July 16, 1945, and used it a few weeks later, on August 6 at Hiroshima and August 9 at Nagasaki, Japan. Shortly thereafter, Japan surrendered.[8]

The Soviet Union soon developed its own bomb in 1949, and the numerical and technological arms race was off and running. In this arms race, the United States always maintained a creative and technological lead and the Soviet Union effectively played catch-up, mimicking each American advance and even building more and bigger warheads and intercontinental ballistic missiles (ICBMs). After the early 1960s, when both superpowers could totally obliterate the other, it became ludicrous to speak of winning the arms race. From that point on, each superpower was simply adding to its overkill capacity and making sure that its nuclear weapons (not its people) could survive a first strike by the other side.

Great Britain and France developed their own nuclear weapons and delivery systems in order to help deter the

> **For Reflection**
>
> The controversy over whether the use of the atomic bomb was morally right or historically necessary still rages. Opponents contend that Japan was on the verge of surrendering anyway and that the bomb was used to prevent the Soviet Union from sharing in the victory in the Pacific. They also question the morality of using an indiscriminate weapon with the intention of killing civilians. Proponents contend that a bloody invasion would have been necessary before Japan would have surrendered, and that the use of the atomic bombs saved tens of thousands of American soldiers. This controversy is likely to be rekindled on the seventy-fifth anniversary of the bombing of Hiroshima and Nagasaki in 2020.

Soviet Union from attacking Western Europe, to enhance their prestige as major players in the world, and to maintain their independence. China, feeling threatened by its Soviet neighbor and desiring global prestige, also developed nuclear weapons. These three nations together have about 1,200 nuclear warheads. For some years, the United States, the Soviet Union (Russia), Great Britain, France, and China constituted the nuclear club of acknowledged nuclear powers. These countries also happen to be the five permanent members of the UN Security Council. This limited increase of nuclear weapons' states left the doctrine of deterrence intact, but proliferation became a concern.

The spread of nuclear weapons has been curbed primarily by the Nuclear Non-Proliferation Treaty (NPT). This 1968 accord took effect in 1970. The NPT binds together the acknowledged nuclear powers with nonnuclear nations. Those without nuclear weapons pledge not to acquire them and to submit to the supervision of the International Atomic Energy Agency (IAEA), which monitors their compliance. Nuclear powers agree to share nuclear energy technology with other nations, under the watchful eye of the IAEA, and to take steps toward reversing the arms race, nuclear disarmament, and a treaty on "general and complete disarmament" (Article VI).

When the Soviet Union splintered into fifteen independent republics in 1991, Ukraine, Kazakhstan, and Belarus became nuclear powers by virtue of having Soviet missiles based in their territory. All three dismantled these weapons and, with the aid of Russia and the United States, removed them to Russia.[9] Thus, all three countries have disarmed and joined the NPT protocol. This is good news, given the historical and current tensions between these countries and Russia, as well as the continuing ethnic and political turmoil within these states.

Four other countries are now recognized as nuclear weapons states. Israel, although it does not officially admit it, has developed and stockpiled about eighty nuclear weapons. India twisted the Atoms for Peace program, which assisted countries in the development of nuclear energy, into a nuclear bomb, which it first tested in 1974. Pakistan, India's neighbor and nemesis, produced and tested a nuclear weapon in 1998. This development led India to conduct further tests to establish its nuclear capability as a deterrent to Pakistan. None of these three had signed the Non-Proliferation Treaty. North Korea unilaterally withdrew from the NPT in 2003 and has tested nuclear bombs five times, in 2006, 2009, 2013, and twice in 2016.[10] This means that nuclear weapons have been introduced into three of the most volatile regions in the world: the Middle East, South Asia, and East Asia.

The Middle East

Israel's nuclear capability has been a major spur for its nondemocratic Arab neighbors to buy or build a nuclear bomb of their own. The Middle East is a volatile area that contains multiple fault lines for war: Israel vs. the Palestinians and the Arab countries, tensions between the Sunni and Shiite branches of Islam and with Muslim extremists, various other ethnic and religious tensions, the desire for political freedom in the face of tyranny that manifested itself in the 2011 Arab Spring, and a gap between the oil-rich minority and the poor majority. Introducing weapons of mass destruction and sophisticated delivery systems such as ballistic missiles and high-tech fighter bombers into this region is an invitation for trouble and tribulation. Yet many of the countries in the region sought to do just that.

In his 2002 State of the Union address to Congress, President George W. Bush identified an "axis of evil"—states that supported terrorism and sought nuclear weapons. Two of the states he identified as part of this axis of evil were in the Middle East: Iraq and Iran (the third was North Korea).

The 2003 preemptory invasion of Iraq was justified by the Bush administration in part because it was thought that Saddam Hussein was developing a nuclear bomb and had stockpiles of chemical and biological weapons. In reality Iraq had been disarmed of weapons of mass destruction after the 1991 Persian Gulf War. No ongoing nuclear weapons program nor any current stockpiles of chemical or biological weapons were found during the invasion.[11] Because of the political disarray left over from the Iraq War (2003–2011), it is unlikely that Iraq would seek to develop weapons of mass destruction in the foreseeable future.

Although a signatory of the NPT, in 2005 the IAEA found Iran's advancing capability to enrich fissionable material to be out of compliance with the agreement. The UN Security Council responded by passing seven resolutions demanding Iran stop its nuclear development activities. Iran unconvincingly contended that it was developing its nuclear energy program (which is allowed by the NPT), not nuclear weapons. Iran was also developing and testing ballistic missiles, also in violation of UN resolutions.

Iran is a majority Shia Muslim country that is a theocratic Islamic republic. The current supreme leader is Ayatollah Ali Khamenei. Iran actively supports terrorist groups such as Hezbollah in Lebanon. An Iranian nuclear weapon would probably further stimulate a nuclear arms race in the Middle East. A nuclear-armed Iran would be threatening and unacceptable to Israel, whose right to exist Iran has publicly denied, and to Iran's Sunni Muslim neighbors, such as Saudi Arabia. Israel threatened to bomb Iran's nuclear facilities, as it had preemptively bombed nuclear sites in Iraq in 1981 and Syria in 2007. The logistics of attacking Iran's more distant and more secure nuclear sites may well have required the aid of the United States to be effective, and probably would have resulted in war with Iran. In 2012, President Obama said that while the United States would not tolerate a nuclear-armed Iran, loose talk of a military response was premature.[12]

Iran's capacity to enrich fissionable material was augmented during the presidency of Mahmoud Amadinejad (2005–2013). When attempts to negotiate a settlement with Iran failed, the United States and the European Union imposed economic sanctions on Iran, including an oil embargo, in 2012. In 2013 Hassan Rouani was elected president of Iran, and under his leadership negotiations with the five permanent members of the UN Security Council plus Germany (P5+1) to settle the dispute moved forward. In mid-July 2015, with the economic sanctions clearly taking a toll, these negotiations yielded a Joint Comprehensive Plan of Action (JCPOA), a twenty-five-year nuclear agreement that limits Iran's nuclear capacity in exchange for relief from the sanctions tied to Iran's refusal to abide by UN resolutions regarding its nuclear activities. By January 2016, Iran had complied with the agreement and sanctions began to be lifted. The Iranians gave up 98 percent of their nuclear material, dismantled more than 1,200 centrifuges, disabling their ability to enrich uranium, and poured concrete into the core of a major plutonium reactor, all in the visible presence of IAEA inspectors.[13]

Opposition to this admittedly imperfect, yet effective, accord continued on the part of Israel, Saudi Arabia, and US congressional Republicans.[14] President Trump repeatedly criticized the Iran Nuclear Agreement during his campaign. Despite personal pleas from European leaders Emmanuel Macron of France, Angela Merkel of Germany, and Theresa May of the United Kingdom, on May 8, 2018, President Trump withdrew the United States from the accord and reinstituted economic sanctions on Iran. Mr. Trump also threatened to impose sanctions on European companies that continue to do business with Iran. Iran said it would continue to abide by the JCPOA as long as the other signatories do. President Trump's decision seems to reduce US options to military force if Iran refuses to comply with US demands.[15]

A third Middle Eastern country that President Bush could have included in his 2002 "axis of evil" was Libya. Muammar al-Qaddafi (1942–2011) certainly supported terrorism and had an active program to develop nuclear weapons and an arsenal of chemical weapons. On December 19, 2003, however, Qaddafi suddenly announced that Libya would dismantle its weapons of mass destruction (WMD) and ballistic missile programs, and did so in 2014 with the independent verification of the IAEA. Qaddafi apparently wanted to normalize relations with the West and avoid the fate suffered by Iraq. The political instability that followed the Libyan civil war of 2011 (during which Qaddafi was killed) makes it unlikely that Libya will revive its WMD or missile programs in the foreseeable future. Thus, one Middle Eastern country voluntarily renounced its aspirations for a nuclear bomb and destroyed its chemical weapons and ballistic missiles.[16]

South Asia

The animosity between India and Pakistan is rooted in the partition that accompanied their independence from the United Kingdom in 1947. At that time Muslims comprised about 25 percent of the population, but nearly every village on the Indian subcontinent had either a Muslim or a Hindu minority. Muhammad Ali Jinnah, the leader of the All-India Muslim League, insisted on the creation of Pakistan in areas where there was a Muslim majority, and Jawaharlal Nehru, who became the first prime minister of India, reluctantly agreed. This resulted in one of the largest mass migrations in history as fourteen million Hindus, Muslims, and Sikhs fled from areas where they were a minority, and in the vengeful slaughter of about 250,000 people.[17] Muslims were a majority of the population in Punjab, the western part of the region, and in Bengal, the eastern part of the region. Thus Pakistan was divided into two parts with India between them. Western Pakistan was a thousand miles from Eastern Pakistan; their peoples shared a religion, but little else, including language and ethnicity. India and Pakistan have fought four wars against each other since their independence in 1947. In the third of those wars (1971), India intervened on behalf of the Bangladesh Liberation Movement, routed the Pakistani army in a fortnight, and East Pakistan became Bangladesh. (The United States supported Pakistan in the Bangladesh Liberation War, and India allied itself with the Soviet Union.)

The other three of those wars between India and Pakistan (in 1947–1948, 1965, and 1999) pertained to a territorial dispute over Kashmir, a conflict that continues to simmer and intermittently erupt. On November 26, 2008, Pakistani militants killed over 160 people in a rampage in Mumbai, India. Such incidents of terrorism and the low-level conflict that persists in Kashmir inflame the hostility between India and Pakistan.[18] Now that both countries have nuclear weapons, eruptions of these tensions tempt India and Pakistan to use them.[19] In both India and Pakistan, the billions of dollars spent on their nuclear arms race and military forces would be better spent on feeding and educating their children, health care for their people, and creating jobs and economic development.

Pakistan is a particularly worrying nuclear-armed country. It is increasing its nuclear arsenal (at least 120 warheads) faster than any other country, and it is adding tactical (or battlefield) nuclear weapons that it might be more tempted to use, especially given India's superiority in conventional armaments and forces. Pakistan has left open the possibility that it would be the first to use nuclear weapons. Tactical nukes are also more likely to find their way into the hands of terrorists. Pakistan has purchased eight submarines from China (for an estimated $5 billion) which could be equipped with nuclear missiles, and has developed the medium-range (1,700 miles) Shaheen III missile capable of striking anywhere in India. At the same time, Pakistan has sunk deeper into economic and political chaos. It is home to a variety of extremist groups, including a Taliban insurgency whose aim is to bring down the government. Pakistan refuses to sign the NPT or the treaty banning nuclear weapons tests, and in the past it has been implicated in the spread of nuclear capability to rogue nations such as North Korea. China, a close ally of Pakistan, and a rival of democratic India, is also adding to its nuclear arsenal (about 250 warheads). The intensifying nuclear arms race in South Asia, and in particular the troubling situation in Pakistan, demands far greater international attention.[20]

East Asia

North Korea, however, is now the world's most worrisome nuclear threat. North Korea (the Democratic People's Republic of Korea) is a deeply impoverished, heavily armed, and totally repressive Communist dictatorship. Since the Armistice Agreement that marked the end of the Korean War (1950–1953), a precarious standoff has existed between North Korea and South Korea (the Republic of Korea), which is now democratic and economically prosperous. Enmity also exists between North Korea and Japan, which occupied Korea for thirty-five years until the end of World War II in 1945. These relationships are further complicated by the proximity of China, North Korea's main ally, economic lifeline, and sometime critic. North Korea is ruled by the Kim dynasty. The Soviets brought Kim Il-Sung to power in 1945, and he established a ruthless Communist government, cut off from the rest of the world, and characterized by a personality cult centered on the supreme leader. He was succeeded by his son Kim Jong-Il in 1994, who was succeeded by his third and youngest son, Kim Jong-Un, in December 2011. The untested, little-known, thirty-something Kim Jong-Un has solidified his power by purging at least seventy senior officials, including his uncle, whom he executed. He is also suspected of ordering the assassination of his oldest brother, Kim Jong-Nam, on February 13, 2017, when VX, a deadly nerve agent, was rubbed on him at Kuala Lumpur International Airport in Malaysia. A UN panel reported in 2014 that the Kim dynasty has committed systematic crimes against humanity during their rule, including executions, torture, rape, deliberate starvation of their people, and almost total suppression of free thought and expression.[21]

North Korea has more than ten nuclear devices. It says it tested a thermonuclear or hydrogen bomb in January 2016, but there is skepticism about that claim.[22] It has developed an intercontinental missile capable of reaching Guam and perhaps the United States. North Korea is also developing submarine-launched ballistic missiles. Its young leader seems erratic and unpredictable. Given its poverty and isolation, North Korea might be prone to sell a nuclear weapon or nuclear technology to another country or to a terrorist group. North Korea is probably the world's most dangerous nuclear threat.[23]

Numerous diplomatic initiatives between North Korea and the United

States, South Korea, Japan, China, and Russia (the Six Parties) had vacil-
lated between stalemate and progress, then fell apart in 2009. In response
to North Korea's nuclear tests and ballistic missile development, the United
Nations imposed sanctions on North Korea in 2013 and stiffened them in
late 2016, both times with the support of China, which is key to enforcing the
sanctions.[24] Since 2009 the United States had made a North Korean commitment to denuclearization a precondition for restarting negotiations. President
Donald Trump changed that.

During his campaign, Donald Trump talked about inviting Kim Jong-Un
to the White House to eat hamburgers around a conference table and make a
deal. In the first year of his presidency President Trump and Supreme Leader
Kim Jong-Un exchanged insults and threats in the context of North Korea's
testing of long-range missiles.[25] Then South Korean president Moon Jae-in
invited North Korea to jointly participate in the 2018 Winter Olympics being
held at Pyeongchang, South Korea, and Mr. Kim sent a delegation headed by
his sister, Kim Yo-Jong. This seemed to break the ice between the two Koreas,
and eventually President Trump accepted an invitation to meet with Mr. Kim
in Singapore on June 12, 2018, where Mr. Kim pledged to denuclearize his
country, but with no specific agreements or timeline.

This thawing of the relations between the United States and North Korea
is a positive development. Kim Jong-Un has taken some confidence-building
measures, such as instituting a moratorium on nuclear and missile tests, demol-
ishing his country's only nuclear testing site, and dismantling a missile engine
testing facility. He complains that the United States has done nothing to recip-
rocate.[26] Many foreign policy experts are skeptical that Mr. Kim will actually
destroy the North's nuclear weapons and missile program, which seem to be his
insurance against forced regime change. Perhaps President Trump and Secretary of State Mike Pompeo, in cooperation with the Six Parties, can work out an
agreement with the realistic goal of freezing North Korean nuclear fuel production and stopping missile and nuclear testing, using positive inducements such
as a lifting of sanctions, economic assistance, the removal of the Terminal High
Altitude Area Defense (THAAD) missile defense system (which also bothers
China),[27] and a peace treaty to replace the Korean War armistice.[28]

Past and Future

It is important to note that there have been some other successes in regard
to nuclear nonproliferation. South Africa developed, tested, and stockpiled a
small number of nuclear weapons, then decided to destroy them and is now
nuclear-free. In the late 1970s and early 1980s, Argentina and Brazil seemed
poised to embark on a nuclear arms race like that between India and Pakistan, but the replacement of their military governments with democracies has
eased the tension between the two countries and resulted in the termination of

their nuclear weapons programs.[29] No African or Latin American country has nuclear weapons.[30] Most nations seem comfortable without nuclear weapons, but all are wary of those that do exist and of the countries that possess them.

At the meeting to renew the NPT on its twenty-fifth anniversary in 1995, the nuclear powers pushed for its indefinite extension. Some of the nonnuclear nations—notably Mexico, Venezuela, Nigeria, and Indonesia—wanted to extend the treaty for fixed periods of time, as in the past. These countries argued that the nuclear powers had not lived up to the nuclear disarmament provisions of the treaty and were unlikely to do so unless they were subjected to continued pressure. The treaty was indefinitely and unconditionally renewed in 1995, but the arguments of the nonnuclear nations retain considerable merit. The NPT regime will work only if there is a genuine consensus of opinion and effective implementation of its provisions. The nuclear-weapons states, in particular, must make good-faith efforts toward the abolition of nuclear weapons.[31] There is a NPT Review Conference held at the UN headquarters every five years. In 2015 the member states were not able to reach a consensus on the Final Document.[32]

ARMS CONTROL

As the arms race developed, so did efforts at arms control, and these efforts bore fruit in various treaties and agreements. We have already seen that the 1968 Non-Proliferation Treaty (NPT) has been effective in keeping the nuclear club rather exclusive. The 1963 Limited Test Ban Treaty prohibited above-ground testing of nuclear weapons. It was signed in the aftermath of the Cuban Missile Crisis, among the tensest moments in the Cold War. The Anti-Ballistic Missile Treaty (ABM) of 1972, which severely curtailed the development of defensive systems to counter a nuclear attack, effectively closed off a whole new direction (i.e., defense) for the arms race. The Strategic Arms Limitation Talks (SALT), which resulted in the 1972 SALT I and 1979 SALT II treaties, slowed the arms race but did not result in the destruction of any nuclear warheads, missiles, or bombers.[33]

The Reagan years (1981–1989) brought a lull in arms-control negotiations, a leap in the arms race, and a corresponding surge in nuclear anxiety. The impasse in arms-control negotiations ended when Mikhail Gorbachev, the Soviet premier, accepted the US position regarding intermediate-range ballistic missiles in Europe. These were missiles based on both sides of the Iron Curtain that could reach targets in Western Europe or in the Soviet Union.[34] The Intermediate-Range Nuclear Forces (INF) Treaty treaty prohibits the testing, production, and possession of land-based ballistic and cruise missiles, armed with either nuclear or conventional warheads, with a range of 500 to 5,500 kilometers. Although the Soviet Union had a substantial lead in the number of missiles and warheads, Gorbachev agreed that both sides would destroy *all* of their intermediate nuclear forces. The INF Treaty (1987) was the first that actually reduced the number of missiles and warheads.[35] Unfortunately in 2014, Russia tested a ground-launched cruise missile that the United States claimed was in violation of the INF Treaty. In the early days of the Trump administration, it was discovered that Putin had secretly deployed this controversial missile.[36]

The INF Treaty gave the two superpowers motivation to resume Strategic Arms Reduction Talks (START), which resulted in two treaties—START I (1991) and START II (1993). START I called for mutual reductions in strategic weapons to about 6,000 each, but its implementation was delayed until 1994 by the dissolution of the Soviet Union on December 25, 1991. START II called for the United States and Russia to dramatically reduce their stockpiles of strategic nuclear warheads (to about 3,500 each) and of tactical nuclear weapons.[37] The US Senate, however, did not ratify START II until January 1996. The treaty could be interpreted as favoring the United States in that it gave the United States a numerical advantage, and it required Russia to dismantle all of its big land-based missiles, while the United States kept many of its advantageous submarine-based missiles. The Russian Duma (Parliament) hesitated to ratify the treaty, giving it only partial assent in 2000. Thus START II was never implemented, and the Clinton administration began a START III process as a way to overcome Russia's concerns.[38]

In 2001 President George W. Bush came into office having stated two clear goals regarding strategic nuclear weapons: to reduce America's nuclear arsenal to about 2,000 strategic warheads and to build a missile defense system. In May 2002, he signed a simple three-page (START I is over 700 pages long) Strategic Offensive Reduction Treaty (SORT, often called the Moscow Treaty) with Russian President Vladimir Putin that committed both sides to reduce their operationally deployed strategic nuclear warheads to no more than 2,200 by 2012. Bush had wanted an informal gentlemen's agreement to this effect to allow maximum flexibility, but both the Russians and the US Senate insisted on a formal treaty. The Senate ratified this treaty and it went into force in 2003.[39]

Although the defensive side of the arms race had been effectively halted by the ABM Treaty in 1972, the idea of a National Missile Defense (NMD) system was revived by President Reagan's "Star Wars" proposal in 1983 and again by a Republican Congress in 1996. President Bush was concerned about a nuclear attack or nuclear blackmail by a rogue state (ruled by unhinged authoritarian regimes) that acquired nuclear weapons. Thus, after announcing its intentions in December 2001, the United States officially terminated its participation in the ABM Treaty on June 13, 2002, and broke ground at an NMD construction site in Fort Greeley, Alaska, two days later.

As we have seen, North Korea has become the rogue state with nuclear weapons and ballistic missiles that Bush feared. Supreme ruler Kim Jong-Un has also vaguely pledged to denuclearize and has a moratorium on nuclear and missile tests. The US NMD system, primarily located at Fort Greeley, Alaska, uses a Ground-based Mid-Course Defense (GMD) that tries to intercept the incoming ICBM in space. This is comparable to hitting a bullet with a bullet in a sea of decoys. Indeed, in eighteen tests conducted in benign conditions favoring success, the interceptor failed to hit its target nine times, or 50 percent of the time.[40] Even if this defensive technology could be perfected, most analysts think that better offensive technology would quickly be developed to defeat it. Furthermore, the NMD would be useless against the more realistic, but still fanciful, threat of a nuclear bomb delivered by small plane, by land (truck or suitcase), or sea (speedboat or freighter).[41] None of America's allies in Europe was in favor of the US renunciation of the ABM Treaty in order to build a NMD system, especially one that is unlikely to protect Europe. China, noting that the threat from rogue nations is questionable, not unreasonably interprets the missile shield as protecting the United States from its rather limited nuclear deterrent. The NMD has strained relations with both friends and foes.

The Missile Defense Agency (MDA) of the Department of Defense is in charge of the NMD system. The Obama administration continued the development and testing of the NMD, increasing the number of interceptors from thirty in 2009 to forty-four by the end of 2017. Since 1985 the United States has spent over $180 billion on the NMD system according to MDA figures. The interceptor missiles are more expensive than the missiles and warheads they are intercepting.[42] Should the NMD system be scrapped, with the United States rejoining the ABM Treaty?

The Moscow Treaty was superseded by New START, which was signed by US President Obama and Russian President Dmitri Medvedev on April 8, 2010, and went into force on February 5, 2011. This treaty requires the United States and the Russian Federation to reduce deployed warheads to 1,500, and to reduce deployed and nondeployed launchers (ICBMs, SLBMs, and bombers) to 800, of which only 700 can be deployed. By February 2018, the deadline for reaching these limits, the United States had reduced its deployed warheads to 1,350 and Russia to 1,444. New START uses a modified and updated version of the verification measures in the 1991 START I treaty, which include on-site inspections, technical means (such as satellite observance), and data exchanges.[43]

In June 2018 the nine states with nuclear weapons possessed approximately 3,964 operationally deployed nuclear weapons. If all nuclear warheads are counted, these states together possessed a total of approximately 14,570 nuclear weapons. The United States (6,550) and Russia (6,850) have approximately 93 percent of the nuclear warheads that remain in existence. Through arms-control agreements the two superpowers of the Cold War era have radically reduced the number of warheads at their disposal from over 50,000 in 1965, yet they maintain sufficient capability for deterrence.[44]

Arms-control agreements have focused on strategic nuclear weapons and have paid little attention to tactical nuclear weapons, which have a lower yield, shorter range, and are designed for battlefield use. In 1991 both the United States and the Soviet Union eliminated from their arsenals many of these tactical nuclear weapons. From approximately 8,000 then, the United States now has around 760 tactical nuclear weapons with about 200 deployed in Europe. Experts think Russia has between 1,000 and 6,000 tactical nuclear weapons. Tactical nuclear weapons raise a number of issues. The yield or power of these weapons varies up to about 300 tons of TNT (the bomb dropped on Hiroshima was equivalent to about 15 kilotons of TNT), but all of them would release deadly radiation, which makes them inherently indiscriminate. The smaller size of the weapons raises safety and security concerns: they could be lost, stolen, or sold more easily. The role of tactical nuclear weapons in US, Russian, or NATO security policies is unclear. The low yield of these weapons threatens to blur the line between conventional and nuclear weapons, and makes the use of nuclear weapons more thinkable and tempting. Any use of a nuclear weapon would likely result in escalation toward nuclear war and mutually assured destruction.[45] Tactical nuclear weapons should be included in arms control and disarmament discussions and agreements.

In December 2009, less than a year into his first term, President Barack Obama was awarded the Nobel Peace Prize "for his extraordinary efforts to strengthen international diplomacy and cooperation between peoples." In his acceptance speech, Obama acknowledged "the considerable controversy your generous decision has generated" because he was at the beginning of his labors on the world stage with few accomplishments, and because he was commander–in-chief of a nation engaged in two wars. The award, then, was an incentive for Obama to fulfill the promise the Nobel committee saw in him. It was based in part on an April 5, 2009, foreign policy speech that he gave in Prague, Czech Republic.[46] There the newly elected US president had committed the only nation to have used nuclear weapons to lead the way toward a "world without nuclear weapons." One would be hard-pressed to argue that Obama had become clearly worthy of his Nobel Peace Prize by the end of his presidency.

A year later Obama returned to Prague to sign the New START treaty. In part to secure the necessary Republican support to ratify the treaty, Obama agreed to a modernization of the US nuclear arsenal, but the president pledged to make no new nuclear arms.[47]

Through the Department of Energy's National Nuclear Security Administration's (NNSA) Life Extension Program (LEP), the US military continually upgrades and refurbishes its existing strategic and tactical delivery systems and their nuclear warheads to last well beyond their originally planned service life and to keep them safe, secure, and reliable. Because of the Comprehensive (Nuclear) Test Ban (CTB) Treaty, this is done without testing the warheads. Despite the LEP, many of these delivery systems and types of warheads are reaching their "sell-by dates," and the United States is planning to replace them with new systems that will be more capable and precise than the originals. This US investment in its nuclear forces is unrivaled by any other nuclear power. The plan proposed by the Obama administration goes well beyond the original idea of modernization, and it certainly seems to break Obama's pledge not to build new nuclear weapons.[48] For example:

- The LEP for the 400 Minuteman III ICBMs has essentially produced a new missile, with expanded targeting options and improved accuracy and survivability.
- The United States currently has fourteen Ohio-class nuclear-powered ballistic missile submarines (SSBN), twelve of which are deployed at any one time. The navy plans to replace these as they are retired with a new Columbia-class SSBN(X), beginning in 2031.
- The US Air Force currently deploys eighteen B-2 Spirit bombers and seventy-two B-52H bombers, thirty of which will be converted to carry only conventional weapons under New START. The Air Force is planning to replace its existing bombers with one hundred new, dual-capable, long-range B-21 bombers, perhaps beginning around 2040.
- The NNSA is currently pursuing a plan to consolidate the existing number of nuclear warhead types from ten down to five. One of the new warhead types, the B61 Model 12, was bomb flight-tested in Nevada in 2015. It has a "dial-a-yield" feature with the lowest of the four settings equivalent to 300 tons of TNT, making its tactical use on a battlefield more tempting. This family of new warhead types tends toward the small, the stealthy, and the accurate.[49]

Is this modernization program still a refurbishment or is the United States creating new nuclear arms? Is it compatible with Obama's commitment to a "world without nuclear weapons"?

The cost of this new nuclear enterprise was estimated at $355 billion during the decade 2014–2023, and about $1 trillion over three decades.[50] One wonders if this nuclear modernization plan is affordable and if such budget priorities would be moral. The amount spent on the US nuclear arms program from 1940 through 1996 is estimated at $5.5 trillion, or 29 percent of all military spending ($18.7 trillion) during that period.[51] From 1996 through 2014 approximately $130 billion was spent on nuclear weapons.[52] Now the United States plans to spend another $1 trillion over three decades on nuclear weapons it would be unthinkable and immoral to ever use. As the Second Vatican Council pointed out as early as 1965, "the arms race is an utterly treacherous trap for humanity, and one which injures the poor to an intolerable degree."[53] Even without being used, nuclear weapons harm humanity and the earth.[54]

Because of the Western sanctions imposed on Russia after its annexation of Crimea in March 2014 and its military incursion into Ukraine, President Putin has shown no interest in further reductions in nuclear arms.[55] The US nuclear modernization plan seems to point in the direction of a renewed nuclear arms race rather than further bilateral or multilateral nuclear disarmament. Thus, progress toward nuclear disarmament was at a standstill by the end of Obama's presidency. The modernization program seemed to enhance the role of nuclear weapons in US security strategy, and further reductions in nuclear weapons seemed politically unlikely.[56]

President Trump has given no indication of having a vision of nuclear abolition. He had not given much attention to arms control through the second year of his administration, but he is committed to the modernization of the US nuclear arsenal.[57]

DETERRENCE OR DISARMAMENT?

There is a fundamental question facing policy makers and citizens in regard to nuclear weapons: deterrence or disarmament?[58] Should the goal be the abolition of nuclear weapons, or should the doctrine of deterrence, based on a limited stockpile of nuclear weapons, continue to guide US foreign policy?

If it is decided that deterrence is the more secure policy (and it appears to have worked thus far), a few hundred or a thousand nuclear warheads probably would be sufficient. Thus, deterrence could be achieved at the level agreed upon by New START (1,500) or even lower. Since the credibility of deterrence depends on a country's ability to strike back after an attack, mobile submarines and bombers as delivery vehicles would be superior to missiles in fixed silos, which are more vulnerable to a first-strike attack.

But if nuclear weapons are unusable in any moral or rational approach to warfare, and if they are dangerous and terrifying in themselves, then why have them at all? Would not the United States and the world be more secure if nuclear weapons were abolished? The difficulty, of course, is that the nuclear genie cannot be put back in the bottle. Humankind will always have the capability to make a nuclear bomb.

While the design of a bomb is not overly daunting, producing bomb-grade fissionable material is a complex process requiring sophisticated and scarce equipment.[59] Thus, a world without nuclear weapons could be maintained through strict controls on producing weapons-grade material. Indeed, although it has not been foolproof, the IAEA does keep track of fissionable material throughout the world. Protocols for managing this doubly dangerous material are already in place, although they undoubtedly should be strengthened.

Catholic social teaching certainly leans in the direction of nuclear disarmament. In their 1983 pastoral letter *The Challenge of Peace*, the American Catholic bishops, following statements by Pope John Paul II, arrived at a "strictly conditioned moral acceptance of nuclear deterrence . . . as a step on the way toward progressive disarmament" (##186–187). Ten years later in their anniversary statement titled *The Harvest of Justice Is Sown in Peace*, the bishops continued to accept deterrence, but only as a step toward a postnuclear form of security that lies in the abolition of nuclear weapons and the strengthening of international law (p. 333). Five years later (1998) a group of seventy-three "Pax Christi USA Bishops" issued a statement on "The Morality of Nuclear Deterrence" that concluded, "Nuclear deterrence as a national policy must be condemned as morally abhorrent because it is the excuse and justification for the continued possession of these horrendous weapons. We urge all to join in taking up the challenge to begin the effort to eliminate nuclear weapons now, rather than relying on them indefinitely." Pope John XXIII seemed to be well ahead of his successors when he wrote the following in his 1963 encyclical *Peace on Earth*:

> Justice, then, right reason and consideration for human dignity and life urgently demand that the arms race should cease, that the stockpiles which exist in various countries should be reduced equally and simultaneously by the parties concerned, that nuclear weapons should be banned, and finally that all come to an agreement on a fitting program of disarmament, employing mutual and effective controls (#112).

The Catholic Church, then, calls for nuclear disarmament, but allows deterrence to stand as a step along the way.

A growing number of diplomats, military leaders, and defense experts in the United States (such as General Andrew Goodpaster, former commander of NATO, General George Lee Butler, former commander-in-chief of the US Strategic Command, Paul Nitze, former arms negotiator, Robert McNamara, former secretary of defense, and General Charles A. Horner, commander of the coalition air forces during the Persian Gulf War) have urged "a fundamental re-evaluation of long-standing assumptions regarding the benefits of nuclear weapons," and total nuclear disarmament as realistic goals.[60] General Horner pointed out the hypocrisy of the United States being the major nuclear power and criticizing other nations for developing nukes. Didn't Jesus suggest that we get the log out of our own eye before we try to remove the speck from our neighbor's eye (Matt 7:1–5)?

On January 4, 2007, George P. Shultz (secretary of state 1982–1989 for President Reagan), William J. Perry (secretary of defense 1994–1997 for President Clinton), Henry A. Kissinger (secretary of state 1973–1977 for presidents Nixon and Ford), and Sam Nunn (Democratic senator from Georgia from 1972 to 1997 and former chair of the Senate Armed Service Committee) published an op-ed piece in the *Wall Street Journal* titled "A World Free of Nuclear Weapons."[61] As we have seen above, President Obama committed the United States to stopping the spread of nuclear weapons and to seeking a world without them in Prague in 2009.[62] The abolition of nuclear weapons is supported by knowledgeable people across the political and ideological spectrum, but, of course, not by everyone.

Indeed, after two negotiation conferences held at the United Nations in New York on March 27–31 and June 15–July 7, the Treaty on the Prohibition of Nuclear Weapons was formally adopted on July 7, 2017. It is open for signature by any member state and enters into legal force ninety days after being ratified by fifty countries.[63] The goal of the Nuclear Ban Treaty is to realize a world free of nuclear weapons. It is an initiative to prohibit the use, possession, development, testing, deployment, and transfer of nuclear weapons under international law. This enterprise is sponsored by the UN General Assembly, not the Security Council, led by six countries: Austria, Brazil, Ireland, Mexico, Nigeria, and South Africa. There were 132 UN member nations that participated in the negotiations. None of the nuclear powers participated, nor did they participate in the series of preliminary meetings, beginning in 2013, on the humanitarian impact of nuclear weapons.[64] The United States led a group of dozens of members in a boycott of the negotiations, with US ambassador to the United Nations, Nikki R. Haley, saying the time was not right to outlaw nuclear weapons.[65]

The New START treaty seemed to move the United States and Russia toward a policy of minimal deterrence, although one might wish for a clearer statement of this objective, a more definite timeline, the removal of ICBMs from high alert, and the destruction (not storage) of warheads and specific delivery systems (such as B-52 bombers).[66] Neither Russia nor the United States seems currently open to making progress on bilateral nuclear arms control. Perhaps, then, despite Ambassador Haley, it is time for a Nuclear Ban Treaty that moves beyond the bilateral approach of SALT and START, and includes all the members, official and de facto, of the nuclear club and of the United Nations.

A first step toward nuclear disarmament would be a reaffirmation, and in some cases the ratification, of *a comprehensive ban on testing nuclear weapons*. In order to win the vote for an indefinite extension of the Non-Proliferation Treaty (NPT), the nuclear powers agreed early in 1996 to reach an accord banning nuclear testing that was overwhelmingly endorsed by the United Nations. In order for the treaty to become universal law, however, all forty-four nations possessing nuclear reactors must sign and ratify the treaty. India and Pakistan refused to sign the treaty, and both tested nuclear weapons in 1998, but not since then. In October 1999, the Republican majority in the US Senate refused to ratify the Comprehensive Test Ban Treaty. China has also not ratified the CTB, but both Washington and Beijing continue to abide by it. Despite the failure to have a universally ratified CTB treaty, the twenty-first century de facto moratorium on nuclear testing has been broken only by North Korea. It is clear that established nuclear powers have no need to test nuclear weapons. It would seem to be in US national interests to have a CTB treaty with the force of law. The United States could exercise leadership by ratifying this treaty.[67]

Other steps toward nuclear disarmament would include a *global ban on the production of fissionable materials* for use in nuclear weapons *and strengthening the International Atomic Energy Agency,* whose role is expanding beyond the constraints of its limited budget. These were the partially realized goals of the four Nuclear Security Summits (2010–2016) sponsored by the Obama administration. These summits were primarily addressing the problem of terrorists getting their hands on a nuclear bomb or enough nuclear material for a dirty bomb. Banning the production of fissionable materials and destroying bomb-grade material that exists would also be key to abolishing nuclear weapons.

A final step would be the mutually agreed-upon and verified destruction of nuclear weapons. The United States and Russia should enter into multilateral discussions with all the nations that have nuclear weapons, under the auspices of the United Nations, aimed at the verified elimination of all nuclear weapons and join the Nuclear Ban Treaty.

The United States foreign-policy establishment seems to vacillate on the issue of nuclear weapons, decrying the efforts of others to acquire them but clinging to our own like a security blanket. Unfortunately, nuclear weapons are more like a grenade than a security blanket. The nuclear NPT clearly commits the nuclear powers to disarm. (The Nuclear Ban Treaty expects to complement the NPT, making the goal of nuclear abolition clearer.) If the United States is a country of integrity that honors the treaties it signs, then the United States has chosen the path of nuclear disarmament. The American Catholic bishops point this out in their 1983 pastoral letter *The Challenge of Peace* (#208). The Obama administration acknowledged this commitment and began slowly moving down the path toward a safer world order, one without the fear of a nuclear holocaust shadowing the future. Both domestic and international political realities hampered progress toward the abolition of nuclear weapons. The contours of that path are clear: stopping the proliferation of nuclear weapons, adherence to the CTB treaty, the destruction of existing weapons-grade fissionable material and a verifiable global ban on its production, strengthening the IAEA, and dismantling all nuclear weapons and their delivery systems.

CHEMICAL AND BIOLOGICAL WEAPONS

Although nuclear weapons are more destructive, chemical and biological weapons share many of the same characteristics:

- They are indiscriminate.
- They can cause the horror of mass death.
- They are difficult to control.
- They are prone to proliferation.
- They are problematic to destroy.

Chemical Weapons

Chemical weapons release chemicals, such as nerve gas or tear gas, which kill or disable people. They have been called the "poor country's atom bomb" because they represent an inexpensive way for a country to acquire weapons of mass destruction for potential leverage in international conflicts. Protective clothing and gas masks can often defend against a chemical threat. Chemical weapons are intrinsically indiscriminate. The results of their use during World War I were so horrible that the *use* of chemical (and biological) weapons was banned by the 1925 Geneva Protocol, which is still in effect. Chemical weapons have only rarely been used in warfare since then. They were intentionally used to massacre civilians in the gas chambers of the concentration camps during the Holocaust but not on the European battlefield in World War II. The United States used napalm and the herbicide Agent Orange in the Vietnam War. Iraq, under Saddam Hussein, used chemical weapons in the Iran–Iraq War (1980–1988) and against the Kurdish residents of Halabja in northern Iraq in 1988, killing nearly everyone in the village. Bashar al-Assad used sarin gas in an attack on the Ghouta area outside Damascus, killing 1,400 people, in August of 2013. Retaliation by the United States was avoided by an international accord in which Syria surrendered its 1,290 metric tons of chemical weapons, which were removed and destroyed by an international coalition, including Russia.[68] Chlorine gas, which has many civilian uses, was not included, and Assad has used chlorine gas as a weapon from early in 2015 through January 2018.[69] President Assad then used the nerve agent sarin, which was included in the agreement, in bombing the town Khan Sheikhun on April 4, 2017, killing more than eighty civilians, including children. Two days later President Trump ordered a retaliatory strike by fifty-nine Tomahawk cruise missiles on the Shayrat airbase near Homs, from which the Syrian chemical attack was launched.[70]

Because many chemicals have both a peaceful use and can also be used in weapons (the bomb set off in Oklahoma City in 1995 was made from chemicals used in the manufacture of fertilizer), only on-site inspection can really control the proliferation of chemical weapons. On-site verification was not included in the agreement with Syria to dispose of its chemical weapons. In 1992 a new Chemical Weapons Convention (CWC) was introduced through the United Nations to ban the *production, possession,* and use of chemical weapons. This convention went into effect in April of 1997. By 2015, 192 states were party to the CWC, and only Egypt, North Korea, South Sudan, and Israel (which signed the CWC but has not ratified it) were not on board. President Assad of Syria sent a letter to the United Nations affirming the CWC with immediate effect in September 2013, but Syria has used chemical weapons many times since then. The Organization for the Prohibition of Chemical Weapons (OPCW), headquartered in The Hague, is responsible for implementing the CWC through on-site inspections and overseeing and verifying the destruction of chemical weapons.[71] The OPCW, which won the Nobel Peace Prize in 2013, reported in May of 2015 that 90 percent of the stockpiles reported by the members of the CWC had been destroyed.[72]

As with nuclear weapons, the dismantling and disposal of chemical weapons has proved to be costly and hazardous. Both Russia and the United States, which had the biggest stockpiles of chemical weapons, failed to meet the 2012 CWC deadline for their destruction. Russia claimed to complete the process in 2017, but then was accused by Britain of using a lethal nerve agent, Novichok, on a former Russian spy and his daughter (both of whom survived) in early 2018. The United States expects to finish destroying its chemical weapons in 2023.[73] The cost of destroying the 30,000 metric-ton US chemical arsenal was an estimated $40 billion.

In its domestic legislation that ratified and implemented the CWC, the United States unilaterally provided itself with three exemptions. This has undermined the treaty by setting a bad example for other countries to follow. Moreover, the majority of the parties to the treaty have not paid their regular assessments or have failed to reimburse the Organization for the Prohibition of Chemical Weapons for the cost of inspections, resulting in a financial crisis. The United States is one of the countries at greatest risk from the spread of chemical weapons, yet it still has not exercised responsible leadership in controlling them.[74]

Biological Weapons

Biological weapons use micro-organisms or biologically derived toxins instead of chemicals. Some organisms, such as the ebola virus, anthrax bacterial spores, or smallpox, can cause fatal diseases; others, such as influenza, can be incapacitating. Deadly viruses could cause an epidemic that would be impossible to control and that might rebound to destroy the nation that used the weapon. To date, biological weapons have not yet been used in warfare.

The use of biological weapons was banned by the 1925 Geneva Protocol. The development, production, and possession of biological weapons and toxins are prohibited by the 1972 Biological Weapons Convention (BWC). The BWC also bans delivery vehicles for such weapons and requires the destruction of any stockpiles of biological arms. As of July 2016 the BWC has been ratified by 175 states and has nine signatory states; thirteen countries are not party to the treaty.[75]

The treaty makes no provision for inspection or verification and specifies no sanctions for violation. This lack of teeth reduces the BWC to little more than a handshake agreement. Consequently, the BWC member states established an Ad Hoc Group in 1994 to develop a system of on-site inspections to monitor compliance with the treaty. As with chemical weapons, the dual use of biological agents can make inspection and verification delicate and difficult. In July of 2001, the US delegation under the George W. Bush administration not only rejected the verification protocol that was on the table but withdrew from the Ad Hoc Group, effectively ending the process.[76] Since the United States is under threat from bioterrorism, one wonders about the wisdom of unilaterally withdrawing from the process to verify compliance with the BWC.

The BWC holds a review conference about every five years. At the sixth review conference in 2006, the member states created an Implementation Support Unit (ISU), consisting of three staff members, housed at the UN Department of Disarmament Affairs in Geneva, to assist with administration and facilitation. The United States and perhaps a dozen other countries engage in biological weapons research, which is not banned by the treaty, ostensibly to deter one another from developing such weapons.[77]

WEAPONS OF LONG-TERM DESTRUCTION

If used, weapons of mass destruction—nuclear, chemical, and biological weapons—cause long-term destruction through radiation, chemicals, and biological agents that linger and spread. Thankfully weapons of mass destruction have been rarely used. There are, however, modern weapons that extend the harm and tragedy of war well beyond the war itself. These "weapons of long-term destruction" (WLTD) include land mines, cluster bombs, and depleted uranium shells. These weapons have actually killed or maimed more victims than have weapons of mass destruction.[78]

Land Mines

Antipersonnel land mines (APMs) are like a buried grenade with a trigger activated by contact or sensor that explodes, sending shrapnel into the immediate area. APMs are designed to maim rather than kill an enemy soldier based on the assumption than an injured soldier requires more resources than a dead one. "Smart mines" that self-destruct or self-deactivate after a set period are available, albeit more expensive, but most land mines remain active until detonated or disarmed. Antivehicle mines have more explosive power to destroy or damage an armored truck, Humvee, or tank. Improvised explosive devices (IEDs) are considered land mines because they function similarly. Land mines, plus cluster bombs and any bombs that fail to explode, become unexploded ordinance (UXO) after a conflict ends, and this debris of war is often not responsibly cleaned up.[79]

Postwar land mines are a scourge for civilians, especially children, and they obstruct reconstruction and economic development efforts. A new mine costs as little as $3, but uprooting a mine can cost between $200 and $1,000, and an arm, a leg, or a life. There are perhaps 100 million mines buried in sixty-four countries around the world, and they have killed or maimed more than 100,000 people, mostly civilians, since 1999. In 2016 there were 8,605 casualties, including 2,089 deaths, from land mines. As in 2015, this marked a sharp increase in the number of casualties, including the most child casualties ever recorded. There were casualties in fifty-two nations and four other areas. Seventy-eight percent of the casualties were civilians, and 42 percent of those were children. As of November 2017, sixty-one states and areas were contaminated by APMs.[80]

The civilian casualties caused by mines are a strong argument for their condemnation, but mines can serve a defensive military purpose. Bernard E. Trainor, a retired Marine lieutenant general and former director of the national security program at Harvard's Kennedy School of Government, conveys the ambiguity of land mines in recounting his experience in the Korean War. As his platoon was taking Hill 59 from Chinese Communist forces, Trainor tripped on a wire. "I heard a 'thip' as it activated a mine, and I steeled myself for the explosion that would rip off my legs. Nothing happened. The mine had failed to function." Two nights later, when the enemy forces tried to recapture the hill, the mines his platoon had planted to protect their position saved them from being overrun. Trainor thinks that trying to outlaw mines would be futile and unverifiable and, since mines can protect American troops in certain circumstances, perhaps immoral.[81] He and others favor the use of sophisticated, "smart" mines that automatically deactivate, along with restrictions on the sale of mines. Other American military officers, however, including General Norman Schwarzkopf (1934–2012), the commander of the Gulf War, and General David C. Jones (1921–2013), a former chair of the Joint Chiefs of Staff, argued that APMs are not essential in modern warfare and ought to be banned.[82]

In 1992 six non-governmental organizations (NGOs) joined together to form the International Campaign to Ban Landmines (ICBL). Sustained by moral outrage at the tragic civilian casualties of land mines during war and after war, and effectively using the internet to inform and organize, the ICBL brought the nations of the world together at Ottawa, Canada, in 1997 to become party to the "Convention on the Prohibition of the Use, Stockpiling, Production and Transfer of Anti-Personnel Mines and on Their Destruction," also called the Mine Ban Treaty or the Ottawa Convention. The Mine Ban Treaty went into effect in 1999, and in November 2017 it had 162 states parties. It provides the framework for eradicating APMs through its comprehensive prohibitions and requirements that states parties clear mined areas within ten years, destroy stockpiles within four years, and provide victim assistance. There are, however, thirty-five countries that are not party to the Mine Ban Treaty, including the United States, Russia, China, India, North Korea, South Korea, Pakistan, Myanmar, Israel, Egypt, Iran, and Syria.[83] The United States argues that it needs APMs to protect its antitank mines in the demilitarized zone in Korea and wants to keep the APM military option open in other situations. Critics contend that concern for discriminate warfare and civilian casualties should motivate the United States (and all countries) to stop producing and using APMs and to destroy stockpiles of these weapons. The ICBL and its founding coordinator, Jody Williams, received the Nobel Peace Prize in 1997.

From 2012 to 2016, about 927 square kilometers were cleared of mines, destroying some 1.1 million APMs and 68,000 antivehicle mines. Twenty-eight states parties to the Mine Ban Treaty and one state not party have completed clearance since 1999, including the once heavily contaminated Mozambique. Funding to support mine action decreased by 23 percent in 2015 and 7 percent in 2016. Collectively, states parties have destroyed more than fifty-three million stockpiled antipersonnel mines, including more than 2.2 million destroyed in 2016. There are eleven countries that reserve the right to produce land mines, and there are nonstate actors that continue to produce improvised explosive devices.[84] Thus, while progress has been made in clearing mines and destroying some stockpiles, mines continue to be sown, especially in areas of active conflict such as Syria and Myanmar. Land mines maim and kill civilians, and especially children, every day.

Cluster Munitions

Cluster munitions, technically called cluster bomb units (CBUs), are horrific weapons. The canisters can be dropped by aircraft or launched by land or sea. Each canister can contain up to 650 bomblets or submunitions which are dispersed over a wide area. Each bomblet contains shrapnel, such as steel pellets, and explodes in mid-air or on impact. Some submunitions have a small parachute to float to the target. Some have heat-seeking technology and armor piercing capability for use against tanks and vehicles (or persons). Its footprint can be as large as two football fields or a square kilometer. A cluster bomb is like a shotgun blast of grenades. It can have a devastating effect on masses of soldiers or a village (antipersonnel), or columns of tanks or vehicles (anti-materiel). The bomblets are often brightly colored and in various shapes resembling batteries, tennis balls, soda cans, or hockey pucks. Too often the bomblet fails to explode, either because it lands on a soft surface or malfunctions. The dud rate in Kosovo and Afghanistan is estimated between 5 and 30 percent. In its conflict with Hezbollah in the summer of 2006, Israel launched some 2.6–4 million submunitions in Lebanon, two-thirds of which were scattered in populated areas. The United Nations estimates that over a million failed to detonate. The United States has used cluster munitions in nearly every conflict from Vietnam to Iraq in 2003, after which it suspended their use. In the bombing of Laos, which ended in 1974, the United States dropped eighty million cluster bomblets, with approximately 10 percent failing to explode. Every month this unexploded ordinance kills two or three Laotian civilians and injures another six or seven.[85]

Handicap International estimates that 98 percent of casualties of cluster munitions are civilians and 27 percent of those are children.[86] This statistic plays an important role in the ethical analysis of cluster munitions by theological ethicist Tobias Winright. Based on the just-war principles of discrimination and proportionality, he concludes that "the use of cluster munitions is not morally justified at this time."[87] In examining whether cluster munitions are *inherently* immoral, he notes that the submunitions are often *designed* to look like batteries, tennis balls, etc., signaling an intent for unexploded ordinance to harm civilians and especially children. In Afghanistan, for example, the United States dropped cluster bombs and humanitarian aid food parcels that were both yellow, leading some civilians to mistake bombs for food, and requiring the United States to broadcast warnings.[88] While such designs are either negligent or intentionally inhumane, it would be possible to design cluster munitions in a different way. It seems to me that the *use* of cluster munitions in any populated area would be indiscriminate and wrong. If cluster munitions were used against a military target in an unpopulated battlefield, it is hard to understand how 98 percent of casualties could be civilians. While cluster bombs may not be inherently evil, their use is often indiscriminate, as is the expected effect of the unexploded ordinance they leave behind.

For this reason, the nations of the world met in Dublin, Ireland, in 2008 to develop the Convention on Cluster Munitions (CCM), an international treaty that prohibits all use, production, transfer, and stockpiling of cluster munitions. The CCM also developed a framework for cooperation to ensure adequate care and rehabilitation for those injured by cluster munitions and their communities, clearance of contaminated areas, and destruction of stockpiles. The CCM went into force on August 1, 2010. To date there are one hundred states parties and nineteen signatories that have joined the convention. Seventy-eight states, however, have not joined the CCM, including the United States, Russia, China, India, Israel, Iran, Saudi Arabia, North Korea, and South Korea.[89] Like land mines, cluster munitions are weapons of long-term destruction that the world would be better off without.

Depleted Uranium Shells

Depleted uranium (DU) is a by-product of the enrichment of natural uranium. It has 60 percent of the radioactivity of uranium, and it is radioactive virtually forever. Because of its high density, it can penetrate most armor. It is plentiful, relatively cheap, and effective. It allows the military to penetrate tanks and other armored vehicles from greater and safer distances.

When a DU shell strikes metal, the DU vaporizes and then settles as dust that can be inhaled, ingested, or enter the body through an open wound. It bioaccumulates up the food chain, becoming more harmful when it reaches humans. The health risks associated with DU include stillbirths, birth defects, kidney malfunction, infertility, and cancer. After over 320 tons (944,000 rounds) of DU were used in the 1991 Gulf War, cancer rates in Iraq increased seven to ten times, and birth deformities increased four- to sixfold.[90] The United States used hundreds of thousands of DU rounds in the 2003 Iraq War. The United States also used 5,265 armor-piercing 30mm DU rounds in an air attack against Islamic State fuel trucks in Syria in November 2015.[91] DU ordinance has also been used in Afghanistan, Bosnia, Kosovo, Kuwait, Serbia, and Somalia. Thus far there is no convention or treaty banning the use of depleted uranium weapons.

Based on the principles of discrimination and proportionality that govern the just conduct of war, it is nearly impossible to imagine the moral use of weapons of mass destruction (WMDs)—nuclear,[92] chemical, and biological weapons—and difficult to imagine the moral use of weapons of long-term destruction (WLTDs) —land mines, cluster munitions, and depleted uranium shells. Ideally, these weapons should be banned, destroyed, and abolished.

TARGETED KILLING AND ARMED DRONES

Drones, technically called unoccupied aerial vehicles (UAVs) or remotely piloted aircrafts (RPAs), were developed by the Department of Defense in the 1970s and 1980s for the purpose of surveillance. The first known use of an armed drone was the killing of a top al-Qaeda military commander, Mohammed Ater, in Afghanistan in November 2001, during the George W. Bush administration. In 2015 the United States possessed perhaps 8,000 drones, most used for surveillance, with 300 or 400 armed. The most common armed drones are the MQ-1 Predator and the MQ-9 Reaper, which usually use modified hellfire missiles. Drones are slow (about one hundred mph), fly low, and are noisy. They would be no match for a sophisticated anti-aircraft defense system. Some models can stay aloft for over twenty-four hours, permitting sustained surveillance. Drones extend the reach of the military into areas difficult to access by troops on the ground. They are operated or piloted remotely, often from the United States, and thus shield military personnel from any risk of physical harm.[93] In 2015 there were about 1,300 prepared pilots, but the extensive use of drones has led to a shortage of pilots and to the use of private contractors for operating reconnaissance missions (they are legally prohibited from firing weapons).[94] After 9/11, the Bush administration authorized about four dozen targeted killings using drones. The Obama administration authorized ten times that number of strikes and institutionalized and normalized the practice. President Trump has increased the tempo of drone strikes, and he seems to be moving to dilute or circumvent the Obama rules of engagement. In particular he has granted military requests to declare parts of Yemen and Somalia as "areas of active hostilities," where more permissive battlefield rules apply.[95] Although criticized worldwide, targeted killing and the use of drones generally seem to be approved of by the American public (there is not much discussion of it, unlike torture), and supported by Congress.

The policy and practice of targeted killing, however, raise a number of ethical issues. Drones are a weapon often used by the United States in such killings, and this new weapon poses additional ethical questions. The principles for conducting war justly will guide this ethical inquiry.

The United States employs armed drones in two different contexts: *counterinsurgency* in "areas of conflict" such as Afghanistan and Iraq by the military, and in *counterterrorism* outside conventional war zones (such as in Pakistan, Yemen, Somalia, and West Africa[96]), conducted by the Central Intelligence Agency (CIA). The military acknowledges and accounts for battlefield strikes, which are required to meet the international criteria for just war and are not especially controversial. The legal and ethical justification for killing terrorists in sovereign nations where the United States is not formally at war is complicated, in part because Congress never updated the 2001 authorization for war in Afghanistan to take account of America's expanded military action against terrorists in Syria, Yemen, Libya, etc. Arbitrarily extending areas of conflict, as President Trump has done, is or should be controversial. The CIA's operations are covert, which by law cannot even be acknowledged by the government.[97]

This lack of transparency remains a major point of contention regarding American policy. For example, Anwar al-Awlaki, a Muslim cleric and native-born American citizen, was targeted and killed by a CIA drone strike in northern Yemen on September 30, 2011. In January 2013, a white paper that summarized a 2010 Justice Department memo arguing the legality of a targeted killing of a US citizen, was leaked to the press and publicly discussed. When that happened, the White House had not even acknowledged killing al-Awlaki fifteen months earlier![98] It is impossible to adequately assess the US policy of targeted killings outside areas of active hostility and the use of drones in these strikes when the policy is secret.

In response to the charge of a lack of transparency, the Obama administration gradually became more open. President Obama capped off a series of public presentations by administration officials with a speech billed as a comprehensive statement on counterterrorism policy on May 23, 2013, at the National Defense University located at Fort McNair in Washington, DC.[99] In that speech Obama announced the declassification of the strike on al-Awlaki and three other strikes where Americans were killed by attack drones. He confirmed that all strikes outside war zones were reported to the proper congressional committees. Obama also announced that the framework that governs US use of force against terrorists developed in his first term had been codified in a Presidential Policy Guidance, often referred to as a "playbook," which he signed the previous day. A nonclassified summary of this document was released the day of the speech, and the document itself was finally declassified and released to the public in August 2016.[100] At the time of Obama's speech, it was also reported that the White House wanted to shift counterterrorist targeted killings from the CIA to the Pentagon in order to make the program somewhat more transparent. This move would increase transparency, reduce duplication, improve efficiency, and make congressional oversight easier.[101] Congressional intelligence committees, however, resisted this good idea, and it was not implemented.[102] President Trump plans to keep both the Pentagon and CIA targeted killing programs, and to allow the CIA to engage in strikes in Afghanistan.[103]

Israel's struggle over the morality of targeted killing has shaped the larger debate. The second Palestinian intifada (or uprising) began in 2000. It was characterized by suicide bombings that targeted civilians in Israel. When the Israel Defense Forces (IDF) began killing Palestinians in the West Bank and Gaza whom the IDF suspected of planning suicide bombings, it precipitated a legal and ethical debate. How could these targeted killings be justified? Two conceptual frameworks were considered: a law enforcement model and a military model. The law enforcement model, which would treat terrorists as criminals, was deemed inapplicable because Palestinians were not under the direct jurisdiction of Israel, and the Palestinian Authority was either incapable or unwilling to move against these terrorists. The level of violence, however, was comparable to that of an armed conflict, although one party was not a state. Terrorists were actively engaged in hostility even if, similar to resistance fighters in World War II, they did not follow the four criteria for combatant status in international law: being subject to a hierarchical command structure, wearing distinguishing uniforms, carrying their weapons overtly, and respecting civilian immunity from direct attack. Thus terrorists were deemed "illegal combatants," subject to direct attack, but not due the privileges of a legal combatant, such as prisoner-of-war (POW) status. A preemptive lethal strike on a person actively engaged in terrorism was justified by self-defense and the defense of innocent targets of planned attacks. This conceptual framework was adapted by the United States after 9/11. It seems to be accepted by terrorists as well, who reject the idea that they are criminals and see themselves as combatants in an armed conflict. Given this, international law, which was developed with the assumption that armed conflict would be either interstate or intrastate, needs to be revised to account for conflicts between states and nonstate armed groups.[104]

Given, then, that a terrorist can be morally targeted under this conceptual framework, what circumstances permit a person to be targeted (put on a "kill list")? Norms for justifying whom to target are one aspect of the just-war *principle of discrimination or non-combatant immunity*. At first only "high-value targets" (HVT), leaders and significant actors in al-Qaeda and its associated groups, were subject to lethal strikes.[105] Eventually, however, even those whose behavior rendered them suspect (so-called signature strikes) were targeted and killed. The United States has also engaged in "double-tap" strikes, where a second strike targets those who render aid to the victims of a previous strike on the assumption that they are also terrorists. It seems to me that neither suspicious behavior nor simply being a military-aged male (MAM) is sufficient for targeting. Signature strikes are not morally justified. Double-tap strikes are wrong and even perverse. Evidence of direct participation in activities that threaten others should be required to target a person. Active participation in terrorist activities would include things such as gathering intelligence, bomb-making, transporting persons to hostilities, planning operations, and so on. Targeted killing is only justified for self-defense and to prevent harm to civilians; it is not justified as punishment or for revenge.[106]

Discrimination means not directly attacking civilians, and proportion puts limits on any indirect collateral damage. Contemporary war tends to result in many more civilian casualties than those of combatants.[107] Thus, the precision of many US weapons, including drones, would seem to be consistent with respect for the principles of discrimination and proportion. President Obama said that there should be "near-certainty that no civilians will be killed or injured" in a lethal strike.[108] Nevertheless, US drone warfare has often been criticized as indiscriminate.

As part of an effort to be more transparent, on July 1, 2016, the Obama administration released its official statistics on targeted killings outside of areas of active hostilities for the period from Obama's first inauguration (January 20, 2009) to December 31, 2015. The report said that 473 strikes had resulted in the deaths of between 2,372 and 2,581 combatants and between 64 and 116 noncombatants.[109] The report acknowledges that the official government civilian death count is far lower than estimates compiled by independent sources, and it offers some possible reasons for this. The report explicitly states that it does not count all military-aged males as combatants. Since the report does not include any specific information about strikes, such as the date, location, and particular numbers regarding combatant and noncombatant casualties, it is impossible to compare the data. Thus, its transparency is limited. Each organization, including the government, has different ways of compiling casualty statistics and different criteria for who is a combatant and a noncombatant. All statistics regarding casualties from targeted killings are educated guesses.[110] Although the figures remain uncertain, they show that these strikes kill many more militants than civilians (a rate of about 14 percent), and it seems civilian casualties from US strikes have been declining since 2013. Drone strikes in particular could be more discriminate than alternatives, such as piloted aircraft, artillery, and cruise missiles, because drones can continue surveillance until the trigger is pulled.[111] The preponderance of evidence is that drone strikes can be considerably more discriminating and more proportionate than other methods of aerial assault.[112] Drones, however, are not inherently discriminating; it depends on how they are used. From the perspective of just conduct in warfare, the lack of accurate, comparable statistics on civilian casualties is worrying.[113] President Trump plans to target not only high-level militants but also foot-soldier jihadists, and to eliminate high-level vetting for proposed strikes by the military and the CIA. He will, however, keep the requirement of "near certainty" that no civilians will be killed.[114]

Wounds and death, however, are not the only harms caused by drones. The psychological and emotional effects on civilian populations from drones can be a form of terrorism. The constant presence of low-flying, noisy drones can increase anxiety to the breaking point of sanity. Collateral damage to buildings and property and personal injury can result in financial ruin for poor families. The covert nature of drone strikes outside war zones means that there is no way to report mistakes or harm and no recourse for compensation. Drone surveillance and strikes can result in feelings of asymmetry, powerlessness, and resentment. In journalist David Rohde's account of his time as a prisoner of the Taliban, he singles out the constant presence of drones as "hell on earth."[115] Psychological trauma is not a new consequence of war, but drones add a new wrinkle.

In this sense the use of drones may be a successful and effective tactic, but a questionable strategy; that is, it may make the just resolution of a conflict less likely.[116] Targeted killing, mostly by drone strikes, has decimated the leadership and infrastructure of terrorist groups such as al-Qaeda and more recently has undermined ISIS (or Islamic State or ISIL).[117] Drones effectively conduct surveillance and kill without putting US military personnel in harm's way, increase the reach of the military, and their precision can make them discriminate and proportionate.[118] The resentment, fear, and anger caused by targeted killings and the use of drones, however, may make drones subject to what retired General Stanley McChrystal calls "counterinsurgency math." If two bad guys are eliminated, how many are left? Maybe more than before since each has relatives and fellow tribesmen who are now potential enemies. This is multiplied when there are civilian casualties of strikes. Those on the receiving end of drone surveillance and targeted strikes can experience them as the profoundly arrogant acts of an untouchable enemy. The covert nature of the US counterterrorism policy leaves terrorist groups in control of public relations. Drone strikes have certainly been used as a recruiting tool for terrorist organizations, and they have stoked an anti-American backlash even in countries not directly affected. Moreover, the very effectiveness and low cost of drone strikes may result in an overreliance on a military solution to terrorism rather than peacebuilding through working for social justice.[119]

Another worrying consequence of drone warfare is the psychological trauma suffered by many of the remote pilots who monitor the surveillance videos and are involved in identifying, tracking, and killing the targets. Drone pilots are exposed to repeated graphic violence, such as beheadings by Islamic State fighters. One drone warrior told of his satisfaction at being able to kill a targeted father while sparing his young son who was with him, then watching the son reassemble the pieces of his father's shattered body. Rather than a sense of detachment afforded by distance, three-fourths report feelings of grief, remorse, and sadness. Given the secrecy of the program, these fighters cannot talk to anyone about their feelings beyond a small circle of insiders. After remotely experiencing horrific violence, drone pilots drive home to their families in the suburbs. This psychological trauma can have incapacitating physical effects. Even the sense of immunity from danger can feel like a violation of the warrior ethic. In studying those involved, psychologists have discovered a phenomenon that they call "moral injury," a sense of transgressing the participants' own deeply held moral beliefs, their conscience. For those involved in this warfare over time, there can be a sense of disillusionment, wondering whether progress is being made and a deep questioning of the morality of the whole endeavor. Some traumatized warriors have sought reconciliation and healing by telling their stories and publicly questioning the morality of the war on terror.[120]

By what legitimate authority does the United States carry out targeted killings in sovereign nations where it is not engaged in armed conflict? Current international norms allow this in three situations: if the sovereign state consents to it, if the UN Security Council authorizes the intervention, or if it is in accord with a nation's right of self-defense against attack. The lack of transparency by the United States in the repeated use of the third justification sets a bad precedent for targeted killing, especially by armed drones, outside of declared zones of hostility. The United States has set itself up as judge, jury, and executioner, the sole arbiter of imminent threat, with no public accountability or impartial evaluation of its decisions. This risks destabilizing the shaky edifice of collective security in the UN Charter. As other nations acquire drone technology, they are likely to use the same justification with the same lack of transparency, undermining sovereignty and threatening the foundations of democracy itself. The situation cries out for a better balance between the principles of self-defense and sovereignty.[121]

Targeted killing is only justified as a last resort, when capture and detention is not feasible. Capture is preferable because it respects life and because the prisoner may yield information under questioning. (Torture is immoral, a violation of human dignity and human rights; it is illegal under international law and US law; and it is ineffective.[122]) Drones, however, eliminate any risk or cost to US military personnel, and thus may tip the interpretation of "feasible" toward targeted killing rather than capture, perhaps undermining the principle of last resort.[123]

In summary: Those actively engaged in terrorism can be considered illegal combatants in an armed conflict. If their capture is not feasible and for the purpose of self-defense and the protection of innocent civilians, it is morally justified to target them for a lethal strike. Such strikes should be discriminate and proportionate. Attack drones can certainly be effective, and they can be more discriminate and proportionate than alternatives. They may also cause psychological trauma that is itself a form of terrorism, and they may in the long term be a counterproductive strategy by making the just resolution of the conflict more difficult. The US lack of transparency regarding the legal and ethical basis of its use of drones for targeted killing outside areas of conflict makes it difficult to evaluate US counterterrorism policy and practice, and it sets a very bad precedent for the more widespread use of drones in the near future.[124]

It is important to say that from the perspective of Christian nonviolence and of just peacemaking, weapons of mass destruction, weapons of long-term destruction, and targeted killing are simply wrong.

CYBERATTACKS AND SPACE DEFENSE

Cyberattacks[125]

Cyberattacks are now ranked as the number one risk facing the United States, ahead of terrorism. Our interconnectedness makes us vulnerable. The US Cyber Command, housed at Fort Meade, Maryland, along with the National Security Administration (NSA), is primarily responsible for securing the country against cyberattacks and planning and implementing US cyberattacks. The Pentagon has empowered the Cyber Command to be more aggressive in defending the country against cyberattacks, including employing frequent raids aimed at disabling cyberweapons.

It is odd, then, that John R. Bolton, days after becoming President Trump's National Security Advisor in April 2018, eliminated the position of White House cybercoordinator, who had overseen the complex mix of cyber activities run by the American government. Mr. Rob Joyce, an experienced expert in US cyber operations, returned to the NSA and was replaced by a young National Security staff member with little experience in this complex field. It is reported that President Trump has shown only a passing interest in cyber affairs. This does not seem to be an administration that is stepping up its game to protect the country from its foremost threat.

The following are some examples of cyberattacks and their consequences. Shortly before Christmas in 2015, Russian hackers (not necessarily the Russian government) executed a cyberattack on Ukraine's electrical grid. The operators of the grid were bewildered. They had no control over their computers and watched as circuits were disconnected and backup systems deleted. When the hackers disconnected the backup electrical system, they were left sitting in the dark. There were blackouts throughout Ukraine.

On May 12, 2017, North Korean hackers released the WannaCry virus, which affected an estimated 200,000 computers in over 100 countries. The hackers demanded a ransom in order to unlock the computer. Notably affected was the National Health Service (NHS) in the United Kingdom. About a third of the 236 NHS sites were affected, and more than 6,900 appointments were canceled.

On April 8, 2008, the Stuxnet computer worm, developed jointly by the United States and Israel, although never acknowledged by either nation, infected Iran's Natanz nuclear facility, causing at least a fifth of its nuclear centrifuges to spin out of control. This cyberattack seriously hampered Iran's program to develop a nuclear weapon. It is thought that the United States may have caused some of North Korea's missile tests to fail through cyberattacks.

Given the risk and damage possible, it is imperative that the United States improve its cyber defenses through steps such as improving technological sophistication and ensuring that nothing digital is on the market without sufficient security. It is also necessary to establish global norms or rules regarding cyberattacks, perhaps through a Geneva Convention–type meeting. The nations that seem most involved in cyberattacks are the United States, Russia, China, North Korea, Iran, and Israel.

Perhaps the just-war tradition can offer some direction toward norms to guide cyber activity.[126] The just-war principle of noncombatant immunity, which prohibits directly intended attacks on civilians, can help guide the morality of cyberattacks. It is often said that it is difficult to know the intent of hackers. In the first two examples above, the effect of the attack is to disrupt and burden the lives of ordinary people and sick people. It has been suggested that perhaps the cyberattack on the Ukraine electrical grid was practice for a more widespread attack, but that makes neither the intent nor the effect justifiable. Such attacks are unethical and should be prohibited by international law.

In the third example, the cyberattack is aimed at a military target with the intent to halt the spread of nuclear weapons or their delivery systems. As far as I am aware, no one was injured or killed in these cyberattacks. Because this is more discriminate and proportionate, it may be more justifiable.

Although apparently it is sometimes possible to identify the general source of a cyberattack with some certainty, it is usually difficult to identify the hackers or to apprehend them. Nevertheless, it would be helpful to identify what is off limits for cyberattacks, such as elections, hospitals, emergency communication systems, and electric power grids, based on the principle of noncombatant immunity.

Space Defense

In June 2018, President Trump called for establishing a sixth branch of the military (joining the Army, Navy, Air Force, Marines, and Coast Guard) focused on space. Whether a new branch is necessary can be debated, and Mr. Trump's boast of establishing "dominance in space" is probably not helpful, but he is correct that space is an important security concern. Satellites help guide aircraft carriers in the Persian Gulf, troops in Afghanistan, drones in Somalia, and gather information on adversaries. Russia is developing antisatellite weapons, and China tested an antisatellite weapon in 2007, destroying one of its own weather satellites. The following year the United States did the same thing.[127]

The UN Outer Space Treaty went into effect in 1967. It makes the exploration and use of outer space open to all countries for the benefit of humanity.[128] It prohibits the stationing of weapons of mass destruction in space. Its spirit would prohibit weapons in space, but it does not explicitly say that. Diplomacy was not mentioned by President Trump, but strengthening the Outer Space Treaty would seem much simpler and more constructive than adding another branch to the military, although verification might be tricky. The United States should be helping preserve outer space as a global commons, free of conflict, and open to all.

FUEL TO THE FIRE: THE TRADE IN CONVENTIONAL ARMS

Few would argue that weapons in themselves start wars. While the arms trade is not the match that ignites conflict, the proliferation of weapons adds fuel to the fire.[129] The availability of armaments can encourage potential belligerents to rely on a military rather than a political solution to their dispute. And once combat begins, the influx of weapons tends to prolong the dispute and magnify the destruction. One thinks of the almost total destruction of Grozny, the capital of Chechnya, in the early months of 1995, or the damage inflicted on Mosul, Iraq, in its liberation from ISIS in 2016–2017. One of the lessons of Rwanda (1994) is that, while artillery may be necessary to destroy buildings, machetes and small arms are sufficient for slaughtering hundreds of thousands of human beings.

Arms transfers have also contributed to escalating a war. The acquisition of missiles, for example, enabled both Iran and Iraq to engage in a variety of escalatory moves during their conflict (1980–1988), such as bombing each other's ports and cities. Both sides used chemical weapons. What would have happened if one or both had nuclear weapons?

The proliferation of conventional arms, therefore, leads to more, longer, and more destructive wars.[130] Adding fuel to the fire of international conflict is hardly conducive to a more peaceful world order. The arms trade, however, is very profitable, and thus the weapons industries and their governments have a vested interest in its continuation. A rudimentary understanding of the mechanics and motivation for the arms trade is essential for deciding whether and how to curtail it.

The Arms Trade

For decades the Soviet Union exported the most weapons (usually accounting for about 40 percent of the world market), while the United States was second, with about a 20-percent share of the sales.[131] In 1991, however, with the Russian economy declining and with the United States' display of the technological superiority of its weapons in the Gulf War, the United States raced past Russia to become the world's premier arms exporter, controlling over 60 percent of the global market in arms exports by 1994.[132]

Global arms sales in 2014 were estimated to be at least $94.5 billion. Between 2011 and 2015, the global transfer of weapons increased by more than in any other five-year period since 1990. The United States and Russia account for 58 percent of the weapons sold in those five years, and the five permanent members of the UN Security Council supplied nearly 75 percent of arms transferred.[133]

The first-tier merchants are full-service suppliers. China, which has a reputation for a willingness to sell anything to anyone, solidified its position as a first-tier supplier by increasing its weapons exports by 6.2 percent from 2011 to 2015. A second-tier of sellers tends to specialize in certain types of weapons and carve out a market niche for themselves. They include smaller countries in Europe, such as the Netherlands, and other nations, such as South Korea, Israel, and Brazil.[134]

The motives for arms transfer involve a push (supply) and a pull (purchase).

Suppliers push weapons for political and economic reasons. Suppliers want to arm their allies or to reward friends through the transfer of weapons. For example, there was an increase in US arms sales and military assistance to countries that aided the post–September 11 "war on terrorism," such as Pakistan, Azerbaijan, Tajikistan, and the Philippines. But it is largely the profit motive that removes restraints on arms transfers. The United States suffers from a serious trade deficit that would be worse without its arms sales. Thus the US government has vigorously supported the arms industry through easing restrictions and fees on foreign weapons purchases, financially assisting friendly nations in buying American armaments, and aiding the US defense industry in research and development.[135] For Russia, the sale of weapons is one of its few sources of hard currency and indeed one of its few exports.

Buyers purchase armaments for security, for aggression, and also for symbolic reasons. Some nations feel the need to defend themselves against enemies or adversaries. Some countries wish to pursue conflict with others to right perceived injustices or to enhance their national self-interest. Repressive governments throughout the world buy or build weapons to defend themselves against their own people. And, unfortunately, high-tech weapons can function as symbols of power, pride, and modernity for developing countries and established powers.

Traffic in conventional weapons steals from the poor even more directly than the nuclear arms race. Countries that can least afford it are buying weapons and building their militaries instead of feeding and educating their people.

Small Arms and Light Weapons

Intrastate conflicts are often fought primarily with small arms and light weapons (SALW). Small arms are categorized as intended for use by individual members of armed forces, such as revolvers, pistols, assault rifles, and light machine guns. Light weapons are intended for use by several members of armed forces serving as a crew, such as heavy machine guns, mounted grenade launchers, portable anti-aircraft and antitank guns and missile systems. There are over 600 million SALW in circulation worldwide. Of the forty-nine conflicts fought in the 1990s, forty-seven were intrastate ethnic and sectarian conflicts waged with small arms.[136]

Thus, assault rifles, grenades, and other such weapons were responsible for the widespread death and suffering, mostly to civilians, which resulted from these and other intrastate conflicts. Such weapons were not even included in the statistics for trade in conventional arms, and little attention had been paid to this particular market. Beginning around 1997, however, there was an explosion of interest by researchers and activists in a movement to curtail the diffusion of small arms and light weapons in the hope of replicating the success of movements such as the International Campaign to Ban Landmines and diminishing the violence of intrastate conflict.[137] In 2001 the UN Security Council held a conference on the illicit trade of SALW. Out of the conference came a Program of Action (PoA) to halt illegal trafficking in SALW. As part of this PoA, UN member states agreed to submit an annual report on the status of this effort in their nation. Between 2002 and 2010, 152 nations out of 192 submitted yearly reports, but the number of submissions dropped off dramatically by 2013, with only thirty-seven nations reporting. In 2006 the Control for Arms campaign initiated by three international NGOs—Amnesty International, International Action Network on Small Arms (IANSA), and Oxfam—successfully pushed the United Nations to work toward an Arms Trade Treaty (ATT). Concerns about SALW were integrated into the ATT.[138]

The Arms Trade Treaty

UN diplomatic conferences in 2012 and 2013 finally produced a treaty, and only Iran, North Korea, and Syria blocked a consensus on the final draft. The UN General Assembly endorsed the ATT with a vote of 156–3 with twenty-three abstentions in the spring of 2013, and the treaty entered into force on December 24, 2014.[139] By June 2017, 130 of 195 UN member states had signed the ATT, and by August 2018, ninety-five had formally accepted the treaty through ratification or accession. The United States and Israel are among the thirty-five nations that have signed the treaty but not ratified it. Notable states among the sixty-five that have not signed the ATT include Russia and China (the second and fifth largest arms exporters), and four of the five largest arms importers: India, Saudi Arabia, Egypt, and China, as well as North Korea, Pakistan, Iran, Iraq, and Canada.[140]

The ATT is a multilateral, legally binding agreement that establishes common standards for the international trade of conventional weapons and seeks to decrease illicit trafficking in arms. It is not really an arms control treaty in that it does not place any restrictions on the types or quantity of weapons that can be traded among nations, nor does it affect a nation's gun safety laws. The ATT requires annual reporting of exports and imports of arms to a treaty secretariat, thereby enhancing transparency. The treaty prohibits transfer authorization for weapons to states that are under a UN Security Council arms embargo or if the exporting nation knows that the weapons would be used for genocide, crimes against humanity, grave breaches of the Geneva Conventions of 1949, or attacks aimed at civilians. It applies to all conventional arms within the seven categories of the UN Register of Conventional Arms (battle tanks, armored combat vehicles, large-caliber artillery systems, combat aircraft, attack helicopters, warships, and missiles and missile launchers), to small arms and light weapons, and to ammunition/munitions used by such weapons.[141]

Curtailing the Arms Trade

The common standards for the trade in conventional weapons and the limits on that trade set out in the Arms Trade Treaty are helpful, but what might an arms control policy look like? Since the United States is now the world's top arms exporter and is reputed to stand for peace, security, and human rights, it is logical to expect American leadership in developing a policy to control the arms trade. In fact just the opposite has occurred—the United States has succumbed to the temptations of profit and politics and resisted steps to control the trade in weapons.

For example, the first Bush administration tried to lobby the five permanent members of the UN Security Council to join a system of multilateral controls on the arms market after the Persian Gulf War (1991). The system quickly broke down when the United States announced billions of dollars of arms sales to Israel, Kuwait, Saudi Arabia, Turkey, and Taiwan—contrary to the agreed-upon regime.[142] This took place in spite of the reality that the arming of Iraq, mostly by Russia and Western Europe, had been an important ingredient in Iraq's invasion of Kuwait, which led to the Gulf War. Arms sales are often a clear case of profit eclipsing prudence.

The four components of an arms control regime are relatively clear:

- The first is *transparency*. The nations of the world need to declare and account for both imports and exports of arms. Records need to be kept in order to understand the dynamics of the arms trade, to defuse arms races based on worst-case conjecture, and to curtail the illicit trafficking of weapons. The annual report of arms exports and imports required by the ATT is a significant step in this direction.
- Second, there need to be *supply-side restraints*. Although high-minded and principled, it is bad business for a country to refuse to sell arms when other nations are eagerly in line to do so. Rather than try to cut off sales "cold turkey," it is probably more realistic to set incremental goals toward the objective of disarmament. For example, a ceiling on volume could be set based on a current percentage of the market. Weapons that are inherently or almost always indiscriminate could be banned from trade.
- Third, *economic conversion* is essential. Unless the military-industrial complex is converted to serve civilian markets, suppliers will not be restrained, and when efforts are made to reduce the arms trade, politicians will continually be faced with the unhappy prospect of the loss of domestic jobs.
- Finally, *regional arms control agreements* can begin to restrain recipients from filling their perceived need for more arms.[143]

Obviously such an arms control regime will need to be connected to a broader effort toward building common security, preventing and resolving conflict, recognizing human rights, diminishing poverty, and promoting democracy.

Putting out fires and preventing them are at least as important as cutting off the fuel.

GUN SAFETY IN THE UNITED STATES

According to the US Centers for Disease Control and Prevention, there were 33,599 deaths by firearms in 2014 and twice that number of injuries. About two-thirds of gun-related deaths were suicides. The tragedy of these statistics was driven home to me by the July 17, 1989, cover story in *Time* magazine, titled "Death by Gun: America's Toll in One Typical Week," which had pictures and stories in a yearbook-like format of the 464 people who suffered gun deaths from May 1 to 7, 1989. With an average of sixteen pictures per page there were twenty-eight pages in the portfolio.[144] Page after page of people killed through guns in one week. And for every person killed, two suffer injuries that are often life altering, physically, such as paralysis, and mentally, such as debilitating post-traumatic stress syndrome.[145] Besides the shocking human costs, the obvious financial costs of gun violence include legal services, medical costs, policing, incarceration, lost earnings and time, as well as many hidden costs. Gun violence is a problem in the United States.[146]

There are over 300 million guns in the United States, or about one per capita, although only about a third of households had a gun in 2014.[147] The gun culture in the United States is rooted in the Second Amendment to the US Constitution, which says, "A well regulated militia, being necessary to the security of a free state, the right of the people to keep and bear arms, shall not be infringed." As interpreted by the June 26, 2008, *District of Columbia et al. v. Heller* Supreme Court majority opinion written by Justice Antonin Scalia, the Second Amendment confers an individual right to possess a firearm for lawful purposes such as self-defense, but that right is not unlimited and can be reasonably restricted.[148] Americans are about ten times more likely to be killed by a gun than people in other developed countries.[149] What can be done to improve public safety in regard to guns in the United States?

The National Rifle Association (NRA) is a nonprofit organization that advocates for the right to bear arms. In doing so it, in effect, lobbies for the gun industry. It is well funded and powerful, influencing federal, state, and local policy. At times, its passion for gun rights can lead to apparently unreasonable policies. Two examples would be the 2005 congressional decision to shield the arms industry from damage suits, a protection no other industry enjoys, and Congress's restriction on the government's ability to conduct basic public health research on gun deaths, as if information and knowledge are harmful. Congress should overturn such senseless and unfair measures.[150]

Both guns and cars typically account for more than 30,000 deaths a year in the United States. Thus a public health approach that treats guns as we do cars and takes evidence-based steps to make them safer seems sensible. The practical goal would be to keep guns out of the hands of high-risk individuals, such as criminals, abusers, terrorists, children, and the severely mentally ill.[151] Federal law already prohibits anyone convicted of a felony or of misdemeanor domestic violence against a spouse or who is subject to a domestic violence restraining order from owning a gun. Anyone who has been involuntarily committed because of mental illness is prohibited from buying a gun. Most mentally ill people are not violent, and our country should better address mental health problems. Still, people who are a threat to themselves or others should not have access to guns.[152] It is bewildering that those on the terrorist watch list are not prohibited from buying a gun, and more than two thousand terrorist suspects purchased a firearm between 2004 and 2014. This glaring omission should be closed.

Federal law requires licensed firearms dealers to perform a background check, but does not require private sellers to do so. The result is that 40 percent of guns in the United States are acquired without a background check. Clearly, universal and comprehensive background checks should be required for all gun purchases and exchanges. Polls show overwhelming public support for this policy, including from about 85 percent of gun owners.[153] Such a system should develop efficient and effective mechanisms for states and institutions to report persons prohibited from owning guns to the National Instant Criminal Background Checks System. This would include those involuntarily committed because of mental illness, those with domestic violence restraining orders, convicted felons, and terrorist suspects. It should also require those who join the prohibited list to surrender their firearms and allow their confiscation by law enforcement.

As with cars, anyone who owns or acquires a gun should be required to register it. Gun owners and users should also need a license, issued when a person has demonstrated that s/he can use a gun responsibly and has passed a background check. There should be serious penalties for not registering a gun or reporting that a registered gun is no longer in your possession. (In Australia, the possession of an unregistered firearm can result in a fine of $220,000 or fourteen years in jail.)[154] Of the guns used in committing a crime, nearly half, and possibly as many as 70 percent, are stolen. Registering guns would be a step in addressing this reality, and it would complement and facilitate universal background checks.[155]

Guns and ammunition designed for the battlefield have no place in our homes or on our streets. Congress should restore the assault weapons ban (in effect from 1994 to 2004), add a ban on "bump stocks," which turn a semiautomatic weapon into an automatic weapon; enact limits on gross ammunition clips that enable mass shootings, and ban the sale of ammunition such as armor-piercing bullets (a clear danger to the police). In many states it may be easier to buy ammunition than cold medicine. California has local laws that require dealers to keep logs of sales and is leading the way in thinking about ammunition and gun safety.[156]

"Gun safety studies have found that a gun in the home is twenty-two times more likely to be used in a family homicide, suicide, or accident than in self-defense."[157] Among the most tragic gun deaths are those involving preschoolers, children, and teenagers who pick up a loaded gun and kill themselves or someone else accidentally.[158] As difficult as it might be to prosecute a grieving family member or friend, gun owners should be held accountable in such cases. A reasonable requirement would be for guns to be kept unloaded and locked up at home, although it can be objected that this makes legitimate self-defense more difficult. This mandate might also prevent some family homicides and suicides. About 85 percent of suicide attempts involving guns are successful, in comparison with only 3 percent using an overdose of drugs. Nearly two-thirds of annual gun deaths are suicides. Education campaigns, especially centered on places where guns are sold, is one response to this tragic toll.[159]

Car manufacturers have taken innovative and effective steps to make cars safer—from air bags, to cameras that allow expanded vision, to sensors that slow or stop a car headed toward a barrier. Arms manufacturers, shielded from liability and protected by the NRA, have not significantly advanced safer "smart gun" technology. They should.[160]

The goal of these policy ideas is to make the most deadly kind of weapons harder to get and to reduce the relentless toll of gun-related deaths and injuries in the United States. The only variable that can explain the high rate of mass shootings in the United States is the presence of a prodigious number of weapons.[161] A system of universal background checks, gun registration, licensing owners and users of firearms, limits on the types of weapons and ammunition sold to civilians, and locking away unloaded guns in the home would not prevent law-abiding people from obtaining guns for lawful purposes such as hunting and self-defense. These policies also conform to the Second Amendment's acknowledgment that those who keep and bear arms should be "well regulated."[162] It is reasonable to think that such policies would reduce the number of gun-related homicides, suicides, and accidents and enhance public safety.

UNITED STATES MILITARY SPENDING

There have been fluctuations in US military spending since the conclusion of World War II, but it increased dramatically after September 11, 2001, with the wars in Afghanistan and Iraq, and still has not returned to pre-9/11 levels. Data on defense spending is dependent on what is counted or not included in the military account. At present, the United States is responsible for about a third of global military spending. This raises the question of how much the United States should spend on defense.

Recent History

The Reagan administration (1980–1988) dramatically increased US military spending in order to counter the perceived threat of the Soviet "evil empire." The deficit spending required by huge military budgets and simultaneous tax cuts was responsible for increasing US debt and for the economic recession at the beginning of the 1990s.

The Cold War ended in the presidency of George H. W. Bush (1989–1993). The Persian Gulf War (1990–1991), to free Kuwait from an Iraqi invasion, however, was fought during this period. After the Gulf War, the United States did decrease its military spending. Early in his presidency, Bill Clinton (1993–2001) managed to get Congress to balance the federal budget, and, by the end of his presidency, aided by the most expansive American economy in history, the United States began to reduce its debt. In inflation-adjusted dollars, defense spending during the 1990s held steady at about the same amount as the average peacetime budgets during the Cold War.[163]

Encouraged by the patriotic mood of the country after September 11, 2001, the Bush administration asked a compliant Congress for a significant increase in military spending in fiscal years (October to October) 2002 and 2003. The Pentagon was able to keep producing the tanks, jet fighters, and aircraft carriers it wanted and to develop the mobile Special Forces units and hi-tech, laser-guided munitions it seeks for the future. The Bush administration's strategy seemed to be permanent military superiority.[164]

President Bush also initiated two wars in response to the September 11, 2001, attacks, in Afghanistan in 2001 and Iraq in 2003, which dramatically increased military spending during his two terms (2001–2009). The United States federal government has spent or obligated 4.8 trillion dollars on the wars in Afghanistan and Iraq. The wars have been paid for almost entirely by borrowing, which, along with borrowing in response to the Great Recession of 2008, has raised the US budget deficit and increased the national debt. Interest payments could total over an estimated $7.9 trillion by 2053.[165]

In President Barack Obama's first term (2009–2013) the war in Iraq (2003–2011) gradually ended, but Obama increased the American troops in Afghanistan from 36,000 to over 80,000, in addition to the 32,000 NATO troops serving there. After Osama bin Laden was killed in Pakistan in May of 2011, the United States and NATO began a withdrawal of troops from Afghanistan that culminated in the formal end of their combat mission there on December 28, 2014. In the summer of 2017, President Trump increased the 8,800 troops that remain there by several thousand, further extending America's longest war. Military spending decreased in President Obama's second term (2013–2017), but remained over $100 billion higher than the annual level prior to 2001.

Part of the reason for a gradual decrease in military spending is the Budget Control Act (BCA) of 2011, which resulted in a process of sequestration or automatic spending cuts. Faced with a need to raise the ceiling on the debt and aware of the hundreds of billions of dollars being added to the debt by deficit spending, President Obama and Congress agreed to a deal to cut the annual deficit in the longer term.[166] The BCA established the bipartisan Joint Select Committee on Deficit Reduction (or Super Committee) which was to develop a plan to decrease the deficit by $1.2 trillion over ten years. If the committee did not come up with a plan, then there would be automatic across-the-board cuts (sequestrations) equally divided between defense and domestic spending beginning in 2013. The Super Committee failed to act, and these automatic annual reductions continue to happen until 2021.[167] The Obama administration's budget for fiscal year 2017 proposed $583 billion for defense spending, allocating $525 billion for the Department of Defense's (DoD) base budget activities (such as payroll and developing and procuring weapon systems), which was 1.2 percent less than enacted for 2016 in order to comply with sequestration, and $59 billion for overseas contingency operations (OCO).[168]

In mid-March 2017, President Trump unveiled his one-page budget proposal for fiscal year 2018. The proposal asked for $54 billion in additional defense spending paid for by cuts to domestic programs, including reductions in the State Department (i.e., diplomacy), low-income housing, famine relief, and no government funding to agencies such as the National Endowments for the Arts and the Humanities, the Appalachian Regional Commission, and the Public Broadcasting System (PBS). The requested increase in defense spending would be about 10 percent more than the BCA budget cap for 2018. In addition to questions about the wisdom of additional defense spending and especially to draconian cuts to diplomacy and to domestic programs, it is difficult to see how the Trump administration's budget proposal could be squared with the requirements of sequestration. President Trump and the Republican Congress also enacted tax cuts.[169]

What Counts as Defense Spending?

There is some disparity in the amount of military spending depending on the source, but most sources count the Department of Defense Base Budget and the Overseas Contingency Operations only. This amount is used to compare the defense spending of various countries and to calculate the world's total military spending. Mandy Smithberger demonstrates that much of what the United States spends on defense is omitted from that amount. US spending on nuclear weapons, for example, is under the Department of Energy; and Veterans Affairs, International Affairs, and Homeland security are also in separate budgets. In any rational accounting of spending for national defense, these sums and others, such as military retirement costs and the share of the interest on the national debt generated by borrowing for defense costs, would logically be included. If included, then the annual US national security budget would be about $1.1 trillion, or almost double the $600-billion-plus amount generally given.[170]

How Much Should the United States Spend on the Military?

When United States military spending is compared to that of other nations, US superiority becomes clear. The United States spent more on its military than the next eight nations combined, and the United States and its close allies (NATO countries, Australia, Japan, and South Korea) will spend considerably more than the rest of the world combined.[171]

Father J. Bryan Hehir, Parker Gilbert Professor of the Practice of Religion and Public Life at Harvard's Kennedy School of Government, routinely points out that a budget is a moral document that indicates the values one espouses. Given the comparatively disproportionate US military spending, it is fair to ask how much should the United States spend on the military. What priority should national defense be given in the budget? These questions have an economic and a political dimension.

As with the arms trade, one justification that the military-industrial complex offers for significant defense spending is that it creates jobs and strengthens the economy. Military spending, however, creates fewer jobs per dollar than does spending in the civilian sector. This is because teachers, social workers, nurses, and construction workers make less on average than do defense workers who weld submarines or program guided missile systems, and because defense work also tends to be less labor intensive than most civilian employment. Military spending produces goods that have little economic benefit. Tanks and submarines drain the economy rather than contribute to it, as trucks and fishing boats do. High military spending reduces long-term economic growth.[172] In particular, the combination of tax cuts and high defense spending creates deficits and debt, and can contribute to a recession, as happened during the Reagan administration. The federal deficit for fiscal year 2018 increased by 17 percent to $779 billion precisely because of tax cuts and military spending.[173]

War has a ruinous effect on the economy, especially if fought on home turf. War destroys people, cities, farms, and factories, and it is exorbitantly expensive. Governments must pay for war by raising taxes, printing more currency (fueling inflation), or by borrowing money (which increases government debt).[174] It was noted above that most of the $4.8 trillion cost of the wars in Afghanistan and Iraq was borrowed.

A further economic concern is balancing defense spending with allocating funds for human development and social needs. In 2015 the world spent $1.676 trillion on the military. In a world where nearly two out of three persons do not have their basic needs met, one wonders if this does not reflect skewed priorities. As already noted, the Second Vatican Council proclaimed, "The arms race is an utterly treacherous trap for humanity, and one which injures the poor to an intolerable degree."[175]

As explained in chapter 3, in 2015, the United Nations developed and accepted seventeen Sustainable Development Goals (SDGs) that member nations are to use as a framework for their agendas and public policies through 2030. These SDGs expand upon the Millennium Development Goals in place from 2001 to 2015. How far could reductions in global military spending take us toward fulfilling these goals? A 2016 report from the Stockholm International Peace Research Institute suggests that about 68 percent of global military spending could fulfill nearly all of the SDGs.[176] Even a 10-percent reduction in global military spending ($167 billion), with the resources allocated toward fulfilling the UN SDGs, would make a significant difference.

From a political perspective the purpose of military spending is the security of the people of a nation or national self-defense. The US military is already far superior to that of any other nation. The United States is building a military that can do anything, anywhere, anytime.[177] Given the comparatively disproportionate US military spending, it would not be surprising if the rest of the world becomes uncomfortable about the possibility of American imperialism, that is, that the United States is aggressively trying to build an empire and exercising power and control, rather than simply defending itself. This raises several questions about American foreign policy and military strategy:

- Has the United States moved from a defensive stance to an aggressive posture?
- Will high military spending unduly expand the influence of the military-industrial complex in American life?
- What is the relationship between "security" and military spending, or spending on social needs such as education, health care, infrastructure, environment, foreign aid, and diplomacy (the United States has about 20,000 diplomatic personnel, but two million soldiers, and it spends about $30 billion on foreign aid, but $600 billion plus on the military[178])?
- Will US military superiority itself create enemies and foster anti-Americanism?
- Does high defense spending abet dangerous nationalism rather than healthy patriotism?
- Is the United States becoming imperialist?

Disproportionate defense spending and an exaggerated emphasis on the military might be sweeping the United States in a direction contrary to its highest ideals.

If the United States' military is clearly superior, and if military spending actually hurts the economy in the long run, and if the government is struggling to balance the budget and control debt, why is defense spending regarded as sacrosanct and untouchable? Perhaps a serious national effort focused on economic conversion and reasonable reductions in defense spending to strategically justifiable levels would immensely strengthen the American economy and allow the United States to increase its support of human development and a healthy earth community. It may be that a healthy economy will be the real measure of success and security in the twenty-first century.

The gospel calls Christians to be peacemakers. Weapons of mass destruction appear to be intrinsically evil, and the trade in armaments prepares the world for war, rather than creating the conditions for peace. In the face of human misery, the amount spent on the military seems skewed and perhaps sinful. If Christians are to be peacemakers, we will need to "beat our swords into plowshares," our tanks into buses, to close the book on war and become skilled in conflict resolution (Isa 2:4).

STUDY QUESTIONS

1. See the questions above about American foreign policy and military strategy.

2. Should the international community be working toward the goal of minimal deterrence or total nuclear disarmament?

3. Should the United States join the conventions or treaties banning land mines and/or cluster bombs?

4. Under what conditions do you think the targeted killing of terrorists is justified? What limits should there be on the use of armed drones? What limits or rules should the international community develop regarding cyberattacks? Should the United States develop a space force?

5. Whom does the trade in conventional weapons benefit? Whom does it harm? How does the military-industrial complex influence our mindset or perspective, even our language? What would economic conversion mean?

Epilogue
_____

CHRISTIAN CITIZENSHIP AND RESOURCES FOR INVOLVEMENT

What good is it my brothers and sisters, if you say you have faith but do not have works? Can faith save you? If a brother or sister is naked and lacks daily food, and one of you says to them, "Go in peace; keep warm and eat your fill," and yet you do not supply their bodily needs, what is the good of that? So faith by itself, if it has no works, is dead. (Jas 2:14–17)

Let love be genuine; hate what is evil, hold fast to what is good; love one another with mutual affection; outdo one another in showing honor. Do not lag in zeal, be ardent in spirit, serve the Lord. Rejoice in hope, be patient in suffering, persevere in prayer. Contribute to the needs of the saints; extend hospitality to strangers. (Rom 12:9–13)

CHRISTIAN CITIZENSHIP

Christian discipleship requires that one work for justice and make peace. This is the social and global dimension of striving to be compassionate. Christians must be *hearers* of the Word, that is, attentive to the presence and call of God in their lives, and *doers* of the Word, actively responding to God's call in the world. This chapter discusses *how* Christians can become constructively involved in working for justice and making peace.

Discipleship requires both an inner journey and an outer journey, both contemplation and resistance.[1] There are at least four dimensions to this journey: growing in knowledge and wisdom, personal conversion and changes in lifestyle, working within a faith community, and public policy advocacy or exercising one's citizenship. Growth in each of these areas contributes to living a life of compassion and justice.

Growing in Knowledge and Wisdom

In Luke's Gospel the transition between the infancy narrative and Jesus's public ministry is accomplished with the statement: "And Jesus increased in wisdom and in years, and in divine and human favor" (Luke 2:52). "To grow in knowledge and wisdom" requires information and education, and it requires the development of a heart and conscience able to discern right from wrong.[2] If knowledge is the queen of virtues, wisdom is the grandmother of virtues— earthy, practical, sensitive, caring, and authentic. Knowledge can be gained from books, but wisdom is born of experience. Wisdom comes from making love, tending to sick children, weathering conflict patiently, and growing older gracefully.

This book has provided a considerable amount of information on global issues. Justice seekers and peacemakers should crave information, constantly searching for truth. In the movie *Gandhi* there is a scene in which hungry peasants oppressed by the landowners ask Gandhi to help them. The first thing Gandhi does upon arrival (after persuading the local magistrate that there is no reason to arrest him) is to carefully document the abuses. Gathering information is a critical first step in working for justice.

Karl Barth, one of the twentieth century's great Protestant theologians, said that the Christian should do theology with the Bible in one hand and a newspaper in the other. An educated person should make it a daily habit to gather the news and keep up with what is going on in the world. (See the Resources section of this chapter for a list of helpful periodicals.) And the Christian should interpret and respond to the news through the perspective of God's Word.

Personal Conversion and Change

Those who are working for justice because of their faith often include "contemplation" in their process of reflection, that is, a conscious listening for God's voice by paying attention to the presence and movement of God's Spirit in our lives and our world. Conversion calls for continual growth.[3]

This growth in the Spirit will inevitably affect the way we live life. An awareness of the simplicity of Jesus's life, of the gap between the rich and the poor, and of the way patterns of human consumption injure the earth and its ecosystems will push the Christian to "live simply so that others can simply live."[4]

Materialism or consumerism is one of the most insidious ideologies of the last part of the twentieth century.[5] Its victims are not only the poor and the planet but also its practitioners. It has often been said that consumerism is a form of idolatry that promises personal fulfillment but yields only frustration and alienation—from God, from one another, and from nature. Thus, a simpler lifestyle is good, first of all, for the one who lives it.

Asceticism and voluntary poverty have deep roots in the Christian tradition. A simple lifestyle is not the pursuit of suffering or hardship for its own sake, but rather a conscious effort to live in harmony with God, the community, and nature. The "Shakertown Pledge," first taken by a group of justice- and peace-minded Christians on a retreat at Shakertown, Kentucky, in 1973, raises the right questions for intentionally moving toward a life of creative simplicity:

> Recognizing that the earth and the fullness thereof is a gift from our gracious God, and that we are called to cherish, nurture, and provide loving stewardship for the earth's resources, and recognizing that life itself is a gift, and a call to responsibility, joy, and celebration, I make the following declarations:
>
> 1. I declare myself to be a world citizen.
> 2. I commit myself to lead an ecologically sound life.
> 3. I commit myself to lead a life of creative simplicity and to share my personal wealth with the world's poor.
> 4. I commit myself to join with others in the reshaping of institutions in order to bring about a more just global society in which all people have full access to the needed resources for their physical, emotional, intellectual, and spiritual growth.
> 5. I commit myself to occupational accountability, and so doing I will seek to avoid the creation of products which cause harm to others.
> 6. I affirm the gift of my body and commit myself to its proper nourishment and physical well-being.
> 7. I commit myself to examine continually my relations with others, and to attempt to relate honestly, morally, and lovingly to those around me.
> 8. I commit myself to personal renewal through prayer, meditation, and study.
> 9. I commit myself to responsible participation in a community of faith.[6]

There are many ways for different persons to apply these commitments to their own lives, but a few examples might stimulate further reflection.

Most people are familiar with steps that they can take to lead a more ecologically sound life—buying a fuel-efficient car, using the car less and walking or bicycling more, turning off lights and turning the thermostat down in the winter and up in the summer, and recycling or not buying products that are packaged in ways harmful to the environment. Some states require deposits on cans and bottles to reduce litter or encourage recycling by having residents separate waste from recyclable materials for pickup. It is surprising that these practices are not universal. Switch to solar or wind power.

Tithing—giving away one-tenth of one's income to either religious institutions and/or to other charities—has biblical roots and represents a practical way to share wealth.[7] Average Americans give only between 1 or 2 percent of their income to charity. Some parishes and churches give a tenth of their collections to the poor and for the causes of justice and peace.

A couple decided to respond to the gospel call to nonviolence. They decided their first step would be to disarm their household. The husband had been in the army and owned three rifles, worth several hundred dollars. They decided that to sell the rifles would have no impact on disarming the world, so they took the rifles into the backyard and ceremoniously broke them into a pile of scrap metal and wood and recycled it. For them, this was a powerful symbol of personal transformation and of a commitment to work to disarm the world. Tax resistance was another step on their journey.

A white couple, deeply committed to racial equality and justice, intentionally moved into an integrated neighborhood. They felt that they could not raise healthy children in the segregated environment of most suburbs.

Occupation or employment can also be signs of Christian vocation. According to Catholic social thought, ideally work should be a meaningful way for us to use talents and gifts to contribute to the community.[8] "The investment of wealth, talent, and human energy should be specially directed to benefit those who are poor or economically insecure."[9]

Nearly any profession or job can be directed toward justice for the poor. A physician can work in an urban clinic or a remote rural area. A lawyer can work for legal aid, promote civil rights, or defend the environment.[10] A business person can make responsibility for customers and employees the number-one priority. A salesclerk can treat customers with respect and hospitality.

Financial investments can also be evaluated with a social conscience. Saving for the future can be reasonable and responsible, but, for example, banks that engage in "redlining" should not receive support. Christians can seek out money market funds or investment portfolios with a social conscience.

Working within a Faith Community

Christians usually seek justice and peace through working within a faith community. A faith community can support the individual Christian in the sometimes risky and often painful struggle to overcome injustice, and it can challenge its members to continue to strive to transform society into a just community. The institutional church can often add clout to efforts to reform society or change social structures or institutions.

The themes of justice and peace should be integrated into the worship and prayer of faith communities. The connections between, for example, the Eucharist and world hunger and the oppression of the poor should always be apparent.[11] The inclusive table fellowship of the Lord demands that Christians oppose segregation and discrimination and the violation of human rights and that they work continuously to feed the hungry and give drink to the thirsty. The memory of Jesus's crucifixion demands Christians stand in solidarity with those who suffer imprisonment, torture, or are killed because they oppose tyranny and want a better life for their communities. Weaving concerns about justice and peace into the worship and the life of a faith community is the responsibility of every member.

The church should be a model or a sign of a just community in the world, but inevitably this community of sinners falls short in this regard. [12] Thus, working for justice includes efforts to transform the institutional church and local congregations as well as efforts to transform the larger society. Are fair wages paid to church employees? Are there equal opportunities for women? Does the church have an "edifice complex" that distracts from a commitment to the poor? Is wealth wasted or hoarded, or spent on the needs of the community and especially the least of these? Are the church's investments made with a social conscience? Is authority exercised in terms of service? Is the faith community engaged in direct service to the poor and courageous advocacy for justice? Are luxury cars in the church parking lot consistent with a preferential option for the poor? Does self-righteousness creep into attitudes and service?

Public Policy Advocacy

Finally, it must be emphasized that public policy advocacy or the exercise of one's citizenship is an essential dimension of Christian discipleship. Christian and church involvement in politics is not only appropriate, it is necessary. Social structures are set up through public policy decisions, and they are changed and reformed through public policy decisions. Working for a society that is more just necessarily involves critical participation in these decisions.

It is important for churches to set up shelters for the homeless and soup kitchens for the hungry and for Christians to work at shelters and soup kitchens. But it is just as important for churches to lobby for affordable housing and for welfare policies that ensure that no one is hungry. Indeed, fundamental social changes regarding housing and feeding the hungry would make shelters and soup kitchens unnecessary. The more just a society is, the less need there is for charity.

The United States has an important constitutional principle that separates the church from the state, but it is often misunderstood. The Constitution takes pains to keep the *institutions* of church and state separate. History has taught us that when the church becomes a secular power, the church is usually corrupted and harms society. Likewise the state has no business forbidding the free exercise of any religion, which is a fundamental human right.

The separation of religion from life, however, or of faith from politics is "pure heresy."[13] A Christian's relationship with God should affect every dimension of life, from what we eat to how we vote. Christian faith *should* influence the exercise of citizenship. The Christian community, the church, has as much right to lobby for its perspective and policy choices as does the National Rifle Association, the American Medical Association, or a coalition of insurance companies. Nor does the Constitution prohibit Christians from exercising their citizenship rights or the church from *proper* involvement in public policy discussions and decisions.

It is important, however, that the church influence public policy in a theologically and politically appropriate manner. The following five guidelines can assist the church in properly participating in politics:[14]

1. The role of the church is to lift up for discussion the *moral* dimensions of public policy issues. Morality should be the consistent focus of the church's social pronouncements.

2. The church should endeavor to be *persuasive* when it enters public policy debate. The church's social analysis must be competent and informed, clear and reasonable. The church cannot rely exclusively on authority or revelation in public debate in a pluralistic society.

3. One of the most persuasive and effective ways for the church to influence public policy is through *example*, by modeling its moral teachings. The church must practice what it preaches. It must incarnate its moral vision through programs and structures that stand as beacons to society.

4. Because of the nature of the church's social mission and the nature of politics, it is almost always prudent for the church to *avoid single-issue politics and to remain clearly nonpartisan*. The church's mission is broad and encompassing, and political issues are complex and interconnected. The pursuit of single-issue politics, on the other hand, is narrow and reductionist, and partisan positions will exclude people of good will and tend to be shortsighted. Thus, ordinarily, the church should avoid endorsing candidates or political parties and avoid evaluating candidates or political platforms on the basis of any single issue.[15]

5. In a pluralistic society public policy and legislation should be able to satisfy the criteria of *feasibility* and *enforceability*. Politics involves building a consensus around a reasonable and viable position. An unenforceable law is a bad law because it lessens respect for the law. A public policy that is forced on an unwilling public is divisive and alienating.

These five guidelines pertain to the church's official involvement in public policy discussions and decisions. The individual Christian's participation in politics is, of course, less constrained and might be more partisan, since individuals speak and act for themselves and not the community.

The primary act of political involvement is to register and to cast an informed and conscientious ballot for candidates who represent values and positions consistent with Christian faith. Financial support and active campaigning for candidates are important ways to participate in the political process. Committed Christians can also choose to run for local, state, or federal offices. Every country certainly needs politicians of integrity who are willing to serve the public and to work for the common good.

Voting and campaigning are only the first steps in shaping public policy. Just as organizations, corporations, and interest groups lobby elected officials in an effort to get their perspectives enacted into legislation and policy, so all citizens should lobby their representatives on behalf of their point of view. Christian citizens should advocate for the poor and oppressed, the powerless and voiceless. Communication with elected representatives through letters, e-mail, phone calls, social media, and visits to elected representatives can influence government policy.[16]

Some people are intimidated by the prospect of writing or lobbying government officials, but there is no reason for this. The president and representatives to the federal or state House and Senate and local government are, after all, *representatives*. Their job is to represent citizens' views in the government, and if they do not, they are held accountable at election time. They should be interested in knowing what people think. Sometimes a dozen or so well-timed correspondents can have a dramatic impact in focusing a representative's attention on a piece of legislation and in shaping his or her views.

An effective communication is courteous, brief, and clear. It is usually best to focus on one issue at a time and to be specific about the legislation or issue under discussion. Most representatives will respond. It is a good idea to write a follow-up message thanking the representative for making such a wise choice or continuing the dialogue on the issue. An example of a lobby letter follows.[17]

Return Address
Date

Dear Senator,

The Women, Infants and Children (WIC) program is in danger of being cut back. I urge you to vote to restore the president's funding request, rather than cut the program by 25 percent.

Every dollar spent on prenatal care under the WIC program saves $3.50 in later Medicaid costs, according the General Accounting Office. Not only does WIC save money, it is also a wise investment in human resources. A 25-percent cut in funding would reduce the number of recipients by nearly 100,000. Given that WIC is one of the country's most successful and cost-effective nutrition intervention programs, this simply does not make sense.

I hope you will vote for women, infants, and children, and that you will encourage your colleagues to do so as well. Please inform me of your position.

Sincerely,

Most senators and congresspersons now have e-mail addresses that are available through internet servers. The website for "Contacting the Congress" (www.contactingcongress.org) makes e-mailing your representative convenient. The president's e-mail address is president@whitehouse.gov. Network, a Catholic social justice lobby, now has a system that allows you to send a preformulated e-mail on timely issues to your representative through its website: www.networklobby.org.

Writing a letter to the editor of a local newspaper or writing an informative op-ed piece can also be an effective way to engage in public policy discussion. Such efforts allow citizens to take a public stand and to educate and encourage others as well.

Direct communication with elected officials can be accomplished by arranging a visit with them, either on a trip to Washington, DC, or in their home district. Government representatives are busy people, but most realize that they must be accessible to the citizens they represent. Their office is more likely to schedule a personal visit with a small group that represents an organization such as Bread for the World or Network. Even if the representative is not available, it is worthwhile to meet with a member of his or her staff.

There are times, of course, when public policy advocacy and social change require steps beyond dialogue. Nonviolent direct confrontation through protest marches, demonstrations, strikes, boycotts, street theater, or civil disobedience can be important steps in transforming society into a just community.[18] Such actions were instrumental in the civil rights and labor movements, for example. In the United States, rights to free speech and to assemble and protest are recognized and generally protected. Still, it requires personal courage to take a public stand or to court arrest on behalf of the poor and for the cause of justice and peace in the midst of controversy. Resistance against tyranny and oppression and standing for liberty and justice for all are among the founding principles of the American nation. Christian citizens should not find it extraordinary to engage in public protest in the name of justice and peace. After all, the church has produced a wealth of prisoners and martyrs, beginning with its founder and his apostles.

In sum, Christian discipleship requires the maturation of compassion, wisdom, and courage. "Go therefore and make disciples of all nations, baptizing them in the name of the Father and of the Son and of the Holy Spirit, and teaching them to obey everything that I have commanded you. And remember, I am with you always, to the end of the age" (Matt 28:19–20).

SUGGESTIONS AND RESOURCES FOR INVOLVEMENT

This section of the chapter aims to steer the reader toward further resources for action and information. The first part offers some suggestions for research projects on justice and peace issues; the second part lists resources for further information and study.

Projects

There are many interesting research projects that can be undertaken in connection with this material. For example:

- Research a country, paying attention to questions of justice and peace.
- A film festival related to a global issue. On colonialism, for example, one could see *Black Robe, Mister Johnson, The Mission,* and *Gandhi.* On Central America, *Romero, Under Fire, El Norte,* and *Choices of the Heart.*
- Research a commodity, such as coffee or sugar, uncovering the justice questions involved in its production and marketing.
- Follow an issue in the news related to justice and peace, keeping a file of clippings from newspapers and news magazines, and summarizing your thoughts on the issue.
- Offer your time and energy to a soup kitchen, shelter, prison, or community agency, and keep a journal of reflections on your experience.
- Identify an issue related to justice or conflict resolution at your school, workplace, community, or household, and try to accomplish some constructive change.
- Do an internship with the legislature, or identify a piece of legislation related to justice and lobby for its passage.
- Start a justice and peace committee at your place of worship, in your local community, or at your school.
- Organize a lecture series on justice and peace issues at your school or for your community.
- Start or join a discussion group on justice and peace issues. If you do, you might use this book as a discussion starter.
- Join an organization working for justice or peace, such as Bread for the World, Network, Catholic Charities, Friends of the Earth, the Sierra Club, Amnesty International, Human Rights Watch, the NAACP, Black Lives Matter, the National Organization for Women, the Fellowship of Reconciliation, Pax Christi USA, etc., and become an activist in this specific cause who is connected to a local and a national group.

For Further Information and Study

The notes to the chapters can steer the reader toward books and articles related to the particular issues addressed in this book. The purpose of this section is to highlight journals, books, and websites that are dedicated in a general way to the themes of justice and peace.

Periodicals and Journals

Many organizations publish a periodical or newsletter to keep their members informed about issues, such as *Bread* (BFW), NETWORK*Connection, Fellowship* (FOR), *Greenpeace Quarterly, Human Rights Quarterly,* and *The Defense Monitor.*

There are other periodicals, such as *Sojourners, Maryknoll, The National Catholic Reporter, The Catholic Worker, The Journal for Peace & Justice Studies, CrossCurrents, America,* and *Commonweal* that regularly address social issues from a Christian perspective.

There are also journals, such as *Current History, The Nation, Foreign Affairs, Foreign Policy,* and *Ethics and International Affairs,* that can provide background information and analysis on global issues. Most libraries carry these sources of information, subscribe to online journals, or can get articles for patrons through interlibrary loan.

A daily newspaper that has good international coverage, such as the *New York Times,* the *Washington Post,* the *Wall Street Journal,* or *The Guardian* can provide a wealth of information.

Sources of Publications

The following is list of sources that provide publications on issues related to justice and peace:

The Worldwatch Institute (http://www.worldwatch.org) publishes an annual report *The State of the World* on the movement toward a sustainable society, as well as other resources.

United States Institute of Peace (www.usip.org) sponsors research and produces publications on global conflict and its resolution.

United Nations Development Programme (www.undp.org) publishes the *Human Development Report,* a thoughtful and statistic-filled annual report on global progress toward human development.

World Resources Institute (www.wri.org) publishes high quality research related to the environment that is available for download.

The *Encyclopedia of Associations,* published annually by the Gale Group, Detroit, provides an annotated guide to more than 24,000 national and international organizations, and can be found in many libraries.

Websites

The internet provides an embarrassment of riches in information about our world and its social, economic, and political conditions. One difficulty is sorting out the gems from the garbage; another is finding what you want. David Ettinger has produced a helpful bibliographic essay on "International Relations Resources on the World Wide Web," in the April 2002 issue of *Choice*

(1353–72) that annotates over one hundred sites. My much more limited goal is to direct readers to sources of demographic information and social and economic indicators for the countries of the world.

A wealth of information is found in the annual *Human Development Report*. The entire report, including the Human Development Index, the Gender Development Index, and other tables, is available online at www.undp.org. Similarly the various publications of the World Bank, including World Development indicators, are available at www.worldbank.org. The *CIA World Factbook*, now simply *The World Factbook*, is an excellent source of information on the various countries of the world (https://www.cia.gov/library/publications/the-world-factbook), and www.globastat.com compiles and ranks countries based on World Factbook data for 140 categories including population, population density, GDP, GDP per capita, debt, economic aid, life expectancy, literacy, and year of independence from colonial powers.

The Economist Intelligence Unit (eiu.com) is a commercial site that offers excellent country-specific information, but much of this data is available free from Economist.com. Country briefings are available at www.economist.com/countries.

Amnesty International's annual human rights reports are available at www.amnesty.org. Data on international security and military expenditure can be found at the Stockholm International Peace Research Institute (SIPRI) at www.sipri.se. Environmental data can be found at the World Resources Institute (www.wri.org).

Excellent maps, which are not subject to any copyright restriction, can be found at the Perry-Castaneda Library Map Collection at the University of Texas: www.lib.utexas.edu/maps. Among the best metasites that provides links to resources in all of the above categories is the WWW Virtual Library for International Affairs Resources created by Wayne A. Selcher of Elizabethtown College, PA, at http://internationalaffairsresources.com.

Notes

Introduction

1. These two opening quotes provide at least a description (rather than a definition) of peace and justice from a Christian perspective. Peace is not merely the absence of war, but the presence of justice and community. The US bishops present a fuller description of justice in National Conference of Catholic Bishops (NCCB), *Economic Justice for All*, ##68–95. The litmus test of the justice of a society is the condition of the poor and the marginalized people (##38, 123). References to official documents of the Catholic Church will use the paragraph or section numbers rather than page numbers.

2. The idea of a "starter" book comes from Adam Daniel Corson-Finnerty, *World Citizen: Action for Global Justice* (Maryknoll, NY: Orbis Books, 1982). For several years, Corson-Finnerty's book informed and transformed my students in a course on "Christianity and Social Justice" in the way I hope this book can.

3. These sentences paraphrase ideas found in NCCB, *Economic Justice for All*.

4. Daniel C. Maguire, *The Moral Choice* (Minneapolis, MN: Winston Press, 1978), chap. 5.

5. Quoted in Michael True, *Justice Seekers, Peace Makers: 32 Portraits in Courage* (Mystic, CT: Twenty-Third Publications, 1985), 96.

6. Fred Kammer, *Doing Faithjustice: An Introduction to Catholic Social Thought* (New York: Paulist Press, 1991), 73.

7. In analyzing the obstacles to justice and peace in the current world situation, this book takes up the task of developing a theology of peace as described by the US bishops in *The Challenge of Peace:* "A theology of peace should ground the task of peacemaking solidly in the biblical vision of the kingdom of God, then place it centrally in the ministry of the Church. It should specify the obstacles in the way of peace, as these are understood theologically and in the social and political sciences. It should both identify the specific contributions a community of faith can make to the work of peace and relate these to the wider work of peace pursued by other groups and institutions in society. Finally, a theology of peace must include a message of hope" (#25).

Chapter One

1. See chapter 5 of the Song of Solomon in the Hebrew Scriptures where the female lover wearies her friends with talk of her beloved.

2. Marcus J. Borg, *Meeting Jesus Again for the First Time* (San Francisco: Harper SanFrancisco, 1994), 31–32. This section on Jesus as a spirit person relies on Borg, *Meeting Jesus Again*, 30–39.

3. All three Synoptic Gospels—Matthew, Mark, and Luke—have accounts of these visions by Jesus.

4. Borg, *Meeting Jesus Again*, 46. This section depends on Borg, chap. 3, "Jesus, Compassion, and Politics"; on Cardinal Walter Kasper, *Mercy: The Essence of the Gospel and the Key to Christian Life* (New York: Paulist Press, 2014); and on Donald P. McNeill, Douglas A. Morrison, and Henri J. M. Nouwen, *Compassion: A Reflection on the Christian Life* (Garden City, NY: Doubleday Image Book, 1982), Part One, "The Compassionate God." See also Monika K. Hellwig, *Jesus: The Compassion of God* (Wilmington, DE: Michael Glazier, 1985).

5. Richard Gula, *Reason Informed by Faith* (New York: Paulist Press, 1989), 185. By this expression Gula means to indicate that Jesus is God's fullest revelation of the invitation of divine love to us and the fullest human response to God.

6. Kasper, *Mercy*, 42; Borg, *Meeting Jesus Again*, 48–49.

7. Kasper, *Mercy*, 51, 48–49. Kasper points out (49) that the revelatory declaration of Exodus 34:6 is repeated in the Hebrew Scriptures in a formulaic way, especially in the Psalms (See Deut 4:31; Pss 86:15; 103:8; 116:5; 145:8; Jon 4:2; Joel 2:13, etc. and Kasper, *Mercy*, 58–59.)

8. Kasper says that what is new in Jesus's message that distinguishes it from the Hebrew Scriptures is its inclusiveness and universality. "There is room for all in God's kingdom; no one is excluded" (*Mercy*, 67–68).

9. See John Shea, *Stories of Faith* (Chicago: Thomas More Press, 1980), chap. 6, for a poetic account of Jesus, the "Son Who Must Die."

10. Borg, *Meeting Jesus Again*, 49. This section on the politics of compassion versus the politics of purity depends on pp. 49–61.

11. Ibid., 51–52.

12. Kasper, *Mercy*, chap. 3, "The Message of the Old Testament"; and Borg, *Meeting Jesus Again*, 58–61.

13. Matt 23:23; Luke 11:42. Borg, *Meeting Jesus Again*, 54.

14. See also Isaiah 1:10–15. This point is made well in Ronald J. Sider, *Rich Christians in an Age of Hunger: A Biblical Study* (New York: Paulist Press, 1977), 80–81.

15. Borg, *Meeting Jesus Again*, 55–57. It is worth noting that Karen Armstrong, the prolific scholar of world religions, argues that there is unanimous agreement on the primacy of compassion in all world religions. See her "Compassion's Fruit," *AARP Magazine* (March/April 2005): 62–64. Armstrong was instrumental in creating the Charter for Compassion in 2009.

16. Borg, *Meeting Jesus Again*, 58.

17. See also Acts 4:32–37.

18. Sider, *Rich Christians*, 101.

19. Ibid., 101–10, quote at 106.

20. Bob Smietana, "Sunday Morning in America Still Segregated—and That's OK with Worshipers," LifeWay Research, January 15, 2015, https://lifewayresearch.com.

21. See Jack Nelson-Pallmeyer, *Brave New World Order* (Maryknoll, NY: Orbis Books, 1992), chap. 8, "Mark, Jesus, and the Kingdom: Confronting World Orders, Old and New"; and Ched Myers, *Binding the Strong Man: A Political Reading of Mark's Story of Jesus* (Maryknoll, NY: Orbis Books, 1988).

22. The Zealots emerge clearly only at the time of the 70 CE revolt against the Romans that led to the destruction of the Temple by the Romans, but their brand of militant nationalism was surely around in Jesus's time. They are mentioned indirectly in the Gospels. The Essenes were a sort of monastic community who retreated to the desert to lead a holy and pure and faithful religious life. The Pharisees, who are prominent in the Gospels, become Jesus's adversaries. See Donald Senior, *Jesus: A Gospel Portrait* (Cincinnati: Pflaum Standard, 1975), chap. 2, "The World of Jesus."

23. Ibid., 47–48.

24. Ms. Egan said this in a personal conversation. For a sense of what she had in mind, see her "The Beatitudes, the Works of Mercy, and Pacifism," in Thomas A. Shannon, ed., *War or Peace?* (Maryknoll, NY: Orbis Books, 1980), 169–87.

25. Walter Wink, *Violence and Nonviolence in South Africa: Jesus' Third Way* (Philadelphia: New Society Publishers, 1987), chap. 2.

26. Ibid., 17.

27. Ibid. Jewish law required the return of a person's coat every evening at sunset so he would have a cover in night, because God is compassionate. See Exod 22:25–27; Deut 24:10–13, 17.

28. Jesus's rejection of dominating power is a key to understanding Jesus and discipleship according to Gula, *Reason Informed by Faith*, 189–97.

29. John Dominic Crossan, *God and Empire: Jesus against Rome, Then and Now* (San Francisco: HarperSanFrancisco, 2007), 94.

30. See Roland Bainton, *Christian Attitudes toward War and Peace* (Nashville: Abingdon Press, 1960), chap. 5; and John Helgeland, Robert J. Daly, and J. Patout Burns, *Christians and the Military: The Early Experience* (Philadelphia: Fortress Press, 1985).

31. Mark J. Allman, *Who Would Jesus Kill? War, Peace, and the Christian Tradition* (Winona, MN: St. Mary's Press [now Anselm Academic], 2008), 83.

32. Mark 1:14–15; Matt 4:17.

33. For a theological discussion of the notion of transformation that is rooted in H. Richard Niebuhr's classic work, *Christ and Culture* (New York: Harper, 1951), see Glen H. Stassen, D. M. Yeager, and John Howard Yoder, *Authentic Transformation* (Nashville: Abingdon Press, 1996).

34. Charles E. Curran, "Conversion: The Central Moral Message of Jesus," in Charles E. Curran, *A New Look at Christian Morality* (Notre Dame, IN: Fides, 1968), 65. See also James P. Hanigan, "Conversion and Christian Ethics," *Theology Today* 40 (April 1983): 33–34.

35. See Suzanne Toton, *World Hunger* (Maryknoll, NY: Orbis Books, 1982), 115–21; and Donal Dorr, *The Social Justice Agenda* (Maryknoll, NY: Orbis Books, 1991).

36. There is no official canon for Catholic social teaching. In Catholic ecclesiastical polity, the official teachings of councils of the whole church (Vatican II), of the popes (social encyclicals), and of Vatican synods carry more weight and authority than those of national conferences of bishops or of individual bishops, yet all of these documents could be considered official Catholic teaching that in some degree should bind or guide a Catholic. For a listing of the papal, conciliar, and synod documents, see J. Milburn Thompson, *Introducing Catholic Social Thought* (Maryknoll, NY: Orbis Books, 2010), 8–11; and Charles Curran, "A Century of Catholic Social Teaching," *Theology Today* 48 (July 1991): 154n2. David J. O'Brien

and Thomas A. Shannon have produced two very helpful collections of documents associated with Catholic social teaching: *Renewing the Earth: Catholic Documents on Peace, Justice, and Liberation* (Garden City, NY: Image Books, Doubleday & Co., 1977); and *Catholic Social Thought: The Documentary Heritage* (Maryknoll, NY: Orbis Books, 1992 [updated/expanded ed., 2010]). The Pontifical Council for Justice and Peace, *Compendium of the Social Doctrine of the Church* (Washington, DC: United States Conference of Catholic Bishops, 2004), offers a Vatican summary or statement of Catholic social teaching.

37. Edward P. DeBerri and James E. Hug, with Peter J. Henriot and Michael J. Schultheis, *Catholic Social Teaching: Our Best Kept Secret*, 4th rev. and exp. ed. (Maryknoll, NY: Orbis Books; Washington, DC: Center for Concern, 2003). In his *Responses to 101 Questions on Catholic Social Teaching* (Mahwah, NJ: Paulist Press, 2001), Kenneth Himes suggests that this perception may be changing.

38. For theological reflection on Catholic social teaching (CST), see, for example, Kenneth Himes, *Responses to 101 Questions on Catholic Social Teaching*, 2nd ed. (Mahwah, NJ: Paulist Press, 2013); Donal Dorr, *Option for the Poor and for the Earth: Catholic Social Teaching*, rev. ed. (Maryknoll, NY: Orbis Books, 2012).

39. In O'Brien and Shannon, *Catholic Social Thought*, 306.

40. NCCB, *Economic Justice for All*, in O'Brien and Shannon, *Catholic Social Thought*, Introduction, #25.

41. Ibid., ##35–36.

42. Pope John XXIII, *Peace on Earth* (*Pacem in Terris*), in O'Brien and Shannon, *Catholic Social Thought*. See also Pope John Paul II, *On the Hundredth Anniversary of "Rerum Novarum"* (*Centesimus Annus*), #47, in O'Brien and Shannon, *Catholic Social Thought*, for a sort of summary statement of human rights.

43. See *Economic Justice for All*, ##79–85; David Hollenbach, "Global Human Rights: An Interpretation of Contemporary Catholic Understanding," in Charles Curran and Richard McCormick, eds., *Official Catholic Social Teaching* (Readings in Moral Theology 5; Mahwah, NJ: Paulist Press, 1986), 366–83; and John Langan, "Human Rights in Roman Catholicism," ibid., 110–29.

44. Peter L. Berger and Thomas Luckman, *The Social Construction of Reality: A Treatise in the Sociology of Knowledge* (New York: Anchor Books, 1967).

45. See Shannon Craigo-Snell and Christopher J. Doucot, *No Innocent Bystanders: Becoming an Ally in the Struggle for Justice* (Louisville, KY: Westminster John Knox Press, 2017), 56–62, passim.

46. Pope John Paul II, *On Social Concern* (*Sollicitudo Rei Socialis*) (1987), in O'Brien and Shannon, *Catholic Social Thought*, #36.

47. Ibid, #37.

48. See Synod of Bishops, *Justice in the World*, in O'Brien and Shannon, *Catholic Social Thought*, 307–8, passim; Pope Paul VI, *Evangelization in the Modern World* (*Evangelii Nuntiandi*), in ibid., ##31, 36; Kammer, *Doing Faithjustice*, chap. 5.

49. Pope John Paul II, *On Social Concern*, #38. See Jacques Delcourt, "The New Status of Solidarity in the Social Teaching of the Catholic Church," in Samuel M. Natale and Francis P. McHugh, eds., *Proceedings of the First International Conference on Social Values*, Held at St. Edmond's College, University of Cambridge, vol. 1 (New Rochelle, NY: Iona College, 1991), 189–96.

50. Pope John Paul II, *On Social Concern*, #39; NCCB, *Economic Justice for All*, #66, and chap. 4, "A New American Experiment: Partnership for the Public Good."

51. Pope Francis, Apostolic Exhortation, *The Joy of the Gospel* (*Evangelii Gaudium*) (2013), ##188–89.

52. The principle of participation is developed in Paul VI, *A Call to Action* (*Octogesima Adveniens*) (1971), ##22, 24; Synod of Bishops, *Justice in the World*, 308, 315–17; John Paul II, *On the Hundredth Anniversary*, ##43, 46–48; and throughout NCCB, *Economic Justice for All*.

53. NCCB, *Economic Justice for All*, #71.

54. John Paul II, *On the Hundredth Anniversary*, ##46–48; NCCB, *Economic Justice for All*, #77, passim; and Canadian Conference of Catholic Bishops, *Ethical Choices and Political Challenges: Ethical Reflections on the Future of Canada's Socio-economic Order*, in David M. Byers, ed., *Justice in the Marketplace: Collected Statements of the Vatican and the U.S. Catholic Bishops on Economic Policy, 1891–1984* (Washington, DC: United States Catholic Conference, 1985), 485.

55. Synod of Bishops, *Justice in the World*, 315–17.

56. The principle of subsidiarity was first articulated by Pope Pius XI in *After Forty Years* (*Quadragesimo Anno*, 1931), ##79–80. See also John Paul II, *On the Hundredth Anniversary*, #48; and NCCB, *Economic Justice for All*, ##99, 124.

57. Pope John XXIII, *Christianity and Social Progress* (*Mater et Magistra*) (1961) in O'Brien and Shannon, *Catholic Social Thought*, ##51–67; NCCB, *Economic Justice for All*, #124. See Kammer, *Doing Faithjustice*, 80, 83. The principle of socialization is related to the principle of solidarity.

58. NCCB, *Economic Justice for All*, ##52, 85–91, passim.

59. Ibid., #24.

60. Vatican II, *Pastoral Constitution on the Church in the Modern World* (1965), in O'Brien and Shannon, *Catholic Social Thought*, #4.

61. The pertinent Medellín conference documents can be found in O'Brien and Shannon, *Renewing the Earth*, 549–84. The Puebla conference documents can be found in John Eagleson and Philip Sharper, eds., *Puebla and Beyond: Documentation and Commentary*, trans. John Drury (Maryknoll, NY: Orbis Books, 1979).

62. These documents are in O'Brien and Shannon, *Catholic Social Thought*. Pope John Paul II returns to the question of development and the "social mortgage" on private property in his encyclical *On the Hundredth Anniversary*, ##30–46. See also Pope Paul VI, *A Call to Action* (*Octogesima Adveniens*), #23.

63. Pope Francis, *The Joy of the Gospel*, #197.

64. Peter J. Henriot, *Opting for the Poor: A Challenge for North Americans* (Washington, DC: Center for Concern, 1990), 24.

65. NCCB, *Economic Justice for All*, #86. Henriot, *Opting for the Poor*, 25, distinguishes between the "needy" and the poor. The needy, of course, should not be neglected, but the poor require our committed attention and action.

66. Henriot, *Opting for the Poor*, 26.

67. This is Kammer's preferred description of this principle (Kammer, *Doing Faithjustice*, chap. 4).

68. Pope Francis, *The Joy of the Gospel*, #198. See #198 also for Francis's description of the option for the poor.

69. This is the critical question raised in Sider's book *Rich Christians*. It is based primarily on the parable of the rich man who overlooked a poor beggar at his gate (Luke 16:19–31) and secondarily in the parable of the rich fool (Luke 12:13–21). Sider explores a "Biblical attitude toward property and wealth" in chap. 5. He concludes that, according to scripture, possessions, although not innately evil, are "positively dangerous because they often encourage unconcern for the poor, because they lead to strife and war, and because they seduce people into forsaking God" (122).

70. See also John Paul II, *On Social Concern*, ##25, 26, 34; *On the Hundredth Anniversary*, #37; *The Ecological Crisis: A Common Responsibility* (also referred to as *Peace with God the Creator, Peace with All of Creation*) *Origins* 19 (1990): 465–68. See also *And God Saw That It Was Good: Catholic Theology and the Environment*, ed. Drew Christiansen and Walter Grazer (Washington, DC: United States Catholic Conference, 1996).

71. Pope Francis's encyclical *Laudato Si': On Care for Our Common Home* is available on the Vatican website. Our Sunday Visitor, the United States Conference of Catholic Bishops, and Paulist Press published paperback editions of the document in 2015. Orbis Books published the document with a commentary by eco-theologian Sean McDonagh, and Paulist Press published a commentary on the encyclical by Kevin W. Erwin, both in 2016.

72. Orbis Books, for example, has a series of publications on theology and ecology.

73. Lynn White Jr., "The Historical Roots of Our Ecological Crisis," *Science* 155, no. 3767 (March 10, 1967): 1203–7. White argues that Western Christianity's interpretation of the "dominion" given to man by God in Genesis as domination may be fundamentally responsible for our ecological crisis.

74. Elizabeth Rosenthal, "Vatican Penance: Forgive Us Our Carbon," *New York Times*, September 17, 2007. See, however, Robert Mickens, "Letter from Rome," *Tablet*, May 1, 2010, 37, which suggests that the Hungarian forest that was to offset Vatican City's carbon emissions has yet to be planted. See Daniel Stone, "How Green Was the Green Pope?" *National Geographic News*, February 28, 2013.

75. J. Milburn Thompson, "The Message of the Encyclical on the Environment: Metanoia," *Today's American Catholic*, August/September, 2015, 16. This essay refers to two op-ed pieces in the *New York Times*: Paul Vallely, "The Pope's Ecological Vow," June 28, 2015; and David Brooks, "Fracking and the Franciscans," June 23, 2015.

76. NCCB, *The Challenge of Peace*, in O'Brien and Shannon, *Catholic Social Thought*, ##71–78, 111–21. See NCCB, *The Harvest of Justice Is Sown in Peace*, in Gerard F. Powers et al., eds., *Peacemaking: Moral and Policy Challenges for a New World* (Washington, DC: United States Catholic Conference, 1994), 317–19.

77. Paul VI, *On the Development of Peoples*, ##87, 76–77. John Paul II, *On Social Concern*, #39, and *On the Hundredth Anniversary*, #52. Pope Francis, *The Joy of the Gospel*: "In the end, a peace which is not the result of integral development will be doomed; it will always spawn new conflicts and various forms of violence" (#219).

78. See Vatican II, *The Pastoral Constitution on the Church in the Modern World*, #85; and NCCB, *The Harvest of Justice Is Sown in Peace*, 316–17.

79. John Paul II, "World Day of Peace Message (January 1, 2002)," *America*, January 7/14, 2002, 8, passim. The pope uses justice and forgiveness as a repeated refrain in this post–September 11 message.

80. Vatican II, *The Pastoral Constitution on the Church in the Modern World,* #80.

81. NCCB, *The Challenge of Peace,* ##160–61, 188, passim.

82. Ibid., ##186, 188.

83. This is not to conclude, however, that the Persian Gulf War was morally justified or that it was conducted justly. See, for example, Thomas C. Fox, *Iraq: Military Victory, Moral Defeat* (Kansas City, MO: Sheed & Ward, 1991); and Kenneth L. Vaux, *Ethics and the Gulf War* (Boulder, CO: Westview Press, 1992). The US bishops themselves differed on these questions.

84. See, for example, John Paul II, *On the Hundredth Anniversary,* #52. This has been a constant theme of the popes' World Day of Peace statements and of their talks and homilies in various settings.

85. Vatican II, *The Pastoral Constitution on the Church in the Modern World,* #81. See also John Paul II, *On Social Concern,* ##23–24.

86. See Vatican II, *The Pastoral Constitution on the Church in the Modern World,* #82; NCCB, *The Challenge of Peace,* ##235–44; John Paul II, *On Social Concern,* ##41–45; NCCB, *The Harvest of Justice Is Sown in Peace,* 325, passim.

87. See, for example, Pax Christi's Peacemaker Pamphlet Series; Mary Ann Luke, ed., *Pilgrims and Seekers: Saints without Pedestals* (Erie, PA: Pax Christi USA, 1995); and Jim Wallis and Joyce Hollyday, eds., *Cloud of Witnesses,* rev. ed. (Maryknoll, NY: Orbis Books, 2005).

Chapter Two

1. Witness the barbaric beheading, disseminated through social media, of two American journalists, James Foley and Steven Sotloff, in August 2014, by the Islamic State of Iraq and Syria (ISIS).

2. See "George Tinker: Survival and Self-Determination, An Interview by Bob Hulteen," in *Cloud of Witnesses,* ed. Jim Wallis and Joyce Hollyday, rev. ed. (Maryknoll, NY: Orbis Books, 2005), 44–45.

3. Edward Countryman, *Americans: A Collision of Histories* (New York: Hill & Wang, 1996), 7.

4. See the two books by Charles C. Mann, *1491: New Revelations of the Americas before Columbus* (New York: Vintage, 2006; and *1493: Uncovering the New World Columbus Created* (New York: Vintage 2012).

5. A few others could be added to this list, such as Ethiopia, which defeated Italian invaders, and Liberia, which had close ties to the United States, and some of the countries in the Persian Gulf. See George Thomas Kurian, ed., *Encyclopedia of the Third World,* 4th ed. (New York: Facts on File, 1992), vol. 3, Appendix I, 2233.

6. Adam Daniel Corson-Finnerty, *World Citizen: Action for Global Justice* (Maryknoll, NY: Orbis Books, 1982), 9.

7. Ibid., 10. Corson-Finnerty is relying on D. K. Fieldhouse, *The Colonial Empires* (New York: Delacorte Press, 1967), 178. See Trevor Getz and Heather Streets-Salter, *Modern Imperialism and Colonialism: A Global Perspective* (Upper Saddle River, NJ: Pearson, 2010), for a contemporary textbook on the topic. See Margaret Kohn, "Colonialism," in *The Stanford Encyclopedia of Philosophy* (Spring 2014), ed. Edward N. Zalta, http://plato.stanford.edu, for a general essay on the topic.

8. This account relies on the summaries in Corson-Finnerty, *World Citizen,* chap. 1, and Paul Vallely, *Bad Samaritans: First World Ethics and Third World Debt* (Maryknoll, NY: Orbis Books, 1990), 85–105.

9. Ross Gandy, *A Short History of Mexico: From the Olmecs to the PRI* (Cuernavaca: Center for Bilingual Multicultural Studies, 1987), 5. This account relies on Gandy and on Corson-Finnerty.

10. Corson-Finnerty, *World Citizen,* 12. See Gandy, *Short History,* 6–7.

11. Gandy, *Short History,* 7.

12. Joseph Collins, "World Hunger: A Scarcity of Food or a Scarcity of Democracy," in Michael T. Klare and Daniel C. Thomas, eds., *World Security: Challenges for a New Century* (New York: St. Martin's Press, 1994), 360.

13. Gandy, *Short History,* 8–9.

14. Corson-Finnerty, *World Citizen,* 11.

15. Vallely, *Bad Samaritans,* 88, quoting Paul Harrison, *Inside the Third World* (London: Penguin Books, 1979).

16. Corson-Finnerty, *World Citizen,* 17. Cf. Vallely, *Bad Samaritans,* 91.

17. Elizabeth Morgan, *Global Poverty and Personal Responsibility* (New York: Paulist Press, 1989), 70–71.

18. Vallely, *Bad Samaritans,* 91; Corson-Finnerty, *World Citizen,* 16.

19. Corson-Finnerty, *World Citizen,* 14; Vallely, *Bad Samaritans,* 96. Chapter 6, below, examines ethnic conflict in Africa.

20. Corson-Finnerty, *World Citizen,* 16. See the film *Out of Africa* (1985), directed by Sydney Pollack, starring Meryl Streep and Robert Redford.

21. See Caroline Elkins, *Imperial Reckoning: The Untold Story of Britain's Gulag in Kenya* (New York: Henry Holt, 2005).

22. Vallely, *Bad Samaritans,* 96.

23. Corson-Finnerty, *World Citizen,* 17; Vallely, *Bad Samaritans,* 93–94.

24. The film *Black Robe* (1991), directed by Bruce Beresford, addresses this issue very well. It is set in French Canada. The film contains some violent scenes.

25. Vallely, *Bad Samaritans,* 99.

26. Ibid., 97.

27. The film *Mister Johnson* (1991), directed by Bruce Beresford, illustrates this point well.

28. Louis Fischer, *Gandhi: His Life and Message to the World* (New York: New American Library, 1954), 65–67. This massacre is also depicted in the film *Gandhi* (1982), directed by Richard Attenborough, starring Ben Kingsley. General Dyer's Indian troops fired 1,650 bullets at unarmed civilians who were trapped in an enclosed area, causing 1,516 casualties and 379 deaths.

29. See Stanley Karnow, *In Our Image: America's Empire in the Philippines* (New York: Ballantine Books, 1989), chaps. 4–7, for a detailed account of this war and its political background.

30. Charles S. Olcott, *The Life of William McKinley* (Boston: Houghton Mifflin, 1916), vol. 2, 110.

31. Karnow, *In Our Image,* 198. William Howard Taft, the first American governor of the Philippines, condescendingly referred to Filipinos as "little brown brothers"

(174). The term captures some of the air of superiority, racism, and self-deceptive benevolence that white Americans brought to US control of the Philippines.

32. Larry Rohter, "Remembering the Past; Repeating It Anyway," *New York Times*, July 24, 1994, 1, 3. See also Michael Duffey, *Sowing Justice, Reaping Peace* (Franklin, WI: Sheed & Ward, 2001), chap. 1.

33. Rohter, "Remembering the Past."

34. Arthur Simon, *Bread for the World* (New York: Paulist Press, 1975), 74–75, 90.

35. *Rerum Novarum* can be found in *Catholic Social Thought: The Documentary Heritage*, ed. David J. O'Brien and Thomas A. Shannon (Maryknoll, NY: Orbis Books, 1992, 2010).

36. Paul Kennedy, *Preparing for the Twenty-First Century* (New York: Random House, 1993), 4–5. My account of Malthus and population is drawn from pp. 3–13.

37. Kennedy, *Preparing*, 8. The three escape hatches are discussed on pp. 6–10.

38. Ibid., 9.

39. Ibid., 10–11.

40. Alvin Toffler, *Future Shock* (New York: Bantam Books, 1970).

41. Thomas L. Friedman, *Thank You for Being Late: An Optimist's Guide to Thriving in an Age of Accelerations* (New York: Farrar, Straus and Giroux, 2016), 19–35, passim. Friedman's book is reviewed by John Micklethwait, "In Search of World Order," *New York Times Book Review*, December 18, 2016, 1, 14. Friedman's column, "Climate Shifts Aren't Limited to the Weather," *New York Times*, August 2, 2017, op-ed page, is a good introduction to the thesis of the book.

42. See Michael Grunwald, "The Second Age of Reason," *Time*, September 8–15, 2014, 37–39, on which this section depends.

43. See Kate Murphy, "We Want Privacy, but Can't Stop Sharing," *New York Times*, October 5, 2014, SR 4.

44. Friedman, *Thank You for Being Late*, 203–43. Friedman relies on James Bessen, *Learning by Doing: The Real Connection between Innovation, Wages, and Wealth* (New Haven, CT: Yale University Press, 2015). Kai-Fu Lee, "The Real Threat of Artificial Intelligence," *New York Times*, June 25, 2017, SR 4, 5. On the Universal Basic Income see Robert Reich, "What If the Government Gave Everyone a Paycheck?" *New York Times Book Review*, July 15, 2018, 1, 20, reviewing Annie Lowrey, *Give People Money: How a Universal Basic Income Would End Poverty, Revolutionize Work, and Remake the World* (New York: Crown, 2018); and Andrew Yang, *The War on Normal People: The Truth About America's Disappearing Jobs and Why Universal Basic Income Is Our Future* (New York: Hachette, 2018).

45. This history of the twentieth century, the World Wars, and the Cold War is common knowledge, but see Joshua S. Goldstein and Jon C. Pevehouse, *International Relations*, 10th ed., 2012–2013 Update (New York: Pearson, 2013), 26–38, 61–63, for a lucid summary.

46. Samuel P. Huntington, "Democracy's Third Wave," *Journal of Democracy* 2, no. 2 (Spring 1991): 12–34; and his book *The Third Wave: Democratization in the Twentieth Century* (Norman: University of Oklahoma Press, 1991), both based on his 1989 Julian J. Rothbaum Lectures at the University of Oklahoma. The first wave of democratization was the century from about 1820 to 1926, and the second wave was after World War II, from about 1946 to 1962. Each of these first two waves was

followed by a reversal. Interestingly, writing in 1990, Huntington characterized the third wave as the "Catholic wave" and pointed to the church's newfound support for democracy at the Second Vatican Council (1962–65) as one of five reasons for increasing democracy among the world's countries. This third wave continued until around 2006. See also Goldstein and Pevehouse, *International Relations*, 94–96.

47. Larry Diamond, "Facing Up to the Democratic Recession," *Journal of Democracy* 26, no. 1 (January 2015): 141–55, at 141. See Freedom House and its annual publication *Freedom in the World* for a country-by-country appraisal of global democracy, www.freedomhouse.org. While not all experts agree completely with Freedom House's criteria for democracy and freedom, its data are universally respected and used.

48. Ibid., 142.

49. Marc F. Plattner, "Is Democracy in Decline?" *Journal of Democracy* 26, no. 1 (January 2015): 5–10, at 7.

50. Plattner, "Is Democracy in Decline," 7–10; Diamond, "Facing Up to the Democratic Recession," 144–55; Francis Fukuyama, "Why Is Democracy Performing So Poorly?" *Journal of Democracy* 26, no. 1 (January 2015): 11–20; and Pippa Norris, "Trump's Global Democracy Retreat," *New York Times*, September 7, 2017, op-ed page.

51. See Alan S. Blinder, *After the Music Stopped: The Financial Crisis, the Response, and the Work Ahead* (New York: Penguin Press, 2013), 23–27, passim.

52. Abhijit Banerjee and Esther Duflo, *Poor Economics: A Radical Rethinking of the Way to Fight Global Poverty* (New York: Public Affairs, 2011), 136–37.

Chapter 3

1. See Katherine Boo, *Behind the Beautiful Forevers: Life, Death, and Hope in a Mumbai Undercity* (New York: Random House, 2012).

2. Anup Shah, "Poverty Facts and Stats," Global Issues, http://www.globalissues.org.

3. United Nations Development Programme, *Human Development Report 2016: Human Development for Everyone*, "Overview," hdr.undp.org, 2–3; Michael P. Todaro, *Economic Development*, 6th ed. (Reading, MA: Addison-Wesley, 1997), 16–18.

4. Joshua S. Goldstein and Jon C. Pevehouse, *International Relations*, 10th ed., 2012–2013 Update (Boston: Pearson, 2013), 21–26.

5. As of July 2016, low-income economies were defined as those with a gross national income (GNI) per capita of $1,025 or less in 2015; lower-middle-income economies have a GNI per capita between $1,026 and $4,035; upper-middle-income economies between $4,036 and $12,475; high-income-economies $12,476 or more. The World Bank Data Blog, "New Country Classifications by Income Level," https://blogs.worldbank.org. See *Human Development Report 2016*, Table 1, Human Development Index and Its Components, 198–201.

6. Freedom House, "Freedom in the World 2018," freedomhouse.org.

7. Jason Hickel, "Exposing the Great 'Poverty Reduction' Lie," *Aljazeera*, August 21, 2014; Shah, "Poverty Facts and Stats."

8. *Human Development Report 2016*, 31.

9. Larry Elliott, "World's Eight Richest People Have Same Wealth as Poorest 50%," www.theguardian.com.

10. Martin Caparros, "Counting the Hungry," *New York Times*, September 28, 2014, SR4.

11. Goldstein and Pevehouse, *International Relations*, 14, 461; "Inequality Index: Where Are the World's Most Unequal Countries?" www.theguardian.com.

12. *Human Development Report 2016*, 30–31.

13. *Human Development Report 2001*, 20, hdr.undp.org.

14. *Human Development Report 2016*, 25.

15. Ibid., Table 1, "Human Development Index and Its Components," 198–201. Vincent Ferraro and Melissa Rosser, "Global Debt and Third World Development," in Michael T. Klare and Daniel C. Thomas, *World Security: Challenges for a New Century* (New York: St. Martin's Press, 1994), 335–36, make a similar point using older data.

16. United Nations, *Millennium Development Goals Report 2015*, July 1, 2015, 3–9; Achilleas Galatsidas and Finbar Sheehy, "What Have the Millennium Development Goals Achieved?" www.theguardian.com.

17. Max Roser and Esteban Ortiz-Ospina, "Global Extreme Poverty," Our World in Data, ourworldindata.org.

18. Nicholas Kristof, "Why 2017 May Be the Best Year Ever," *New York Times*, January 22, 2017, op-ed page.

19. Homi Kharas and Wolfgang Fengler, "Global Poverty Is Declining but Not Fast Enough," *Brookings Institute*, November 7, 2017; Jason Hickel, "Exposing the Great 'Poverty Reduction' Lie"; *Human Development Report 2016*, 26, 30.

20. The United Nations, "Transforming Our World: The 2030 Agenda for Sustainable Development," September 2015, https://sustainabledevelopment.un.org; *Human Development Report 2016*, 45–47.

21. Thomas L. Friedman, *The Lexus and the Olive Tree* (New York: Farrar, Straus and Giroux, 1999), xiv.

22. *Human Development Report 1996*, 5, hdr.undp.org.

23. *Human Development Report 1999*, 1. "Globalization with a Human Face" is the subtitle for the *Human Development Report 1999*, hdr.undp.org.

24. Friedman, *Lexus and Olive Tree*, 85–86, xviii.

25. Ibid., xv; *Human Development Report 2016*, 35.

26. *Human Development Report 2016*, 35.

27. Ibid., 35–38.

28. Friedman, *Lexus and Olive Tree*, 86–87.

29. Ibid., 87, 161.

30. *Human Development Report 2016*, 33–35.

31. Elizabeth Hinson-Hasty, *The Problem of Wealth: A Christian Response to a Culture of Affluence* (Maryknoll, NY: Orbis Books, 2017), 6–7, 82–83.

32. *Human Development Report 1999*, 2. "The fundamental moral criterion for all economic decisions and policies is this: they must be at the service of all people, especially the poor"; *Economic Justice for All*, # 24.

33. Hinson-Hasty, *The Problem of Wealth*, 8–22, 213–14. Hinson-Hasty critiques "economism" (the reduction of all things to economics) in chap. 3, and "social developmentalism" and "neoliberalism" in chap. 4.

34. *Economic Justice for All*, ##1, 5.

35. Global Justice Now, October 17, 2018, http://www.globaljustice.org.uk, for 2017, based on *CIA World Factbook 2017* and *Fortune Global 500*.

36. Bob Herbert, "Nike's Pyramid Scheme," *New York Times,* June 10, 1996, op-ed page.

37. Jason Hickel, "Aid in Reverse: How Poor Countries Develop Rich Countries," *The Guardian*, January 14, 2017, based on a study by Global Financial Integrity (GFI, http://www.gfintegrity.org) and the Centre for Applied Research at the Norwegian School of Economics; and Kathy McAfee, "Why the Third World Goes Hungry: Selling Cheap, Buying Dear," *Commonweal,* June 15, 1990, 380.

38. James B. McGinnis, *Bread and Justice: Toward a New International Economic Order* (New York: Paulist Press, 1979), chaps. 8–12. E. F. Schumacher, *Small Is Beautiful: Economics as If People Mattered* (New York: Harper & Row, 1973). Goldstein and Pevehouse, *International Relations*, 352–53, "Debate about Foreign Direct Investment"; Michael P. Todaro and Stephen C. Smith, *Economic Development*, 12th ed. (Boston: Pearson, 2015), 736–43.

39. "Sweatshops in Bangladesh," War on Want, https://waronwant.org; Jim Sessions, "Cross-border Blues," *Forum for Applied Research and Public Policy* 14 (Spring, 1999): 58–64; David Schilling, "*Maquiladora* Workers Deserve a Sustainable Living Wage," *Interfaith Center on Corporate Responsibility Brief* 23, no. 10 (1995): 3B. Sam Dillon, "At U.S. Door, Huddled Masses Yearn for Better Pay," *New York Times*, December 4, 1995, A4.

40. Jim Yardley, "Report on Deadly Factory Collapse in Bangladesh Finds Widespread Blame," *New York Times*, May 22, 2013.

41. "Sweatshops in Bangladesh."

42. Michelle Chen, "Was Your Smartphone Built in a Sweatshop?" *The Nation*, January 2, 2018.

43. Larry Rohter, "To U.S. Critics, a Sweatshop; to Hondurans, a Better Life," *New York Times*, July 18, 1996, A1, A14; Nipa Banerjee, "The Ethics of Buying Clothes Produced in Sweatshops," Center for International Policy Studies Blog, February 26, 2018, https://www.cips-cepi.ca. See also Christopher Blattman and Stefan Dercon, "Everything We Know about Sweatshops Was Wrong," *New York Times*, April 27, 2017, op-ed page, for a different perspective based on their research in Ethiopia.

44. Felicity Lawrence, "The Sweatshop Generation," *The Guardian*, June 12, 2002, 17.

45. Abigail McCarthy, "By the Sweat of Kid's Brows," *Commonweal*, June 1, 1996, 7–8. Steven Greenhouse, "Sporting Goods Concerns Agree to Combat Sale of Soccer Balls Made by Children," *New York Times*, February 14, 1997, A12.

46. Banerjee, "The Ethics of Buying Clothes"; Larry Rohter, "To U.S. Critics," A14. Kaushik Basu, "The Poor Need Child Labor," *New York Times*, November 29, 1994, op-ed page.

47. David Moberg, "Bringing Down Niketown," *The Nation* 268 (June 7, 1999): 15–19; Steven Greenhouse, "Voluntary Rules on Apparel Labor Proving Elusive," *New York Times*, February 1, 1997, 1, 7; Steven Greenhouse, "Accord to Combat Sweatshop Labor Faces Obstacles," *New York Times*, April 13, 1997, 1, 20; "A Modest Start on

Sweatshops," *New York Times*, April 16, 1997, editorial; Abigail McCarthy, "Kinder, Gentler Sweatshops," *Commonweal* 124, June 6, 1997, 6–7.

48. On the August 2017 Nike agreement, see the ASAS website, http://usas.org. Jeffrey C. Isaac, "Thinking about the Anti-Sweatshop Movement," *Dissent* 36 (Fall 2001): 100–108; Dana O'Rourke, "Sweatshops 101," *Dollars and Sense* 237, Sept./Oct. 2001, 14–19.

49. "Statistics and Facts on the U.S. Apparel Industry," Statista, www.statista. com.

50. Moberg, "Bringing Down Niketown," 18.

51. Amy Merrick, "Why Students Aren't Fighting Forever 21," *New Yorker*, June 6, 2014.

52. Steven Kull, "American Support for Foreign Aid in the Age of Trump," *Brookings*, July 31, 2017, https://www.brookings.edu. The May 2017 opinion poll was by the Program for Public Consultation (PPC) of the University of Maryland. There is bipartisan support for foreign aid in Congress. Thus the actual 2018 fiscal budget approved by Congress did not cut foreign aid as much as the Trump administration proposed. See also Ann M. Simmons, "U.S. Foreign Aid: A Waste of Money or a Boost to World Stability? Here Are the Facts," *Los Angeles Times*, May 10, 2017.

53. Kull, "American Support for Foreign Aid"; Simmons, "U.S. Foreign Aid"; and "Development Aid Rises Again in 2016 but Flows to Poorest Countries Dip," OECD, November 4, 2017, www.oecd.org.

54. "U.S. Drops to 4th in Aid to Developing Countries," *Hartford Courant*, June 18, 1996, reporting on an OECD report.

55. "Development Aid Rises Again," OECD; "Military Expenditure," Stockholm International Peace Research Institute (SIPRI), May 2, 2018, www.sipri.org. US military spending in 2016 was $610 billion or 3.1 percent of GDP, which accounted for 35 percent of global military spending.

56. "The Russian Federation's Official Development Assistance," OECD.org (2017).

57. Junyi Zhang, "Chinese Foreign Assistance Explained," *Brookings*, July 19, 2016, https://www.brookings.edu; Adam Taylor, "China Treats Its Foreign Aid Like a State Secret. New Research Aims to Reveal It," *Washington Post*, October 11, 2017, reporting on research by AidData; Maria Abi-Habib, "How China Got Sri Lanka to Cough Up a Port," *New York Times*, June 26, 2018, A1, 6.

58. Goldstein and Pevehouse, *International Relations*, 486, 489.

59. Ibid., 490–92.

60. Frances Robles, "FEMA Was Sorely Unprepared for Puerto Rico Hurricane, Report Says," *New York Times*, July 13, 2018, A15. The official death toll, which was listed at 64, was raised to 2,975 nearly a year later. Sheri Fink, "Nearly a Year after Hurricane Maria, Puerto Rico Revises Death Toll to 2,975," *New York Times*, August 28, 2018.

61. See Jeffrey D. Sachs, "When Foreign Aid Makes a Difference," *New York Times*, Feb. 3, 1997, op-ed page, and his book *The End of Poverty: Economic Possibilities for Our Time* (New York: Penguin Books, 2006).

62. Todaro and Smith, *Economic Development*, 600–677, esp. 630–62; Goldstein and Pevehouse, *International Relations*, 472–74.

63. *Human Development Report 2016*, 26–27; Goldstein and Pevehouse, *International Relations*, 461–68.

64. Goldstein and Pevehouse, *International Relations*, 472–73.

65. "Exports of Goods and Services as Percent of GDP," World Bank (2017), http://www.worldbank.org; Goldstein and Pevehouse, *International Relations*, 481–82; *Human Development Report 2002*, 33, hdr.undp.org.

66. *Human Development Report 2002*, 33; Goldstein and Pevehouse, *International Relations*, 294–98, 481–82; Heinz Strubenhoff, "The WTO's Decision to End Agricultural Export Subsidies Is Good News for Farmers and Consumers," *Brookings*, February 8, 2016, https://www.brookings.edu.

67. McGinnis, *Bread and Justice*, 89–91; Goldstein and Pevehouse, *International Relations*, 295.

68. *Human Development Report 2002*, 33.

69. See J. Milburn Thompson, "Progressive Christians Should Not Oppose the Expansion of NAFTA," *Journal for Peace and Justice Studies* 10 (2000): 1–27; and James McBride and Mohammed Aly Sergie, "NAFTA's Economic Impact," Council on Foreign Relations Backgrounder, October 4, 2017, https://www.cfr.org.

70. Mark Landler and Alan Rappeport, "President Hails Revised Nafta Trade Deal, and Sets Up a Showdown with China," *New York Times*, October 2, 2018, A1, 5; and Jim Tankersley, "Trump Just Ripped Up NAFTA: Here's What's in the New Deal," *New York Times*, October 2, 2018, A5.

71. Goldstein and Pevehouse, *International Relations*, 294–98.

72. Veronique de Rugy, "Why the U.S. Should Drop All Tariffs," *New York Times*, June 21, 2018, op-ed page.

73. Joseph Collins, "World Hunger: A Scarcity of Food or a Scarcity of Democracy?" in Klare and Thomas, eds., *World Security*, 363.

74. Ibid., 364.

75. M. A. Thomas, "Getting Debt Relief Right," *Foreign Affairs* 80, Sept./Oct., 2001, 36.

76. "Heavily Indebted Poor Country Initiative," World Bank, January 9, 2018, http://www.worldbank.org; "Can Debt Relief Make a Difference?" *Economist* 357, November 18, 2000, 85.

77. "Debt Data by Region," World Bank (2018), http://www.worldbank.org.

78. Thomas, "Getting Debt Relief Right," 36–46, documents this point with considerable detail; see also Marcelo M. Giugale, *Economic Development: What Everyone Needs to Know*, 2nd ed. (New York: Oxford University Press, 2017 [orig., 2014]), 190–93; Robert Snyder, "Proclaiming Jubilee—For Whom?" *Christian Century* 116, June 30, 1999, 682–85; David Malin Roodman, "Ending the Debt Crisis," in Lester R. Brown et al., *State of the World 2001* (New York: W. W. Norton, 2001), 163.

79. Goldstein and Pevehouse, *International Relations*, 478–80, at 479.

80. "Global South Debt Payments Increase Almost 50% in Two Years," Jubilee Debt Campaign, March 13, 2017, https://jubileedebt.org.uk.

81. Friedman, *Lexus and Olive Tree*, 247–63.

82. *Human Development Report 1996*, 5.

83. For a challenging essay on this point, see David Bentley Hart, "Christ's Rabble:

The First Christians Were Not Like Us," *Commonweal*, October 7, 2016, 18–21; and Simeon Zahl and David Bentley Hart, "Suggestions or Commands? An Exchange on David Bentley Hart's 'Christ's Rabble,'" *Commonweal*, December 16, 2016, 9–12. See also Hinson-Hasty, *The Problem of Wealth*, 27–46.

84. Arantxa Guerena, *Unearthed: Land, Power, and Inequality in Latin America* (Oxfam, November 2016), 13, 21–25, https://www.oxfam.org.

85. Max Roser, "Global Economic Inequality," Our World in Data (updated October 2016), https://ourworldindata.org.

86. Eduardo Porter and Karl Russell, "It's an Unequal World. It Doesn't Have to Be," *New York Times*, December 14, 2017, an analysis of World Wealth and Income Database 2017, http://wid.world, in Business Day.

87. Thomas Piketty, *Capital in the Twenty-First Century*, trans. Arthur Goldhammer (Cambridge, MA: Belknap Press of Harvard University, 2014), 20–27; Giugale, *Economic Development*, 66.

88. *Human Development Report 1996*, 5–6; Giugale, *Economic Development*, 67.

89. *Human Development Report 2001*, 17.

90. Giugale, *Economic Development*, 67. See, for example, Jane Meyer, *Dark Money: The Hidden History of the Billionaires Behind the Rise of the Radical Right* (New York: Doubleday, 2016).

91. Porter and Russell, "It's an Unequal World."

92. Based on *Human Development Report 1996*, 6–8.

93. Abhijit V. Banerjee and Esther Duflo, *Poor Economics: A Radical Rethinking of the Way to Fight Global Poverty* (New York: PublicAffairs, 2011), 157–81. More recently Mr. Yunus has gotten entangled in Bangladesh's complex politics.

94. Jacob Poushter, "Internet Access Growing Worldwide but Remains Higher in Advanced Countries," Pew Research Center, February 22, 2016; *Human Development Report 2001*, 3. "Making New Technologies Work for Human Development" is the subtitle and theme of this edition of this *Human Development Report*.

95. Nicholas D. Kristof and Sheryl WuDunn, *Half the Sky: Turning Oppression into Opportunity for Women Worldwide* (New York: Vintage, 2009), passim; Goldstein and Pevehouse, *International Relations*, 433–34, 473–74; *Human Development Report 1996*, 32–36, discussing the "gender-related development index" and the "gender empowerment measure."

96. Goldstein and Pevehouse, *International Relations*, 475–76; John Kenneth Galbraith, *The Good Society: The Humane Agenda* (Boston: Houghton Mifflin, 1996), chap. 17.

97. Giugale, *Economic Development*, 68.

98. Sarah Jacobs, "Just Nine of the World's Richest Men Have More Wealth Than the Poorest 4 Billion People," *Independent*, January 17, 2018; "The Billionaires 2018" *Forbes*, March 6, 2018.

99. This quote from Gandhi is found on an Oxfam poster on the environment. He states elsewhere: "The rich have a superfluous store of things which they do not need, and which are therefore neglected and wasted; while millions are starved to death for want of sustenance. If each retained possession only of what he needed, no one would be in want, and all would live in contentment. As it is the rich are discontented no less

than the poor" (M. K. Gandhi, *Non-Violent Resistance* [New York: Schocken Books, 1951], 46).

100. This paragraph is based on Banerjee and Duflo, *Poor Economics*, vii–xi and 1–16. Since this section relies primarily on this one source I will put page numbers from this book in parentheses rather than use multiple endnotes.

101. Programs that focus on eradicating a particular disease that affects the poor can also be included in the "low hanging fruit" in public health. The Carter Center and the Bill and Melinda Gates Foundation have sponsored such programs with significant success. Donald G. McNeil Jr., "Now in Sight: Success Against an Infection That Blinds," *New York Times*, July 17, 2018, D1, 6, tells the story of a U.S.A.I.D.-funded global program focused on trachoma, the world's leading infectious cause of blindness, which is making significant progress at reasonable cost.

102. Geeta Anand, "Fighting Truancy among India's Teachers, with a Pistol and Stick," *New York Times*, February 20, 2016, A1, 6. This is the story of Manoj Mishra, who is cracking down on truant teachers in India's most populous state, Uttar Pradesh. Mr. Mishra discovered that some of the teachers lived more than a thousand miles away, and one had not been to his school for six years.

103. Ali Akbar Natiq, "Where Democracy Is a Terrifying Business" *New York Times*, July 17, 2018. This is a story illustrating how elections in Pakistan are a way for the rich to oppress the poor.

104. *Human Development Report 1996*, 26. Goldstein and Pevehouse, *International Relations*, 185–87.

105. Dom Hélder Câmara, *Spiral of Violence* (London: Sheed & Ward, 1971).

106. Eileen Egan, "The Beatitudes, the Works of Mercy, and Pacifism," in Thomas Shannon, ed., *War or Peace?* (Maryknoll, NY: Orbis Books, 1980), 173–75.

Chapter Four

1. United Nations Development Programme, *Human Development Report 1996* (New York: Oxford University Press, 1996).

2. Lynn White Jr., "The Historical Roots of the Ecological Crisis," *Science* 155 (March 10, 1967): 1203–7.

3. Genesis 1:28. See also Genesis 9:1–7, where God repeats the admonition to subdue the earth and gives humanity the animals to eat as well.

4. See, for example, Mary Evelyn Jegen and Bruno V. Manno, eds., *The Earth Is the Lord's: Essays on Stewardship* (New York: Paulist Press, 1978); and Carolyn Thomas, *Gift and Response: A Biblical Spirituality for Contemporary Christians* (New York: Paulist Press, 1994), 10–12.

5. Michael J. Himes and Kenneth R. Himes, *Fullness of Faith: The Public Significance of Theology* (New York: Paulist Press, 1993), chap. 5.

6. See James A. Nash, *Loving Nature: Ecological Integrity and Christian Responsibility* (Nashville: Abingdon Press, 1991), chap. 3, for a discussion of the claim against Christianity, and chaps. 4 and 5, for a constructive theological response.

7. Thomas Berry, *The Dream of the Earth* (San Francisco: Sierra Club Books, 1988); *The Great Work: Our Way into the Future* (New York: Three Rivers Press, 1999); *Christian Future and the Fate of the Earth* (Maryknoll, NY: Orbis Books, 2009).

8. See Bill Davis and George Sessions, *Deep Ecology: Living as if Nature Mattered* (Salt Lake City: Gibbs Smith, 1985); and Arne Naess, "Sustained Development and Deep Ecology," in J. Ronald Engel and Joan Gibb Engel, eds., *Ethics of Environment and Development: Global Challenge, International Response* (Tucson: University of Arizona Press, 1990). The "Deep Ecology" perspective rejects an anthropocentric approach that seeks to reform human behavior toward the environment; it advocates a more radical view that recognizes the unity of humans, plants, animals, and the earth. It calls for a new ecological consciousness, a change in human understanding of the relationship of humans and the ecosystem. The ecosystem itself becomes the primary value.

9. See Drew Christiansen, "Ecology, Justice, and Development," *Theological Studies* 51 (March 1990): 76–79. See also Pamela Smith, *What Are They Saying about Environmental Ethics* (New York: Paulist Press, 1997), for an excellent overview of these diverse positions.

10. This statement of values and perspective depends on Himes and Himes, *Fullness of Faith*, chap. 5; and on Pope Francis, *Laudato Si': On Caring for Our Common Home* (The Holy See [vatican.va], 2015).

11. This is based on an illustration by theologian John Haught. See Brian G. Henning, *Riders in the Storm: Ethics in an Age of Climate Change* (Winona, MN: Anselm Academic, 2015), 26.

12. Peter Brannen, "When Life on Earth Nearly Vanished," *New York Times*, July 30, 2017, SR 2.

13. Elizabeth Kolbert, *The Sixth Extinction: An Unnatural History* (New York: Picador, 2014), 14–19, chap. 4. This section depends in part on Kolbert. In 1980, Luis and Walter Alvarez correctly hypothesized that this extinction event was caused by a six-mile wide asteroid colliding with Earth in Mexico's Yucatan Peninsula. See Luis W. Alvarez et al., "Extraterrestrial Cause for the Cretaceous-Tertiary Extinction," *Science* 208 (1980): 1095–1108.

14. Kolbert, *The Sixth Extinction*, 230–34; chap. 7, especially 237–38, 246–47.

15. Ibid., 165–68. The Living Planet Index Report for 2016 indicates that vertebrate populations' abundance plummeted by 58 percent between 1970 and 2012, and is on track to reach 67 percent by 2020 (wwf.panda.org). See Damian Carrington, "World on Track to Lose Two-Thirds of Wild Animals by 2020, Major Report Warns," *The Guardian*, October 27, 2016.

16. The idea of a new epoch called the Anthropocene was first suggested by Paul Crutzen, a Dutch chemist who shared a Nobel Prize for discovering the effects of ozone-depleting compounds, in "Geology of Mankind," *Nature* 415 (January 2002): 23. The International Commission on Stratigraphy (ICS) administers the geologic time scale. Jan Zalasiewicz, a geologist at the University of Leicester in England, is chairing a thirty-five-member Anthropocene Working Group (AWG) to explore the official designation of a new epoch. Key questions are *whether* we have entered a new epoch and, if so, *when* did it begin? At the 35th International Geological Congress in South Africa in August 2016, the AWG, on a vote of thirty to three with two abstentions, recommended approval of the new Anthropocene epoch. The recommendation would need a 60 percent majority of both the ICS and the International Union of Geological Sciences (IUGS) for approval. The AWG continues to work on the date, location, and primary evidence to present. Bill

McKibben suggests something similar when he argues that the planet that humans have created today is so different from the climatic "sweetest of sweet spots" of the Holocene that it needs a new name: Eaarth (Bill McKibben, *Eaarth: Making a Life on a Tough New Planet* [New York: Henry Holt, 2010], 1–3).

17. Thomas Berry, *The Great Work: Our Way into the Future* (New York: Three Rivers Press, 1999), 3.

18. Ibid., 8.

19. Intergovernmental Panel on Climate Change (IPCC), *Climate Change 2013: The Physical Science Basis,* Working Group I (WGI) Contribution to the Fifth Assessment Report (Cambridge: Cambridge University Press, 2013), "Summary for Policy Makers," 4.

20. See John Houghton, *Global Warming: The Complete Briefing,* 5th ed. (Cambridge: Cambridge University Press, 2015), 17–33, 50–53, 266–67; Justin Gillis, "Climate Change Is Complex. We've Got Answers to Your Questions," *New York Times,* September 24, 2017, A22; and Henning, *Riders in the Storm,* 53–55.

21. Houghton, *Global Warming,* 9–10, 137–43; Henning, *Riders in the Storm,* 31–32.

22. The American Association for the Advancement of Science (AAAS) Climate Science Panel, *What We Know: The Reality, Risks and Response to Climate Change* (2014), 3. See also Henning, *Riders in the Storm,* 61–64, on the gap between scientific consilience and public perception in the United States.

23. John Noble Wilford, "Ages-Old Icecap at North Pole Is Now Liquid, Scientists Find," *New York Times,* August 19, 2000, A1, A13. See also Eugene Linden, "The Big Meltdown," *Time,* September 4, 2000, 52–56.

24. See National Oceanic and Atmospheric Administration (NOAA), National Centers for Environmental Information, State of the Climate, Global Analysis, Annual Reports, 2016, https://www.ncdc.noaa.gov.

25. This is the theme of McKibben, *Eaarth.*

26. Houghton, *Global Warming,* 163. The following depends primarily on 162–217 in Houghton.

27. Nicholas Kristof, "As Trump Denies Climate Change, These Kids Die," *New York Times,* January 8, 2017, op-ed page.

28. Henning, *Riders in the Storm,* 21–25. The lower numbers for 1950 are based on data from the National Climatic Data Center (NCDC). The higher numbers for 2000–2009 are based on more thorough analysis by the National Center for Atmospheric Research.

29. This paragraph is based on the United Nations Office for Disaster Risk Reduction (UNISDR) and the Centre for Research on the Epidemiology of Disasters (CRED), *The Human Cost of Weather-Related Disasters 1995–2015* (UNISDR, 2015, www.unisdr.org), 5.

30. Houghton, *Global Warming,* 200; Brad Plumer, "Assessing the Economic Bite from Rising Temperatures," *New York Times,* June 30, 2017, A16; Brad Plumer and Nadja Popovich, "Tracking Possible Trajectory of a World of Sweltering Days," *New York Times,* June 23, 2017, A10; and Salman Masood and Mike Ives, "As the Scorchers Multiply in Asia, Mercury Records Fall and Climate Concern Rises," *New York Times,* June 18, 2017, A8.

31. Nadja Popovich, "Hotter Summers, Once Exceptional, Become the Norm," *New York Times*, July 29, 2017, A4.

32. Tatiana Schlossberg, "Climate Change Blamed for Half of Increased Fire Danger," *New York Times*, October 11, 2016, A11; Matt Richtel and Fernanda Santos, "Wildfires, Once Confined to a Season, Burn Earlier and Longer," *New York Times*, April 13, 2016, A1, 3.

33. Houghton, *Global Warming*, 149–50. See also Henning, *Riders in the Storm*, 32–34; Norimitsu Onishi, "Drought Deepens South Africa's Malaise," *New York Times*, December 27, 2015, A6, A9.

34. Somini Sengupta, "Hotter, Drier, Hungrier: How Global Warming Punishes the World's Poorest," *New York Times*, March 12, 2018, A1, 7.

35. Nic Wertz and Elisabeth Malkin, "Hundreds Missing as Cleanup Begins in Guatemala," *New York Times*, October 5, 2015, A4; Aurelien Breeden, "France: Riviera Cleans Up after Deadly Flooding," *New York Times*, October 6, 2015, A8.

36. Doyle Rice, "Biblical Flooding Becoming More Common: South Carolina's 1-in-a 1000 Year Rain Is 6th in U.S. since 2010," *USA Today*, October 6, 2015; Richard Fausset and Alan Blinder, "End to Rain Is in Sight, but Floods to Continue," *New York Times*, October 6, 2015, A10, A19.

37. Michael Wines, "Study Sees a Higher Risk of Storms on the Horizon," *New York Times*, September 24, 2013, reporting on Noah S. Diffenbaugh, Martin Scherer, and Robert J. Trapp, "Robust Increases in Severe Thunderstorm Environments in Response to Greenhouse Forcing," *Proceedings of the National Academy of Sciences* 110, no. 41 (October 8, 2013): 16361–66.

38. Houghton, *Global Warming*, 150–53; Adam Sobel, "Where Are the Hurricanes?" *New York Times*, July 15, 2016, op-ed page.

39. Henry Fountain, "Forests Protect the Climate. A Future with More Storms Would Mean Trouble," *New York Times*, March 13, 2018, D1, 6.

40. Scientists are working on the question of whether a particular weather event was influenced by climate change. See, for example, Heidi Cullen, "Solving the Weather/Climate Puzzle," *New York Times*, March 12, 2016; and Henry Fountain, "Climate Swat Team," *New York Times*, August 2, 2016, D1, D3.

41. Houghton, *Global Warming*, 169. This section depends on pp. 164–75. The projection of a one meter average sea level rise by 2100 is based on the IPCC report, and it is widely reported in the literature on this topic. See Justin Gillis, "Greenhouse Gas Linked to Floods along U.S. Coasts," *New York Times*, February 23, 2016, A1, 10.

42. Kenneth Chang, "Snow Down and Heat Up in the Arctic Report Says," *New York Times*, December 18, 2014, A 5; Damian Carrington, "Arctic Sea Ice Shows Surprise Revival in a Cool Year," *The Guardian*, July 21, 2015, 5; Henry Fountain and John Schwartz, "Spiking Temperatures in the Arctic Startle Scientists," *New York Times*, December 22, 2016, A4.

43. Henry Fountain, "Alaska's Permafrost Is Thawing," *New York Times*, August 24, 2017, A1, 12; Kendra Pierre-Louis, "Beavers Thaw Permafrost as They Head Farther North," *New York Times*, December 21, 2017, A13.

44. Justin Gillis and Kenneth Chang, "Scientists Warn of Rising Oceans from Polar Melt," *New York Times*, May 13, 2014, A1, 8; Kenneth Chang, "The Big Melt

Accelerates," *New York Times*, May 20, 2014, Dl, D5; Jon Gertner, "The Secrets in the Ice," *New York Times Magazine*, November 15, 2015, 48-57, 80-81, at 50, 55, 57.

45. Justin Gillis, "Ice-Sheet Melt Seen Harming Cities by 2100," *New York Times*, March 31, 2016, A1,10, reporting on Robert M. DeConto and David Pollard, "Contribution of Antarctica to Past and Future Sea-Level Rise," *Nature* 531, March 31, 2016, 591–97; Richard Alley, "The Thwaites Glacier," *New York Times*, April 23, 2017, SR6.

46. This section on the consequences of rising sea levels depends primarily on Gardiner Harris, "As Seas Rise, Millions Cling to Borrowed Time and Dying Land," *New York Times*, March 20, 2014, A1, 10–11; Nicholas Kristof, "Swallowed by the Sea," *New York Times*, January 21, 2018, op-ed page; and Houghton, *Global Warming*, 170–75.

47. See Russell Shorto, "How to Think Like the Dutch in a Post-Sandy World," *New York Times Magazine*, April 13, 2014, 20–23; and Michael Kimmelman, "Dutch Face Rising Seas. The World Is Watching," *New York Times*, June 16, 2017, A1, 8–9.

48. See Justin Gillis, "Global Warming's Marker: Coastal Inundation Has Begun," *New York Times*, September 4, 2016, A1, 22–23.

49. See the Academy Award–nominated film *Sun Come Up* (2011), directed by Jennifer Redfearn. It tells the story about the relocation struggles of the Carteret Islanders, a community living on a remote island chain in the South Pacific Ocean, and now some of the world's first climate change refugees.

50. Christine Hauser, "An Oozing, Often Toxic, Symptom of Climate Change in Fast-Warming Waters," *New York Times*, August 30, 2018, A11.

51. See, for example, Edward Wong and Mia Li, "China's Growth Is Threatening Its Wetlands, Scientists Find," *New York Times*, October 20, 2015, A4.

52. Kolbert, *The Sixth Extinction*, 114. This section on ocean acidification depends primarily on *Sixth Extinction*, chaps. 6 and 7, especially 113–14, 120–24, 130–42.

53. Ibid., 123–24.

54. Ibid., 129–30, 141–42; Kendra Pierre-Louis and Brad Plumer, "Global Warming's Toll on Coral Reefs: As if They're 'Ravaged by War,'" *New York Times*, January 5, 2018, A9.

55. This section depends on Food and Agriculture Organization—United Nations (FAO-UN), *Livestock's Long Shadow: Environmental Issues and Options* (Rome: FAO, 2006); Jim Mason and Peter Singer, *The Ethics of What We Eat: Why Our Food Choices Matter* (Emmaus, PA: Rodale, 2006), esp. 23–68; and John H. Sniegocki, "Christian Ethics and Dietary Choices," *Clergy Journal* 85 (July/August 2009): 12–14, which is an abridged version of a paper given at the 2009 meeting of the College Theology Society (CTS).

56. FAO-UN, *Livestock's Long Shadow*, executive summary, xx.

57. Eugene Linden, "The Death of Birth," *Time*, January 2, 1989, 32.

58. FAO-UN, *Livestock's Long Shadow*, executive summary, xxi and 79–124.

59. Sniegocki, "Christian Ethics and Dietary Choices," 17–19.

60. See Nicholas Kristoff, "The Unhealthy Meat Market," *New York Times*, March 13, 2014, op-ed page.

61. FAO-UN, *Livestock's Long Shadow*, executive summary, xxiii–xxiv, 221–66.

On the politics of reforming industrial agriculture see Michael Pollan, "Why Did the Obamas Fail to Take on Corporate Agriculture?" *New York Times Magazine*, October 9, 2016, 41–50, 81–83.

62. Sniegocki, "Christian Ethics and Dietary Choices," 14; CTS paper, 19–31; Rebecca Smithers, "Vast Animal Crops to Satisfy Our Meat Needs Are Destroying Planet," *The Guardian*, October 5, 2017. See David Gelles, "Clearing the Cages, but Maybe Not the Conscience," *New York Times*, July 17, 2016, for a practical and moral discussion of cage-free laying hens.

63. FAO-UN, *FAO Assessment of Forests and Carbon Stocks, 1990–2015* (Rome: FAO, 2015); FAO-UN, *Global Forest Resources Assessment 2015* (Rome, 2015), esp. 2–5, "1990–2015: Twenty-Five Years in Review," which summarizes the forty-eight-page document.

64. Brad Plumer, "To Slow Deforestation, Study Offers an Easy Fix," *New York Times*, July 21, 2017, A9.

65. Kolbert, *The Sixth Extinction*, 151–53; also see chaps. 8 and 9; Linden, "The Death of Birth," 32.

66. Edward O. Wilson, "Threats to Biodiversity," *Scientific American* 261, September 1989, 108.

67. Kolbert, *The Sixth Extinction*, 157–62. See Nicholas St. Fleur, "Study Finds Broad Threats to Amazon Tree Species," *New York Times*, November 21, 2015, A3.

68. Kevin J. O'Brien, *An Ethics of Biodiversity: Christianity, Ecology, and the Variety of Life* (Washington, DC: Georgetown University Press, 2010), 3; Wilson, "Threats to Biodiversity," 112; Linden, "The Death of Birth," 32; Kolbert, *The Sixth Extinction*, 165–68.

69. Linden, "The Death of Birth," 33. This phenomenon is dramatized in two films: *Medicine Man* (1992), directed by John McTiernan and starring Sean Connery; and *The Emerald Forest* (1985), directed by John Boorman. The latter focuses on the plight of indigenous people who live in tropical forests.

70. Wilson, "Threats to Biodiversity," 114; Elisabeth Malkin, "Guatemalans Living Off Forests Get Task of Saving Them," *New York Times*, November 26, 2015, A16.

71. Malia Wollan and Spencer Lowell, "Arks of the Apocalypse," *New York Times Magazine*, July 16, 2017, 34–45.

72. Edward O. Wilson, "The Global Solution to Extinction," *New York Times*, March 13, 2016, SR7. See also Edward O. Wilson, *Half-Earth: Our Planet's Fight for Life* (New York: Liveright Publishing, 2016).

73. Coral Davenport, "Nations Approve Landmark Climate Accord in Paris," *New York Times*, December 13, 2015, A1, 19; and Coral Davenport, "A Climate Deal, 6 Fateful Years in the Making," *New York Times*, December 14, 2015, A1, 5, are the primary sources for these paragraphs on the making of the Paris Agreement.

74. A federal waiver allows California to set its own auto emissions standards, and twelve other states now follow California's standards. The California Air Resources Board (CARB) is sticking with the Obama auto emissions goals. See Hiroko Tabuchi, "U.S. Climate Change Policy: Made in California," *New York Times*, September 27, 2017, A1, 18.

75. Coral Davenport and Alissa J. Rubin, "Trump Signs Rule to Block Efforts Aiding Climate," *New York Times*, March 29, 2017, A1, 19.

76. Michael R. Bloomberg, "Climate Progress, without Trump," *New York Times*, March 31, 2017, op-ed page; Brad Plumer, "California's Ambitious Agenda to Cut Greenhouse Gas Emissions," *New York Times*, July 27, 2017, A13. Withdrawing from the Paris climate agreement is actually a nearly four-year process, which Trump has pledged to follow. See Brad Plumer, "U.S. Won't Actually Be Leaving the Paris Climate Deal Anytime Soon," *New York Times*, June 8, 2017, A22.

77. Steven Erlanger et al., "Leaders Pledge Climate Action Without Trump," *New York Times*, July 9, 2017, A1, 8.

78. Coral Davenport, "Major Climate Report Describes a Strong Risk of Crisis as Early as 2040," *New York Times*, October 7, 2018, which discusses the IPCC report, *Global Warming of 1.5 Degrees C.* (2018). On the choice of the target for avoiding the worst consequences of climate change and the reasonableness of reaching it see Houghton, *Global Warming*, 279–87.

79. Houghton, *Global Warming*, 272–76; Justin Gillis, "Climate Talks Also Focus on Saving World Forests," *New York Times*, December 11, 2015, A6, 23.

80. Jacques Leslie, "Soil Power! The Dirty Way to a Green Planet," *New York Times*, December 3, 2017, SR7; Moises Velasquez-Manoff, "Can Dirt Save the Earth?" *New York Times Magazine*, April 12, 2018, 28–35, 59, 61.

81. Houghton, *Global Warming*, 276–78.

82. Hiroko Tabuchi, "The World Is Embracing S.U.V.s. That's Bad News for the Climate," *New York Times*, March 6, 2018, B1, 2; J. Milburn Thompson, "Pro & Con: Should Americans Purchase Sport Utility Vehicles? No. That's Profligate Consumption," *Hartford Courant*, January 24, 1998, op-ed page. On energy and carbon dioxide savings in transport see Houghton, *Global Warming*, 307–10.

83. On energy conservation and efficiency in buildings and appliances, see Houghton, *Global Warming*, 300-307.

84. Ibid., 281, 281–87, where Houghton argues for a zero carbon economy.

85. The following analysis depends on Bill McKibben, "The Reckoning: Global Warming's Terrifying New Math," *Rolling Stone* 1162, August 2, 2012, 52, 54–58, 60. See also Sammy Roth, "The Cry: 'Keep It in the Ground,'" *USA Today*, April 17, 2016.

86. Nearly everyone suggests that putting a price on carbon (through a carbon tax, cap-and-trade system, etc.) would be a positive step in slowing global warming. Because of Republican climate-change deniers and political deference to the fossil-fuel industry, this has been politically impossible so far in the United States. And Pope Francis warns that buying and selling carbon credits can be a "new form of speculation" and a "ploy which permits maintaining excessive consumption." (*Laudato Si'*, #171). Pope Francis may be correct, and his emphasis on excessive consumption is a point well taken. Nevertheless, putting a price on carbon can be effective and helpful.

87. Randall Smith, "A New Divestment Focus on Campus: Fossil Fuels," *New York Times*, September 5, 2013; Bill McKibben, "Cashing Out from the Climate Casino," *New York Times*, December 15, 2017, op-ed page; and Bill McKibben, "New York City Just Declared War on the Oil Industry," *The Guardian*, January 11, 2018, op-ed page.

Moved by Pope Francis's environmental encyclical *Laudato Si'*, perhaps Catholic universities' financial advisers will take the lead in this divestment campaign.

88. Hiroko Tabuchi, "As Beijing Joins Climate Fight, Chinese Companies Build Coal Plants," *New York Times*, July 2, 2017, A10.

89. Somini Sengupta, "Oil Producer. Climate Ally. Norway Is a Paradox." *New York Times*, June 18, 2017, A6.

90. "Britain Joins the Shift to Electric Cars," *New York Times*, July 31, 2017, editorial; Stephen Castle, "To Fight Pollution, Britain Will Ban Sales of New Diesel and Gas Cars by 2040," *New York Times*, July 27, 2017, A6; Bill Vlasic and Neal E. Boudette, "GM and Ford Lay Out Plans to Expand Electric Models," *New York Times*, October 3, 2017, A1, 19.

91. Houghton, *Global Warming*, 311–12. Some argue that methane leaks in the process of producing and distributing natural gas nullifies the CO2 saved by burning natural gas. Even if natural gas is the least polluting fossil fuel, it is a short-term solution. See Clifford Kraus, "Future of Natural Gas Hinges on Stanching Methane Leaks," *New York Times*, July 12, 2016, B1.

92. Houghton, *Global Warming*, 312–13.

93. Peter Thiel, "The New Atomic Age We Need," *New York Times*, November 28, 2015, op-ed page, argues on behalf of nuclear energy but without addressing the environmental concerns.

94. Helen Caldicott, *Nuclear Madness* (Brookline, MA: Autumn Press, 1978), 65 and passim.

95. Henry Fountain, "Finns Work to Entomb the Nuclear Waste of Reactors," *New York Times*, June 13, 2017, D1. The article contrasts the popular acceptance of the transparent Onkalo project with the resistance to the Yucca Mountain proposal in Nevada.

96. See William Colgan et al., "The Abandoned Ice Sheet Base at Camp Century Greenland, in a Warming Climate," *Geophysical Research Letters* (August 4, 2016). See Damian Carrington, "Arctic Stronghold of Vital Seeds Partially Flooded after Permafrost Melts," *The Guardian*, May 20, 2017, 19.

97. Brad Plumer, "Glut of Natural Gas Pressures Nuclear Power, and Climate Goals, Too," *New York Times*, June 14, 2017, A17.

98. Matthew L. Wald, "Demolition of Nuclear Plant Illustrates Problems Involved," *New York Times*, May 14, 2002, A16.

99. Thiel, "The New Atomic Age We Need"; Houghton, *Global Warming*, 314; and Diane Cardwell, "America's Retreat from Atomic Power," *New York Times*, February 19, 2017, BU1, 4; Brad Plumer, "U.S. Nuclear Comeback Stalls as Two Reactors Are Abandoned," *New York Times*, August 1, 2017, A1, 6; Brad Plumer, "As U.S. Backs Off of Nuclear Power, Georgia Wants to Keep Building Reactors," *New York Times*, September 1, 2017, B2.

100. Houghton, *Global Warming*, 314; "A Renewable Energy Boom," *New York Times*, April 4, 2016, editorial.

101. Ernesto Londono, "Chile's Energy Transformation Is Powered by Wind, Sun, and Volcanos," *New York Times*, August 13, 2017, A6.

102. Houghton, *Global Warming*, 315–16.

103. Ibid., 316–20.

104. Ibid., 321–22; Justin Gillis, "Trump Can't Stop Energy Transition," *New York Times*, January 3, 2017, D1, D3.

105. Houghton, *Global Warming*, 322–28. As noted above, the fossil-fuel industry will resist renewable energy. One of the emerging obstacles to solar energy is overt and subtle opposition from utilities. See Hiroko Tabuchi, "After Rapid Growth, Rooftop Solar Programs Dim under Pressure from Utility Lobbyists," *New York Times*, July 9, 2017, 13.

106. Houghton, *Global Warming*, 328–29, 332–36.

107. Eduardo Porter, "Planet-Cooling Technology May Be Earth's Only Hope," *New York Times*, April 5, 2017, B1, B4; Jon Gertner, "Pandora's Umbrella: Are We Really Ready to Intentionally Alter Our Environment in Order to Fight Climate Change?" *New York Times Magazine* (The Climate Issue), April 23, 2017, 59–63. This section is based on these articles.

108. Houghton, *Global Warming*, 251–52.

109. John Schwartz, "Global Fuel Subsidies Dwarf Funding Commitment to Climate Change," *New York Times*, December 6, 2015, A9.

110. Houghton, *Global Warming*, 329–33. On investment in research and development, see also Coral Davenport and Nick Wingfield, "The Billionaire Statesman: Bill Gates Takes on Climate Change with Nudges and a Powerful Rolodex," *New York Times*, December 9, 2015, B1.

111. Houghton, *Global Warming*, 256, 297, 300, 339, 341. Divestment in fossil fuels and investment in carbon-free energy sources is key.

112. Houghton, *Global Warming*, 286; Davenport, "Nations Approve Landmark Climate Accord," A19. This commitment of rich countries to poor nations at the Paris climate agreement is partially undermined by President Trump's withdrawal of the United States from the accord.

113. Justin Gillis, "A Path for Climate Change Beyond Paris," *New York Times*, December 1, 2015, D1, 2; "The Electric Car Revolution," *New York Times*, July 18, 2017, editorial. See the Deep Decarbonization Pathways Project website at deepcarbonization.org.

114. Justin Gillis, "Short Answers to Hard Climate Questions," *New York Times*, December 1, 2015, D6.

115. See Paul Krugman, "Wind, Sun and Fire," *New York Times*, February 1, 2016, op-ed page, who argues that modest policy changes could implement "a renewable-energy revolution."

116. Max Roser and Esteban Ortiz-Ospina, "World Population Growth," Our World in Data (2013, 2017), https://ourworldindata.org.

117. United Nations Department of Economic and Social Affairs, Population Division (UN-ESA) *World Population Prospects: The 2015 Revision* (New York: United Nations, 2015), "Key Findings and Advance Tables," 2; Sam Jones and Mark Anderson, "World Population Heading for 10bn by 2050," *The Guardian*, July 30, 2015, 17.

118. David Kinsella, Bruce Russett, and Harvey Starr, *World Politics: The Menu for Choice*, 10th ed. (Boston, MA: Wadsworth, Cengage Learning, 2013), 405–6; Nathan

Keyfitz, "The Growing Human Population," *Scientific American* 261, September 1989, 122.

119. UN-ESA, *World Population Prospects: The 2015 Revision*, Interactive Data, Total Fertility Tables, http://esa.un.org.

120. UN-ESA, *World Population Prospects: The 2015 Revision*, "Key Findings and Advance Tables," 1. India's population is expected to surpass that of China by 2023 and to continue growing to about 1.7 billion by 2050, while China's population will decrease slightly from 1.4 billion in the 2030–2050 period (4).

121. Paul Kennedy, *Preparing for the Twenty-First Century* (New York: Random House, 1993), 32–33.

122. Based on 2009 data from the US Energy Information Administration, http://www.eia.gov.

123. Pope Francis, *Laudato Si'*, #50.

124. Kinsella, Russett, and Starr, *World Politics*, 359; Eugene Linden, "Remember the Population Bomb? It's Still Ticking," *New York Times*, June 18, 2017, SR4.

125. UN-ESA, *World Population Prospects: The 2015 Revision*, "Key Findings and Advance Tables," 4.

126. Janet Ranganathan, "The Global Food Challenge Explained in 18 Graphics," World Resources Institute blog, December, 2013, http://www.wri.org.

127. Kinsella, Russett, and Starr, *World Politics*, 411–12.

128. Ranganathan, "The Global Food Challenge"

129. UN-ESA, *World Population Prospects: The 2015 Revision*, Interactive Data, Population Density Table, http://esa.un.org.

130. Richard W. Mansbach, *The Global Puzzle: Issues and Actors in World Politics* (Boston: Houghton Mifflin, 1994), 515.

131. Dennis Pirages, "Demographic Change and Ecological Security," in Michael T. Klare and Daniel C. Thomas, *World Security: Challenges for a New Century* (New York: St. Martin's Press, 1994), 318–22; Robert Engelman, Brian Halweil, and Danielle Nierenberg, "Rethinking Population, Improving Lives" in Christopher Flavin et al., *State of the World 2002* (New York: W. W. Norton, 2002), 130–31.

132. UN-ESA, *World Urbanization Prospects, 2014 Revision*, "Highlights,"1, https://esa.un.org.

133. Pirages, "Demographic Change and Ecological Security," 319, 322.

134. Goldstein, *International Relations*, 410–12.

135. Ibid.

136. William K. Stevens, "Poor Lands' Success in Cutting Birth Rate Upsets Old Theories," *New York Times*, January 2, 1994, 1, 8.

137. Anastasia Toufexis, "Too Many Mouths," *Time*, January 2, 1989, 50. This issue of *Time* was devoted to the ecological crisis by recognizing the Earth as "Planet of the Year."

138. John F. Burns, "Bangladesh, Still Poor, Cuts Birth Rate Sharply," *New York Times*, September 10, 1994, A10. Amartya Sen, "Population: Delusion and Reality," *New York Review of Books*, September 22, 1994, 71, wonders if economic and social development will not be necessary for Bangladesh to lower its fertility rate to around 2 percent, which would begin to stabilize its population.

139. Bill Keller, "Zimbabwe Taking a Lead in Promoting Birth Control," *New York Times*, September 4, 1994, 16.

140. Sen, "Population: Delusion and Reality," 63–64; Charles F. Westoff, "Finally, Control Population," and Ellen Chesler, "Stop Coercing Women," *New York Times Magazine*, February 6, 1994, 30–33.

141. John Bongaarts et al., *Family Planning Programs for the 21st Century: Rationale and Design* (New York: Population Council, 2012).

142. See Charles E. Curran, "Population Control: Methods and Morality," in his *Issues in Sexual and Medical Ethics* (Notre Dame, IN: University of Notre Dame Press, 1978), 168–197; Charles E. Curran, ed., *Contraception: Authority and Dissent* (New York: Herder & Herder, 1969); and "*Humanae Vitae* at Fifty: An Unhealed Wound," a special issue of *Commonweal*, June 15, 2018, 9–24. In general, the Christian churches in the Protestant or Reformed traditions do not oppose contraception or birth control, although most do oppose abortion.

143. Neil MacFarquhar, "With Iran Population Boom, Vasectomy Receives Blessing," *New York Times*, September 8, 1996, 1, 14. See Burns, "Bangladesh, Still Poor, Cuts Birth Rate Sharply," A10; and Engelman et al., "Rethinking Population," 141–42.

144. Toufexis, "Too Many Mouths," 50. See Goldstein, *International Relations*, 409, 413.

145. Engelman et al., "Rethinking Population," 137–47.

146. Jeffrey Kluger and Andrea Dorfman, "The Challenges We Face," *Time* 160, August 26, 2002, A7.

147. Goldstein and Pevehouse, *International Relations*, 389; William C. Clark, "Managing Planet Earth," *Scientific American* 261, September 1989, 47.

148. Coral Davenport, "Economies Can Still Rise as Carbon Emissions Fade," *New York Times*, April 7, 2016, A3; Sophie Yeo and Simon Evans, "The 35 Countries Cutting the Link Between Growth and Emissions," A Policy Document from Carbon Brief, April 5, 2016, www.carbonbrief.org.

149. Kinsella, Russett, and Starr, *World Politics*, 423–27. This section depends on Kinsella, Russett, and Starr. In the 5th ed. of *World Politics: The Menu for Choice* (New York: W. H. Freeman, 1996), 460, Russett and Starr illustrate this point with statistics on life expectancy rather than infant mortality.

150. Nash, *Loving Nature*, 200-202.

151. Pope Francis, *Laudato Si'*, ##175, 196. On sustainable development, see ##159–62, 194. See also J. Milburn Thompson, "The Message of the Encyclical on the Environment: Metanoia," *Today's American Catholic*, August/September 2015, 16.

152. Bill McKibben, "Buzzless Buzzword," *New York Times*, April 10, 1996, op-ed page. McKibben argues that "sustainability" requires inner development rather than outer growth, and requires restraint, self-discipline, and other-directedness.

153. The Basel Convention website (www.basel.int); Annie Leonard, *The Story of Stuff: The Impact of Overconsumption on the Planet, Our Communities, and Our Health—And How We Can Make It Better* (New York: Free Press, 2010), 227.

154. US Environmental Protection Agency website, www.epa.gov/laws-regulations/toxic-substance-control-act, and www.epa.gov/superfund.

155. Nicholas Kristof, "Are You a Toxic Waste Disposal Site?" *New York Times*, February 14, 2016, op-ed page; Nathaniel Rich, "The Lawyer Who Became Dupont's Worst Nightmare," *New York Times Magazine*, January 10, 2016, 36–45, 57–61.

156. Leonard, *Story of Stuff*, 207–217; John Langone, "A Stinking Mess," *Time*, January 2, 1989, 45.

157. Center for Sustainable Systems at the University of Michigan, Factsheets, "Municipal Solid Waste" (css.snre.umich.edu).

158. Dolly Shin for the Earth Engineering Center (EEC) at Columbia University, *Generation and Disposition of Municipal Solid Waste (MSW) in the United States: A National Survey*, executive summary, January 3, 2014, www.seas.columbia.edu; Edward Hume, *Garbology: Our Dirty Love Affair with Trash* (New York: Avery, 2012), 4–5, 308–11.

159. Leonard, *Story of Stuff*, 190–99, 233–36, 161–63, 245–46.

160. Center for Sustainable Systems at the University of Michigan, Factsheets, "Municipal Solid Waste," css.umich.edu/factsheets; John Tierney, "Recycling Is Garbage," *New York Times Magazine*, June 10, 1996, 28, 48, 51; Langone, "A Stinking Mess," 45.

161. Shin (EEC), *Generation and Disposition of Municipal Solid Waste*, executive summary.

162. John Tierney, "The Reign of Recycling," *New York Times*, October 4, 2015, SR1, 4.

163. Melissa Eddy, "Germans Are World Champions of Recycling," *New York Times*, November 29, 2016, A7.

164. Center for Sustainable Systems at the University of Michigan, Factsheets, "Municipal Solid Waste"; Leonard, *Story of Stuff*, which is skeptical about the environmental value of WTE (215), and opposed to incinerators and burning trash in general (212–17).

165. Tierney, "Recycling Is Garbage," 28, 51; Leonard, *Story of Stuff*, 207–9.

166. Center for Sustainable Systems at the University of Michigan, Factsheets, "Municipal Solid Waste"; Leonard, *Story of Stuff*, 207–9.

167. Ivan Amato, "Can We Make Garbage Disappear?" *Time*, November 8, 1999, 116; and Eric Roston, "New War on Waste," *Time*, August 26, 2002, 28–31.

168. This section is based on the Edwards Peacemaking Lecture that I presented at the Louisville Presbyterian Theological Seminary on October 21, 2010. The presentation was revised and published as "Linking Peace and the Environment in Catholic Social Teaching," *Journal for Peace and Justice Studies* 22 (Spring 2012), 3–18, at 8–18. This is a modified version of that publication.

169. Pope John Paul II, World Day of Peace Message, "The Ecological Crisis: A Common Responsibility" (or "Peace with God the Creator, Peace with All of Creation") (1990), #12. See Robert Jarrett, "The Environment: Collateral Victim and Tool of War," *Bioscience* 53 (September 2003): 880–82, which reviews two books on this topic, J. E. Austin and C. E. Burch, eds., *The Environmental Consequences of War: Legal, Economic, and Scientific Perspectives* (Cambridge: Cambridge University Press, 2000); and T. H. Hastings, *Ecology of War and Peace: Counting Costs of Conflict* (Lanham, MD: University Press of America, 2000). Jarrett notes that both books identify "the same basic list of principal environmental harms derived from war" (882).

170. Thomas Stock and Karlheinz Lohs, eds., *The Challenge of Old Chemical Munitions and Toxic Armament Wastes*, SIPRI Chemical and Biological Warfare Studies #16 (New York: Oxford University Press, 1997).

171. John Cairns Jr., "War and Sustainability," *International Journal of Sustainable Development and World Ecology* 10 (September 2003): 188; and Laurie Johnston, "Just War and Environmental Destruction," in *Can War Be Just in the 21st Century?* ed. Tobias Winright and Laurie Johnston (Maryknoll, NY: Orbis Books, 2015), 98–99.

172. Mark J. Allman and Tobias Winright, *After the Smoke Clears: The Just War Tradition and Postwar Justice* (Maryknoll, NY: Orbis Books, 2010), 165–72.

173. Gary E. Machlis and Thor Hanson, "Warfare Ecology," *Bioscience* 58 (September 2008): 729–36, at 729, 731.

174. George E. Clark, "War and Sustainability: The Economic and Environmental Costs," *Environment* 50 (Jan./Feb., 2008): 3–4; Karl Mathiesen, "What's the Environmental Impact of Modern War?" *The Guardian*, November 6, 2014. November 6 is the United Nation's International Day for Preventing the Exploitation of the Environment in War.

175. Allegra Stratton, "[British Defense Secretary] Fox Reveals £260 m [$416 m] Cost of Libya Campaign," *The Guardian*, June 24, 2011, 4.

176. Michael J. Mills, Owen B. Toon, Richard P. Turco et al., "Massive Global Ozone Loss Predicted Following Regional Nuclear Conflict," *Proceedings of the National Academy of Sciences of the United States of America* 105 (April 8, 2008): 5307–12.

177. Pope Benedict XVI, World Day of Peace Message, "If You Want to Cultivate Peace, Protect Creation" (2010), #11.

178. John Schwartz, "A New Tool to Analyze War's Effect on the Planet," *New York Times*, August 22, 2015 A4; and Rachel Nuwer, "War's Other Victims: Animals" *New York Times*, January 16, 2018, D5.

179. Michael T. Klare. *Resource Wars: The New Landscape of Global Conflict* (New York: Metropolitan Books, Henry Holt, 2001); Chester A. Crocker, Fen Osler Hampson, and Pamela Aall, "The Center Cannot Hold: Conflict Management in an Era of Diffusion," in Crocker, Hampson, and Aall, eds., *Managing Conflict in a World Adrift* (Washington, DC: United States Institute of Peace Press, 2015), 9–10.

180. Pope Francis, *Laudato Si'*, ## 31, 48, 57; Pope Benedict XVI, "If You Want to Cultivate Peace," ##9, 10.

181. Klare, *Resource Wars*, 1–25, at 25.

182. Thomas F. Homer-Dixon, "Environmental Scarcity, Mass Violence, and the Limits to Ingenuity," *Current History* 95 (November 1996): 359–65, at 362.

183. Thomas F. Homer-Dixon, "Environmental Scarcity and Intergroup Conflict," in Michael T. Klare and Daniel C. Thomas, eds., *World Security: Challenges for a New Century*, 2nd ed. (New York: St. Martin's Press, 1994), 351–52; and Thom Shanker, "Why We Might Fight, 2011 Edition," *New York Times*, December 12, 2010, WK3, which discusses the five nation competition over the Arctic and its resources.

184. Nils Petter Gleditsch, "Climate Change, Environmental Stress, and Conflict," in Crocker, Hampson, and Aall, eds., *Managing Conflict in a World Adrift*, 147–68, at 151, 160.

185. Somini Sengupta, "Warming, Water Crisis, Then Unrest: How Iran Fits a Pattern," *New York Times*, January 19, 2018, A4.

186. Homer-Dixon, "Environmental Scarcity, Mass Violence," 359; and Thomas F. Homer-Dixon, *Environment, Scarcity, and Violence* (Princeton, NJ: Princeton University Press, 2001). Homer-Dixon's research on environmental scarcity and violent conflict during the 1990s is significant, but also ambiguous, controversial, and disputed. See, for example, Nils Peter Gleditsch and Henrik Udal, "Ecoviolence? Links between Population Growth, Environmental Scarcity, and Violent Conflict in Thomas Homer-Dixon's Work," *Journal of International Affairs* 56 (Fall 2002), 282–302; Idean Salehyan, "From Climate Change to Conflict? No Consensus Yet," *Journal of Peace Research* 45 (May 2008): 315–26; and Magnus Theisen, "Blood and Soil? Resource Security and International Armed Conflict Revisited," *Journal of Peace Research* 45 (November 2008): 801–18.

187. Homer-Dixon, "Environmental Scarcity, Mass Violence," 360–61.

188. Ibid., 361.

189. Gleditsch, "Climate Change," 161.

190. Pope Francis, *Laudato Si'*, # 25; Pope Benedict XVI, "If You Want to Cultivate Peace," #4. See the *New York Times* series "Carbon's Casualties," 2016.

191. Thomas F. Homer-Dixon, Jeffrey H. Boutwell, and George W. Rathjens, "Environmental Change and Violent Conflict," *Scientific American* 268, February 1993, 38.

192. Michael Renner, "Breaking the Link Between Resources and Repression," in Christopher Flavin et al., eds., *State of the World 2002: A Worldwatch Institute Report on Progress Toward a Sustainable Society* (New York: W. W. Norton, 2002), 149–73, esp. 150; and Michael Renner, *The Anatomy of Resource Wars* (Worldwatch Paper 162, October 2002).

193. Coral Davenport, "Climate Change Deemed Growing Threat by Military Researchers," *New York Times*, May 14, 2014, A18; Coral Davenport, "Pentagon Signals Security Risks of Climate Change," *New York Times*, October 14, 2014, A14. There is now a non-partisan Washington think tank, The Center for Climate and Security, climateandsecurity.org.

Chapter Five

1. Malcolm Linton, "War Wounds," *Time* 154, September 13, 1999, 36–39.

2. Jack Donnelly, *International Human Rights*, 4th ed. (Boulder, CO: Westview Press, 2013), 6.

3. Because of concerns about sovereignty, the United States has only ratified the Covenant on Civil and Political Rights in 1992. Although the United States generally abides by the provisions of these covenants, it refuses to subject itself to outside scrutiny. See Donnelly, *International Human Rights*, 8, 133–35.

4. See Stephen P. Marks, "Promoting Human Rights," in Michael T. Klare and Daniel C. Thomas, eds., *World Security: Trends and Challenges at Century's End* (New York: St. Martin's Press, 1991), 297–99, for a comparable list.

5. Donnelly, *International Human Rights*, 14.

6. Ibid., 14–16.

7. Ibid., 77–83.

8. Oliver Burkman and Richard Norton-Taylor, "Newborn World Court Fights for Survival," *The Guardian*, July 1, 2002, 15.

9. Jack Donnelly, "International Human Rights after the Cold War," in Michael T. Klare and Daniel C. Thomas, eds., *World Security: Challenges for a New Century*, 2nd ed. (New York: St. Martin's Press, 1994), 237.

10. Barbara Crossette, "U.N. Reports Latin America Suffers Fewer 'Disappeared,'" *New York Times*, May 25, 1997, 4. See "Freedom in the World" at www.freedomhouse. org.

11. Larry Diamond, "Facing Up to the Democratic Recession," *Journal of Democracy* 26 (January 2015): 148. See the section on "The Ebb and Tide of Democracy" in chap. 2 above.

12. Donnelly, *International Human Rights* (Boulder, CO: Westview Press, 1993), 150.

13. Donnelly, "International Human Rights after the Cold War," 241.

14. Donnelly, *International Human Rights* (1993), 101. Donnelly calls this an attitude of "American exceptionalism." See ibid., 4th ed. (2013), 114–15.

15. "A Record of Torture and Lies," *New York Times*, December 10, 2014, editorial. See also Mark Mazzetti, "Senate Panel Faults CIA over Brutality and Deceit in Terrorism Interrogations," *New York Times*, A1, A12.

16. See Stephen Grey, *Ghost Plane: The True Story of the CIA Torture Program* (New York: St. Martin's Press, 2006); and Jane Mayer, "Outsourcing Torture," *New Yorker* 81, February 14, 2005, 106–23, for exposés of this aspect of the Bush administration's torture program.

17. George Hunsinger, "Torture Is the Ticking Time Bomb: Why the Necessity Defense Fails," *Journal for Justice and Peace Studies* 17, no. 2 (Fall 2008): 2–21, at 12–13.

18. John Perry, *Torture: Religious Ethics and National Security* (Maryknoll, NY: Orbis Books, 2005), 14. Perry examines the experience of the tortured (chap. 5) and torturers (chap. 4).

19. The sections on the ethics and the legality of torture are based on J. Milburn Thompson, "Catholic Social Teaching and the Ethics of Torture," *Journal for Justice and Peace Studies* 17, no. 2 (Fall 2008): 22–42, especially 23–26.

20. Perry, *Torture*, 36.

21. David P. Gushee, "Against Torture: An Evangelical Perspective," *Theology Today* 63 (2006): 349–64, at 359.

22. Gushee, "Against Torture," 357. Fleming Rutledge, "My Enemy, Myself," *Theology Today* 63 (2006): 382, where she talks of torture as bullying, taking advantage of a relative superiority of strength.

23. Gushee, "Against Torture," 358–59; Elizabeth Johnson, "You Did It to Me," *America* 196, February 26, 2007, 14–17.

24. Perry, *Torture*, chap. 4, explores the moral guilt of the torturer.

25. The Advisory Committee on Social Witness Policy (ACSWP) of the Presbyterian Church, USA, *Resolution on Human Rights in a Time of Terrorism and Torture*, approved by the 217th General Assembly, 2006, 11; Johnson, "You Did It to Me," 14–17.

26. Patrick McCormick, "The Scourge of Abu Ghraib," *U.S. Catholic* 69, August 2004, 46–49, at 49.

27. See Appendix C, 1241, of *The Torture Papers: The Road to Abu Ghraib*, ed.

Karen L. Greenberg and Joshua L. Dratel (New York: Cambridge University Press, 2005), for a list of "Torture Related Laws and Conventions," and internet addresses where they are available.

28. Thompson, "Catholic Social Teaching and the Ethics of Torture," 26.

29. Andrew C. McCarthy, "Torture: Thinking about the Unthinkable," *Commentary* 118, July/August 2004, 27.

30. Hunsinger, "Torture Is the Ticking Time Bomb," 13–14.

31. "Prosecute Torturers and Their Bosses," *New York Times*, December 22, 2014, editorial.

32. See Vatican II, *Gaudium et Spes: Pastoral Constitution on the Church in the Modern World*, in O'Brien and Shannon, *Catholic Social Thought*, #27; US Conference of Catholic Bishops, *Forming Consciences for Faithful Citizenship* (November 14, 2007), ##23, 64, 88 (www.usccb.org). See also Pontifical Council for Justice and Peace, *Compendium of the Social Doctrine of the Church* (Washington, DC: United States Conference of Catholic Bishops, 2004), #404.

33. Thompson, "Catholic Social Teaching and the Ethics of Torture," 33.

34. Some of the Catholic bishops in Chile eventually issued orders of excommunication for torturers and those who ordered torture during the period of military rule (1973–1990). See William T. Cavanaugh, *Torture and Eucharist: Theology, Politics, and the Body of Christ* (Oxford, UK: Blackwell Publishers, 1998), 252–64.

35. See Glenn Greenwald, *No Place to Hide: Edward Snowden, the NSA, and the U.S. Surveillance State* (New York: Metropolitan Books, 2014).

36. Donnelly, *International Human Rights* (1993), 238.

37. David Hollenbach, "Global Human Rights: An Interpretation of the Contemporary Catholic Understanding," in David Hollenbach, *Justice, Peace, and Human Rights: American Catholic Social Ethics in a Pluralistic World* (New York: Crossroad, 1988), 91.

38. Michael J. Himes and Kenneth R. Himes, *Fullness of Faith: The Public Significance of Theology* (New York: Paulist Press, 1993), 64. See Donnelly, *International Human Rights* (2013), 24–25, 27.

39. Donnelly, *International Human Rights* (1993), 19–28. Ibid., 4th ed. (2013), chap. 2, esp. 19–22. Natural Law and Kantian philosophies would logically provide stronger bases for human rights than utilitarian or Marxist philosophies.

40. NCCB, *Economic Justice for All*, in O'Brien and Shannon, eds., *Catholic Social Thought*, #25, and passim.

41. See Meghan J. Clark, *The Vision of Catholic Social Thought: The Virtue of Solidarity and the Praxis of Human Rights* (Minneapolis: Fortress Press, 2014), 2–3, chap. 2, passim. Clark emphasizes the link between solidarity and human rights, rooted in the relational nature of human beings created in the image and likeness of the Trinity, which gives the Catholic theory of human rights a personalistic and a communitarian flavor.

42. Himes and Himes, *Fullness of Faith*, chap. 3, "The Trinity and Human Rights," 55–73.

43. Richard W. Mansbach, *The Global Puzzle: Issues and Actors in World Politics* (Boston: Houghton Mifflin, 1994), 539.

44. David Hollenbach, *Claims in Conflict: Retrieving and Renewing the Catholic Human Rights Tradition* (New York: Paulist Press, 1979), 203. Hollenbach presents a detailed schema for interpreting human rights at 89–100, passim.

45. Ibid., 204.

46. Donnelly, *International Human Rights* (1993), 37–38. Ibid., 4th ed. (2013), chap. 3, especially 44–45. Donnelly is a major source for this section.

47. The whole idea of human rights is inimical to a strong conception of cultural relativism. This is, however, a much debated philosophical issue. It should be noted that Catholic theology has little difficulty with the idea of universal moral norms and principles, but there is much discussion of their interpretation and implementation.

48. Donnelly, *International Human Rights* (1993), 38.

49. Nicholas D. Kristof and Sheryl WuDunn, *Half the Sky: Turning Oppression into Opportunity for Women Worldwide* (New York: Vintage Books, 2009), xvii. See also the PBS documentary of the same title, based on the book.

50. "Gender Wage Gap" (2017) https://data.oecd.org; *OECD Factbook 2013: Economic, Environmental and Social Statistics*, Special Chapter on Gender Equality, under "Jobs and Wages," OECD iLibrary.

51. Owen R. Jackson, *Dignity and Solidarity: An Introduction to Peace and Justice Education* (Chicago: Loyola University Press, 1985, 1990), 178. NCCB, *Economic Justice for All*, ##178–80.

52. See Ellen Barry, "Battling Tradition with Defiance: Indian Women Seeking to Work Confront Taboos and Threats," *New York Times*, January 31, 2016, A1, A10–12, about the struggle of a group of Indian women to work outside of the home.

53. *Global Gender Gap Report 2016*, published by the World Economic Forum (www.weforum.org), 7. This report also ranks countries overall and in each of the four areas. The United States ranked 45th overall, 73rd in political empowerment, 1st in education, 62nd in health, and 26th in economic participation and opportunity.

54. *Human Development Report 2014*, 175, hdr.undp.org; Katrin Bennhold and Rick Gladstone, "Over 70 Nations Have Been Led by Women, So Why Not the U.S.?" *New York Times*, November 11, 2016, A11; Ernesto Londono, "President Bachelet of Chile Is the Last Woman Standing in the Americas," *New York Times*, July 24, 2017, A1, 6.

55. Alexandra Zavis, "Women's History Month . . . A Reality Check," *Courier-Journal*, March 22, 2015, H1.

56. Kristoff and WuDunn, *Half the Sky*, 67–68.

57. Nicholas Kristof, "Save My Wife," *New York Times*, September 17, 2006, op-ed page; and Nicholas Kristof, "Prudence's Struggle Ends," *New York Times*, September 24, 2006, op-ed page. See also Kristof and WuDunn, *Half the Sky*, 109–13.

58. World Health Organization (WHO), Maternal Mortality Fact Sheet, February 16, 2018. Surprisingly, the United States is an outlier regarding progress in maternal mortality. See, for example, "America's Shocking Maternal Deaths," *New York Times*, September 4, 2016, editorial.

59. Tabassum Firoz et al. for the Maternal Morbidity Working Group, "Measuring Maternal Health: Focus on Maternal Morbidity," *Bulletin of the World Health Organization* 91 (published online: August 6, 2013), 794–96.

60. Kristof and WuDunn, *Half the Sky*, chap. 6, 93–102.

61. Nicholas Kristof, "They Call This Pro-Life?" *New York Times*, April 23, 2017, op-ed page; Gardiner Harris and Somini Sengupta, "Trump Rule on Abortion Will Affect Much More," *New York Times*, May 16, 2017, A15.

62. Kristof and WuDunn, *Half the Sky*, chaps. 1 and 2.

63. Ibid., 82–83; Nicholas Kristof, "Her Father Shot Her in the Head," *New York Times*, January 31, 2016, op-ed page, the story of a Pakistani woman who is the subject of a short documentary titled "A Girl in the River: The Price of Forgiveness," directed by Sharmeen Obaid-Chinoy, which won an Academy Award in 2016.

64. Kristof and WuDunn, *Half the Sky*, 61–67; Mujib Mashal and Zahra Nader, "In Lawless Afghan Province, 'NoValue' and No Justice for Women," *New York Times*, July 9, 2017, A6.

65. Kristof and WuDunn, *Half the Sky*, 70–79.

66. Somini Sengupta, "One by One, Marry-Your-Rapist Laws Are Falling in the Middle East," *New York Times*, July 23, 2017, A1, 9; Nicholas Kristof, "An American 13-Year-Old, Pregnant and Married to Her Rapist," *New York Times*, June 3, 2018, SR3.

67. United Nations Office of the High Commissioner for Human Rights, "Rape: Weapon of War." Kristoff and WuDunn, *Half the Sky*, 84–87, 216–19.

68. Rukmini Callimachi, "Enslaving Young Girls, The Islamic State Builds a Vast System of Rape," *New York Times*, August 13, 2015, A1, A12–13; and Rukmini Callimachi et al., "2018 Nobel Peace Prize Awarded to Congolese Doctor [Denis Mukwege] and Yazidi Activist [Nadia Murad]," *New York Times*, October 5, 2018.

69. Jodi Kantor and Megan Twohey, "Harvey Weinstein Paid Off Sexual Harassment Accusers for Decades," *New York Times*, October 6, 2017, A1.

70. Carole J. Sheffield, "Sexual Terrorism," in Jo Freeman, ed., *Woman: A Feminist Perspective* (Mountain View, CA: Mayfield, 1989), 3–19; Charlotte Bunch and Roxanna Carrillo, "Global Violence against Women: The Challenge to Human Rights and Development," in Michael T. Klare and Daniel C. Thomas, *World Security: Challenges for a New Century* (New York: St. Martin's Press, 1994), 261.

71. United Nations Children's Fund (UNICEF), *Female Genital Mutilation/ Cutting: A Global Concern* (New York: UNICEF Pamphlet, 2015); Pam Belluck and Joe Cochrane, "Female Genital Cutting: Not Just 'An African Problem,'" *New York Times*, February 5, 2016, A6. See also World Health Organization, Female Genital Mutilation Fact Sheet, January 31, 2018. The United Nations Population Fund (UNFPA) and UNICEF sponsor a joint program on eliminating female genital mutilation/cutting.

72. Kristoff and WuDunn, *Half the Sky*, 221–29. For an argument that this cultural practice should be tolerated, see Richard A. Shweder, "What about 'Female Genital Mutilation'? and Why Understanding Culture Matters in the First Place," *Daedalus* 129 (Fall 2000): 209–32.

73. Celia W. Dugger, "African Ritual Pain: Genital Cutting," *New York Times*, October 5, 1996, 1, 6, 7, at 6; Kristof and WuDunn, *Half the Sky*, 123.

74. Neil MacFaquar, "Mutilation of Egyptian Girls, Despite Ban, It Goes On," *New York Times*, August 8, 1996, A3.

75. Jina Moore, "She Ran from the Cut, and Helped Thousands of Other Girls

Escape, Too," *New York Times*, January 14, 2018, A9. See also the story of Fauziya Kassindja as told by Celia W. Dugger, "A Refugee's Body Is Intact but Her Family Is Torn," *New York Times*, September 11, 1996, A1, B6–7. Fauziya Kassindja, with her attorney Layli Miller Bashir (now Layli Miller-Muro), published her story in a book titled *Do They Hear You When You Cry?* (New York: Delacorte Press, 1998).

76. World Health Organization, Female Genital Mutilation Fact Sheet, January 31, 2018; Celia W. Dugger, "New Law Bans Genital Cutting in United States," *New York Times*, October 12, 1996, A1, 28.

77. A similar program was begun in Senegal by Molly Melching, an educator from Danville, Illinois, in 1991 called Tostan, which means "breakthrough" in the local language. See Kristof and WuDunn, *Half the Sky*, 124–29; and Celia W. Dugger, "Senegal Curbs a Bloody Rite, African-Style," *New York Times*, October 16, 2011, 1, 12.

78. The University of Saint Joseph (West Hartford, CT), the women's college where I taught from 1982–2001, was founded in 1932 by the Sisters of Mercy because there was no opportunity for women to acquire a college education in the area at that time. It became co-ed in 2018.

79. UN Report on Millennium Development Goal #2, To achieve universal primary education by 2015.

80. UN Department of Economic and Social Affairs, *The World's Women 2010: Trends and Statistics*, chap. 3, Education, Key Findings, https://unstats.un.org.

81. *Human Development Report 1996*, 32–34. These same points are confirmed in *Human Development Report 2001*, 15–16.

82. For example, women often suffer from harsh discrimination in Islamic societies, but many scholars of Islam argue that the Qu'ran can be interpreted to support the equality of women. See Elaine Sciolino, "The Many Faces of Islamic Law," *New York Times*, October 13, 1996, E4; and Riffat Hassan, "Women in Islam and Christianity: A Comparison," *Concilium* (1994, no. 3): 18–22; Kristof and WuDunn, *Half the Sky*, chap. 9, "Is Islam Misogynistic?" The Catholic Church affirms the equality of women and men and condemns discrimination against women. See, for example, Pope John XXIII, *Pacem in Terris*, #41; and the National Conference of Catholic Bishops, "To Live in Christ Jesus: A Pastoral Reflection on the Moral Life," (Washington, DC: United States Catholic Conference, 1976), 24–25. The Vatican, however, consciously uses exclusive language in most of its official documents, and the Catholic Church (along with the Orthodox churches, and some Protestant denominations) does not ordain women. This practice results in most of the power and leadership in the hands of men.

83. Bunch and Carrillo, "Global Violence against Women," 256. See Kristof and WuDunn, *Half the Sky*, chap. 14, "What You Can Do"; and Valerie M. Hudson and Dara Kay Cohen, "Women Are a National Security Issue," *New York Times*, December 26, 2016, op-ed page.

84. Alex Mikulich, "Where Y'at Race, Whiteness, and Economic Justice? A Map of White Complicity in the Economic Oppression of People of Color," in *The Almighty and the Dollar: Reflections on "Economic Justice for All,"* ed. Mark J. Allman (Winona, MN: Anselm Academic, 2012), 198–201. See also Michelle Alexander, *The New Jim Crow: Mass Incarceration in the Age of Colorblindness* (New York: New Press, 2012), 23.

85. Corson-Finnerty, *World Citizen*, 67.

86. Dee Brown, *Bury My Heart at Wounded Knee: An Indian History of the American West* (New York: Bantam Books, 1970).

87. Ibid., 86–89. Films that dramatize this tragic history include *Little Big Man*, directed by Arthur Penn and starring Dustin Hoffman (1970), and *Dances with Wolves*, directed by and starring Kevin Costner (1990).

88. Jackson, *Dignity and Solidarity*, 188–89. For insight into the reality of slavery in the southern United States, see Alex Haley, *Roots* (Garden City, NY: Doubleday, 1976), and the made-for-TV movie (1977) based on this book; and Solomon Northup, *12 Years a Slave* (New York: Atria Books/37 Ink, 2013 [orig., 1853]) and the film of the same title, directed by Steve McQueen (2014).

89. Edward Ball, "Slavery's Enduring Resonance," *New York Times*, March 15, 2015, SR5.

90. Alexander, *The New Jim Crow*, 28–30; Gregory P. Downs, "The Dangerous Myth of Appomattox," *New York Times*, April 12, 2015, SR12.

91. Alexander, *The New Jim Crow*, 30–35, at 35.

92. Campbell Robertson, "History of Lynchings in the South Documents Nearly 4000 Names," *New York Times*, February 10, 2015, A11; "Lynching as Racial Terrorism," *New York Times*, February 11, 2015, editorial page; and "The Horror of Lynchings Lives On," *New York Times*, December 4, 2016, editorial page.

93. Ira Katznelson, "Who Really Got Handouts," *New York Times*, August 13, 2017, SR2. See John Howard Griffin, *Black Like Me* (New York: New American Library, 1960, 1961) for a moving account of the daily life of blacks in the segregated South.

94. See Taylor Branch, *Parting the Waters: America in the King Years 1954–63* (New York: Simon & Schuster, 1988), for a thorough account of the early civil rights movement, or David J. Garrow, *Bearing the Cross: Martin Luther King, Jr. and the Southern Christian Leadership Conference* (New York: William Morrow, 1986). Two recent films dramatize the period of the civil rights movement: *Lee Daniels's The Butler*, directed by Lee Daniels (2014); and *Selma*, directed by Ava DuVernay (2015).

95. "Voting Rights by the Numbers," *New York Times*, April 19, 2015, editorial page; and "A Movement to End Racist Voting Laws," *New York Times*, October 5, 2016, editorial page.

96. Bryan M. Massingale, *Racial Justice and the Catholic Church* (Maryknoll, NY: Orbis Books, 2010), 4–9.

97. This paragraph is based on Massingale, *Racial Justice and the Catholic Church*, chap. 1, "What Is Racism," 1–42.

98. Alexander, *The New Jim Crow*, 2. This section is based upon Alexander.

99. It is not only a prior conviction that is eroding the right to vote for African Americans but state laws developed in the wake of the 2013 *Shelby County v. Holder* Supreme Court decision that invalidated a key provision of the 1965 Voting Rights Act. See Jim Rutenberg, "A Dream Undone: Inside the 50-Year Campaign to Roll Back the Voting Rights Act," *New York Times Magazine*, August 2, 2015, cover story; and William Barber II, "The Retreat from Voting Rights," *New York Times*, April 28, 2016, op-ed page.

100. John Eligon and Mitch Smith, "After Protests for Racial Justice, Activists Ask: What Next?" *New York Times*, August 16, 2015, A14.

101. Ball, "Slavery's Enduring Resonance," SR5; Leonard Pitts, "Walter Scott, Is He Just Another 'Isolated Incident'?" *Courier-Journal*, April 13, 2015, op-ed page.

102. Katie Rogers, "FBI Investigating Police Accounts of Black Woman's Death in Custody," *New York Times*, July 16, 2015; Charles M. Blow, "Questions about the Sandra Bland Case," *New York Times*, July 22, 2015, op-ed page. Kimberle Williams Crenshaw and Andrea Ritchie, *Say Her Name: Resisting Police Brutality against Black Women* (African American Policy Forum and Center for Intersectionality and Social Policy Studies, 2015) document more than seventy unarmed black women killed by police since 2012, and tell their lesser known stories (www.aapf.org).

103. Julie Bosman, Mitch Smith, and Michael Wines, "Videos of Police Shootings Give Few Easy Answers," *New York Times*, June 26, 2017, A10; Jess Bidgood, "No Third Trial for Ex-Officer Who Killed Driver, Cincinnati Prosecutor Says," *New York Times*, July 19, 2017, A20.

104. Ibram X. Kendi, "Black Deaths, American Lies," *New York Times*, June 25, 2017, op-ed page; Michael Eric Dyson, "Racial Violence on the Screen," *New York Times*, August 6, 2017, op-ed page.

105. See Justin Wolfers, Kevin Quealy, and David Leonhardt, "1.5 Million Black Men, Missing from Daily Life" *New York Times*, April 21, 2015, A1, A3.

106. There are several films that dramatize apartheid in South Africa: *A Dry White Season* (1989), directed by Euzhan Palcy; *A World Apart* (1988), directed by Chris Menges; *Mandela* (1987), directed by Philip Saville; *Invictus* (2010), directed by Clint Eastwood and starring Morgan Freeman and Matt Damon; and *Mandela: Long Walk to Freedom* (2014), directed by Justin Chadwick and based on Nelson Mandela's autobiography, *Long Walk to Freedom* (Boston: Little, Brown, 1994).

107. Corson-Finnerty, *World Citizen*, 66–67.

108. Sathianathan Clarke, Deenabandhu Manchala, and Philip Vinod Peacock, eds., *Dalit Theology for the Twenty-First Century: Discordant Voices, Discerning Pathways* (Oxford: Oxford University Press, 2010).

109. See J. Milburn Thompson, *Catholic Social Thought* (Maryknoll, NY: Orbis Books, 2010), 41–46, for the story of American theologian John Courtney Murray, S.J., and the development of the *Declaration on Religious Freedom* at Vatican II.

110. Kim Hjelmgaard, "Violence Against Jews Surges: Anti-Semitic Attacks up 40 Percent in 2014," *USA Today*, April 16, 2015, 1B; David Brooks, "How to Fight Anti-Semitism," *New York Times*, March 24, 2015, op-ed page; "Anti-Semitism in the Soccer Stands," *New York Times*, April 19, 2015, editorial page.

111. Alissa J. Rubin and Aurelien Breeden, "France Announces Plan to Fight Racism," *New York Times*, April 18, 2015, A10.

112. The World Watch List gives an overview of Christian persecution worldwide.

Chapter Six

1. Steven Pinker, *The Better Angels of Our Nature: Why Violence Has Declined* (New York: Penguin Books, 2012), argues that violence is in fact declining.

2. See Mark Allman, *Who Would Jesus Kill? War, Peace, and the Christian Tradition* (Winona, MN: St. Mary's Press, 2008); and Lisa Sowle Cahill, *Love Your Enemies: Discipleship, Pacifism, and Just War Theory* (Minneapolis: Fortress Press, 1994).

3. See Glen H. Stassen, *Just Peacemaking: Transforming Initiatives for Justice and Peace* (Louisville, KY: Westminster/John Knox Press, 1992); and Glen Stassen, ed., *Just Peacemaking: The New Paradigm for the Ethics of War and Peace* (Cleveland: Pilgrim Press, 2008).

4. Tobias Winright and Laurie Johnston, eds., *Can War Be Just in the 21st Century? Ethicists Engage the Tradition* (Maryknoll, NY: Orbis Books, 2015).

5. This phrase is from Michael T. Klare, *Resource Wars: The New Landscape of Global Conflict* (New York: Metropolitan Books, Henry Holt, 2001).

6. Francis Fukuyama, "The End of History," *National Interest*, Summer 1989, 3–18.

7. Joshua S. Goldstein and Jon C. Pevehouse, *International Relations*, 10th ed., 2012–13 update (New York: Pearson, 2013), 160–68.

8. Ted Robert Gurr and Barbara Harff, *Ethnic Conflict in World Politics* (Boulder, CO: Westview Press, 1994), 5.

9. Ibid., 144; see also 18–26; Gidon Gottlieb, *Nation Against State: A New Approach to Ethnic Conflicts and the Decline of Sovereignty* (New York: Council on Foreign Relations, 1993), xii. Most often the nation lives in the territory it claims as its homeland, as with the Slovenes and Croats in the former Yugoslavia, or the Kurds in parts of Turkey, Iraq, Iran, and Syria. But the claim can also be primarily historical, as with the Jews toward Israel prior to 1948.

10. Walker Connor, "From Tribe to Nation?" *History of European Ideas* 13 (1991): 6. Walker Connor, "The Specter of Ethno-Nationalist Movements Today," *PAWSS Perspectives* 1 (April 1991): 2.

11. Connor, "From Tribe to Nation," 9. Myth is used here in the sense of a story that sets up a people, not the sense of a widely held false belief.

12. Walker Connor, "Beyond Reason: The Nature of the Ethnonational Bond," *Ethnic and Racial Studies* 16 (July 1993): 382.

13. Walker Connor, "When Is a Nation?" *Ethnic and Racial Studies* 13 (January 1990): 97–98.

14. Connor, "The Specter of Ethno-Nationalist Movements Today," 4.

15. Michael Ignatieff, *Blood and Belonging: Journeys into the New Nationalism* (New York: Farrar, Straus and Giroux, 1993), 37–38.

16. Bruce Russett and Harvey Starr, *World Politics* (New York: W. H. Freeman, 1996), 54.

17. Connor, "Beyond Reason," 374–75; Connor, "The Specter of Ethno-Nationalist Movements Today," 3; and Gottlieb, *Nation Against State*, 35.

18. Gurr and Harff, *Ethnic Conflict in World Politics*, 5.

19. Gottlieb, *Nation Against State*, 78, referring to the Genocide Convention of 1948.

20. Goldstein and Pevehouse, *International Relations*, 166–68.

21. Gurr and Harff, *Ethnic Conflict in World Politics*, 17.

22. Ted Robert Gurr, *Political Rebellion: Causes, Outcomes and Alternatives* (New York: Routledge, 2015), 133. This book is a collection of key essays on the major themes of Gurr's work and thought.

23. Gurr, *Political Rebellion*, 124–40.

24. Ted Robert Gurr, "Minorities and Nationalists: Managing Ethnopolitical

Conflict in the New Century," in *Turbulent Peace: The Challenges of Managing International Conflict*, ed. Chester A. Crocker et al. (Washington, DC: United States Institute of Peace, 2001), 164–66.

25. Sumantra Bose, "National Self-Determination Conflicts: Explaining Endurance and Intractability," in *Managing Conflict in a World Adrift*, ed. Chester A. Crocker et al. (Washington, DC: United States Institute of Peace, 2015), 169–83.

26. This section depends on Michael J. Himes and Kenneth R. Himes, *Fullness of Faith: The Public Significance of Theology* (Mahwah, NJ: Paulist Press, 1993), chap. 6, "Incarnation and Patriotism," 125–56, and chap. 7, "The Communion of Saints and an Ethic of Solidarity," 157–83.

27. Ibid., 130.

28. John Paul II, "On Social Concern" (*Sollicitudo Rei Socialis*, December 30, 1987), in *Catholic Social Thought: The Documentary Heritage*, ed. David J. O'Brien and Thomas A. Shannon (Maryknoll, NY: Orbis Books, 1992, 2010), #38.

29. Himes and Himes, *Fullness of Faith*, 146.

30. Jean Bethke Elshtain, "Identity, Sovereignty, and Self-Determination," in *Peacemaking: Moral and Policy Challenges for a New World*, ed. Gerard F. Powers et al. (Washington, DC: United States Catholic Conference, 1994), 101–4.

31. Gurr and Harff, *Ethnic Conflict in World Politics*, 139–44; Gottlieb, *Nation Against State*, 31.

32. Goldstein and Pevehouse, *International Relations*, 168–69; David Little, "Religious Nationalism and Human Rights," in *Peacemaking*, ed. Powers et al., 88–89.

33. David Little, *Sri Lanka: The Invention of Enmity* (Washington, DC: United States Institute of Peace Press, 1994), 103–7; Mark Juergensmeyer, "Religious Nationalism: A Global Threat?" *Current History* 95 (November 1996): 372–76.

34. Ted Robert Gurr, "Communal Conflicts and Global Security," *Current History* 94 (May 1995): 214; Douglas M. Johnston, "Religion and Conflict Resolution," *Fletcher Forum of World Affairs* 20 (Winter 1996): 53.

35. NCCB, "The Harvest of Justice Is Sown in Peace," in *Peacemaking*, ed. Powers et al., 329. Quote is from John Paul II, "To Build Peace, Respect Minorities," 1989 World Day of Peace Message, *Origins* 18, December 29, 1988, 469.

36. See Michael K. Duffey, *Sowing Justice, Reaping Peace: Case Studies of Racial, Religious, and Ethnic Healing Around the World* (Chicago: Sheed & Ward, 2001); and Mark Juergensmeyer, *Terror in the Mind of God: The Global Rise of Religious Violence* (Berkeley: University of California Press, 2000).

37. John W. Mulhall, *America and the Founding of Israel: An Investigation of the Morality of America's Role* (Los Angeles: Deshon Press, 1995), 60–72.

38. Ibid., 137–62.

39. Ibid., 163–66.

40. Michael K. Duffy, *Sowing Justice*, 118–23. The hope associated with the Oslo peace process effectively ended the first intifada.

41. Sara Roy, "Why Peace Failed: An Oslo Autopsy," *Current History* 101 (January 2002): 8–16.

42. Duffy, *Sowing Justice*, 127, 130–31; Thomas L. Friedman, "The New Math," *New York Times*, January 15, 2003, op-ed page. In the end about one thousand Israelis and three thousand Palestinians were killed in the second intifada.

43. Jeremy Pressman, "The Second *Intifada*: Background and Causes of the Israeli-Palestinian Conflict," *Journal of Conflict Studies* 23, no. 2 (Fall 2003): 114–41.

44. Steven Erlanger, "Hamas Routs Ruling Faction, Casting Pall on Peace Process," *New York Times*, January 27, 2006.

45. Mark Joseph Stern, "How Did Hamas Come to Power in Gaza?" *Slate*, November 19, 2012; Declan Walsh and David M. Halbfinger, "Unity Deal Offers Hope for Palestinians and Respite for Gaza," *New York Times*, October 13, 2017, A1, 6.

46. Jefferson Morley, "Israeli Withdrawal from Gaza Explained," *Washington Post*, August 10, 2005; and William Booth and Ruth Eglash, "A Decade Later, Many Israelis See Gaza Pullout as a Big Mistake," *Washington Post*, August 15, 2015.

47. Peter Beaumont, "Possible War Crimes in Gaza, Says UN," *The Guardian*, June 23, 2015, 14; "For the Sake of Those Who Suffered in Gaza's Vicious War, There Has to Be Accountability on Both Sides," *The Guardian*, June 23, 2015, editorial.

48. Jodi Rudoren and Isabel Kershner, "Arc of a Failed Deal: How Nine Months of Mideast Talks Ended in Disarray," *New York Times*, May 28, 2014.

49. Peter Baker and Julie Hirschfeld Davis, "U.S. Finalizes Deal to Give Israel $38 Billion in Military Aid," *New York Times*, September 14, 2016, A6.

50. Peter Baker, "A Defiant Israel Vows to Expand Its Settlements," *New York Times*, December 27, 2016, A1, 10; and Somini Sengupta and Rick Gladstone, "Rebuffing Israel, U.S. Allows U.N. Censure over Settlements," *New York Times*, December 24, 2016, A1, 7.

51. Secretary of State John Kerry, "Remarks on Middle East Peace," December 28, 2016, https://2009-2017.state.gov/secretary/remarks/2016/12/266119.htm.

52. Roger Cohen, "Why Israeli-Palestinian Peace Failed," *New York Times*, December 24, 2014, op-ed page.

53. Max Fisher, "The Two-State Solution: What It Is and Why It Hasn't Happened," *New York Times*, December 30, 2016, A8; "Is Israel Abandoning a Two-State Solution?" *New York Times*, December 30, 2016, editorial; "Stop the Settlements," *Commonweal*, January 27, 2017, 5, editorial.

54. David M. Halbfinger, "Israel Feels Pride but Senses Peril as U.S. Moves Embassy," *New York Times*, May 14, 2018, A1.

55. David M. Halbfinger and Isabel Kershner, "Israeli Law Declares the Country 'The Nation-State of the Jewish People,'" *New York Times*, July 20, 2018, A1, 8.

56. George A. Lopez, "The Sanctions Dilemma," *Commonweal*, September 11, 1998, 12.

57. Mark Thompson, "The Forgotten War," *Time*, September 23, 2002, 43–44.

58. Council on Foreign Relations, "The War in Afghanistan, 1999–2017, Timeline," https://www.cfr.org.

59. Information on the prelude to the Iraq War is based in part on Jonathon Stein and Tim Dickinson, "Lie by Lie: A Timeline of How We Got into Iraq," *Mother Jones*, September–October 2006, http://www.motherjones.com.

60. Daniel Benjamin, "Saddam Hussein and Al Qaeda Are Not Allies," *New York Times*, September 30, 2002, op-ed page.

61. "Trying to eliminate Saddam, extending the ground war into an occupation of Iraq, would have violated our guideline about not changing objectives in midstream, engaging in 'mission creep,' and would have incurred incalculable human and political

costs. Apprehending him was probably impossible. . . . Had we gone the invasion route, the U.S. could conceivably still be an occupying power in a bitterly hostile land." See George Bush and Brent Scowcroft, "Why We Didn't Remove Saddam," *Time*, March 2, 1998, and in Bush and Scowcroft, *A World Transformed* (New York: Alfred A. Knopf, 1998), 498. According to the Global Policy Forum, *Time* magazine removed the Bush-Scowcroft essay from its site.

62. Stein and Dickinson, "Lie by Lie." On the Bush administration's justification for the war in Iraq, see President George W. Bush's speech to the nation on March 17, 2003.

63. Council on Foreign Relations, "The Iraq War Timeline, 2003–2011," https://www.cfr.org.

64. Regarding the incorrect contention that Iraq had weapons of mass destruction, see the testimony of David Kay, the former chief US weapons inspector in Iraq, before the Senate on January 24, 2004. On the disconnect between Iraq and al-Qaeda, see *The 9/11 Commission Report* (New York: W. W. Norton, 2004). For a critical appraisal of the Bush administration's justification for the preemptive war in Iraq and of its bungled conduct of the early occupation, see Thomas E. Ricks, *Fiasco: The American Military Adventure in Iraq, 2003 to 2005* (New York: Penguin Press, 2006).

65. Seymour M. Hersh, "Torture at Abu Ghraib," *New Yorker* 80, May 10, 2004, 42–53.

66. Council on Foreign Relations, "The Iraq War Timeline, 2003–2011"; Joseph E. Stiglitz and Linda J. Blimes, "The True Cost of the Iraq War: $3 Trillion and Beyond," *Washington Post*, September 5, 2010; Nicholas Kristof, "Trump's Talk Worries Me, Like the Talk before the Iraq War," *New York Times*, March 22, 2018, op-ed page.

67. Scott Anderson, "Fractured Lands: How the Arab World Came Apart," *New York Times Magazine*, August 14, 2016, 1–58, at 13; Robert F. Worth, *A Rage for Order: The Middle East in Turmoil, from Tahir Square to Isis* (New York: Farrar, Straus and Giroux, 2016), 3–13, and 223–33; and Amnesty International, "The Arab Spring: Five Years On, Timeline," https://www.amnesty.org.

68. Worth, *A Rage for Order*, 127–69; Anderson, "Fractured Lands," 38–39. On the Arab Spring in Egypt, see the documentary film *The Square* (2013), by Jehane Noujain, which won three Emmy awards and was nominated for an Academy Award.

69. Worth, *A Rage for Order*, 36–60; Anderson, "Fractured Lands," 17–18, 26, 30–32. Jo Becker and Eric Schmitt, "As Trump Wavers on Libya, an ISIS Haven, Russia Presses On," *New York Times*, February 7, 2018, A1, 8–9.

70. This section on Yemen prior to and during the Arab Spring is based on Worth, *A Rage for Order*, 96–124.

71. Nick Cumming-Bruce, "[U.N.] War Crimes Report on Yemen Accuses Saudi Arabia and U.A.E.," *New York Times*, August 29, 2018, A6; "Why Are U.S. Bombs Killing Civilians in Yemen?" *New York Times*, August 29, 2018, editorial.

72. This account is based on "Yemen Crisis: Who Is Fighting Whom?" BBC News, January 30, 2018, http://www.bbc.com/.

73. Worth, *A Rage for Order*, 61–95, at 67–69; "Syria's Civil War Explained from the Beginning," *Aljazeera*, February 8, 2018, http://www.aljazeera.com, which is updated regularly.

74. Worth, *A Rage for Order*, 81–86. The percentage of the population of various

minorities in based on Anderson, "Fractured Lands," 20, and Ken Stammerman, "The Arab Spring," a continuing education course taught in Fall 2016 at Bellarmine University. Various sources disagree on the percentages, but everyone acknowledges the sectarian and ethnic divisions in Syria that fuel the civil war.

75. This is Worth's main theme in chap. 3 of *A Rage for Order*. See also "Syria's Civil War Explained," especially the section on "What Caused the Uprising."

76. "Syria's Civil War Explained," the section on "International Involvement."

77. "The Rise and Fall of ISIL Explained," *Aljazeerha*, June 20, 2017, www. aljazeera.com; Anderson, "Fractured Lands," 44.

78. See the personal account by Nadia Murad, *The Last Girl: My Story of Captivity, and My Fight Against the Islamic State* (New York: Tim Duggan Books, 2017). Ms. Murad shared the Nobel Peace Prize in 2018 for her efforts against rape as a weapon of war.

79. Anderson, "Fractured Lands," 44–47; Cameron Glenn, "Timeline: The Rise, Spread, and Fall of the Islamic State," The Wilson Center, https://www.wilsoncenter. org, July 5, 2016, updated December 19, 2017.

80. Anderson, "Fractured Lands," 44–49, 55–56; Council on Foreign Relations, Global Conflict Tracker, "Civil War in Syria," and "War Against the Islamic State in Iraq," (updated, February 21, 2018), https://www.cfr.org.

81. Azadeh Moaveni, "The Lingering Dream of an Islamic State," *New York Times*, January 14, 2018, SR7.

82. Sewell Chan, "What's Behind Turkey's Attack on American-Allied Kurds in Syria?" *New York Times*, January 23, 2018, A6; Eric Schmitt and Rod Nordland, "U.S. Loses Fighting Partner, the Kurds, after Turkish Assault," *New York Times*, March 1, 2018, A13; "Syria's Civil War Explained," the sections on "Rebel Groups," and "The Situation Today."

83. Gurr and Harff, *Ethnic Conflict in World Politics*, 30.

84. Ibid., 31; Ignatieff, *Blood and Belonging*, 179.

85. Marvin Zonis, "The Dispossessed: A Review of *A Modern History of the Kurds* by David McDowall (New York: I. B. Tauris/St. Martin's Press, 1996)," *New York Times Book Review*, March 10, 1996, 15.

86. Ignatieff, *Blood and Belonging*, 194–98; Zonis, "The Dispossessed," 15; Anderson, "Fractured Lands," 18–20.

87. Celestine Bohlen, "War on Rebel Kurds Puts Turkey's Ideals to Test," *New York Times*, July 16, 1995, 3; Celestine Bohlen, "In Turkey, Open Discussion of Kurds Is Casualty of Effort to Confront War," *New York Times*, October 29, 1995, 20; Ignatieff, *Blood and Belonging*, 199–212; Zonis, "The Dispossessed," 14.

88. Anderson, "Fractured Lands," 48, 55–57. Anderson tells the story of the Arab Spring through six figures, one of whom is Dr. Azar Mirkhan, a practicing urologist and an Iraqi peshmerga commander. The Mirkhans are affiliated with the Barzani tribal alliance. Azar's father, Heso, and older brother, Ali, are both revered warriors who died in battle in 1983 and 1994, respectively. It is only after repeated prodding that Azar admits to Anderson that Heso and Ali were actually killed by rival Kurdish peshmerga (57).

89. Ibid., 18–19.

90. Loveday Morris, "How the Kurdish Independence Referendum Backfired Spectacularly," *Washington Post*, October 20, 2017.

91. Margaret Coker, "Kurds Reach Accord with Iraq after Vote for Independence," *New York Times*, March 22, 2018, A4.

92. Elizabeth Tsurkov, "Israel's Deepening Involvement with Syria's Rebels," War on the Rocks, February 14, 2018, https://warontherocks.com; "Syria's Civil War Explained," the section on "International Involvement."

93. "Syria's Civil War Explained," Introduction; Margaret Coker et al., "In Idlib, Final Offensive in Syrian War May Come at Horrific Cost to Civilians," *New York Times*, September 3, 2018, A7.

94. Neil MacFarquhar, "Russia's Biggest Problem in Syria: Its Ally, President Assad," *New York Times*, March 9, 2018, A1, 8.

95. This account is based on Worth, *A Rage for Order*, 196–220.

96. Borzou Daragahi, "Belt-Tightening Demands Put Tunisia's Democracy at Risk," *New York Times*, May 4, 2018, A10.

97. Tim Pat Coogan, *The Troubles: Ireland's Ordeal 1966–1996 and the Search for Peace* (Boulder, CO: Roberts Rinehart, 1996), 12–25.

98. Michael MacDonald, *Children of Wrath: Political Violence in Northern Ireland* (Cambridge, UK: Polity Press, 1986), 54.

99. See Ignatieff, *Blood and Belonging*, chap. 6.

100. MacDonald, *Children of Wrath*, 25.

101. Ibid., 75–79; Ronnie Munck, "The Making of the Troubles," *Journal of Contemporary History* 27 (April 1992): 215–28; Sabine Wichert, "The Role of Nationalism in the Northern Ireland Conflict," *History of European Ideas* 16 (January 1993): 110–14.

102. Sean Clarke, James Sturke, and Jenny Percival, "Timeline: Northern Ireland," *The Guardian*, March 10, 2009. See the film *The Journey* (2017), directed by Nick Hamm, for an imaginative re-creation of the forging of a relationship between Rev. Ian Paisley and Martin McGuinness.

103. John Darnton, "After a Massacre in Ulster, Another Season of Fear," *New York Times*, November 1, 1993, A1, A12; Brendan O'Leary and John McGarry, *The Politics of Antagonism: Understanding Northern Ireland*, 2nd ed. (London: Athlone Press, 1996), 12–13.

104. Alan Cowell, "50 Years Later, Troubles Still Cast 'Huge Shadow' over Northern Ireland," *New York Times*, October 5, 2018, A4; Iain McDowell, "Stormont Deadlock: Need to Know Guide," BBC News NI, February 5, 2018; Stephen Castle, "With Good Friday Agreement under Threat, Voters Urged to 'Stand Up,'" *New York Times*, April 10, 2018, A10.

105. This section is based on two articles, J. Milburn Thompson, "Brexit: A Warning for the United States," *Today's American Catholic*, August/September 2016, 1, 3; and Thompson, "UK Journal: Election, Brexit and Terrorism," *Today's American Catholic*, August/September 2017, 5, which are based primarily on the extensive and continuing coverage of Brexit in the *New York Times* and *The Guardian*.

106. Peter S. Goodman, "In Britain, Austerity Is Changing Everything," *New York Times*, May 28, 2018, A1, 6, 7.

107. Stephen Castle, "Latest Stumbling Block in the Brexit Talks: The Irish Border," *New York Times*, December 5, 2017, A9; Castle, "Why Can't the U.K. Solve the Irish Border Problem in Brexit?" *New York Times*, March 1, 2018, A7.

108. Katrin Bennhold, "How Brexit Hurts: Nurses and Doctors Leaving London," *New York Times*, November 23, 2017, A1, 10–11; Kimoko de Freytas-Tamura, "Exodus of Foreign Workers Leaves British Employers in the Lurch," *New York Times*, December 17, 2017, A5.

109. Jon Stone, "Brexit: Theresa May Agrees to Pay 39 bn. Pounds Divorce Bill to the EU," *Independent*, December 8, 2017; Stephen Castle, "E.U. Leaders Accept 'Divorce Deal' with Britain and New Phase of Talks," *New York Times*, December 16, 2017, A5.

110. Stephen Castle, "UK's Next Brexit Agony: What Sort of Trade Deal?" *New York Times*, December 18, 2017, A6; Stephen Castle, "Brexit Nightmare: 17-Mile Traffic Jam at the Dover Border," *New York Times*, June 4, 2018, A8.

111. Stephen Castle, "Theresa May Says U.K. Has to Face Hard Facts on Brexit," *New York Times*, March 3, 2018, A6.

112. Michael J. Abramowitz, *Freedom in the World 2018: Democracy in Crisis*, Freedom House Annual Report, https://freedomhouse.org. See also Peter S. Goodman, "Post-World War II Order Is under Assault from the Powers That Built It," *New York Times*, March 27, 2018, A1, 6.

113. Abramowitz, *Freedom in the World 2018*, 2–6; Declan Walsh, "As Strongmen Steamroll Their Opponents, U.S. Is Silent," *New York Times*, February 2, 2018, A1, 10.

114. Anshel Pfeffer, "Netanyahu, the Icon of the World's Strongmen," *New York Times*, May 20, 2018, SR4, 5; Halbfinger and Kershner, "Israeli Law Declares the Country," A1, 8.

115. Bret Stephens, "The Rise of Euro-Putinism," *New York Times*, March 17, 2018, op-ed page; See also Steven Lee Myers, "The Poison Putin Spreads," *New York Times*, March 18, 2018, SR 6, 7; Abramowitz, *Freedom in the World 2018*, 5.

116. Steven Erlanger, "In Eastern Europe, Populism Lives, Widening a Split in the E.U.," *New York Times*, November 29, 2017, A8.

117. E. J. Dionne, "Populism Isn't the Villain," *Commonweal*, March 8, 2018, https://www.commonwealmagazine.org.

118. Piotr H. Kosicki, "Poland Turns Right: A New Government, an Old Nativism," *Commonweal*, July 8, 2016, 10–11; "Poland's Tragic Turn," *New York Times*, December 22, 2016, editorial; and Marc Santora, "After a President's Shocking Death, a Suspicious Twin Reshapes a Nation," *New York Times*, June 17, 2018, A1, 11.

119. Patrick Kingsley, "As Worst Fears Rise of Autocrats, Hungary Shows What's Possible," *New York Times*, February 11, 2018, A1,10; Patrick Kingsley, "Safe in Hungary, Viktor Orban Pushes His Message across Europe," *New York Times*, June 5, 2018, A1, 6.

120. Robert Tait, "Czech Government Resigns as PM Fights Corruption Allegations," *The Guardian*, January 17, 2018; Robert Tait, "Czech Protesters Inflamed by Police Role for Communist MP," *The Guardian*, March 5, 2018; Marc Santora, "Young Slovaks Buck a Trend, Protesting to Save Their Democracy," *New York Times*, March 18, 2018, A9.

121. Bulcsu Hunyati and Csaba Molnar, "Central Europe's Faceless Strangers:

The Rise of Xenophobia," Freedom House, Nations in Transit Brief (June 2016), 1–6, at 4. See Paul Krugman, "Why It Can Happen Here," *New York Times*, August 28, 2018, op-ed page, which argues that the United States is close to becoming another Poland or Hungary.

122. Chris Buckley and Steven Meyers, "China's Xi Wins Constitutional Backing for New Strongman Era," *New York Times*, March 12, 2018, A5.

123. Hannah Beech, "Cambodia's Ruler Tightens Grip, Energized by Beijing's Blessings," *New York Times*, March 19, 2018, A1, 9.

124. James A. Millward, "Is China a Colonial Power?" *New York Times*, May 6, 2018, SR7; and Brook Larmer, "Is China the World's New Colonial Power?" *New York Times Magazine,* May 7, 2017, 20ff.

125. Richard C. Paddock, "In Malaysia, Old Prime Minister Promises a New Order," *New York Times*, May 11, 2018, A1, 6.

126. Dexter Filkins, "Turkey's Vote Effectively Makes Erdogan a Dictator," *New Yorker,* April 17, 2017.

127. Walsh, "As Strongmen Steamroll Their Opponents, U.S. Is Silent," A1, 10; Declan Walsh and Nour Youssef, "As Sisi Silences Critics, Hope Fades That Egypt's Crackdown Will Ease," *New York Times*, May 24, 2018, A6.

128. The suggestion of an "inclusive populism" is based on Richard D. Kahlenberg, "The Bobby Kennedy Pathway," *New York Times*, March 18, 2018, SR 5, which is in turn based on Kahlenberg's "The Inclusive Populism of Robert Kennedy," A Century Foundation Report, March 16, 2018, https://tcf.org.

129. See ReclaimingJesus.org for the statement. David Brooks makes a similar point from a more philosophical perspective in "Donald Trump Is Not Playing by Your Rules," *New York Times*, June 12, 2018, op-ed page.

130. This section is based on Kim Hjelmgaard, ""Crimeans Say They're Cozy in Russian Fold," *USA Today*, January 8, 2017; "Ukraine Crisis: What's Going On in Crimea?" BBC News, August 12, 2016; and "Crimea Profile" BBC News, January 17, 2018.

131. "Ukraine Crisis"; Alisa Sopova, "How's Life in the War Zone? Not Great," *New York Times*, May 27, 2018, SR10.

132. "Kashmir: Fast Facts," CNN (updated, March 25, 2018); Sameer Yasir, "Deadly Clashes in Kashmir between Indian Army and Militants," *New York Times*, April 2, 2018, A6; "Conflict between India and Pakistan," Council on Foreign Relations (updated, April 10, 2018), https://www.cfr.org. The Indian government is secretive about the number of troops in Kashmir, and some suggest that as many as eighty thousand people have died in the conflict.

133. Celia W. Dugger, "India Ends Kashmir Truce; Seeks Top-Level Pakistan Meeting," *New York Times*, May 24, 2001, A12.

134. Ian Johnson, "Xi Jinping and China's New Era of Glory," *New York Times*, October 15, 2017, SR2.

135. "China and Tibet," *Human Rights Watch World Report 2018*; Chris Buckley, "China Is Detaining Muslims [Uighurs] in Vast Numbers. The Goal: 'Transformation,'" *New York Times*, September 9, 2018, A1, 10.

136. Max Fisher, "Trump, Taiwan, and China: The Controversy Explained," *New York Times*, December 4, 2016, A18.

137. Austine Ramzy, "China Conducts War Games, and Taiwan Is the Target," *New York Times*, April 19, 2018, A9.

138. "Territorial Disputes in the South China Sea," Council on Foreign Relations Global Conflict Tracker (updated on April 20, 2018); "South China Sea and the Rule of Law," *New York Times*, July 13, 2016, editorial.

139. Nick Cumming-Bruce, "Myanmar Generals Should Face Genocide Charges Over Rohingya, U.N. Says," *New York Times*, August 28, 2018, A4; Nicholas Kristof, "Is This Genocide?" *New York Times*, December 17, 2017, SR1, 4–5. There were over fifty articles on Myanmar and the Rohingya in *New York Times* between 2015 and April 2018.

140. "Myanmar Country Profile," BBC News (updated April 12, 2018); "Burma," *The CIA World Factbook*, April 16, 2018.

141. Gardiner Harris, "Myanmar Is Intensifying Violence against Ethnic Minorities, U.S. Says," *New York Times*, May 30, 2018, A7.

142. "Burma," *The CIA World Factbook*; Kristof, "Is this Genocide?"; "Myanmar's Killing Fields," *Frontline*, PBS (May 8, 2018), pbs.org, produced and reported by Evan Williams.

143. Max Fisher, "Myanmar, Once a Hope for Democracy, Now a Study in How It Fails," *New York Times*, October 20, 2017, A11; Nicholas Kristof, "I Saw a Genocide in Slow Motion," *New York Times*, March 4, 2018, SR1, 4; Michael Schwartz, "U.S. Holocaust Museum Revokes Award to Aung Saw Suu Kyi," *New York Times*, March 8, 2018, A4.

144. John McCain and Angelina Jolie, "America Should Lead in Saving the Rohingya," *New York Times*, March 9, 2018, op-ed page. Senators McCain (R-AR) and Ben Cardin (D-MD) have sponsored S2060, The Burma Human Rights and Freedom Act of 2018, which includes many of these recommendations. See Kristof, "I Saw a Genocide in Slow Motion"; also Max Fisher, "Rohingya of Myanmar Learn That 'Never Again' Doesn't Always Apply," *New York Times*, November 14, 2017, A7, for a political analysis of why the global community is not responding to crimes against humanity in Myanmar.

145. Ian Fisher et al., "Chaos in Congo: A Primer: Many Armies Ravage Rich Land in the 'First World War' of Africa," *New York Times*, February 6, 2000, A1, 10-11.

146. Alex De Waal and Rakiya Omaar, "The Genocide in Rwanda and the International Response," *Current History* 94 (April 1995): 156. The number of Tutsi killed is disputed. De Waal and Omaar say 750,000 people were slaughtered. *New York Times* now consistently reports that at least 500,000 Tutsi were killed during this period. Nevertheless, this massacre was an act of genocide. The estimate of the number of refugees resulting from this event (mostly Hutu) likewise varies from one million to two million.

147. "Political Crisis in Burundi," Council on Foreign Relations, Global Conflict Tracker (May 23, 2018).

148. Elias O. Opongo, "Just War and Its Implications for African Conflicts," in *Can War Be Just in the 21st Century?* ed. Tobias Winright and Laurie Johnston (Maryknoll, NY: Orbis Books, 2015), chap. 10, at 145–46.

149. "Rwanda Country Profile," BBC News, August 6, 2017; "Rwanda," *The CIA World Factbook*, April 24, 2018.

150. Jina Moore, "Leader of Burundi Aims to Remain in Power after 3 Terms," *New York Times*, May 18, 2018, A7; "Political Crisis in Burundi," Council on Foreign Relations.

151. Opongo, "Just War and Its Implications," 144–45; John Kiess," Civilian Vulnerability in Contemporary War: Lessons from the War in the Democratic Republic of Congo," in *Can War Be Just in the 21st Century?*, ed. Winright and Johnston, 156–68.

152. "DR Congo Country Profile," BBC News, December 6, 2017; "Congo, Democratic Republic of," *The CIA World Factbook*, April 24, 2018; and Diana Zeyner Alhindawi and Jina Moore, "Motive for Mass Killings in Congo Is Mystery, but the Suffering Is Clear," *New York Times*, April 29, 2018, A8.

153. "Sudan Country Profile, BBC News, January 8, 2018; "Sudan," *The CIA World Factbook*, May 1, 2018.

154. "Darfur Genocide," World without Genocide (2016), http://worldwithout genocide.org.

155. "Famine Stalks South Sudan," *New York Times*, March 7, 2018, editorial; "South Sudan Profile—Timeline," BBC News, January 17, 2018; "South Sudan," *The CIA World Factbook*, May 2, 2018; "Civil War in South Sudan," Council on Foreign Relations Global Conflict Tracker (updated May 10, 2018); Opongo, "Just War and Its Implications," 143–44.

156. "Somalia Civil War," Global Security (updated March 4, 2018), https://www.globalsecurity.org; "Somalia Country Profile," BBC News, January 4, 2018; "Somalia," *The CIA World Factbook*, May 1, 2018.

157. See the film *Black Hawk Down* (2001), directed by Scott Ridley, based on the book by Mark Bowden, for a sense of the fighting that occurred in the 1993 Battle of Mogadishu. Andrew Bacevich, "The Lessons of Black Hawk Down," *New York Times*, October 4, 2018, op-ed page.

158. "Ethiopia Country Profile" BBC News, April 3, 2018; "Eritrea Country Profile," BBC News, May 8, 2018; "Ethiopia," *The CIA World Factbook*, May 7, 2018; "Eritrea," *The CIA World Factbook*, May 1, 2018. Selam Gebrekidan, "Ethiopia and Eritrea Declare an End to Their War," *New York Times*, July 10, 2018, A7.

159. Virginia Comoli, "The Evolution and Impact of Boko Haram in the Lake Chad Basin," Humanitarian Practice Network, October 2017, https://odihpn.org; Ben Taub, "The Emergency: Lake Chad," *New Yorker*, December 4, 2017; "Boko Haram in Nigeria," Council on Foreign Relations Global Conflict Tracker (May 11, 2018); and the country profiles for Nigeria, Cameroon, Niger, and Chad in *The CIA World Factbook*, May 2018.

160. Taub, "The Emergency."

161. Mareike Kuerschner, "Conflict in West African States," E-International Relations Students, March 15, 2013, http://www.e-ir.info.

162. "Biafra War," GlobalSecurity.org; "Biafra at 50: Nigeria's Civil War Explained," BBC video, July 7, 2017.

163. "Liberia—First Civil War—1989-1996," GlobalSecurity.org, November 7, 2011; "Liberia—Second Civil War—1997-2003, GlobalSecurity.org, November 7, 2011; Ruth Maclean, "Ex-footballer George Weah to Become Liberia's President," *The Guardian*, December 28, 2017.

164. Victoria Brittain, "Foday Sankoh: Obituary," *The Guardian*, July 30, 2003; "Sierra Leone Profile—Timeline" BBC News, April 5, 2018; "Sierra Leone: Civil War and Post Civil War" *Encyclopaedia Britannica* (April 2018), https://www.britannica.com; Norimitsu Onishi, "In Ruined Liberia, Its Despoiler Sits Pretty," *New York Times*, December 7, 2000, A1, A20.

165. "Ivory Coast Country Profile," BBC News, January 10, 2018; "Cote d'Ivoire," *The CIA World Factbook*, May 1, 2018.

166. Foday Sanhoh died in UN custody while awaiting his trial on charges of war crimes. Charles Taylor was convicted of war crimes and sentenced to fifty years in prison. Laurent Gbagbo and his wife, Simone, are imprisoned at The Hague for crimes against humanity.

167. "Mali," *The CIA World Factbook*, May 1, 2018; "Destabilization of Mali," Council on Foreign Relations, Global Conflict Tracker (May 22, 2018).

168. Tim McDonnell, "What's the World's Fastest Growing Economy? Ghana Contends for the Crown," *New York Times*, March 11, 2018, A4; "Ghana Overview," World Bank, April 19, 2018; "Ghana Country Profile," BBC News; "Ghana," *The CIA World Factbook*, May 1, 2018.

169. "Zimbabwe Country Profile," BBC News, February 15, 2018; "Zimbabwe," *The CIA World Factbook*, May 1, 2018; Norimitsu Onishi and Alan Cowell, "With Mugabe's Era Ending in Zimbabwe, a Warning Echoes in Africa," *New York Times*, November 16, 2017, A1, 6, 7.

170. "Angola," *The CIA World Factbook*, May 1, 2018; "Angola Country Profile," BBC News, March 7, 2018; Norimitsu Onishi, "Angola's Corrupt Building Boom," *New York Times*, June 25, 2017, A14.

171. "South Africa, *The CIA World Factbook*, May 1, 2018; "South Africa Country Profile," BBC News, April 2, 2018.

172. "South Africa's Protesters Have It Right," *New York Times*, April 8, 2017, editorial; Norimitsu Onishi and Selam Gebrekidan, "'They Eat Money': How Mandela's Political Heirs Grow Rich Off Corruption," *New York Times*, April 16, 2018, A1, 8, 9, 10; Norimitsu Onishi and Selam Gebrekidan, "Corruption Gutted South Africa's Tax Agency. Now the Nation Is Paying the Price," *New York Times*, June 10, 2018, A1, 10, 11.

173. See the annual "Corruption Perceptions Index," produced by Transparency International, www.transparency.org.

174. See Dionne Searcey, "Angolan President, in Power Nearly Four Decades, Says He'll Step Down," *New York Times*, March 12, 2016, A8; Jeffrey Gettleman, "'Africa Rising'? 'Africa Reeling' May Be a More Fitting Slogan Now," *New York Times*, October 18, 2016, A9; Dionne Searcey, "Why Democracy Prevailed in Gambia," *New York Times*, January 31, 2017, A7.

175. It is eye opening to compare an ethnic map of Africa with a territorial map.

176. Carlotta Gall, "Jihadists Deepen Collaboration in North Africa," *New York Times*, January 2, 2016, A1, 6.

177. Jeffrey Gettleman, "Loss of Fertile Land Fuels 'Looming Crisis' across Africa," *New York Times*, July 30, 2017, A1, 10, 11.

178. *Freedom in the World 2018*, Freedom House, http://freedomhouse.org.

179. Danielle Renwick, "Venezuela in Crisis," Council on Foreign Relations,

March 23, 2018; "How Venezuela's Crisis Developed and Worsened," BBC News, May 21, 2018; "Venezuela," *The CIA World Factbook*, May 22, 2018; Max Fisher and Amanda Taub, "How Venezuela Stumbled to the Brink of Collapse," *New York Times*, May 15, 2017, A4; William Neuman and Clifford Kraus, "Workers Flee and Thieves Loot Venezuela's Reeling Oil Giant," *New York Times*, June 15, 2018, A1, 6; Nicholas Casey, "Forecast for Inflation in Venezuela: 1,000.000%," *New York Times*, July 24, 2018, A9.

180. Claire Felter and Danielle Renwick, "U.S.–Cuba Relations," Council on Foreign Relations, January 19, 2018; "Cuba Country Profile," BBC News, May 1, 2018; "Cuba," *The CIA World Factbook*, May 1, 2018.

181. "Colombia Country Profile," BBC News, May 31, 2018; "Colombia," *The CIA World Factbook*, May 16, 2018; Susan Abad and Nicholas Casey, "In Colombia, Far-Right and Hard-Left Candidates Will Vie for Presidency," *New York Times*, May 28, 2018, A5.

182. Jens Manuel Krogstand, "Five Facts about Mexico and Immigration to the U.S.," Pew Research Center Fact Tank, February 11, 2016.

183. "Criminal Violence in Mexico," Council on Foreign Relations Global Conflict Tracker (June 1, 2018); "Mexico Country Profile," BBC News, May 16, 2018; "Mexico," *The CIA World Factbook*, May 16, 2018.

184. See "List of Wars Involving the United States," Wikipedia.

185. Jeff Desjardins, "U.S. Military Deployments by Country," Visual Capitalist, March 18, 2017, https://www.visualcapitalist.com. Kristen Bialik, "U.S. Active-Duty Military Presence Overseas Is at Its Smallest in Decades," Pew Research Center Fact Tank, August 22, 2017.

186. NCCB, *The Harvest of Justice Is Sown in Peace*, 336.

187. Kenneth R. Himes, "Humanitarian Intervention and the Just War Tradition," in *Can War Be Just in the 21st Century?*, ed. Winright and Johnston, 54–55.

188. J. Bryan Hehir, "Intervention: From Theories to Cases," *Ethics and International Affairs* 9 (1995): 3–6; Kenneth R. Himes, "The Morality of Humanitarian Intervention," *Theological Studies* 55 (1994): 84–85, 92–93.

189. Hehir, "Intervention," 8; Himes, "The Morality of Humanitarian Intervention," 97.

190. Hehir, "Intervention," 13. See Brian Larkin, "U.S. Military Interventions in Central and South America in the Twentieth Century," Peace and Justice, August 3, 2013, http://peaceandjustice.org.uk.

191. Himes, "The Morality of Humanitarian Intervention," 97.

192. See J. Milburn Thompson, "Purposeful Intervention, Christian Ethics, and the Case of Haiti," *Journal for the Study of Peace and Conflict* (1997–98), 65–77.

193. Himes, "Humanitarian Intervention and the Just War Tradition," 55–57; Himes, "Catholic Social Thought and Humanitarian Intervention," in *Peacemaking*, ed. Powers et al., 218–20; NCCB, *The Harvest of Justice Is Sown in Peace*, 337.

194. The church affirms both just war and pacifism as options for Christians. See *Gaudium et Spes: The Pastoral Constitution on the Church in the Modern World* (1965) in *Catholic Social Thought*, ed. O'Brien and Shannon, ##79–80; NCCB, *The Challenge of Peace* (1983), ##66–121.

195. See Richard B. Miller, "Casuistry, Pacifism, and the Just War Tradition in

the Post-Cold War Era," in *Peacemaking*, ed. Powers et al., 205–9; Robert Phillips and Duane L. Cady, *Humanitarian Intervention: Just War vs. Pacifism* (Lanham, MD: Rowman & Littlefield, 1996); and Himes, "Catholic Social Thought and Humanitarian Intervention," 224–35.

196. Hehir, "Intervention," 7–8; Cady, *Humanitarian Intervention*, 61–62; NCCB, *The Harvest of Justice Is Sown in Peace*, 337.

197. David Rieff, "Were Sanctions Right?," *New York Times Magazine*, July 27, 2003.

198. Hehir, "Intervention," 8.

199. Himes, "Humanitarian Intervention and the Just War Tradition," 62. This essay explores the six just-war criteria and humanitarian intervention at 61–64.

200. See Hehir, "Intervention," 9, 11–13; Himes, "The Morality of Humanitarian Intervention," 100–101.

201. Hehir, "Intervention," 9; Himes, "The Morality of Humanitarian Intervention," 98–100.

202. This is the argument of Robert Phillips in *Humanitarian Intervention*. See also J. Milburn Thompson, "Why Send in the Troops? Christian Ethics and Humanitarian Intervention," *Theology: Expanding the Borders: The Annual of the College Theology Society*, 43, ed. Maria Pilar Aquino and Roberto S. Goizueta (Mystic, CT: Twenty-Third Publications, 1998), 320–33.

203. Himes, "Catholic Social Teaching and Humanitarian Intervention," 227. See also Mark J. Allman and Tobias L. Winright, *After the Smoke Clears: The Just War Tradition and Post War Justice* (Maryknoll, NY: Orbis Books, 2010), which argues for a *jus post bellum* or post-war justice phase of the just war theory, 143–72.

204. Himes, "The Morality of Humanitarian Intervention," 101–4; Hehir, "Intervention," 13.

205. Hehir, "Intervention," 10–11; Himes, "The Morality of Humanitarian Intervention," 101–2.

206. Glen H. Stassen, *Just Peacemaking: Transforming Initiatives for Justice and Peace* (Louisville, KY: Westminster/John Knox Press, 1992); Glen H. Stassen, ed., *Just Peacemaking: Ten Practices for Abolishing War* (Cleveland: Pilgrim Press, 1998); and Glen H. Stassen, ed., *Just Peacemaking: The New Paradigm for the Ethics of War and Peace*, new ed. (Cleveland: Pilgrim Press, 2008).

207. Stassen, *Just Peacemaking: Transforming Initiatives*, 89–113.

208. J. Milburn Thompson, "Humanitarian Intervention, Just Peacemaking, and the United Nations," *Concilium, 2001/2: The Return of the Just War*, ed. Maria Pilar Aquino and Dietmar Mieth (London: SCM Press, 2001), 83–93.

209. Himes, "Humanitarian Intervention and the Just War Tradition," 57–58; Allman and Winright, *After the Smoke Clears*, 38–40, 177; Opongo, "Just War and Its Implications," 150–55; International Commission on Intervention and State Sovereignty, *The Responsibility to Protect* (Ottawa: International Development Research Centre, 2001), http://www.idrc.ca.

210. "Text of President Bush's Speech," *Courier-Journal*, September 21, 2001, op-ed page.

211. John Paul II, "Message for World Peace Day, January 1, 2002," *America* 186, January 7–14, 2002, 8.

212. James Burtchaell, "A Moral Response to Terrorism," in James Burtchaell, *The Giving and Taking of Life: Essays Ethical* (South Bend, IN: University of Notre Dame Press, 1989), 213–16. This section depends heavily on this essay. See also Edward LeRoy Long Jr., *Facing Terrorism: Responding as Christians* (Louisville, KY: Westminster John Knox Press, 2004), which explores whether terrorism is warfare or crime, 11–15, and presents a Crusade Model, 44–49, 85–93, and a Law Enforcement Model, 50–54, 81–85, of counterterrorism.

213. Burtchaell says, "But for whoever must respond morally to a terrorist act, it surely makes a difference whether it is the work of a tyrant or of the tyrant's victims" ("A Moral Response to Terrorism," 216). See also Juergensmeyer, *Terror in the Mind of God*, 9–10.

214. In this regard, Ishai Menuchin, a major in the Israel Defense Forces Reserves and a leader of the soldiers' movement for selective refusal, wrote in an essay in the *New York Times:* "After 35 years of Israel's occupation of the West Bank and Gaza, the two sides seem only to have grown accustomed to assassinations, bombings, terrorist attacks, and house demolitions. Each side characterizes its own soldiers as either 'defense forces' or 'freedom fighters' when in truth these soldiers take part in war crimes on a daily basis" ("Saying No to Israel's Occupation," March 9, 2002, op-ed page). Menuchin and others, while continuing to serve in Israel's defense forces, are selectively refusing to obey orders to go into the West Bank or Gaza or to commit what they judge to be war crimes.

215. John Kelsay, "Bin Laden's Reasons," *Christian Century*, February 27–March 6, 2002, 26.

216. Ibid., 29. This chilling quote is taken directly from the February 23, 1998 statement "Jihad Against Jews and Crusaders," by the World Islamic Front, which is reprinted in "Bin Laden's Reasons." Kelsay points out how this *fatwa* twists and misinterprets the Qur'an.

217. Andrew Curry, "Here Are the Ancient Sites ISIS Has Damaged and Destroyed," *National Geographic*, September 1, 2015.

218. "What Is 'Islamic State'?" BBC News, December 2, 2015.

219. Burtchaell, "A Moral Response to Terrorism," 228.

220. Richard Falk, "A Just Response," *The Nation* 273, October 8, 2001, 11–15; J. Bryan Hehir, "What Can Be Done? What Should Be Done?" *America* 185, October 8, 2001, 9–12; Susan Sontag, "Real Battles and Empty Metaphors," *New York Times*, September 10, 2002, op-ed page; Paul Krugman, "The Long Haul," *New York Times*, September 10, 2002, op-ed page.

221. On the third and fourth points, see Long, *Facing Terrorism*, 60–75, and 53–54.

222. Stassen, ed., *Just Peacemaking: Ten Practices*; Stassen, "Turning Attention to Just Peacemaking Initiatives That Prevent Terrorism," *Bulletin of the Council of Societies for the Study of Religion* 31, no. 3 (September 2001): 59–65; Long, *Facing Terrorism*, 55–59, 77–81.

223. Seymour M. Hersh, "Torture at Abu Ghraib," *New Yorker*, May 10, 2004; Jane Meyer, "Outsourcing Torture: The Secret History of America's 'Extraordinary Rendition' Program," *New Yorker*, February 14, 2005; Max Fisher, "A Staggering Map of the 54 Countries That Reportedly Participated in the CIA's Rendition Program," *Washington Post*, February 5, 2013.

224. The pastoral message of the United States Conference of Catholic Bishops titled, "Living with Faith and Hope after September 11," November 14, 2001, available at www.usccb.org, while affirming the right of the state to defend itself, stresses the importance of spreading the benefits of globalization to all and especially to the poor and those working for the global common good through constructive diplomacy in the Israeli–Palestinian conflict, by removing economic sanctions on Iraq, by affirming human rights, by reversing the spread of weapons of mass destruction and reducing the US role in the arms trade, and by strengthening the UN and other international institutions.

225. Stassen, "Turning Attention," 61.

226. Juergensmeyer, *Terror in the Mind of God*, xvii. See also Long, *Facing Terrorism*, 36–40.

Chapter Seven

1. Michael T. Klare, "Deadly Convergence: The Arms Trade, Nuclear/Chemical/ Missile Proliferation, and Regional Conflict in the 1990s," in *World Security: Trends and Challenges at Century's End*, ed. Michael Klare and Daniel Thomas (New York: St. Martin's Press, 1991), 170–196.

2. Rakiya Omaar, "Somalia: At War with Itself," *Current History* 91 (October 1991): 231.

3. This description is based on Ronald Sider and Richard Taylor, *Nuclear Holocaust & Christian Hope* (Downers Grove, IL: InterVarsity Press, 1982), chap. 1; Richard McSorley, *Kill? For Peace?* (Washington, DC: Georgetown University, Center for Peace Studies, 1977), chap. 1; John Hershey, *Hiroshima* (New York: Bantam, 1956); and informational material from Physicians for Social Responsibility, including the film *The Last Epidemic: Medical Consequences of Nuclear Weapons and Nuclear War* (1981).

4. Jonathan Schell, *The Fate of the Earth* (New York: Knopf, 1982), 181–82. Originally published in *New Yorker*, February 15, 1982, 45. Mr. Schell died in March 2014. His book is a key resource for understanding the moral and spiritual significance of nuclear weapons.

5. Bruce G. Blair, "Hacking Our Nuclear Weapons," *New York Times*, March 14, 2017, op-ed page. Eric Schlosser, *Command and Control: Nuclear Weapons, the Damascus Accident, and the Illusion of Safety* (New York: Penguin Books, 2013), is about the effort to ensure that nuclear weapons do not go off by accident, by mistake, or any other unauthorized means.

6. The film *Crimson Tide* (1995), directed by Tony Scott, starring Denzel Washington and Gene Hackman, dramatizes both the possibility of a change for the worse in Russia and the power of the captain of a nuclear submarine.

7. See Bill Keller, "Nuclear Nightmares," *New York Times Magazine*, May 26, 2002, 22–29, 51, 54–57.

8. On the controversy about using the atomic bomb, see Guy Alperovitz, "Use of the Atomic Bomb Was Not Inevitable," *Hartford Courant*, October 23, 1994, C1, C4; Ronald Takaki, *Hiroshima: Why America Dropped the Atomic Bomb* (Boston: Little, Brown, 1995).

9. "Belarus Gives Up Last Nuclear Missile," *Hartford Courant*, November 1996, A7; Jane Perlez, "Sunflower Seeds Replace Ukraine's Old Missile Sites," *New York Times*, June 5, 1996, A5.

10. A good source of information on the status of programs regarding weapons of mass destruction and their delivery systems in various countries is the organization Nuclear Threat Initiative, https://www.nti.org.

11. C. J. Chivers, "The Secret Casualties of Iraq's Abandoned Chemical Weapons," *New York Times*, October 14, 2014, A1, tells the story of US troops frequently stumbling on, and on at least six occasions being exposed to, deteriorating chemical weapon remnants from abandoned programs from the 1980s (the time of the Iran/Iraq War), which had been built in collaboration with the West.

12. Helene Cooper, "'Loose Talk of War' Only Helps Iran, President Says," *New York Times*, March 5, 2012, A1.

13. See the summary at Nuclear Threat Initiative, www.nti.org; David E. Sanger, "Iran Meets Terms of Nuclear Deal, Ending Sanctions," *New York Times*, January 17, 2016, A1, 11.

14. See John R. Bolton, "To Stop Iran's Bomb, Bomb Iran," *New York Times*, March 25, 2015, op-ed page, which appeared about a week before the early April 2015 breakthrough toward an agreement with Iran. Mr. Bolton became President Trump's third National Security Adviser on April 9, 2018.

15. Mark Landler, "Trump Abandons Iran Nuclear Deal He Long Scorned," *New York Times*, May 9, 2018, A1; "After the Iran Deal," *Commonweal*, June 1, 2018, editorial, 5.

16. See the summary at Nuclear Threat Initiative, www.nti.org.

17. This is dramatically presented in the film *Gandhi* (1982), directed by Richard Attenborough and starring Ben Kingsley.

18. Mira Kamdar, "Years of Mourning the Losses in Mumbai," *New York Times*, December 1, 2013, SR10; Hari Kumar and Ellen Barry, "Three Indian Soldiers Are Killed on Border of India and Pakistan," *New York Times*, November 23, 2016, A11.

19. "Another Face-Off for Nuclear-Armed Rivals," *New York Times*, January 17, 2013, editorial.

20. "Nuclear Fears in South Asia," *New York Times*, April 6, 2015, editorial; "The Pakistan Nuclear Nightmare," *New York Times*, November 8, 2015, editorial.

21. "North Korea's Horrors," *New York Times*, May 21, 2015, editorial.

22. A nuclear device uses fission to split an atom. A thermonuclear or hydrogen bomb uses fusion to fuse two or more atoms into a larger atom, and is more powerful. See David E. Sanger and William J. Broad, "North Korea's Nuclear Strength, Encapsulated in an Online Ad for Lithium," *New York Times*, April 4, 2017, A1, A9.

23. Mark Landler, "North Korea Nuclear Effort Seen as a Top Threat to the U.S.," *New York Times*, February 10, 2016, A10; and Joel S. Wit, "How to Stop North Korea," *New York Times*, September 13, 2016, op-ed page. See also Nuclear Threat Initiative; and Arms Control Association, "Chronology of U.S.–North Korea Nuclear and Missile Diplomacy," https://www.armscontrol.org, which is very detailed.

24. Somini Sengupta and Jane Perlez, "U.N. Stiffens Sanctions on North Korea," *New York Times*, December 1, 2016, A4; and "North Korea's Nuclear Enabler," *New York Times*, September 10, 2016, editorial.

25. Max Fisher, "North Korea Crazy? Worse, It's Calculating," *New York Times*, September 11, 2016, A6, 9; Max Fisher, "Multiple Options for Striking North Korea, All Highly Risky," *New York Times*, March 19, 2017, A10.

26. Choe San-Hun, "Kim Jong-un Says He Wants Denuclearization in Trump's Current Term," *New York Times*, September 7, 2018, A10.

27. Chris Buckley, "Why U.S. Antimissile System in South Korea Worries China," *New York Times*, March 12, 2017, A8.

28. Choe San-Hun, "North Korea Weaponizes Its Deal with Trump to Tangle Talks," *New York Times*, October 13, 2018, A7; James Clapper, "Ending the Dead End in North Korea," *New York Times*, May 20, 2018, SR3; "North Korea, the Big Negotiating Challenge," *New York Times*, February 20, 2017, editorial.

29. Matias Spektor, "The Long View: How Argentina and Brazil Stepped Back from a Nuclear Race," *Americas Quarterly* (Fall 2015), https://www.americasquarterly.org.

30. Nuclear Threat Initiative, on the 1996 Treaty of Pelindaba, which established a Nuclear Weapons Free Zone in Africa; and on the 1967 Tlatelolco Treaty, which banned nuclear weapons in Latin America and the Caribbean; www.nti.org.

31. Joseph Cirincione, ""The Non-Proliferation Treaty and the Nuclear Balance," *Current History* 94 (May 1995): 201–6; Barbara Crossette, "Discord over Renewing Pact on Spread of Nuclear Arms," *New York Times*, April 17, 1995, A1; Zachary S. Davis, "Nuclear Proliferation and Nonproliferation Policy in the 1990s," in *World Security: Challenges for a New Century*, Second Edition, ed. Michael T. Klare and Daniel C. Thomas (New York: St. Martin's Press, 1994), 106–33; "A Nuclear Milestone," *New York Times*, May 12, 1995, editorial.

32. Nuclear Threat Initiative, NPT Review Conference 2015, https://www.nti.org.

33. Paul Walker, *Seizing the Initiative: First Steps to Disarmament* (Philadelphia: American Friends Service Committee, 1983), 8–16; Joshua S. Goldstein and Jon C. Pevehouse, *International Relations*, 10th ed., 2012–13 update (New York: Pearson, 2013), 219–22.

34. *Strategic* nuclear weapons are those that can be delivered from one superpower to the other with a range over two thousand miles. *Intermediate* nuclear weapons have a shorter, yet significant range. They could be fired from France to Russia, for example, or from Russia to China. *Tactical* nuclear weapons are designed for battlefield use. Their range is shorter and they have less power, although there is no such thing as a nuclear weapon that is genuinely discriminate in its blast effect or radiation effect.

35. Allan S. Krass, "Death and Transfiguration: Nuclear Arms Control in the 1980s and 1990s," in *World Security*, ed. Klare and Thomas (1991), 75–79.

36. Michael R. Gordon, "Russia Secretly Deploys a Missile, Violating a Treaty and Challenging Trump," *New York Times*, February 15, 2017, A18; "A Cornerstone of Peace at Risk," *New York Times*, April 3, 2017, editorial.

37. Alan S. Krass, "The Second Nuclear Era: Nuclear Weapons in a Transformed World," in *World Security*, Second Edition, ed. Klare and Thomas (1994), 92–93.

38. Peter Gray, *Briefing Book on U.S. Leadership and the Future of Nuclear Arsenals* (Washington, DC: Council for a Livable World Education Fund, 1996), 12; Steven Erlanger, "After 3-Year Wait, START II Wins Senate Approval but Still Faces Russian Opposition," *New York Times*, January 27, 1996, 5; Mikhail Gorbachev, "NATO's

Plans Threaten START II," *New York Times*, February 10, 1996, op-ed page; Thomas L. Friedman, "It's Unclear," *New York Times*, June 2, 1997, op-ed page.

39. The Nuclear Threat Initiative, "Strategic Offensive Reductions Treaty (SORT)," https://www.nti.org; the Arms Control Association, "U.S. Missile Defense Programs at a Glance," https://www.armscontrol.org.

40. Leonid Nersisyan, "America vs. Russia: Will Missile Defense Help in a Global Nuclear War?" National Interest, October 20, 2016, https://nationalinterest. org; Laura Grego, George N. Lewis, and David Wright, *Shielded from Oversight: The Disastrous U.S. Approach to Strategic Missile Defense* (Union of Concerned Scientists, July 2016), https://www.ucsusa.org; and Helene Cooper and Eric Schmitt, "U.S. Test of a Missile Interceptor Fails off the Hawaiian Coast, Officials Say," *New York Times*, February 1, 2018, A10.

41. Jessica Stern, "Preventing Portable Nukes," *New York Times*, April 10, 1996, op-ed page.

42. Arms Control Association, "U.S. Missile Defense Programs at a Glance."

43. The Nuclear Threat Initiative, "New START Treaty," www.nti.org.

44. Arms Control Association, "Nuclear Weapons: Who Has What at a Glance," https://www.armscontrol.org.

45. Amy L. Woolf, "Nonstrategic Nuclear Weapons," Congressional Research Service, March 23, 2016, at Summary, https://fas.org.

46. "Remarks by President Obama in Prague as Delivered," https://obamawhite house.archives.gov.

47. William J. Broad and David E. Sanger, "Smaller Bombs Are Adding to Nuclear Fear," *New York Times*, January 12, 2016, A1.

48. Arms Control Association, "U.S. Nuclear Modernization Programs," https://www.armscontrol.org.

49. Ibid.; William J. Broad and David E. Sanger, "U.S. Ramping Up Major Renewal in Nuclear Arms," *New York Times*, September 22, 2014, A1; Broad and Sanger, "Smaller Bombs."

50. All three sources listed in n. 49 state these cost estimates.

51. Stephen I. Schwartz, "The Costs of U.S. Nuclear Weapons," Nuclear Threat Initiative, October 1, 2008, http://www.nti.org. This issue brief is based on Stephen I. Schwartz, *Atomic Audit: The Costs and Consequences of U.S. Nuclear Weapons since 1940* (Washington, DC: Brookings Institution Press, 1998). Also see Matthew L. Wald, "Big Price Tag for A-Bombs, Study Finds: 50 Year Cost to U.S. Is Almost $4 Trillion," *New York Times*, July 12, 1995.

52. Based on a chart on "Nuclear Spending" imbedded in Broad and Sanger, "U.S. Ramping Up Major Renewal in Nuclear Arms."

53. *The Pastoral Constitution on the Church in the Modern World*, in *The Documents of Vatican II*, ed. Walter Abbott, trans. Joseph Gallagher (London: Geoffrey Chapman, 1966), #81.

54. Matthew L. Wald, "Study Finds Destruction in the Making of A-Bombs," *New York Times*, July 26, 1995, A12, reports on a study produced over six years by the International Physicians for the Prevention of Nuclear War, winners of the Nobel Peace Prize in 1985, on the environmental damage from the nuclear weapons program. See Arjun Makhijani and Katherine Yih, eds., *Nuclear Wastelands: A Global Guide*

to Nuclear Weapons Production and Its Health and Environmental Effects (Cambridge, MA: MIT Press, 1995).

55. Broad and Sanger, "U.S. Ramping Up Major Renewal in Nuclear Arms."

56. John Feffer, "Obama's Nuclear Paradox," Foreign Policy in Focus (June 1, 2016), http://fpif.org; R. Jeffrey Smith, "Obama's Broken Pledge on Nuclear Weapons," *Foreign Policy,* March 30, 2016, https://foreignpolicy.com; Bruce Blair, "How Obama Could Revolutionize Nuclear Weapons Strategy Before He Goes," *Politico Magazine,* June 22, 2016, https://www.politico.com; Josh Rogin, "Obama Plans Major Nuclear Policy Changes in His Final Months," *Washington Post,* July 10, 2016.

57. Rick Gladstone, "Urging Nuclear Upgrade to Face 'Bellicose' Russia," *New York Times,* March 23, 2017, A4.

58. The question could be posed as dominance, deterrence, or disarmament. I am assuming the idea of nuclear dominance, with the implication of winning a nuclear war, is absurd. Humanity and the Earth would lose in a nuclear war.

59. Goldstein and Pevehouse, *International Relations,* 209–11.

60. Cirincione, "The Non-Proliferation Treaty and the Nuclear Balance," 205. See Selig S. Harrison, "Zero Nuclear Weapons. Zero," *New York Times,* February 15, 1995, op-ed page; Gray, *Briefing Book,* which presents the debate about deterrence or disarmament and argues for the latter. See Richard N. Haass, "It's Dangerous to Disarm," *New York Times,* December 11, 1996, op-ed page, for a dissenting view.

61. See Philip Taubman, *The Partnership: Five Cold Warriors and Their Quest to Ban the Bomb* (New York: HarperCollins, 2012).

62. See President Barack Obama, "How We Can Make Our Vision of a World Without Nuclear Weapons a Reality," *Wall Street Journal,* March 30, 2016, op-ed page, for another statement by Obama on the abolition of nuclear weapons on the eve of the fourth World Security Summit held in Washington, DC.

63. Rick Gladstone, "The U.N. Adopts a Treaty to Ban Nuclear Weapons. Now Comes the Hard Part," *New York Times,* July 8, 2017, A7.

64. International Campaign to Abolish Nuclear Weapons (ICAN), "Nuclear Ban Treaty Negotiations in 2017," www.icanw.org; "Proposed Nuclear Weapons Ban Treaty," Nuclear Threat Initiative, April 5, 2017, https://www.nti.org. For a critique of this initiative, see Matthew Harries, "The Real Problem with a Nuclear Ban Treaty," Carnegie Endowment for International Peace, March 15, 2017, https://carnegieendowment.org.

65. Somini Sengupta and Rick Gladstone, "United States and Allies Boycott U.N. Talks for a Treaty to Ban Nuclear Weapons," *New York Times,* March 28, 2017, A10.

66. Philip Taubman, "No Need for All These Nukes," *New York Times,* January 8, 2012, SR4.

67. The Arms Control Association, "No Going Back: Twenty Years since the Last U.S. Nuclear Test," *Issue Briefs* 3, no. 14 (September 20, 2012), especially the section "Time to Finish the Job," https://www.armscontrol.org.

68. See Peter Baker, "Deal on Syria's Chemical Weapons Comes Back to Haunt Obama," *New York Times,* April 10, 2017, A14, for a retrospective look at this agreement after President Assad used Sarin gas again in April, 2017.

69. Jared Maslin, "Assad's Regime Is Still Using Chemical Weapons," *Time,* September 14, 2016; Rick Gladstone, "Syria Used Chlorine Bombs Systematically in

Effort to Retake Aleppo, Report Says," *New York Times*, February 14, 2017, A9; Michael Schwirtz, "U.S. Accuses Syria of Chemical Weapons Use," *New York Times*, January 24, 2018, A9. Sarah Everts, "A Brief History of Chemical War," *Distillations* (Spring 2015), https://www.sciencehistory.org; Organization for the Prohibition of Chemical Weapons, "Brief History of Chemical Weapons Use," https://www.opcw.org.

70. Anne Barnard, "Syrian Nerve Gas Attack That Led to Missile Strike Appears to Be One of a Series," *New York Times*, May 2, 2017, A7.

71. Goldstein and Pevehouse, *International Relations*, 214–15; The Arms Control Association, "The Chemical Weapons Convention at a Glance," and "Chemical Weapons Convention Signatories and States-Parties," both October 2015, https://www.armscontrol.org.

72. Alan Cowell, "Chemical Weapons Watchdog Wins Nobel Peace Prize," *New York Times*, October 12, 2013; Rick Gladstone, "Monitors Report a 90% Decline in Stockpiles of Chemical Arms," *New York Times*, May 29, 2015, A6.

73. Ellen Barry, "Russia, Praised for Scrapping Chemical Weapons, Now Under Watchdog's Gaze," *New York Times*, March 22, 2018, A5; Andrew Higgins, "Russia Destroys Chemical Weapons and Faults the U.S. for Not Doing So," *New York Times*, September 28, 2017, A8.

74. Jonathan B. Tucker, "The Chemical Weapons Convention: Has It Enhanced U.S. Security?" *Arms Control Today* 31, April 2001, 8–12, https://www.armscontrol.org.

75. The Arms Control Association, "The Biological Weapons Convention (BWC) at a Glance," September 2012, and "The Biological Weapons Convention Signatories and States-Parties," July 2016, https://www.armscontrol.org.

76. Jonathan B. Tucker, "Putting Teeth in the Biological Weapons Convention," *Issues in Science and Technology* 18 (Spring 2002): 71–77; Susan Wright, "U.S. Vetoes Verification," *Bulletin of the Atomic Scientists* 58 (March/April 2002): 24–26; Arms Control Association, "The BWC at a Glance," https://www.armscontrol.org.

77. Goldstein and Pevehouse, *International Relations*, 215–16; Arms Control Association, "The BWC at a Glance"; Donald G. McNeil Jr., "White House Issues New Regulations for Dangerous Biological Research," *New York Times*, September 25, 2014, A14.

78. Mark J. Allman, *Who Would Jesus Kill? War, Peace, and the Christian Tradition* (Winona, MN: Saint Mary's Press, 2008), 230–33, at 230.

79. Ibid., 230–31; International Campaign to Ban Landmines (ICBL), *Landmine Monitor 2017*, www.the-monitor.org; Mujib Mashal, "Left-behind Explosives Taking Toll on Afghan Children," *New York Times*, February 7, 2017, A4; Niki Kitsantonis, "Bomb Removal in Greece Forces 72,000 from Homes," *New York Times*, February 13, 2017, A3, about defusing a WWII bomb below a gas station.

80. ICBL, *Landmine Monitor*, 2. See, for example, Norimitsu Onishi, "In an Angolan Town, Land Mines Still Lurk 'Behind Every Bush,'" *New York Times*, April 27, 2017, A4.

81. Bernard E. Trainor, "Land Mines Saved My Life," *New York Times*, March 27, 1996, op-ed page. Lt. Gen. Trainor also served as chief military correspondent for *New York Times* and was a military analyst for NBC. He has written three books with Michael R. Gordon on the Gulf War and the Iraq War.

82. Barbara Crossette, "Pact on Land Mines Stops Short of Total Ban," *New York Times*, May 4, 1996, 4.

83. ICBL, *Landmine Monitor*, 1, list of States Parties and non-signers on x.

84. Ibid., 2–4.

85. Tobias Winright, "The (Im)morality of Cluster Munitions," in *Can War Be Just in the 21st Century?* ed. Tobias Winright and Laurie Johnston (Maryknoll, NY: Orbis Books), 2015, 29–49, at 30–34. Geneva International Centre for Humanitarian Demining (GICHD, https://www.gichd.org) and Implementation Support Unit, Convention on Cluster Munitions (ISU CCM, www.clusterconvention.org), *A Guide to Cluster Munitions*, 3rd ed. (Geneva, May 2016), chaps. 1 and 2, 15–42. Speaking in Laos in September, 2016, President Obama stated that between 1963 and 1974 the United States dropped two million tons of bombs on Laos, more than used on Germany and Japan combined in WWII, making the Michigan-sized country the most heavily bombed country in history. Obama announced a doubling of American funding to remove unexploded ordinance. Scott Shane, "The Not-So-Secret War: A Review of *A Great Place to Have a War*, by Joshua Kurtantzick," *New York Times Book Review*, February 5, 2017, 12.

86. *Circle of Impact: The Fatal Footprint of Cluster Munitions on People and Communities* (Handicap International, May 2007), http://www.handicap-international.us. This statistic is based on admittedly incomplete data.

87. Winright, "The (Im)morality of Cluster Munitions," 38–49, at 49.

88. Ibid., 45–46.

89. *Cluster Munition Monitor 2016*, www.the-monitor.org; *A Guide to Cluster Munitions*, 43–56.

90. Mark J. Allman and Tobias L. Winright, *After the Smoke Clears: The Just War Tradition and Post War Justice* (Maryknoll, NY: Orbis Books, 2010), 166–67. These health statistics show correlation rather than causation. The harmful health effects of DU are debated. Another good source of information on DU is the International Coalition to Ban Uranium Weapons, www.bandepleteduranium.org/.

91. Samuel Oakford, "The United States Used Depleted Uranium in Syria," *Foreign Policy*, February 14, 2017, https://foreignpolicy.com.

92. This is the consistent conclusion of the US Catholic Bishops in *The Challenge of Peace: God's Promise and Our Response* (1983). See the ##131–61, especially ##131, 136, 147, 148, 150, 153, 160.

93. Kenneth R. Himes, *Drones and the Ethics of Targeted Killing* (Lanham, MD: Rowman & Littlefield, 2016), 11–13. Himes is a key source for this section.

94. Michael S. Schmidt, "Air Force, Short of Drone Pilots, Use Contractors to Fight Terror," *New York Times*, September 6, 2016, A1, A6.

95. "The Danger of Drones," *New York Times*, March 16, 2017, editorial.

96. The Trump administration added West Africa to places where armed drones are used by stationing them in Niger. This increased the number of troops stationed in Niger as well. See Helene Cooper and Eric Schmitt, "Niger Approves U.S. Drone Flights, Expanding Pentagon's Role in Africa," *New York Times*, December 1, 2017, A9.

97. Himes, *Drones and the Ethics of Targeted Killing*, 163.

98. Ibid., xi, 89–93.

99. Ibid., 85–119, analysis of President Obama's speech at 105–12. Barack Obama,

"Remarks by the President at the National Defense University" (May 23, 2013), https://obamawhitehouse.archives.gov.

100. Charlie Savage, "U.S. Releases Drone Strike 'Playbook' for Targeting Terrorism Suspects," *New York Times*, August 7, 2016, A10. The online version of this article has a link to the document "Procedures for Approving Direct Action Against Terrorist Targets Located Outside the United States and Areas of Active Hostilities."

101. Himes, *Drones and the Ethics of Targeted Killing*, 163–65.

102. Greg Miller, "Lawmakers Seek to Stymie Plan to Shift Control of Drone Campaign from CIA to Pentagon," *Washington Post*, January 15, 2014; Mark Mazetti and Matt Apuzzo, "Deep Support in Washington for C.I.A.'s Drone Missions," *New York Times*, April 26, 2015, A1, 4.

103. Charlie Savage and Eric Schmitt, "Trump Poised to Drop Some Limits on Drone Strikes and Commando Raids," *New York Times*, September 22, 2017, A1, 10.

104. Himes, *Drones and the Ethics of Targeted Killing*, 122–25, and 51–84, esp. 69–70 and 81–83.

105. Ibid., 6, 151.

106. Ibid., 125–28. Himes says double-tap strikes are "morally dubious." See also Tobias L. Winright and Mark J. Allman, "Obama's Drone Wars: A Case to Answer," *Tablet*, August 18, 2012, 6–7, at 7.

107. See Andreas Wenger and Simon J. M. Mason, "The Civilianization of Armed Conflict: Trends and Implications," *International Review of the Red Cross* 90, no. 872 (December 2008): 835–52.

108. President Obama, "Remarks by the President at the National Defense University."

109. Charlie Savage and Scott Shane, "U.S. Reveals Death Toll from Airstrikes Outside War Zones," *New York Times*, July 2, 2016, A1. This article has a link to "Summary of Information Regarding U.S. Counterterrorism Strikes Outside Areas of Hostile Activities," a document released by the Director of National Intelligence, https://www.dni.gov. See also Scott Shane, "Drone Strike Statistics Answer Few Questions, and Raise Many," *New York Times*, July 4, 2016, A1; and "The Secret Rules of the Drone War," *New York Times*, July 10, 2016, editorial.

110. There is, however, no evidence to corroborate the fifty civilians to one militant claim suggested by David Kilcullen and Andrew McDonald Exum, "Death from Above, Outrage Down Below," *New York Times*, May 16, 2009, op-ed page, which is sometimes cited by drone critics. A more realistic estimate would be for every one hundred combatants killed, fourteen civilians are killed.

111. See the film *Eye in the Sky* (2016), directed by Gavin Hood, and starring Alan Rickman and Helen Mirren, for a dramatic enactment of the difficult decisions regarding discrimination and proportion posed by a drone strike. One wonders, however, if the "soda straw" optics of drones might exclude the context of surveillance more than the film suggests.

112. Himes, *Drones and the Ethics of Targeted Killing*, 125–41.

113. Daniel M. Bell, "The Drone Wars and Just War," *Journal of Lutheran Ethics* 14, no. 6 (June 2014), https://www.elca.org, paragraphs 16–25, at 19.

114. Savage and Schmitt, "Trump Poised to Drop Some Limits," A1,10.

115. Rohde is quoted in Paul Lauritzen, "'Lawful but Awful': The Moral Perils of

Drone Warfare," *Commonweal*, January 23, 2015, 16–18, at 18. On the psychological trauma of living under drones, also see Himes, *Drones and the Ethics of Targeted Killing*, 141–42.

116. Bell, "The Drone Wars and Just War," paragraphs 9–15.

117. Adam Goldman and Eric Schmitt, "U.S. Silences Voices of ISIS One at a Time," *New York Times*, November 25, 2016, A1, A3; Rukmini Callimachi, "3 Operatives from ISIS Are Killed in U.S. Strike," *New York Times*, December 14, 2016, A8.

118. Michael V. Hayden, "The Case for Drones," *New York Times*, February 21, 2016, op-ed page.

119. Himes, *Drones and the Ethics of Targeted Killing*, 145–50.

120. Eyal Press, "The Wounds of the Drone Warrior," *New York Times Magazine*, June 17, 2018, 30–37, 47, 49.

121. Himes, *Drones and the Ethics of Targeted Killing*, 152–65; Winright and Allman, "Obama's Drone Wars," 7; Brian Stiltner, "A Taste of Armageddon: When Warring is Done by Drones and Robots," in *Can War Be Just in the 21st Century?* ed. Winright and Johnston, 14–28, at 25–26.

122. See J. Milburn Thompson, "Catholic Social Teaching and the Ethics of Torture," *Journal for Peace and Justice Studies* 17 (2008): 22–42.

123. Himes, *Drones and the Ethics of Targeted Killing*, 142–44.

124. Already America's enemies, such as the Islamic State and al-Qaeda, are using modified off-the-shelf drones for surveillance and attack. Better resourced groups and countries will use more sophisticated drones. Precedent will matter. See Eric Schmitt, "Pentagon Tests Lasers and Nets to Combat a Vexing Foe: ISIS Drones," *New York Times*, September 24, 2017, A1, 12.

125. This section is based on the work of David E. Sanger, a *New York Times* journalist who explores the intersections of technology and international security. His book *The Perfect Weapon: War, Sabotage, and Fear in the Cyber Age* (New York: Crown, 2018) is the basis for two of his articles in the *New York Times*, "Why Hackers Aren't Afraid of Us," June 17, 2018, A4; and "Pentagon Puts Cyberwarriors on the Offensive, Increasing Risk of Conflict," June 18, 2018, A1,13. It is also the basis for Nicholas Kristof, "To Hackers, We're Bambi in the Woods," *New York Times*, July 5, 2018, op-ed page. *The Perfect Weapon* was reviewed by Paul R. Pillar, "Cyberwarfare— The Latest Technology of Destruction," *New York Times Book Review*, July 1, 2018, 10.

126. See Robert H. Latiff," Rebooting the Ethical Soldier," *New York Times*, July 15, 2018, SR4, which explores ethical soldiering in the age of high-tech warfare, although he doesn't directly address cyberwarfare.

127. This brief section is based on Helene Cooper, "A Space Force? The Idea May Have Merit, Some Say," *New York Times*, June 24, 2018, A17; "Trump in Space," *New York Times* July 28, 2018, editorial; and Karl Grossman, "Space Force: Stealing the Heavens for War," *W.A.M.M. Newsletter* 36 (Fall 2018): 2–3, 8–9.

128. "Outer Space Treaty," U.N Office for Outer Space Affairs, www.unoosa.org.

129. Michael T. Klare, "Adding Fuel to the Fire: The Conventional Arms Trade in the 1990s," in *World Security*, Second Edition, ed. Klare and Thomas (1994), 134–54, at 147.

130. Klare, "Adding Fuel to the Fire," 147–48; Klare, "Deadly Convergence," 186–87.

131. Mark R. Amstutz, *International Conflict and Cooperation: An Introduction to World Politics* (Madison, WI: Brown & Benchmark, 1995), 383.

132. Charles M. Sennott, "Armed for Profit: The Selling of U.S. Weapons," *Boston Globe*, February 11, 1996, A Special Report, B2.

133. Stockholm International Peace Research Institute, *SIPRI Yearbook 2016* (Oxford, UK: Oxford University Press, 2016), chap. 15. See Saed Kamali Dehgham, "Global Arms Trade Reaches Highest Point since the Cold War Era," *The Guardian*, February 19, 2017, which is based on the SIPRI data.

134. Klare, "Adding Fuel to the Fire," 139–42.

135. Sennott, "Armed for Profit," B2; Michael T. Klare and Lora Lumpe, "Fanning the Flames of War: Conventional Arms Transfers in the 1990s," in *World Security: Challenges for a New Century*, Third Edition, ed. Michael T. Klare and Yogesh Chandrani (New York: St. Martin's Press, 1998), 160–79, at 72.

136. "Small Arms and Light Weapons (SA/LW)," http://www.globalsecurity.org.

137. Jeffrey Boutwell and Michael T. Klare, eds., *Light Weapons and Civil Conflict: Controlling the Tools of Violence* (New York: Rowman & Littlefield, 1999). See also the International Action Network on Small Arms (IANSA), which is a global movement against gun violence, https://www.iansa.org.

138. Anant Mishra, "Guns, Weapons, and Illegal Trade," *International Policy Digest*, January 5, 2015, https://intpolicydigest.org.

139. "The Arms Trade Treaty at a Glance," Arms Control Association, January 2016, https://www.armscontrol.org.

140. "Arms Trade Treaty," United Nations Office for Disarmament Affairs, https://www.un.org/disarmament.

141. "The Arms Trade Treaty at a Glance," Arms Control Association.

142. Klare and Lumpe, "Fanning the Flames of War," 161–63.

143. Klare, "Adding Fuel to the Fire," 148–51; Klare and Lumpe, "Fanning the Flames of War," 172–76. Regarding the control of light weapons, see Jeffrey Boutwell and Michael T. Klare, "Light Weapons and Civil Conflict: Policy Options for the International Community," in Boutwell and Klare, *Light Weapons and Civil Conflict*, 217–30.

144. See also "1,515 Mass Shootings in 1,735 Days: America's Gun Crisis in One Chart," *The Guardian*, October 2, 2017, for an equally thought-provoking chart.

145. Francis X. Clines, "The Wounded Fight On to Survive in Aurora," *New York Times*, July 9, 2017, op-ed page. The Brady Campaign to Prevent Gun Violence documents that there are an average of 315 people shot every day in the United States, ninety-three of them die, and 222 are injured: http://www.bradycampaign.org.

146. If there are an average of 30,000 gun deaths per year in the United States that would mean about 577 per week. Thus the 464 in *Time's* cover story is now atypical.

147. Tom W. Smith and Jaesok Son, *General Social Survey Final Report: Trends in Gun Ownership in the United States, 1972–2014* (NORC at the University of Chicago, March 2015), www.norc.org.

148. See Abner J. Mikva and Lawrence Rosenthal, "Tough Gun Laws Are

Constitutional," *New York Times*, February 24, 2016, op-ed page; and http://gun-control.procon.org.

149. Erin Grinshteyn and David Hemenway, "Violent Death Rates: The US Compared with Other High-income OECD Countries, 2010," *American Journal of Medicine* 129 (March 2016): 266–73.

150. "A Pro Bono Dream Team Takes On the N.R.A.," *New York Times*, December 18, 2016, editorial.

151. Nicholas Kristof, "Some Inconvenient Gun Facts for Liberals," *New York Times*, January 17, 2016, op-ed page; Nicholas Kristof with Bill Marsh, "How to Reduce Shootings," *New York Times*, November 9, 2017, op-ed page.

152. "Keep Guns Away from Abusers," *New York Times*, January 17, 2016, editorial; "Mental Illness and Gun Violence," *New York Times*, December 15, 2015, editorial; "Congress Says, Let the Mentally Ill Buy Guns," *New York Times*, February 16, 2017, editorial.

153. Nicholas Kristof, "On Guns, We're Not Even Trying," *New York Times*, December 2, 2015, op-ed page. Kristof refers to Colleen Barry et al., "Two Years after Newtown—Public Opinion on Gun Policy Revisited," *Preventive Medicine* 79 (October 2015): 55–58.

154. Mikva and Rosenthal, "Tough Gun Laws Are Constitutional"; Isabella Kwai, "Australia Has Collected 12,500 Guns in Amnesty," *New York Times*, August 13, 2017, A11.

155. Charles M. Blow, "Focus on Illegal Guns," *New York Times*, January 11, 2016, op-ed page.

156. Ian Urbina, "California Tries New Tack on Gun Violence: Ammunition Control," *New York Times*, September 10, 2018, A1, 13.

157. "Despair about Guns Is Not an Option," *New York Times*, December 13, 2015, editorial.

158. Jack Healy et al., "Guns in Tiny Hands: In a Week, Four Toddlers Shoot Themselves," *New York Times*, May 6, 2016, A1, A12; Ryan Foley et al., "Accidental Shootings Put Kids in Early Graves," *USA Today*, October 14, 2016. Shootings by preschoolers happen at a pace of two per week. See also Peter Manseau, "Trigger Warnings," *New York Times*, February 28, 2016, SR6.

159. The Hidden Gun Epidemic: Suicides," *New York Times*, January 9, 2017, editorial; "Guns and the Rising Rate of Suicide," *New York Times*, December 14, 2015, editorial.

160. "Despair about Guns Is Not an Option."

161. Max Fisher and Josh Keller, "What Explains Mass Shootings? International Comparisons Suggest an Answer," *New York Times*, November 8, 2017, A15.

162. Mikva and Rosenthal, "Tough Gun Laws Are Constitutional."

163. Sennott, "Armed for Profit," B4. Although the amount of military spending held steady, as a percentage of GDP military spending decreased by nearly half, from 6.3 percent of GDP in 1986 to 3.6 percent in 1996. The number of personnel in uniform declined by about 25 percent in the 1990s.

164. Michael T. Klare, "Endless Military Superiority," *The Nation* 275, July 15, 2002, 12–16.

165. "The Costs of War," the Watson Institute of International and Public Affairs at Brown University, September, 2016., https://watson.brown.edu.

166. The national *debt* is the total amount the United States owes from past borrowing. Like any debt, the country pays interest on this amount. The annual *deficit* is the amount the government spends over what it takes in in a given year. The country must borrow this amount, which is then added to the national debt. Congress puts a ceiling on the debt in an attempt to control it, and Congress must routinely vote to raise this ceiling when the deficit requires it. If Congress refused to raise the ceiling on the debt, the government cannot borrow more money and will cease to function.

167. Annie Lowrey, "Why Sequestration Is Poised to Kill Trump's Budget," *Atlantic*, March 16, 2017, https://www.theatlantic.com.

168. Congressional Budget Office, *An Analysis of the Obama Administration's Final Future Years Defense Program*, April 2017, Summary, 1, https://www.cbo.gov.

169. Lowrey, "Why Sequestration Is Poised to Kill Trump's Budget"; David Smith and Dominic Rushe, "President's First Budget Cuts Holes in Social Safety Net to Fund Border Wall," *The Guardian*, May 24, 2017, 17; Helene Cooper, "White House Pushes Military Might over Humanitarian Aid in Africa," *New York Times*, June 26, 2017, A8.

170. Mandy Smithberger, "America's $1.1 Trillion National Security Budget," Center for Defense Information, May 24, 2017, at POGO, http://www.pogo.org.

171. See SIPRI (Stockholm International Peace Research Institute), "Military Expenditure Database," https://www.sipri.org. See also K. K. Rebecca Lai et al., "Is the Military Big Enough?" *New York Times*, March 27, 2017, A13.

172. Goldstein and Pevehouse, *International Relations*, 193, 222–24, at 222.

173. Jim Tankersley, "Federal Deficit Rises 17%, to $779 Billion," *New York Times*, October 16, 2018, B7.

174. Goldstein and Pevehouse, *International Relations*, 222.

175. The Pastoral Constitution on the Church in the Modern World (1965) in *The Documents of Vatican II*, ed. Walter M. Abbott, S.J., trans. Joseph Gallagher (New York: Geoffrey Chapman, 1966), #81.

176. SIPRI, "Media Backgrounder: Military Versus Social Expenditure: The Opportunity Cost of World Military Spending," April 5, 2016, https://www.sipri.org.

177. Klare, "Endless Military Superiority."

178. Goldstein and Pevehouse, *International Relations*, 193.

Epilogue

1. See James W. Douglass, *Resistance and Contemplation: The Way of Liberation* (New York: Dell, 1972); Robert H. King, *Thomas Merton and Thich Nhat Hanh: Engaged Spirituality in an Age of Globalization* (New York: Continuum, 2001); and Joseph Nangle, *Engaged Spirituality: Faith Life in the Heart of the Empire* (Maryknoll, NY: Orbis Books, 2008).

2. See 1 Kings 3:3–15, where Solomon asks God for the gift of wisdom.

3. Charles E. Curran, "Conversion: The Central Moral Message of Jesus," in Charles E. Curran, *A New Look at Christian Morality* (Notre Dame, IN: Fides, 1968), 50–52.

4. This quote is attributed to Gandhi, but I cannot find the source. It may, however, be from St. Elizabeth Ann Seton, the first American-born saint.

5. See John F. Kavanaugh, *Following Christ in a Consumer Society: The Spirituality of Cultural Resistance*, rev. ed. (Maryknoll, NY: Orbis Books, 1991).

6. Adam Daniel Finnerty, *No More Plastic Jesus: Global Justice and Christian Lifestyle* (Maryknoll, NY: Orbis Books, 1977), 97.

7. Ronald J. Sider, *Rich Christians in an Age of Hunger: A Biblical Study* (New York: Paulist Press, 1977), 92–93.

8. NCCB, *Economic Justice for All*, ##97–98; and John Paul II, *On Human Work* (*Laborens Exercens*), ##6, 9, 10, in David J. O'Brien and Thomas A. Shannon, *Catholic Social Thought: The Documentary Heritage* (Maryknoll, NY: Orbis Books, 1992, 2010).

9. NCCB, *Economic Justice for All*, #92.

10. See the films *A Civil Action* (1998), directed by Steven Zaillian, starring John Travolta; and *Erin Brockovich* (2000), directed by Steven Soderbergh, starring Julia Roberts.

11. See Joseph A. Grassi, *Broken Bread and Broken Bodies: The Lord's Supper and World Hunger* (Maryknoll, NY: Orbis Books, 1985); and Monica K. Hellwig, *The Eucharist and the Hunger of the World*, 2nd rev. ed. (Kansas City: Sheed & Ward, 1992).

12. "While the Church is bound to give witness to justice, she recognizes that everyone who ventures to speak to people about justice must first be just in their eyes. Hence we must undertake an examination of the modes of acting and of the possessions and lifestyle found within the Church herself." See Synod of Bishops, *Justice in the World*, in O'Brien and Shannon, *Catholic Social Thought* (2010), 312.

13. Arthur Simon, *Christian Faith and Public Policy: No Grounds for Divorce* (Grand Rapids: Eerdmans, 1987), 12, and chap. 5.

14. See J. Milburn Thompson, "A Theological Perspective on Church and Politics in the United States," in Samuel M. Natale and Francis P. McHugh, eds., *Proceedings of the First International Conference on Social Values*, vol. 2 (New Rochelle, NY: Iona College Press, 1991), 37–44, at 39–41.

15. See Timothy Keller, "How Do Christians Fit into the Two-Party System? They Don't," *New York Times*, September 30, 2018, op-ed page.

16. See Simon, *Christian Faith and Public Policy*, 104–13. Arthur Simon is a founding member and past executive director of Bread for the World.

17. The following letter is based upon "Jesse Helms Mocks the Senate," *New York Times*, February 10, 1997, editorial. See www.fns.usda.gov/wic/ for more information about the WIC program.

18. See Gene Sharp, *The Politics of Nonviolent Action*, 3 vols., esp. vol. 2, *The Methods of Nonviolent Action* (Boston: Porter Sargent, 1973); and Elizabeth Morgan, *Global Poverty and Personal Responsibility* (New York: Paulist Press, 1989), 148–53.

Index

Abbas, Mahmoud, 159
abortion, 19, 134
Abu Ghraib, and US torture, 119, 126, 164, 205
Afghanistan, US war in, 250
Africa
    Chinese foreign aid to, 64
    ethnic conflict in, 185–93
    European colonization of, 29, 30
    female genital cutting in, 137, 138
African National Congress, opposition to apartheid, 192
Afwerki, Isaias, 188
age of acceleration, 38
Agent Orange, 113, 228
agricultural productivity, and Malthusian trap, 37
Ahmed, Abiy, 188
Airbnb, 38
Akufo-Addo, Nana, 191
Alaska, climate change in, 86
algae blooms, and climate change, 88
Allende, Salvador, 34
All-India Muslim League, 216
al-Qaeda, 163–68, 234, 237, 238, and terrorism, 202–5
Amadinejad, Mahmoud, 215
Amazon, 38
Americas, "discovery" of, 24
Amnesty International, 123, 245
Anglo-Boer wars, 192
Angola
    civil war in, 191, 192
    US military assistance to, 209
animals, cruel treatment of, 89, 90

Annan, Kofi, 185
Antarctica, climate change in, 87
Anthony, Major Scott, 141
Anthropocene epoch, 80–82
anthropocentrism, 19, 80
Anti-Ballistic Missile Treaty (ABM, 1972), 219, 220, 221
anticommunism, 42
    of the United States, 196, 197
    and US human rights record, 124
antidebt campaigns, 68, 69
anti-Muslim sentiment, 148
antipersonnel mines (APMs), 230, 231
anti-Semitism, 13, 131, 148, 158, 162
antiterrorism, and military intervention, 197
antivehicle mines, 231
apartheid, 13, 31, 76, 119, 120, 131, 146, 192
Aquino, Corazon, 207
Arabs, displacement of, in Palestine, 158
Arab Spring, 44, 165–72, 214
Arafat, Yasser, 158, 159
Arakan Rohingya Salvation Army (ARSA), 184
Arbour, Louise, 122
Arctic, and melting of sea ice, 86
arms control regime, components of, 246
arms control, 219–24
arms race, 20, 42, 210
arms trade, 242–44
Arms Trade Treaty (ATT), 245, 246
artificial intelligence (AI), 39

329